abc
of airports and airliners
JBT
G-A
3/6 by Ow
abc
Civil Aircraft
Recognition
A
B
2/6
abc
LONDON
AIRPORT

ABC
CIVIL
AIRCRAFT
MARKINGS
by J.W.R. Taylor
AN Ian Allan PUBLICATION
2/-
ABC
CIVIL
AIRCRAFT MARKINGS
An Ian Allan Publication
2/6

First published 1948-1957
Reprinted 2025

ISBN 9781800353428

All rights reserved. No part of this book may be reproduced or transmitted in any form or by any means, electronic or mechanical, including photocopying, recording or by any information storage and retrieval system, without permission from the Publisher in writing.

© Crécy Publishing 2025

Printed in Turkey by Pelikan Print

Published by Crécy Publishing Ltd
1a Ringway Trading Est, Shadowmoss Rd
Manchester M22 5LH

Visit the Crécy Publishing website at www.crecy.co.uk

Copyright

Illegal copying and selling of publications deprives authors, publishers and booksellers of income, without which there would be no investment in new publications. Unauthorised versions of publications are also likely to be inferior in quality and contain incorrect information. You can help by reporting copyright infringements and acts of piracy to the Publisher or the UK Copyright Service.

Contents

Introduction 4

1 Airports and Airliners (1948).............................7

2 Civil Aircraft Markings (1950).......................103

3 Civil Aircraft Recognition (1955)...................179

4 London Airport (1957) 255

5 Civil Aircraft Markings (1952).......................301

Introduction

Ian Allan published the first of the iconic 'abc' titles in 1942, a listing of railway locomotive serial numbers which quickly sold-out despite the wartime deprivations. His publishing empire began to flourish in post-war Britain and other transport subjects, including aviation, were soon added to the growing stable of abc books.

In 1948, Owen Thetford authored the Ian Allan "abc of airports and airliners" which described the UK's major airports, their flight timetables and the airliners that flew from these airfields. Some of these – for example Croydon and Pengam Moors – would close within a few years of this book being published, whilst others – such as London Heathrow, Manchester Ringway and Aberdeen Dyce – have today grown out of all recognition.

In 1950, Ian Allan turned to the renowned John WR Taylor to produce the first edition of 'Civil Aircraft Markings' to support the new and growing hobby of aircraft spotting. Essentially a listing of aircraft registrations of the UK (and overseas visiting aircraft), an enthusiast could now confirm the exact aircraft type and the owner. Even the great JWRT could have had no idea that 75 years later, 'CAM' would still be an annual publication and still carrying essentially the same information – albeit for many thousands more civil aircraft than existed back then.

JWRT also soon produced 'abc Civil Aircraft Recognition' – a detailed record of the civil aircraft to be seen in the UK at the time, covering everything from the many pre-war light aircraft still flying then, through the converted wartime bombers, flying boats and early post-war piston engine airliners, through to the leading edge of technology of the day in the form of the de Havilland Comet.

Later in the 1950s, Ian Allan published its abc guide to London Airport (or 'LAP' as it was called before becoming better known as 'Heathrow' or LHR). This fascinating publication marks the zenith of the great piston and turbo-prop engine airliners – the Britannia, DC-7, Stratocruiser and Constellation, all stalwarts of airline fleets before the wave of jet airliners replaced them forever. This book is also a window into a different era of air travel – when making an airline flight was a life event, not a regular chore.

This facsimile reprint from the Ian Allan archives covers five abc titles:

abc of airports and airliners (1948)
abc Civil Aircraft Markings (1950)
abc Civil Aircraft Recognition (1955)
abc London Airport (1957)
abc Civil Aircraft Markings (1952)

It's not difficult to see why so many aviation historians and enthusiasts regard the 1950s as the 'Golden Era' of civil airliners. For any aircraft 'spotter' of the time, these abc books were as essential as a notebook and a good pair of binoculars. Today, this reprint is a historical record, a glimpse into the past and an unashamed slice of nostalgia. Enjoy!

The Crécy Publishing editorial team

Ian Allan
abc of
airports
and
airliners
JBT
G-A
3/6   by Owen G. Thetford

CONTENTS.

	Pages
Introduction	3
Airlines Operating Services to and from the British Isles	5
Company Fleet Lists...	7
Check List of Fleets Employed by Major Air Charter Firms in Great Britain ...	21
Alphabetical Guide to Airliner Registrations of all Nationalities	26
List of Arrivals and Departures at Airports in the U.K. (With Maps of airports):—	
Aberdeen	36
Belfast	37
Blackpool	38
Cardiff	39
Croydon	40
Dublin	41
Edinburgh	42
Gatwick	42
Liverpool	43
London	44
Manchester	57
Northolt	58
Prestwick	61
Renfrew	64
Ronaldsway	68
Shannon	69
Southampton	71
Descriptions of All Airliners in Regular Service, with Silhouettes for Instant Recognition ...	73
Associate Companies of B.E.A. operating internal routes in Great Britain	Inside back cover

A B C
OF
AIRPORTS
AND
AIRLINERS

By

O. G. Thetford

LONDON

Ian Allan Ltd

1948

Left: American Overseas Airlines Lockheed Constellation NC 90925 *Flagship America*.
A.O.A. operates seven Constellations on the New York-London services.

Centre Upper: American Overseas Airlines Skymaster *Flagship Shannon* NC 90910 arriving from New York.

Centre Lower: A Douglas Dakota of Aer Lingus at Northolt.
Below: Douglas Dakota F-BAXA, one of thirty-six Dakotas operated by Air France on European routes.

(*Photos: A. S. C. Lumsden*

INTRODUCTION.

SINCE the Ministry of Civil Aviation first made available the Public Enclosures at Britain's major airports the attendance figures have been increasing by leaps and bounds and it is now sufficiently clear that not only the young aircraft enthusiasts but many members of the wider public are finding interest and relaxation in this form of pastime. Indeed, there can be few people of any age who fail to be fascinated sooner or later by the spectacle of airliners of all nationalities arriving and departing with clockwork regularity. It is not so very long ago since the crossing of the Atlantic by air or a flight from England to Australia earned front-page headlines in every newspaper. Nowadays, within the space of an hour at London Airport, the spectator can see Constellations from India, Australia, South America and New York, Canadairs from Montreal, Skymasters from South Africa and Yorks from the Gold Coast. Likewise at Northolt, clustered on the arrival apron at any time of the day there are airliners from Sweden, Switzerland, Italy, Holland, Greece, Eire and Czechoslovakia.

No spectator however can have his entire interest aroused unless he has some understanding and knowledge of the events he is witnessing and the supply of such needful information is a facility lacking at most airports. The present handbook it is hoped will satisfy this requirement. In preparing it, the author's intention has been twofold, inasmuch as it aims at equal interest for the knowledgeable professional spotter and the average uninformed member of the public.

The enthusiast will find that it lists for the first time the registration letters and individual aircraft names of the fleets of every airline company operating into the British airports, and includes photographs of all current types of airliners in the livery of every company. In obtaining the photographs I have had the co-operation of Mr. Alec S. C. Lumsden of the British Air Line Pilots' Association, to whom I wish to take this opportunity of expressing my thanks. Mr. Lumsden's enthusiasm in the task has been unbounded and his keen appreciation of the collector's requirements is, I think, adequately reflected in the rarity-value of many of the pictures.

In addition to the foreign airliners, the entire fleets of the three British airline corporations are, of course, listed, and there is also a check list of British charter companies operating multi-engined aircraft with details of the fleets.   Charter aircraft fall generally into the airliner class and as in the course of their multifarious duties they are likely to be seen at any airport at any time, it has been thought advisable to include them.

The reader approaching the book innocent, in the main, of things aeronautical, will find that there is included an "A to Z" list of the registration letters of every scheduled airliner liable to be seen at any airport in the British Isles, which identifies at a glance the type and nationality of the aircraft and the company to which it belongs.   To promote further a knowledge of the different types of aircraft there is a set of outline recognition drawings, accompanied by notes of general interest and what the Americans usually describe as " pertinent data " relating to every airliner type currently operating on scheduled air routes.

Of direct utility to both categories of reader is the section devoted to the various airports, arranged alphabetically from Aberdeen (Dyce) to Southampton (Eastleigh).   This section contains tables listing times of arrival and departure of the various companies' services and also stating the point of departure or alternatively the destination of the aircraft.   The times quoted are those of the official summer schedules issued by the airline companies concerned and the frequencies are in most instances liable to reduction after October, though the routes operated remain unchanged.   The map provided for most of the airports shows clearly the layout of the administrative buildings and the direction and length of the runways.

In conclusion, I wish to offer my thanks to Mr. Charles W. Cain who, in his capacity as Editor of "The Aeroplane Spotter", granted his permission for the publication in this book of the various silhouettes appearing in the section devoted to the description of the current types of airliners in service.

O. G. T.

July, 1948.

4

Company Name	Nationality	Year Founded	Airports Used in U.K.
A.B. Aerotransport ..	Swedish	1919	Northolt Prestwick
Aer Lingus	Irish	1936	Northolt Manchester Liverpool Renfrew Dublin Shannon
Air France	French	1933	London Manchester Prestwick Shannon
Air India International ..	Indian	1948	London
Alitalia	Italian	1947	Northolt
American Overseas Airlines	American	1942	London Prestwick Shannon
British European Airways Corporation	British	1946	Northolt Aberdeen Belfast Blackpool Edinburgh Liverpool Manchester Renfrew Ronaldsway
British Overseas Airways Corporation	British	1940	London Prestwick Shannon Southampton
British South American Airways Corporation ..	British	1946	London
Central African Airways	Rhodesian	1946	London
Ceskoslovenske Aerolinie (C.S.A.)	Czech	1946	London Northolt
Cie Air Transport ..	French	1946	Croydon Gatwick
Cobeta	Belgian	1947	Manchester Prestwick

13

Company Name	Nationality	Year Founded	Airports Used in U.K.
Det Danske Luftfartselskab (D.D.L.)	Danish	1918	Northolt Prestwick
Det Norske Luftfartselskab (D.N.L.)	Norwegian	1919	Northolt Prestwick
Flota Aerea Mercante Argentina (F.A.M.A.) ..	Argentine	1946	London
Hellenic Airlines ..	Greek	1947	Northolt Prestwick
Iberia	Spanish	1930	London
Icelandic Airways ..	Icelandic	1944	Prestwick
Iraqi Airways	Iraqi	1945	London
Koninklijke Luchtvaart Maatschappij (K.L.M.)	Dutch	1919	London Manchester Prestwick Dublin
Luxembourg Airlines ..	Luxembourg	1947	Northolt
Pan American World Airways	American	1927	London Prestwick Shannon
Panair do Brasil	Brazilian	1930	London
Qantas Empire Airways ..	Australian	1934	London
South African Airways ..	South African	1931	London
Sabena	Belgian	1923	London Dublin Shannon
Scandinavian Airlines System	Merger of D.D.L., D.N.L. and A.B.A.	1946	Northolt Prestwick
Swissair	Swiss	1922	London Northolt Shannon
Trans-Canada Airlines ..	Canadian	1937	London Prestwick Shannon
Trans - World Airlines (Registered as Transcontinental and Western Air Inc.)	American	1930	Shannon

A.B. AEROTRANSPORT FLEET.

(Component of Scandinavian Airways System).

DOUGLAS DC-6 CLOUDMASTERS.

SE-BDA	Agnar Viking	SE-BDF	Alvar Viking
SE-BDB	Agne Viking	SE-BDL	Ambjörn Viking
SE-BDC	Alf Viking	SE-BDM	Anund Viking
SE-BDD	Algaut Viking	SE-BDO	Arngrim Viking
SE-BDE	Alrek Viking		

DOUGLAS DC-4 SKYMASTERS.

SE-BBA	Sigtrygg Viking	SE-BBE	Svavar Viking
SE-BBC	Sigvard Viking	SE-BBF	Sverker Viking
SE-BBD	Styrbjorn Viking	SE-BBG	Not yet named

DOUGLAS DC-3 DAKOTAS.

SE-BAA	Arne Viking	SE-BBH	Helge Viking
SE-BAB	Bele Viking	SE-BBI	Ivar Viking
SE-BAC	Folke Viking	SE-BBK	Kare Viking
SE-BAL	Lage Viking	SE-BBL	Loke Viking
SE-BAS	Sture Viking	SE-BBM	Magne Viking
SE-BAT	Torbjörn Viking	SE-BBN	Nore Viking
SE-BAU	Ubbe Viking	SE-BBO	Orvar Viking
SE-BAW	Vidar Viking		

DOUGLAS C-47 DAKOTA FREIGHTERS.

SE-BAZ	Esbjörn Viking	SE-BBR	Rörek Viking
SE-BBP	Torgny Viking		

AER LINGUS FLEET.

AIRSPEED CONSULS.

EI-ADB	Unnamed	EI-ADC	Unnamed

DOUGLAS DC-3 DAKOTAS.

EI-ACD	Unnamed	EI-ACL	St. Declan
EI-ACE	St. Colmcille	EI-ACM	St. Fintan
EI-ACF	St. Kieran	EI-ACT	St. Colman
EI-ACG	St. Malachy	EI-ADW	Unnamed
EI-ACH	Unnamed	EI-ADX	Unnamed
EI-ACI	St. Aidan	EI-ADY	Unnamed
EI-ACK	St. Albert		

AIR FRANCE FLEET

DOUGLAS DC-4 SKYMASTERS.

F-BBDA	Ciel de Bretagne	F-BBDI	Ciel de Provence
F-BBDB	Ciel de Touraine	F-BBDJ	Ciel Ile de France
F-BBDD	Ciel de Bourgogne	F-BBDK	Ciel de Normandie
F-BBDE	Ciel de Picardie	F-BBDL	Ciel d'Alsace
F-BBDF	Ciel d'Artois	F-BBDM	Ciel de Gascogne
F-BBDG	Ciel de Champagne	F-BBDN	Ciel de Lorraine
F-BBDH	Ciel de Bearn	F-BBDO	Ciel de Savoie

DOUGLAS C-54A SKYMASTER FREIGHTERS.

F-BELC	F-BELD	F-BELE	F-BELF

LOCKHEED CONSTELLATIONS.

F-BAZA	F-BAZI	F-BAZL	F-BAZO
F-BAZB	F-BAZJ	F-BAZM	F-BAZP
F-BAZC	F-BAZK	F-BAZN	F-BAZQ
F-BAZD			

LANGUEDOC 161s.

F-BATB	F-BATO	F-BATU	F-BCUG
F-BATC	F-BATP	F-BATV	F-BCUH
F-BATD	F-BATQ	F-BATX	F-BCUI
F-BATE	F-BATR	F-BATZ	F-BCUJ
F-BATG	F-BATS	F-BCUA	F-BCUK
F-BATI	F-BATT	F-BCUB	F-BCUL
F-BATJ	F-BCUK	F-BCUE	F-BCUM
F-BATN	F-BCUL	F-BCUF	F-BCUO

DOUGLAS DC-3 DAKOTAS.

F-BAIE	F-BAOE	F-BAXK	F-BCYQ
F-BAIF	F-BAXA	F-BAXL	F-BCYR
F-BAIG	F-BAXB	F-BAXM	F-BCYS
F-BAIH	F-BAXE	F-BAXP	F-BCYT
F-BAII	F-BAXF	F-BAXR	F-BCYU
F-BAIJ	F-BAXG	F-BAXS	F-BCYV
F-BAOA	F-BAXH	F-BBBA	F-BCYX
F-BAOC	F-BAXI	F-BBBE	F-BEFM
F-BAOD	F-BAXJ	F-BCYP	F-BEFN

DE HAVILLAND DRAGON RAPIDES.

F-BEDX	F-BEDY	F-BEDZ

CONSOLIDATED CATALINA FLYING-BOATS.

F-BBCB	F-BBCC	F-BBCD

LATECOERE 631 FLYING-BOATS.

F-BANU	Guillaumet	F-BDRA	Unnamed

AIR INDIA INTERNATIONAL FLEET.

LOCKHEED CONSTELLATIONS.

| VT-CQP | Malabar Princess | | VT-CQS | Mogul Princess |
| VT-CQR | Rajput Princess | | | |

ALITALIA FLEET.

AVRO LANCASTRIANS.

(On loan from B.O.A.C.)

I-DALR	Borea		I-AHCB	Grecale
I-AHBX	Maestrale		I-AHCD	Scirocco
I-AHBY	Libeccio			

S.I.A.I. MARCHETTI S.M. 95s.

I-DALJ	Cristoforo Colombo		I-DALN	Sebastiano Caboto
I-DALK	Amerigo Vespucci		I-DALO	Ugolino Vivaldi
I-DALL	Marco Polo			

AMERICAN OVERSEAS AIRLINES FLEET.

(On services to Great Britain)

DOUGLAS C-54E SKYMASTERS.

NC 90901	Flagship Stockholm		NC 90905	Flagship Glasgow
NC 90902	Flagship London		NC 90906	Flagship Copenhagen
NC 90903	Flagship Oslo			

DOUGLAS C-54G SKYMASTERS.

NC 90910	Flagship Shannon		NC 90913	Flagship Amsterdam
NC 90911	Flagship Reykjavik		NC 90915	Flagship Gander
NC 90912	Flagship Prestwick		NC 90909	Flagship Keflavik

LOCKHEED L-49 CONSTELLATIONS.

NC 90921	Flagship Sweden		NC 90925	Flagship Americ
NC 90922	Flagship Denmark		NC 90926	Flagship Eire
NC 90923	Flagship Great Britain		NC 90927	Flagship Norway
NC 90924	Flagship Holland			

BRITISH EUROPEAN AIRWAYS FLEET.

VICKERS VIKING 1Bs.

G-AHPL	Verdant		G-AHPS	Verity
G-AHPM	Verderer		G-AIVB	Vernal
G-AHPN	Ventnor		G-AIVC	Vernon
G-AHPO	Venture		G-AIVD	Vetcran
G-AHPP	Venus		G-AIVF	Vibrant
G-AHPR	Verily		G-AIVG	Viceroy

G-AIVH	Vicinity	G-AJBO	Vintage
G-AIVI	Victor	G-AJBP	Vintner
G-AIVJ	Victoria	G-AJBS	Virgo
G-AIVK	Victory	G-AJBT	Viper
G-AIVL	Vigilant	G-AJBU	Virtue
G-AIVM	Vigorous	G-AJBV	Viscount
G-AIVN	Violet	G-AJBW	Vista
G-AIVO	Villian	G-AJBX	Vital
G-AJBM	Vincent	G-AJBY	Vitality
G-AJBN	Vindictive	G-AJCE	Vivacious

VICKERS VIKING IA (CREW TRAINING).

G-AHOY	Vanity

DOUGLAS DC-3 DAKOTAS.

G-AGHJ	G-AGIW	G-AHCT	G-AJHY
G-AGHL	G-AGIX	G-AHCU	G-AJHZ
G-AGHS	G-AGJZ	G-AHCV	G-AJIA
G-AGIP	G-AGYX	G-AHCW	G-AJIB
G-AGIS	G-AGZB	G-AHCX	G-AJIC
G-AGIU	G-AGZD	G-AHCY	

DOUGLAS DC-3 DAKOTA FREIGHTERS.

G-AGJV	G-AGJW	G-AGYZ	G-AHCZ

DE HAVILLAND DRAGON RAPIDES.

G-AFEZ	G-AGSK	G-AHKS	G-AHXV
G-AFRK	G-AGUP	G-AHKT	G-AHXW
G-AGJG	G-AGUR	G-AHKU	G-AHXX
G-AGPH	G-AGUU	G-AHKV	G-AHXY
G-AGSH	G-AGUV	G-AHLL	G-AHXZ

B.E.A. EXPERIMENTAL HELICOPTER UNIT.

Bell 47B	G-AKFA	Sikorsky S.51	G-AJOR
Bell 47B	G-AKFB	Sikorsky S.51	G-AJOV
Sikorsky S.51	G-AKCU		

BRITISH OVERSEAS AIRWAYS FLEET

LOCKHEED CONSTELLATIONS.

G-AHEJ	Bristol II	G-AHEM	Balmoral
G-AHEK	Berwick II	G-AHEN	Baltimore
G-AHEL	Bangor II	G-AKCE	Belfast

AVRO LANCASTRIAN FREIGHTERS.

G-AGLS	Nelson	G-AGMG	Nicosia
G-AGLT	Newcastle	G-AGMJ	Naseby
G-AGLW	Northampton	G-AGMK	Newbury
G-AGLY	Norfolk	G-AGMM	Nepal
G-AGMA	Newport	G-AKPY	Not yet named
G-AGMB	Norwich	G-AKPZ	Not yet named
G-AGME	Newhaven	G-AKRB	Not yet named

Upper: Latest type of airliner in service with Air France, the Languedoc 161.   Illustrated is F-BATC, a familiar London Airport visitor.
Lower: Air India International Constellation *Malabar Princess* at London Airport on arrival from Bombay.

Upper: S.I.A.I. Marchetti S M. 95 airliner of the Italian company Alitalia, five of which operate between Northolt and Rome.
Lower: D.H. Rapide of British European Airways.   B.E.A. Rapides operate mainly on the Scottish island services.

11

British European Airways operate over 30 Vickers Viking IB airliners on European routes. With the familiar red "Speed-Key" insignia on nose and fin, G-AJBT *Viper* is illustrated. All B.E.A. Vikings have names beginning with "V".

Douglas Dakota G-AGJV of B.E.A. at Northolt.

Avro Lancastrian, now employed as freighter by B.O.A.C. to Johannesburg and Sydney.

AVRO YORKS.

G-AGJA	Mildenhall	G-AGNX	Moray
G-AGJB	Marathon	G-AGNY	Melrose
G-AGJC	Malmesbury	G-AGNZ	Monmouth
G-AGJD	Mansfield	G-AGOA	Montrose
G-AGJE	Middlesex	G-AGOB	Milford
G-AGNL	Mersey	G-AGOC	Malta
G-AGNM	Murchison	G-AGOD	Midlothian
G-AGNN	Madras	G-AGOE	Medway
G-AGNO	Manton	G-AGOF	Macduff
G-AGNP	Manchester	G-AGSL	Morley
G-AGNS	Melville	G-AGSM	Malvern
G-AGNT	Mandalay	G-AGSN	Marlow
G-AGNU	Montgomery	G-AGSO	Marston
G-AGNV	Morville	G-AGSP	Malborough
G-AGNW	Morecambe		

CONSOLIDATED LIBERATOR II FREIGHTERS.

G-AGJP	G-AHYD	G-AHYF
G-AHYB	G-AHYE	G-AHYG

DOUGLAS DC-3 DAKOTAS.

G-AGGA	G-AGKA	G-AGKJ	G-AGND
G-AGHE	G-AGKB	G-AGKK	G-AGNE
G-AGHF	G-AGKC	G-AGKL	G-AGNF
G-AGHH	G-AGKE	G-AGKN	G-AGNG
G-AGHM	G-AGKF	G-AGMZ	G-AGNK
G-AGHN	G-ACKG	G-AGNB	G-AGZC
G-AGHO	G-AGKH	G-AGNC	G-AGZE
G-AGIZ	G-AGKI		

SHORT S.45 SOLENT FLYING-BOATS.

G-AHIL	Salisbury	G-AHIT	Severn
G-AHIM	Scarborough	G-AHIU	Solway
G-AHIN	Southampton	G-AHIV	Salcombe
G-AHIO	Somerset	G-AHIW	Stornoway
G-AHIR	Sark	G-AHIX	Sussex
G-AHIS	Scapa	G-AHIY	Southsea

SHORT S.25 SANDRINGHAM VII FLYING-BOATS.

G-AKCO	St. George	G-AKCR	Not yet named
G-AKCP	St. David		

SHORT S.25 SANDRINGHAM V (" PLYMOUTH CLASS ") FLYING-BOATS.

G-AHYY	Portsmouth	G-AHZE	Portsea
G-AHZA	Penzance	G-AHZF	Poole
G-AHZC	Pembroke	G-AHZG	Pevensey
G-AHZD	Portmarnock	G-AJMZ	Perth

SHORT S.25 SUNDERLAND III (" HYTHE CLASS ") FLYING-BOATS.

G-AGER	Hadfield	G-AGHZ	Hawkesbury
G-AGEU	Hampshire	G-AGIA	Haslemere
G-AGEW	Hanwell	G-AGJJ	Henley
G-AGHX	Harlequin	G-AGJK	Howard

G-AGJL	Hobart	G-AGKW	Hotspur
G-AGJM	Hythe	G-AGKX	Himalaya
G-AGJN	Hudson	G-AGKY	Hungerford
G-AGJO	Honduras	G-AGKZ	Harwich
G-AGKV	Huntingdon	G-AGLA	Hunter

BOEING STRATOCRUISERS.

The following registration letters have been announced as reserved for use on the B.O.A.C. Stratocruisers now building in the U.S.A., but it is to be noted that these are provisional and liable to alteration. No names have yet been decided for these aircraft which are to come into service on B.O.A.C.'s Atlantic route during 1949.

G-AKGH	G-AKGJ	G-AKGM
G-AKGI	G-AKGK	

BRITISH SOUTH AMERICAN AIRWAYS FLEET.

AVRO TUDOR IVs.

G-AHNJ	Star Panther	G-AHNN	Star Leopard
G-AHNK	Star Lion		

AVRO YORK 1Gs.

G-AHEX	Star Venture	G-AHFD	Star Mist
G-AHEY	Star Quest	G-AHFE	Star Vista
G-AHFA	Star Dale	G-AHFF	Star Gleam
G-AHFB	Star Stream	G-AHFG	Star Haze
G-AHFC	Star Dew	G-AHFH	Star Glitter

AVRO LANCASTRIAN IIs.

G-AKFF	Star Flight	G-AKTB	Star Glory
G-AKFG	Star Traveller	G-AKTC	Star Fortune
G-AKMW	Star Bright	G-AKTG	Star Crest

AVRO LANCASTRIAN IIIs.

G-AGWI	Star Land	G-AGWL	Star Guide

AVRO LANCASTER FREIGHTERS.

G-AGUJ	Star Pilot	G-AGUM	Star Ward

AIRSPEED OXFORD.

G-AIVY	Star Mentor

CENTRAL AFRICAN AIRWAYS FLEET.

(Operating on special flights into Great Britain).

VICKERS VIKINGS.

VP-YEW	VP-YEY	VP-YHT
VP-YEX	VP-YHJ	

CIE AIR TRANSPORT FLEET.

(Operating into Great Britain).

BEECH 18 EXPEDITERS.

F-BEDB	F-BEDD
F-BEDC	F-BEDE

BRISTOL 170s.

F-BEND	F-8ENH
F-BENF	

COBETA FLEET.

(Operated by Cobeta and owned by John Mahieu Aviation of Brussels).

DOUGLAS DC-3 DAKOTA.

OO-APC

LOCKHEED HUDSON.

OO-API

C.S.A. FLEET.

(On services to Great Britain).

DOUGLAS DC-3 DAKOTAS.

OK-WAA	OK-WDC	OK-WDL	OK-WDU
OK-WCN	OK-WDE	OK-WDN	OK-WDV
OK-WCO	OK-WDF	OK-WDO	OK-WDW
OK-WCP	OK-WDG	OK-WDP	OK-WDY
OK-WCR	OK-WDH	OK-WDQ	OK-WDZ
OK-WCS	OK-WDI	OK-WDR	OK-XDH
OK-WCT	OK-WDJ	OK-WDS	OK-XDN
OK-WDA	OK-WDK	OK-WDT	

D.D.L. FLEET.

(Component of Scandinavian Airways System).

DOUGLAS DC-6s.

OY-AAE	
OY-AAF	

DOUGLAS DC-4 SKYMASTERS.

OY-DFI	Dan Viking
OY-DFO	Rolf Viking

VICKERS VIKINGS.

OY-DLA	Tor Viking	OY-DLO	Tormund Viking
OY-DLE	Torleif Viking	OY-DLU	Torlak Viking

DOUGLAS DC-3 DAKOTAS.

OY-DCA	Arv Viking	OY-DDA	Sven Viking
OY-DCE	Gorm Viking	OY-DDE	Erik Viking
OY-DCO	Orm Viking	OY-DDI	Roar Viking
OY-DCU	Ulf Viking	OY-DDY	Trym Viking
OY-DCY	Sten Viking		

DOUGLAS C-47 DAKOTA FREIGHTERS.

OY-AAB	Regnar Viking	OY-AYB	Bjorn Viking
OY-AOB	Bjarke Viking	OY-DDO	Odd Viking
OY-AUB	Bjarne Viking	OY-DDU	Leif Viking

JUNKERS JU 52 FREIGHTER.

OY-DFU   Uffe Viking

15

D.N.L. FLEET.

(Component of Scandinavian Airways System).

DOUGLAS DC-6s.

LN-LAG   *Sverre Viking* | LN-LAH   *Harald Viking*

DOUGLAS DC-4 SKYMASTERS.

LN-IAD   *Haakon Viking* | LN-IAE   *Olav Viking*

DOUGLAS DC-3 DAKOTAS.

LN-IAF	*Nordfugl*		LN-IAN	*Nordvind*
LN-IAG	*Nordegg*		LN-IAO	*Nordodd*
LN-IAH	*Nordheim*		LN-IAP	*Nordpol*
LN-IAI	*Nordis*		LN-IAR	*Nordkapp*
LN-IAK	*Nordkyn*		LN-IAS	*Nordpil*
LN-IAL	*Nordlys*		LN-IAT	*Nordtind*
LN-IAM	*Nordvard*			

SHORT SANDRINGHAM VI FLYING-BOATS.

LN-IAU	*Bamse Brakar*		LN-LAI	*Jutulen*
LN-IAW	*Bukken Bruse*			

F.A.M.A. FLEET.

(Note.: " G.B." indicates aircraft used most on routes to Great Britain).

AVRO YORKS.

LV-AFV (G.B.)		LV-AFZ (G.B.)
LV-AFY (G.B.)		

AVRO LANCASTRIANS.

LV-ACU (G.B.)		LV-ACV (G.B.)

DOUGLAS DC-4B SKYMASTERS.

LV-ABP (G.B.)		LV-AEU (G.B.)
LV-ABS (G.B.)		LV-AFD (G.B.)

DOUGLAS DC-4A SKYMASTERS.

LV-ABI		LV-ABO
LV-ABM		LV-ABR
LV-ABN		LV-ADH

VICKERS VIKINGS.

LV-AEW		LV-AFL		LV-AFI
LV-AEV		LV-AFF		LV-AFU

HELLENIC AIRLINES FLEET.

CONSOLIDATED LIBERATOR.

SX-DAA   *Maid of Athens*

DOUGLAS DC-3 DAKOTAS.

SX-BBA		SX-BBC
SX-BBB		SX-BBD

IBERIA FLEET.

DOUGLAS DC-2s.

EC-AAA	EC-AAD
EC-AAB	

DOUGLAS DC-4 SKYMASTERS.

EC-ACD	EC-ACF
EC-ACE	

D.H. DRAGON RAPIDES.

EC-AAV	EC-BAC
EC-AAS	EC-BAG

DOUGLAS DC-3 DAKOTAS.

EC-ABC	EC-ABQ
EC-ABK	EC-ACG
EC-ABL	EC-ACH
EC-ABM	EC-ACI
EC-ABP	EC-ACX
EC-ABN	

JUNKERS JU 52/3ms.

EC-AAH	EC-AAU
EC-AAI	EC-ABSJ
EC-AAK	EC-ABR
EC-AAL	

IRAQI AIRWAYS FLEET.

(Operating into Great Britain).

VICKERS VIKINGS.

YI-ABP	YI-ABQ	YI-ABR

K.L.M. FLEET.

LOCKHEED L-49 CONSTELLATIONS.

PH-TAU	Utrecht	PH-TDA	Arnhem
PH-TAV	Venlo	PH-TEN	Nijmegen
PH-TAW	Walcheren	PH-TEO	Overloon

LOCKHEED L-749 CONSTELLATIONS.

PH-TDB	Batavia	PH-TDH	Holland
PH-TDC	Curacao	PH-TEP	Pontianak
PH-TDD	Delft	PH-TER	Roermond
PH-TDE	Eindhoven	PH-TES	Soerabaja
PH-TDF	Franeker	PH-TET	Tilburg
PH-TDG	Gouda		

DOUGLAS DC-6s.

PH-TPB	Prins Bernhard	PH-TPM	Prinses Marijke
PH-TPI	Prinses Irene	PH-TPP	Prinses Margriet
PH-TPJ	Prinses Juliana	PH-TPT	Prinses Beatrix

DOUGLAS DC-4 SKYMASTERS.

PH-TAP	Paramaribo	PJ-TAR	Rotterdam
PH-TCE	Edam	PJ-TAS	Schiedam
PH-TCF	Friesland	PJ-TAT	Twenthe

DOUGLAS C-54 SKYMASTERS.

(Note. —" F " indicates freighters).

PH-TAH	PH-TEY (F)	PH-TLO
PH-TAM	PH-TEZ (F)	PH-TLW
PH-TBU	PH-TLK	PH-TSC

DOUGLAS DC-3 [DAKOTAS.

(**Note.**—" F " indicates freighter ;   " P " photographic aircraft ; " T " trainer and freighter).

PH-TAY	PH-TBM (P)	PH-TCK (T)	PH-TDU
PH-TAZ	PH-TBP	PH-TCL	PH-TDV
PH-TBG	PH-TBV	PH-TCS	PH-TDW
PH-TBI	PH-TBX	PH-TCT	PH-TDZ
PH-TBK (T)	PH-TBY	PH-TCU	PH-TEU
PH-TBH (T)	PH-TBZ	PH-TDS	PH-TEW (T)
PH-TBL	PH-TCI	PH-TDT	

(Dakotas in West Indies Division).

PJ-ALA	Ala Blanca	PJ-ALE (F)	PJ-ALI (P)
PJ-ALB	Blauwduif	PJ-ALG (P)	PJ-ALP
PJ-ALC	Chuchubi	PJ-ALH (P)	
PJ-ALD	Dekla		

CONVAIR 240 LINERS.

These aircraft are to replace Dakotas on many European routes of K.L.M. and are to commence delivery from the U.S.A. in the summer. Deliveries are expected to be completed before the end of 1948.   K.L.M. announces that the Convairs will be named after Dutch painters.

PH-TEA	PH-TED	PH-TEG	PH-TEK
PH-TEB	PH-TEE	PH-TEH	PH-TEL
PH-TEC	PH-TEF	PH-TEI	PH-TEM

LUXEMBOURG AIRLINES FLEET.

DOUGLAS DC-3 DAKOTAS.

LX-LAA	LX-LAB

PAN AMERICAN WORLD AIRWAYS FLEET.

(Atlantic Division).

LOCKHEED L-49 CONSTELLATIONS.

NC 88832	Clipper Flora Temple	NC 88856	Clipper Paul Jones
NC 88833	Clipper Bald Eagle	NC 88857	Clipper Flying Mist
NC 88836	Clipper Mayflower	NC 88859	Clipper Flying Eagle
NC 88837	Clipper Challenger	NC 88861	Clipper Winged Arrow
NC 88838	Clipper Donald McKay	NC 88865	Clipper White Falcon
NC 88846	Clipper Great Republic	NC 88868	Clipper Golden Fleece
NC 88847	Clipper Hotspur	NC 86527	Clipper Glory of the Skies
NC 88850	Clipper Intrepid	NC 86529	Clipper Romance of the Skies
NC 88855	Clipper Invincible	NC 86530	Clipper America

DOUGLAS DC-4 SKYMASTERS.

NC 88919	Clipper Panama	NC 88945	Clipper Gladiator
NC 88927	Clipper Skylark		

DOUGLAS DC-3 DAKOTAS.

NC 54227	Clipper Pan American	NC 79009	Clipper Undaunted
NC 79008	Clipper Robin Hood	NC 79010	Clipper Live Yankee

PANAIR DO BRASIL FLEET.

(Operating into Great Britain).
LOCKHEED CONSTELLATIONS.*

PP-PCB	PP-PCG	PP-PDA
PP-PCF	PP-PCR	

Q.E.A. FLEET.

(Operating into Great Britain).
LOCKHEED CONSTELLATIONS.

VH-EAA	Ross Smith	VH-EAC	Harry Hawker
VH-EAB	Lawrence Hargrave	VH-EAD	Chas. Kingsford Smith

SOUTH AFRICAN AIRWAYS FLEET.

(On services to Great Britain).
DOUGLAS DC-4 SKYMASTERS.

ZS-AUA	Tafelberg	ZS-BMH	Lebomba
ZS-AUG	Drakensberg	ZS-BWN	Swartberg
ZS-BMF	Amatola	LS-AU3	Outeniqua
ZS-BMG	Magaliesberg		

S.A.B.E.N.A. FLEET.

DOUGLAS DC-6s.

OO-AWA	OO-AWC
OO-AWB	

DOUGLAS DC-4 SKYMASTERS.

OO-CBI	OO-CBN
OO-CBJ	OO-CBO
OO-CBK	OO-CBP
OO-CBL	OO-CBQ
OO-CBM	

DOUGLAS DC-3 DAKOTAS.

OO-AUL	OO-AUV
OO-AUM	OO-AUX
OO-AUN	OO-AUY
OO-AUO	OO-AUZ
OO-AUP	OO-AWF
OO-AUQ	OO-AWG
OO-AUR	OO-AWK
OO-AUS	OO-AWN
OO-AUT	

D.H. DOVES.

OO-AWD	OO-AWE

SWISSAIR FLEET.

DOUGLAS DC-4 SKYMASTERS.

HB-ILA	HB-ILI
HB-ILE	HB-ILO

DOUGLAS DC-2s.

HB-ITE	HB-ITO

DOUGLAS DC-3 DAKOTAS.

HB-IRA	HB-IRI
HB-IRB	HB-IRK
HB-IRD	HB-IRL
HB-IRE	HB-IRM
HB-IRF	HB-IRN
HB-IRG	HB-IRO
	HB-IRX

CONVAIR 240 LINERS.†

HB-IRP	HB-IRS
HB-IRR	HB-IRT

* Panair do Brazil Constellations are known to the company as the [Bandeirante or "Pioneer" Class.
† On order from U.S.A., delivery expected before the end of 1948.

TRANS-CANADA AIRLINES FLEET.

(Operating into Great Britain).

CANADAIR DC-4M-2 NORTH STARS.

CF-TFA	CF-TFF	CF-TFK	CF-TFP
CF-TFB	CF-TFG	CF-TFL	CF-TFQ
CF-TFC	CF-TFH	CF-TFM	CF-TFR
CF-TFD	CF-TFI	CF-TFN	CF-TFS
CF-TFE	CF-TFJ	CF-TFO	CF-TFT

CANADAIR DC-4M-1 NORTH STARS.*

CF-TEK	CF-TEM	CF-TEP
CF-TEL	CF-TEO	CF-TEQ

TRANS-WORLD AIRLINE FLEET.

(Operating through Shannon).

LOCKHEED L-49 CONSTELLATIONS.

NC 86506	Star of Dublin	NC 90814	Star of Cairo
NC 86511	Star of Paris	NC 90815	Star of Lisbon
NC 86536	Star of Rome	NC 90816	Star of Geneva

LOCKHEED L-749 CONSTELLATIONS.

NC 91201	Star of New York	NC 91207	Star of Missouri
NC 91202	Star of Pennsylvania	NC 91208	Star of Massachusetts
NC 91203	Star of Ohio	NC 91209	Star of New Mexico
NC 91204	Star of Indiana	NC 91210	Star of Delaware
NC 91205	Star of Michigan	NC 91211	Star of Arizona
NC 91206	Star of Illinois	NC 91212	Star of California

DOUGLAS C-54B SKYMASTERS.

NC 34538	The Shalimar	NC 44994	The Alhambra
NC 34537	The Citadel	NC 86571	The Gates of Suez
NC 34577	The Moulein Pagoda		

DOUGLAS C-54E SKYMASTERS.

NC 45341	The Taj Mahal	NC 45344	The Colosseum
NC 45342	The Shamrock	NC 45345	The Arc de Triomphe
NC 45343	The Sphinx	NC 45346	The Acropolis

DOUGLAS C-54G SKYMASTERS.

NC 14747	The Bombay Merchant	NC 79067	The Shanghai Merchant
NC 79066	Unnamed		

* On loan from R.C.A.F., to be returned shortly.

Many charter companies are now operating their aircraft on regular scheduled internal airlines, details of which will be found on another page. To comply with the terms of the Civil Aviation Act, such companies are operating as associates of British European Airways.

Charter aircraft included in this list are either operating such internal services or are available for long-distance charter and freight work. Light aircraft, and aircraft available merely for local and pleasure flights have been excluded, and these can be found in the companion book " A.B.C. OF BRITISH AIRCRAFT MARKINGS."

AIR CHARTER LTD. FLEET.

(Aircraft based at Croydon and Bovingdon).

AIRSPEED CONSUL.

G-AJGH

D.H. DRAGON RAPIDES.

G-AFHY	G-AJFU

AIR CONTRACTORS LTD. FLEET.

(Aircraft based at Bovingdon).

DOUGLAS DAKOTAS.

G-AIWC	G-AIWE
G-AIWD	

AIR ENTERPRISES LTD. FLEET.

(Aircraft based at Croydon and Gatwick).

AIRSPEED CONSUL.

G-AJLJ

D.H. DRAGON RAPIDES.

G-AFMJ	G-AKOA
G-AKNX	G-AKOB
G-AKNY	G-AKRS
G-AKNZ	

AIR NAVIGATION AND TRADING CO. LTD. FLEET.

(Aircraft based at Squire's Gate).

D.H. DRAGON RAPIDES.

G-AKOY	G-AKZT
G-AKSG	

SUPERMARINE SEA OTTERS.

G-AKRG	G-AKYH

AIR TRANSPORT (CHARTER) (C.I.) LTD. FLEET.

(Aircraft based at Jersey).

DOUGLAS DAKOTAS.

G-AJBH	G-AKIL
G-AJBG	

D.H. DRAGON RAPIDES.

G-AFFB	G-AIUL
G-AGWC	

AIRWORK LTD. FLEET.

(Aircraft based at Blackbushe).

BRISTOL FREIGHTER.

G-AHJD

VICKERS VIKINGS.

G-AIXR	G-AJFR
G-AIXS	G-AJFS
G-AJFP	G-AJFT

(Aircraft based at Gatwick).

AIRSPEED CONSUL.

G-AIKR

BIRKETT AIR SERVICES LTD. FLEET.

(Aircraft based at Croydon).

AIRSPEED CONSUL.

G-AJLK

D.H. DRAGON RAPIDES.

G-AJBJ	G-AJDN

BLUE LINE AIRWAYS LTD. FLEET.

(Aircraft based at Tollerton, Nottingham).

AVRO ANSONS.

G-AJFX	G-AKFL
G-AKFK	G-AKFM

BRITISH AIR TRANSPORT LTD. FLEET.

(Aircraft based at Croydon and Redhill, Surrey).

AIRSPEED CONSULS.

G-AHEH	G-AIDZ
G-AHFS	G-AIEA
G-AIDY	

AVRO ANSONS.

G-AHKH	G-AIWV
G-AIWW	G-AIXU

D.H. FLAMINGO.

G-AFYH

A number of Flamingo aircraft are being reconditioned and will appear in service shortly. These aircraft are listed below :—

G-AFYF	G-AFYK
G-AFYJ	G-AFYL

BRITISH AVIATION SERVICES LTD. FLEET.

(Including Silver City Airways, Ltd.).

(Aircraft based at Blackbushe).

AIRSPEED CONSULS.

G-AHRK	G-AJBF

AVRO LANCASTRIAN.

G-AHBV

D.H. DOVES.

G-AIWF	G-AKJP
G-AKJG	

BRISTOL FREIGHTER.

G-AGVC

BRISTOL WAYFARER.

G-AHJC

LOCKHEED LODESTAR.

G-AJAW

DOUGLAS DAKOTAS.

G-AJAV	G-AIRH

BRITISH NEDERLAND AIR SERVICES LTD. FLEET.

(Aircraft based at Bovingdon).

DOUGLAS DAKOTAS.

G-AJZD	G-AJZX

MILES AEROVAN IV.

G-AISI

BROOKLANDS AVIATION LTD. FLEET.

(Aircraft based at Sywell, Northants and Shoreham, Sussex).

D.H. DRAGON RAPIDES.

G-AJHO	G-AJHP

CAMBRIAN AIR SERVICES FLEET.

(Aircraft based at Cardiff Airport).

D.H. DRAGON RAPIDES.

G-AGZJ	G-AKUC
G-AKUB	

CHARTAIR LTD. FLEET.

(Aircraft based at Croydon Airport).

AIRSPEED CONSULS.

G-AIKO	G-AIUR
G-AIKX	G-AIUX
G-AIOM	G-AJGG

CIRO AVIATION FLEET.

(Aircraft based at Gatwick Airport).

D.H. DRAGON RAPIDES.

G-AFMA	G-AKGV

DOUGLAS DAKOTAS.

G-AIJD	ZS-BYX
G-AKJN	

CULLIFORD AIRLINES LTD. FLEET.

(Aircraft based at Squire's Gate).

AVRO ANSON.

G-AIXO

MILES AEROVAN.

G-AJZG

DENNIS AVIATION LTD. FLEET.

(Aircraft based at Croydon and Gatwick).

AIRSPEED CONSULS.

G-AHMB	G-AIOR

HORNTON AIRWAYS LTD. FLEET.

(Aircraft based at Heston).

AIRSPEED CONSULS.

G-AIOP	G-AIUW
G-AIUV	

D.H. DRAGON RAPIDE.

G-AIUO

DOUGLAS DAKOTA.

G-AKLL

HUNTING AIR TRAVEL LTD. FLEET.

(Aircraft based at Croydon and Gatwick).

D.H. DOVES.

G-AJBI	G-AJDP

D.H. DRAGON RAPIDES.

G-AHPU	G-AHWF

VICKERS VIKINGS.

G-AHPI	G-AHPJ

INTERNATIONAL AIRWAYS LTD. FLEET.

(Aircraft based at Croydon Airport).

AIRSPEED CONSULS.

G-AHXP	G-AIUU
G-AIIS	G-AJGB
G-AIOL	

AVRO ANSONS.

G-AGUH	G-AITL

ISLAND AIR CHARTERS LTD. FLEET.

(Aircraft based at Jersey).

D.H. DRAGON RAPIDES.

G-AHPT	G-AJFK

ISLAND AIR SERVICES LTD. FLEET.

(Aircraft based at St. Mary's, Scilly Isles and Croydon).

D.H. DRAGON RAPIDES.

G-AGSJ	G-AIOY

KEARSLEY AIRWAYS LTD. FLEET.

(Aircraft based at Stansted Airport).

DOUGLAS DAKOTAS.

G-AKAR	G-AKOZ
G-AKDT	

LANCASHIRE AIRCRAFT CORPORATION FLEET.

(Aircraft based at Squire's Gate, Blackpool ; Yeadon, Leeds and Bovingdon, Herts).

AIRSPEED CONSULS.

G-AHMD	G-AHZW
G-AHZV	

D.H. DRAGON RAPIDES.

G-AHEA	G-AJKY
G-AJKW	G-AKNV
G-AJKX	G-AKNW

HANDLEY PAGE HALIFAXES.

G-AIHV	*Air Trader*
G-AIHX	*Air Explorer*
G-AIHY	*Unnamed*
G-AJZY	*Air Monarch*
G-AJZZ	*Air Viceroy*
G-AKEC	*Air Voyager*

L.A.M.S. LTD. FLEET.

(Aircraft based at Stansted Airport).

HANDLEY PAGE HALIFAX FREIGHTERS.

G-AHZK	G-AIWJ
G-AHZL	G-AIWK
G-AHZO	G-AIWP

MANX AIR CHARTERS LTD. FLEET.

(Aircraft based at Ronaldsway, Isle of Man).

D.H. DRAGON RAPIDES.

G-AJGV	G-AKIF
G-AKGY	G-AKSE

MORTON AIR SERVICES LTD. FLEET.

(Aircraft based at Croydon Airport and Speke, Liverpool).

AIRSPEED CONSULS.

G-AHFT	G-AIOS
G-AHJX	G-AIOU
G-AIAH	G-AIOW

D.H. DOVES.

G-AKST	G-AKSU

D.H. DRAGON RAPIDES.

G-AGWP	G-AHIA
G-AGWR	G-AKUS

NEWMAN AIRWAYS FLEET.

(Aircraft based at Croydon Airport).

D.H. DRAGON RAPIDE.

G-AKPA

NORTHERN AIR CHARTER LTD. FLEET.

(Aircraft based at Woolsington, Newcastle-on-Tyne and Greatham, West Hartlepool).

AIRSPEED CONSULS.

G-AJGA	G-AJLH

D.H. DRAGON RAPIDE.

G-AKNN

NORTH SEA AIR TRANSPORT FLEET.

(Aircraft based at Hanworth, Feltham, Middlesex).

AVRO ANSON.

G-AIRX

D.H. DRAGON RAPIDES.

G-AHAG	G-AHTY
G-AHGD	G-AIWG
G-AHLU	G-AIWZ

LOCKHEED 12A.

G-AGDT

LOCKHEED 14.

G-AGBG

OLLEY AIR SERVICE LTD. FLEET.

(Aircraft based at Croydon Airport).

AIRSPEED CONSULS.

G-AIUY	G-AJLR
G-AJGD	

D.H. DOVES.

G-AJOT	G-AKSK
G-AKJR	

D.H. DRAGON RAPIDES.

G-AGSI	G-AKSB
G-AHGG	G-AKSD
G-AIYE	

PATRICK-DUVAL AVIATION SERVICES FLEET.

(Aircraft based at Elmdon Airport, Birmingham).

AIRSPEED CONSULS.

G-AIOT	G-AIOV

MILES AEROVANS.

G-AJKP	G-AJOF

SCOTTISH AIRLINES FLEET.

(Aircraft based at Prestwick Airport).

AIRSPEED OXFORD.

G-AHDZ

CONSOLIDATED LIBERATORS

G-AHDY	G-AHZP
G-AHZH	G-AHZR

DOUGLAS DC-3 DAKOTAS.

G-AGWS	G-AGZG
G-AGZF	G-AJVY

FOKKER F.22.

G-AFZP

SIVEWRIGHT AIRWAYS LTD. FLEET.

(Aircraft based at Barton Airport and Ringway Airport, Manchester).

AVRO XIX ANSONS.

G-AHXK	G-AHYN

D.H. DRAGON RAPIDES.

G-AJMY	G-AKMG

DOUGLAS DC-3 DAKOTAS.

G-AKAY	G-AKSM

SKYWAYS LTD. FLEET.

(Aircraft based at Dunsfold, Surrey).

AVRO LANCASTRIANS.

G-AGLV	*Sky Lane*
G-AHBT	*Sky Ranger*
G-AHBZ	*Sky Ambassador*
G-AHCC	*Sky Chieftain*
G-AJPP	*Sky Consort*

AVRO LANCASTER FREIGHTERS.

G-AKAB	*Sky Trainer*

AVRO YORKS.

G-AHFI	*Sky Way*
G-AHLV	*Sky Courier*

D.H. DOVE.

G-AHRB	*Sky Maid*

DOUGLAS DC-3 DAKOTAS.

G-AGBD	*Sky Hawk*
G-AICV	*Sky Liner*

DOUGLAS DC-4 SKYMASTERS.

G-AJPL	*Sky Wisdom*
G-AJPO	*Sky Alliance*
G-AJPM	*Sky Freedom*
G-AJPN	*Sky Champion*

D.H. DRAGON RAPIDE.

G-AHFJ	*Sky Trail*

LOCKHEED 12A.

G-AGWN	Unnamed

SOUTHERN AIRCRAFT (GATWICK) LTD. FLEET.

(Aircraft based at Gatwick Airport).

AVRO ANSON.

G-AKEW

D.H. DRAGON RAPIDES.

G-AJTU | G-AKOO

TRENT VALLEY AVIATION LTD. FLEET.

(Aircraft based at Tollerton, Nottingham).

DOUGLAS DC-3 DAKOTA.

G-AJPF

ULSTER AVIATION LTD. FLEET.

(Aircraft based at Newtownards Airport, Belfast).

AIRSPEED CONSUL.

G-AIKT

D.H. DRAGON RAPIDES.

G-AGIF | G-AHLN

MILES AEROVANS.

G-AJKU | G-AJTD

WESTERN AIRWAYS FLEET.

(Aircraft based at Weston-super-Mare).

AVRO ANSONS.

G-AIOB	G-AITJ
G-AITK	

WESTMINSTER AIRWAYS FLEET.

(Aircraft based at Blackbushe, Surrey and Croydon Airport).

AIRSPEED CONSULS.

G-AJLI | G-AJNG

DOUGLAS DC-3 DAKOTAS

G-AJAY | G-AJAZ

WORLD AIR FREIGHT FLEET.

(Aircraft based at Bovingdon).

HANDLEY PAGE HALIFAX FREIGHTERS.

G-AJNZ | G-AKGZ

CF—CANADA.

Registration	Type
CF-TEK	
CF-TEL	Canadair
CF-TEM	North Star I
CF-TEO	of Trans-Canada
CF-TEP	Air Lines
CF-TFA	
CF-TFB	
CF-TFC	
CF-TFD	
CF-TFE	
CF-TFF	
CF-TFG	
CF-TFH	
CF-TFI	Canadair
CF-TFJ	North Star II
CF-TFK	of Trans-Canada
CF-TFL	Air Lines
CF-TFM	
CF-TFN	
CF-TFO	
CF-TFP	
CF-TFR	
CF-TFS	
CF-TFT	

EC—SPAIN.

Registration	Type
EC-AAA	Douglas DC-2
EC-AAB	of Iberia
EC-AAD	
EC-AAH	
EC-AAI	Junkers
EC-AAK	Ju 52/3m
EC-AAL	of Iberia
EC-AAU	
EC-AAV	D.H. Dragon
EC-AAS	Rapide of Iberia
EC-ABC	
EC-ABK	
EC-ABM	Douglas Dakota
EC-ABN	of Iberia
EC-ABP	
EC-ABQ	
EC-ACD	Douglas
EC-ACE	Skymaster
EC-ACF	of Iberia
EC-ACG	
EC-ACH	Douglas Dakota
EC-ACI	of Iberia
EC-ACX	
EC-BAC	D.H. Dragon
EC-BAG	Rapide of Iberia

EI—EIRE.

Registration	Type
EI-ACD	
EI-ACE	
EI-ACF	
EI-ACG	
EI-ACH	Douglas Dakota
EI-ACI	of Aer Lingus
EI-ACK	
EI-ACL	
EI-ACM	
EI-ACT	
EI-ADB	Airspeed Consul
EI-ADC	of Aer Lingus
EI-ADW	Douglas Dakota
EI-ADX	of Aer Lingus
EI-ADY	

F—FRANCE.

Registration	Type
F-BAIE	
F-BAIF	
F-BAIG	Douglas Dakota
F-BAIH	of Air France
F-BAII	
F-BAIJ	
F-BANU	Latecoere 631 of Air France
F-BAOA	
F-BAOC	Douglas Dakota
F-BAOD	of Air France
F-BAOE	
F-BATB	
F-BATC	
F-BATD	
F-BATE	
F-BATG	
F-BATI	
F-BATJ	
F-BATN	
F-BATO	
F-BATP	Languedoc 161
F-BATQ	of Air France
F-BATR	
F-BATS	
F-BATT	
F-BATU	
F-BATV	
F-BATX	
F-BATZ	
F-BAXA	
F-BAXB	
F-BAXE	
F-BAXF	
F-BAXG	
F-BAXH	
F-BAXI	Douglas Dakota
F-BAXJ	of Air France
F-BAXK	
F-BAXL	
F-BAXM	
F-BAXP	
F-BAXR	
F-BAXS	
F-BAZA	
F-BAZB	
F-BAZC	
F-BAZD	
F-BAZI	
F-BAZJ	Lockheed
F-BAZK	Constellation
F-BAZL	of Air France
F-BAZM	
F-3AZN	
F-BAZO	
F-BAZP	
F-BAZQ	
F-BBBA	Douglas Dakota
F-BBBE	of Air France
F-BBCB	Consolidated
F-BBCC	Catalina
F-BBCD	of Air France

Registration	Type
F-BBDA	
F-BBDB	
F-BBDD	
F-BBDE	
F-BBDF	
F-BBDG	
F-BBDH	Douglas
F-BBDI	Skymaster
F-BBDJ	of Air France
F-BBDK	
F-BBDL	
F-BBDM	
F-BBDN	
F-BBDO	
F-BCUA	
F-BCUB	
F-BCUE	
F-BCUF	
F-BCUG	
F-BCUH	Languedoc 161
F-BCUI	of Air France
F-BCUJ	
F-BCUK	
F-BCUL	
F-BCUM	
F-BCUO	
F-BCYP	
F-BCYQ	
F-BCYR	
F-BCYS	Douglas Dakota
F-BCYT	of Air France
F-BCYU	
F-BCYV	
F-BCYX	
F-BDRA	Latecoere 631 of Air France
F-BEDB	
F-BEDC	Beech
F-BEDD	Expeditor
F-BEDE	of Air Transport
F-BEDX	D.H. Dragon
F-BEDY	Rapide
F-BEDZ	of Air France
F-BEFM	Douglas Dakota
F-BEFN	of Air France
F-BELC	Douglas
F-BELD	Skymaster
F-BELE	of Air France
F-BELF	
F-BEND	Bristol 170
F-BENF	of Air Transport
F-BENH	

G—GREAT BRITAIN

Registration	Type
G-AFEZ	D.H. Dragon Rapide of British European Airways
G-AFFB	D.H. Dragon Rapide of Air Transport (Charter) (C.I.)
G-AFHY	D.H. Dragon Rapide of Air Charter Ltd.

Upper: A Consolidated Liberator freighter of B.O.A.C. as employed on the route to Montreal via Prestwick.
Lower: British Overseas Airways has six Lockheed Constellations on the Atlantic route and has recently purchased five more for the route to Australia.   Here is *Berwick* G-AHEK.

(*Photos: A. S. C. Lumsden*

Upper: Avro York G-AGOF *Macduff* of British Overseas Airways Corporation. B.O.A.C. Yorks fly to the Middle East, West Africa and Singapore.
Lower: One of the 30 Douglas Dakotas still in service with B.O.A.C. Dakotas operate the route from London Airport to Cairo.

27

Short Sandringham flying-boat G-AHYY *Portsmouth*, one of 10 "Plymouth" Class boats used by B.O.A.C. on the Dragon Route to the Far East and Japan, departing from Berth 50, Southampton.

(*Photos: B.O.A.C.*

Short Solent G-AHIN *Southampton* which made the inaugural flight of B.O.A.C.'s new Springbok flying-boat service to South Africa in May, 1948.

G-AFMA	D.H. Dragon Rapide of Ciro's Aviation Ltd.
G-AFMJ	D.H. Dragon Rapide of Air Enterprises Ltd.
G-AFRK	D.H. Dragon Rapide of British European Airways
G-AFYH	D.H. Flamingo of British Air Transport Ltd.
G-AFZP	Fokker F.22 of Scottish Airlines
G-AGBG	Lockheed 14 of North Sea Air Transport Ltd.
G-AGDT	Lockheed 12a of North Sea Air Transport Ltd.
G-AGER, G-AGEU, G-AGEW	Short "Hythe" Flying-boat of B.O.A.C.
G-AGGA, G-AGHE, G-AGHF, G-AGHH, G-AGHM, G-AGHN, G-AGHO	Douglas Dakota of B.O.A.C.
G-AGHJ, G-AGHL, G-AGHS	Douglas Dakota of British European Airways
G-AGHX, G-AGHZ, G-AGIA	Short "Hythe" Flying-boat of B.O.A.C.
G-AGIF	D.H. Dragon Rapide of Ulster Aviation Ltd.
G-AGIP, G-AGIS, G-AGIU, G-AGIW, G-AGIX	Douglas Dakota of British European Airways
G-AGIZ	Douglas Dakota of B.O.A.C.
G-AGJA, G-AGJB, G-AGJC, G-AGJD, G-AGJE	Avro York of B.O.A.C.
G-AGJG	D.H. Dragon Rapide of British European Airways
G-AGJJ, G-AGJL, G-AGJM, G-AGJN, G-AGJO	Short "Hythe" Flying-boat of B.O.A.C.
G-AGJP	Consolidated Liberator of B.O.A.C.
G-AGJV, G-AGJW, G-AGJZ	Douglas Dakota of British European Airways
G-AGKA, G-AGKB, G-AGKC, G-AGKE, G-AGKF, G-AGKG, G-AGKH, G-AGKI, G-AGKJ, G-AGKK, G-AGKL, G-AGKN	Douglas Dakota of B.O.A.C.
G-AGKV, G-AGKW, G-AGKX, G-AGKY, G-AGKZ, G-AGLA	Short "Hythe" Flying-boat of B.O.A.C.
G-AGLS, G-AGLT	Avro Lancastrian of B.O.A.C.
G-AGLV	Avro Lancastrian of Skyways Ltd.
G-AGLW, G-AGLY, G-AGMA, G-AGMB, G-AGME, G-AGMG, G-AGMK, G-AGMM	Avro Lancastrian of B.O.A.C.
G-AGMZ, G-AGNB, G-AGNC, G-AGND, G-AGNE, G-AGNF, G-AGNG, G-AGNK	Douglas Dakota of B.O.A.C.
G-AGNL, G-AGNM, G-AGNN, G-AGNO, G-AGNP, G-AGNS, G-AGNT, G-AGNU, G-AGNV, G-AGNW, G-AGNX, G-AGNY, G-AGNZ, G-AGOA, G-AGOB, G-AGOC, G-AGOD, G-AGOE, G-AGOF	Avro York of B.O.A.C.
G-AGPH, G-AGSH	D.H. Dragon Rapide of British European Airways
G-AGSI	D.H. Dragon Rapide of Olley Air Service Ltd.
G-AGSJ	D.H. Dragon Rapide of Island Air Services Ltd.
G-AGSK	D.H. Dragon Rapide of British European Airways
G-AGSL, G-AGSM, G-AGSN, G-AGSO, G-AGSP	Avro York of B.O.A.C.
G-AGUH	Avro Anson of International Airways Ltd.
G-AGUJ, G-AGUM	Avro Lancaster of British South American Airways
G-AGUP, G-AGUR, G-AGUU, G-AGUV	D.H. Dragon Rapide of British European Airways
G-AGVC	Bristol Freighter of British Aviation Services Ltd.
G-AGWC	D.H. Dragon Rapide of Air Transport (Charter) (C.I.)
G-AGWI, G-AGWL	Avro Lancastrian of British South American Airways
G-AGWN	Lockheed 12a of Skyways Ltd.
G-AGWP, G-AGWR	D.H. Dragon Rapide of Morton Air Services Ltd.
G-AGWS	Douglas Dakota of Scottish Airlines
G-AGYX, G-AGYZ, G-AGZB, G-AGZD	Douglas Dakota of British European Airways
G-AGZF, G-AGZG	Douglas Dakota of Scottish Airlines
G-AGZJ	D.H. Dragon Rapide of Cambrian Air Services Ltd.
G-AHAG	D.H. Dragon Rapide of North Sea Air Transport Ltd.
G-AHBT	Avro Lancastrian of Skyways Ltd.
G-AHBV	Avro Lancastrian of British Aviation Services Ltd.

G-AHBZ G-AHCC	Avro Lancastrian of Skyways Ltd.
G-AHCT G-AHCU G-AHCV G-AHCW G-AHCX G-AHCY G-AHCZ	Douglas Dakota of British European Airways
G-AHDY	Consolidated Liberator of Scottish Airlines
G-AHDZ	Airspeed Oxford of Scottish Airlines
G-AHEA	D.H. Dragon Rapide of Lancashire Aircraft Corporation
G-AHEH	Airspeed Consul of British Air Transport Ltd.
G-AHEJ G-AHEK G-AHEL G-AHEM G-AHEN	Lockheed Constellation of B.O.A.C.
G-AHEX G-AHEY G-AHFA G-AHFB G-AHFC G-AHFD G-AHFE G-AHFF G-AHFG G-AHFH	Avro York of British South American Airways
G-AHFI	Avro York of Skyways Ltd.
G-AHFJ	D.H. Dragon Rapide of Skyways Ltd.
G-AHFT	Airspeed Consul of Morton Air Services Ltd.
G-AHGD	D.H. Dragon Rapide of North Sea Air Transport Ltd.
G-AHGG	D.H. Dragon Rapide of Olley Air Service Ltd.
G-AHIA	D.H. Dragon Rapide of Morton Air Services Ltd.
G-AHIL G-AHIM G-AHIN G-AHIO G-AHIR G-AHIS G-AHIT G-AHIU G-AHIV G-AHIW G-AHIX G-AHIY	Short Solent Flying-boat of B.O.A.C.
G-AHJC	Bristol Wayfarer of British Aviation Services Ltd.
G-AHJD	Bristol Freighter of Airwork Ltd.
G-AHJX	Airspeed Consul of Morton Air Services Ltd.
G-AHKH	Avro Anson of British Air Transport Ltd.
G-AHKS G-AHKT G-AHKU G-AHKV G-AHLL	D.H. Dragon Rapide of British European Airways
G-AHLN	D.H. Dragon Rapide of Ulster Aviation Ltd.
G-AHLU	D.H. Dragon Rapide of North Sea Air Transport
G-AHLV	Avro York of Skyways Ltd.
G-AHMB	Airspeed Consul of Dennis Aviation Ltd.
G-AHMD	Airspeed Consul of Lancashire Aircraft Corporation
G-AHNJ G-AHNK G-AHNN	Avro Tudor IV of British South American Airways
G-AHOY	Vickers Viking of British European Airways
G-AHPI G-AHPJ	Vickers Viking of Hunting Air Travel Ltd.
G-AHPM G-AHPN G-AHPO G-AHPR G-AHPS	Vickers Viking of British European Airways
G-AHPT	D.H. Dragon Rapide of Island Air Charters Ltd.
G-AHPU	D.H. Dragon Rapide of Hunting Air Travel Ltd.
G-AHRB	D.H. Dove of Skyways Ltd.
G-AHRK	Airspeed Consul of British Aviation Services Ltd.
G-AHTY	D.H. Dragon Rapide of North Sea Air Transport Ltd.
G-AHWF	D.H. Dragon Rapide of Hunting Air Travel Ltd.
G-AHXK	Avro Anson of Sivewright Airways Ltd.
G-AHXP	Airspeed Consul of International Airways Ltd.
G-AHXV G-AHXW G-AHXX G-AHXY G-AHXZ	D.H. Dragon Rapide of British European Airways
G-AHYB G-AHYD G-AHYE G-AHYF G-AHYG	Consolidated Liberator of B.O.A.C.
G-AHYN	Avro Anson of Sivewright Airways Ltd.
G-AHYY G-AHZA G-AHZC G-AHZD G-AHZE G-AHZF G-AHZG	Short "Plymouth" Flying-boat of B.O.A.C.
G-AHZH	Consolidated Liberator of Scottish Airlines
G-AHZK G-AHZL G-AHZO	Handley Page Halifax of L.A.M.S. Ltd.
G-AHZP G-AHZR	Consolidated Liberator of Scottish Airlines
G-AHZV G-AHZW	Airspeed Consul of Lancashire Aircraft Corporation
G-AIAH	Airspeed Consul of Morton Air Services Ltd.
G-AIBF	Airspeed Consul of British Aviation Services Ltd.
G-AICV	Douglas Dakota of Skyways Ltd.
G-AIDY G-AIDZ G-AIEA	Airspeed Consul of British Air Transport Ltd.
G-AIHV G-AIHX G-AIHY	Handley Page Halifax of Lancs. Aircraft Corporation
G-AIIS	Airspeed Consul of International Airways Ltd.
G-AIJD	Douglas Dakota of Ciro's Aviation Ltd.

Registration	Operator
G-AIKO	Airspeed Consul of Chartair Ltd.
G-AIKR	Airspeed Consul of Airwork Ltd.
G-AIKT	Airspeed Consul of Ulster Aviation Ltd.
G-AIKX	Airspeed Consul of Chartair Ltd.
G-AIOB	Avro Anson of Western Airways
G-AIOL	Airspeed Consul of International Airways Ltd.
G-AIOM	Airspeed Consul of Chartair Ltd.
G-AIOP	Airspeed Consul of Hornton Airways Ltd.
G-AIOR	Airspeed Consul of Dennis Aviation Ltd.
G-AIOS	Airspeed Consul of Morton Air Services Ltd.
G-AIOT	Airspeed Consul of Patrick-Duval Aviation Services
G-AIOU	Airspeed Consul of Morton Air Services Ltd.
G-AIOV	Airspeed Consul of Patrick-Duval Aviation Services
G-AIOW	Airspeed Consul of Morton Air Services Ltd.
G-AIOY	D.H. Dragon Rapide of Island Air Services
G-AIRH	Douglas Dakota of British Aviation Services Ltd.
G-AIRX	Avro Anson of North Sea Air Transport Ltd.
G-AISI	Miles Aerovan of British Nederland Air Services Ltd.
G-AITJ G-AITK	Avro Anson of Western Airways Ltd.
G-AITL	Airspeed Consul of International Airways Ltd.
G-AIUL	D.H. Dragon Rapide of Air Transport (Charter) (C.I.)
G-AIUO	D.H. Dragon Rapide of Hornton Airways Ltd.
G-AIUR	Airspeed Consul of Chartair Ltd.
G-AIUU	Airspeed Consul of International Airways Ltd.
G-AIUV G-AIUW	Airspeed Consul of Hornton Airways Ltd.
G-AIUX	Airspeed Consul of Chartair Ltd.
G-AIUY	Airspeed Consul of Olley Air Service Ltd.
G-AIVB G-AIVC G-AIVD G-AIVF G-AIVG G-AIVH G-AIVI G-AIVJ G-AIVK G-AIVL G-AIVM G-AIVN G-AIVO	Vickers Viking of British European Airways
G-AIVY	Airspeed Oxford of British South American Airways
G-AIWC G-AIWD G-AIWE	Douglas Dakota of Air Contractors Ltd.
G-AIWF	D.H. Dove of British Aviation Services Ltd.
G-AIWG	D.H. Dragon Rapide of North Sea Air Transport
G-AIWJ G-AIWK G-AIWP	Handley Page Halifax of L.A.M.S. Ltd.
G-AIWV	Avro Anson of British Air Transport Ltd.
G-AIWZ	D.H. Dragon Rapide of North Sea Air Transport
G-AIXO	Avro Anson of Culliford Air Lines Ltd.
G-AIXR G-AIXS	Vickers Viking of Airwork Ltd.
G-AIXU	Avro Anson of British Air Transport Ltd.
G-AIYE	D.H. Dragon Rapide of Olley Air Service Ltd.
G-AJAV	Douglas Dakota of British Aviation Services Ltd.
G-AJAW	Lockheed Lodestar of British Aviation Services Ltd.
G-AJAY G-AJAZ	Douglas Dakota of Westminster Airways Ltd.
G-AJBG G-AJBH	Douglas Dakota of Air Transport (Charter) (C.I.)
G-AJBI	D.H. Dove of Hunting Air Travel Ltd.
G-AJBJ	D.H. Dragon Rapide of Birkett Air Services Ltd.
G-AJBM G-AJBN G-AJBP G-AJBS G-AJBT G-AJBU G-AJBV G-AJBW G-AJBX G-AJBY G-AJCE	Vickers Viking of British European Airways
G-AJDN	D.H. Dragon Rapide of Birkett Air Services Ltd.
G-AJDP	D.H. Dove of Hunting Air Travel Ltd.
G-AJFK	D.H. Dragon Rapide of Island Air Charters
G-AJFP G-AJFR G-AJFS G-AJFT	Vickers Viking of Airwork Ltd.
G-AJFU	D.H. Dragon Rapide of Air Charter Ltd.
G-AJFX	Avro Anson of Blue Line Airways
G-AJGA	Airspeed Consul of Northern Air Charter Ltd.
G-AJGB	Airspeed Consul of International Airways Ltd.
G-AJGD	Airspeed Consul of Olley Air Service Ltd.
G-AJGG	Airspeed Consul of Chartair Ltd.
G-AJGH	Airspeed Consul of Air Charter Ltd.
G-AJGV	D.H. Dragon Rapide of Manx Air Charters Ltd.
G-AJHO G-AJHP	D.H. Dragon Rapide of Brooklands Aviation Ltd.

31

G-AJHY G-AJHZ G-AJIA G-AJIB G-AJIC	Douglas Dakota of British European Airways	G-AJVY	Douglas Dakota of Scottish Airlines	G-AKIF	D.H. Dragon Rapide of Manx Air Charters Ltd.
G-AJKP	Miles Aerovan of Patrick-Duval Aviation Services	G-AJZD	Douglas Dakota of British- Nederland Air Services Ltd.	G-AKIL	Douglas Dakota of Air Transport (Charter) (C.I.)
G-AJKU	Miles Aerovan of Ulster Aviation Ltd.	G-AJZG	Miles Aerovan of Culliford Air Lines Ltd.	G-AKJG	D.H. Dove of British Aviation Services Ltd.
G-AJKW G-AJKX G-AJKY	D.H. Dragon Rapide of Lancs. Aircraft Corporation	G-AJZX	Douglas Dakota of British- Nederland Air Services Ltd.	G-AKJN	Douglas Dakota of Ciro's Aviation Ltd.
G-AJLH	Airspeed Consul of Northern Air Charter Ltd.	G-AJZY G-AJZZ	Handley Page Halifax of Lancs. Aircraft Corporation	G-AKJP	D.H. Dove of British Aviation Services Ltd.
G-AJLI	Airspeed Consul of Westminster Airways Ltd.	G-AKAB	Avro Lancaster of Skyways Ltd.	G-AKJR	D.H. Dove of Olley Air Service Ltd.
G-AJLJ	Airspeed Consul of Air Enterprises Ltd.	G-AKAR	Douglas Dakota of Kearsley Airways Ltd.	G-AKLL	Douglas Dakota of Hornton Airways Ltd.
G-AJLK	Airspeed Consul of Birkett Air Services Ltd.	G-AKAY	Douglas Dakota of Sivewright Airways Ltd.	G-AKMW	Avro Lancaster of British South American Airways
G-AJLR	Airspeed Consul of Olley Air Service Ltd.	G-AKCE	Lockheed Constellation of B.O.A.C.	G-AKNN	D.H. Dragon Rapide of West Cumberland Air Services
G-AJMY	D.H. Dragon Rapide of Sivewright Airways Ltd.	G-AKCO G-AKCP G-AKCR	Short Sandringham VII of B.O.A.C.	G-AKNV G-AKNW	D.H. Dragon Rapide of Lancs. Aircraft Corporation
G-AJMZ	Short " Plymouth " Flying-boat of B.O.A.C.	G-AKDT	Douglas Dakota of Kearsley Airways Ltd.	G-AKNX G-AKNY G-AKNZ G-AKOA G-AKOB	D.H. Dragon Rapide of Air Enterprises Ltd.
G-AJNG	Airspeed Consul of Westminster Airways Ltd.	G-AKEC	Handley Page Halifax of Lancs. Aircraft Corporation	G-AKOO	D.H. Dragon Rapide of Southern Aircraft Ltd.
G-AJNZ	Handley Page Halifax of World Air Freight Ltd.	G-AKEW	Avro Anson of Southern Aircraft Ltd.	G-AKOY	D.H. Dragon Rapide of Air Navigation & Trading Ltd.
G-AJOF	Miles Aerovan of Patrick-Duval Aviation Services	G-AKFF G-AKFG	Avro Lancastrian of British South American Airways	G-AKOZ	Douglas Dakota of Kearsley Airways Ltd.
G-AJOI	Miles Aerovan of Sivewright Airways Ltd.	G-AKFK G-AKFL G-AKFM	Avro Anson of Blue Line Airways	G-AKPA	D.H. Dragon Rapide of New- man Airways
G-AJOT	D.H. Dove of Olley Air Service Ltd.	G-AKGH G-AKGI G-AKGJ G-AKGK G-AKGM	Boeing Stratocruiser of B.O.A.C.	G-AKPY G-AKPZ G-AKRB	Avro Lancastrian of B.O.A.C.
G-AJPF	Douglas Dakota of Trent Valley Aviation Ltd.	G-AKGV	D.H. Dragon Rapide of Ciro's Aviation Ltd.	G-AKRG	Supermarine Sea Otter of Air Navigation & Trading Ltd.
G-AJPL G-AJPM G-AJPN G-AJPO	Douglas Skymaster of Skyways Ltd.	G-AKGY	D.H. Dragon Rapide of Manx Air Charters Ltd.	G-AKRS	D.H. Dragon Rapide of Air Enterprises Ltd.
G-AJPP	Avro Lancastrian of Skyways Ltd.	G-AKGZ	Handley Page Halifax of World Air Freight Ltd.	G-AKSB G-AKSD	D.H. Dragon Rapide of Olley Air Service Ltd.
G-AJTU	D.H. Dragon Rapide of Southern Aircraft Ltd.				

G-AKSE	D.H. Dragon Rapide of Manx AirCharters Ltd.	
G-AKSG	D.H. Dragon Rapide of Air Navigation & Trading Ltd.	
G-AKSK	D.H. Dove of Olley Air Service Ltd.	
G-AKSM	Douglas Dakota of Sivewright Airways Ltd.	
G-AKST / G-AKSU	D.H. Dove of Morton Air Services Ltd.	
G-AKTC / G-AKTG	Avro Lancastrian of British South American Airways	
G-AKUB / G-AKUC	D.H. Dragon Rapide of Cambrian Air Services	
G-AKUS	D.H. Dragon Rapide of Morton Air Services Ltd.	
G-AKYH	Supermarine Sea Otter of Air Navigation & Trading Ltd.	
G-AKZT	D.H. Dragon Rapide of Air Navigation & Trading Ltd.	

HB—SWITZERLAND

HB-ILA / HB-ILE / HB-ILI / HB-ILO	Douglas Skymaster of Swissair	
HB-IRA / HB-IRB / HB-IRD / HB-IRE / HB-IRF / HB-IRG / HB-IRI / HB-IRK / HB-IRL / HB-IRM / HB-IRN / HB-IRO	Douglas Dakota of Swissair	
HB-IRP / HB-IRR / HB-IRS / HB-IRT	Convair 240 Liner of Swissair	
HB-IRX	Douglas Dakota of Swissair	
HB-ITE / HB-ITO	Douglas DC-2 of Swissair	

LN—NORWAY.

LN-IAD / LN-IAE	Douglas Skymaster of D.N.L. (S.A.S.)	
LN-IAF / LN-IAG / LN-IAH / LN-IAI / LN-IAK / LN-IAL / LN-IAM / LN-IAN / LN-IAO / LN-IAP / LN-IAR / LN-IAS / LN-IAT	Douglas Dakota of D.N.L. (S.A.S.)	
LN-IAU / LN-IAW	Short Sandringham VI of D.N.L. (S.A.S.)	
LN-LAG / LN-LAH	Douglas DC-6 of D.N.L. (S.A.S.)	
LN-LAI	Short Sandringham VI of D.N.L. (S.A.S.)	
LN-KAD / LN-KAE / LN-KAF / LN-KAG	Junkers Ju 52/3m of D.N.L. (S.A.S.)	

LV—ARGENTINE.

LV-ABI / LV-ABM / LV-ABN / LV-ABO / LV-ABP / LV-ABQ / LV-ABR / LV-ABS	Douglas Skymaster of F.A.M.A.	
LV-ACU / LV-ACV	Avro Lancastrian of F.A.M.A.	
LV-ADH / LV-AEU	Douglas Skymaster of F.A.M.A.	
LV-AEW / LV-AEV	Vickers Viking of F.A.M.A.	
LV-AEU / LV-AFD	Douglas Skymaster of F.A.M.A.	
LV-AFL / LV-AFF / LV-AFI / LV-AFU	Vickers Viking of F.A.M.A.	
LV-AFV / LV-AFY / LV-AFZ	Avro York of F.A.M.A.	

I X—LUXEMBOURG

LX-LAA / LX-LAB	Douglas Dakota of Luxembourg Airlines	

NC—U.S.A.

NC 14747		
NC 34537 / NC 34558 / NC 34577 / NC 44994 / NC 45341 / NC 45342 / NC 45343 / NC 45344 / NC 45345 / NC 45346	Douglas Skymaster of Trans-World Airline	
NC 54227 / NC 79008 / NC 79009 / NC 79010	Douglas Dakota of Pan American Airways	
NC 79066 / NC 79067	Douglas Skymaster of Trans-World Airline	
NC 86506 / NC 86511	Lockheed Constellation of Trans-World Airline	
NC 86527 / NC 86529 / NC 86530	Lockheed Constellation of Pan American Airways	
NC 86571	Douglas Skymaster of Trans-World Airline	
NC 88832 / NC 88833 / NC 88836 / NC 88837 / NC 88838 / NC 88846 / NC 88847 / NC 88850 / NC 88855 / NC 88856 / NC 88857 / NC 88859 / NC 88861 / NC 88865 / NC 88868	Lockheed Constellation of Pan American Airways	
NC 88919 / NC 88927 / NC 88945	Douglas Skymaster of Pan American Airways	
NC 90814 / NC 90815 / NC 90816	Lockheed Constellation of Trans-World Airline	
NC 90901 / NC 90902 / NC 90903 / NC 90905 / NC 90906 / NC 90909 / NC 90910 / NC 90911 / NC 90912 / NC 90913 / NC 90915	Douglas Skymaster of American Overseas Airlines	

NC 90921	
NC 90922	
NC 90923	Lockheed
NC 90924	Constellation
NC 90925	of American
NC 90926	Overseas
NC 90927	Airlines
NC 91201	
NC 91202	
NC 91203	
NC 91204	Lockheed
NC 91205	Constellation
NC 91206	of Trans-World
NC 91207	Airline
NC 91209	
NC 91210	
NC 91211	
NC 91212	

OK—CZECHO-SLOVAKIA.

OK-WAA	
OK-WCN	
OK-WCO	
OK-WCP	
OK-WCR	
OK-WCS	
OK-WCT	
OK-WDA	
OK-WDC	
OK-WDE	
OK-WDF	
OK-WDG	
OK-WDH	
OK-WDI	
OK-WDJ	Douglas Dakota
OK-WDK	of C.S.A.
OK-WDL	(Czech Airlines)
OK-WDN	
OK-WDO	
OK-WDP	
OK-WDQ	
OK-WDR	
OK-WDS	
OK-WDT	
OK-WDU	
OK-WDV	
OK-WDW	
OK-WDY	
OK-WDZ	
OK-XDH	
OK-XDN	

OO—BELGIUM.

OO-AUL	
OO-AUM	
OO-AUN	
OO-AUO	
OO-AUP	
OO-AUQ	
OO-AUR	Douglas Dakota
OO-AUS	of Sabena
OO-AUT	
OO-AUV	
OO-AUX	
OO-AUY	
OO-AUZ	
OO-AWA	Douglas DC-6
OO-AWB	of Sabena
OO-AWC	

OO-AWD	D.H. Dove
OO-AWE	of Sabena
OO-CBI	
OO-CBJ	
OO-CBK	
OO-CBL	
OO-CBM	Douglas
OO-CBN	Skymaster
OO-CBO	of Sabena
OO-CBP	
OO-CBQ	
OO-AWF	
OO-AWG	Douglas Dakota
OO-AWK	of Sabena
OO-AWN	

OY—DENMARK.

OY-AAB	Douglas Dakota of D.D.L. (S.A.S.)
OY-AAE	Douglas DC-6 of
OY-AAF	D.D.L. (S.A.S.)
OY-AOB	
OY-AUB	
OY-AYB	
OY-DCA	
OY-DCE	
OY-DCO	
OY-DCU	Douglas Dakota
OY-DCY	of D.D.L.
OY-DDA	(S.A.S.)
OY-DDE	
OY-DDI	
OY-DDO	
OY-DDU	
OY-DDY	
OY-DFI	Douglas
OY-DFO	Skymaster of D.D.L. (S.A.S.)
OY-DFU	Junkers Ju 52/3m of D.D.L. (S.A.S.)
OY-DLA	
OY-DLE	Vickers Viking
OY-DLO	of D.D.L. (S.A.S.)
OY-DLU	

PH—HOLLAND.

PH-TAH	
PH-TAM	
PH-TAP	Douglas
PH-TAR	Skymaster
PH-TAS	of K.L.M.
PH-TAT	
PH-TAU	Lockheed
PH-TAV	Constellation
PH-TAW	of K.L.M.
PH-TAY	
PH-TAZ	
PH-TBG	
PH-TBH	
PH-TBI	Douglas Dakota
PH-TBK	of K.L.M.
PH-TBL	
PH-TBM	
PH-TBP	
PH-TBU	Douglas Sky-master of K.L.M.

PH-TBV	
PH-TBX	Douglas Dakota
PH-TBY	of K.L.M.
PH-TBZ	
PH-TCE	Douglas Sky-master of K.L.M.
PH-TCF	
PH-TCI	
PH-TCK	
PH-TCL	Douglas Dakota
PH-TCS	of K.L.M.
PH-TCT	
PH-TCU	
PH-TDA	
PH-TDB	
PH-TDC	
PH-TDD	Lockheed
PH-TDE	Constellation
PH-TDF	of K.L.M.
PH-TDG	
PH-TDH	
PH-TDS	
PH-TDT	
PH-TDU	Douglas Dakota
PH-TDV	of K.L.M.
PH-TDW	
PH-TDZ	
PH-TEA	
PH-TEB	
PH-TEC	
PH-TED	
PH-TEE	
PH-TEF	
PH-TEG	Convair 240
PH-TEH	Liner of K.L.M.
PH-TEI	
PH-TEK	
PH-TEL	
PH-TEM	
PH-TEN	
PH-TEO	
PH-TEP	Lockheed
PH-TER	Constellation
PH-TES	of K.L.M.
PH-TET	
PH-TEU	Douglas Dakota
PH-TEW	of K.L.M.
PH-TEY	Douglas Sky-master of K.L.M.
PH-TEZ	
PH-TPB	
PH-TPI	
PH-TPJ	Douglas DC-6
PH-TPM	of K.L.M.
PH-TPP	
PH-TPT	
PH-TLK	
PH-TLO	Douglas Sky-master of K.L.M.
PH-TLW	
PH-TSC	

PP—BRAZIL.

PP-PCB	
PP-PCF	Lockheed
PP-PCG	Constellation of
PP-PCR	Panair do Brasil
PP-PDA	

SE—SWEDEN.

SE-BAA
SE-BAB
SE-BAC
SE-BAL
SE-BAS } Douglas Dakota of A.B.A. (S.A.S.)
SE-BAT
SE-BAU
SE-BAW
SE-BAZ

SE-BBA
SE-BBC
SE-BBD
SE-BBE } Douglas Skymaster of A.B.A. (S.A.S.)
SE-BBF
SE-BBG

SE-BBH
SE-BBI
SE-BBK
SE-BBL
SE-BBM
SE-BBN } Douglas Dakota of A.B.A. (S.A.S.)
SE-BBO
SE-BBP
SE-BBR

SE-BDB
SE-BDC
SE-BDD
SE-BDE
SE-BDF } Douglas DC-6 of A.B.A. (S.A.S.)
SE-BDL
SE-BDM
SE-BDO

SX—GREECE.

SX-BBA
SX-BBB
SX-BBC } Douglas Dakota of Hellenic Airlines
SX-BBD

SX-DAA } Consolidated Liberator of Hellenic Airlines

VH—AUSTRALIA.

VH-EAA
VH-EAB } Lockheed Constellation of Qantas Empire Airways
VH-EAC
VH-EAD

VP—SOUTHERN RHODESIA.

VP-YEW
VP-YEX
YP-YEY } Vickers Viking of Central African Airways
VP-YHJ
VP-YHT

VT—INDIA.

VT-CQS
VT-CQT } Lockheed Constellation of Air India International
VT-CQU

YI—IRAQ.

YI-ABP
YI-ABQ } Vickers Viking of Iraqi Airways
YI-ABR

ZS—SOUTH AFRICA

ZS-AUA
ZS-AUG
ZS-BMF } Douglas Skymaster of South African Airways
ZS-BMG
ZS-BMH
ZS-BWN

An outstanding publication

★ AIRCRAFT ANNUAL ★

Edited by J. W. R. Taylor

Commends itself by the excellence of its illustrations and articles, contributed by such famous authorities as Sir Alan Cobham, T. O. M. Sopwith, and C. G. Grey.

Stiff cover—96 pages—Seven shillings and sixpence

Obtainable from W. H. Smith & Son, Wyman's and leading booksellers everywhere or direct from the publishers.

35

DYCE AIRPORT (ABERDEEN).

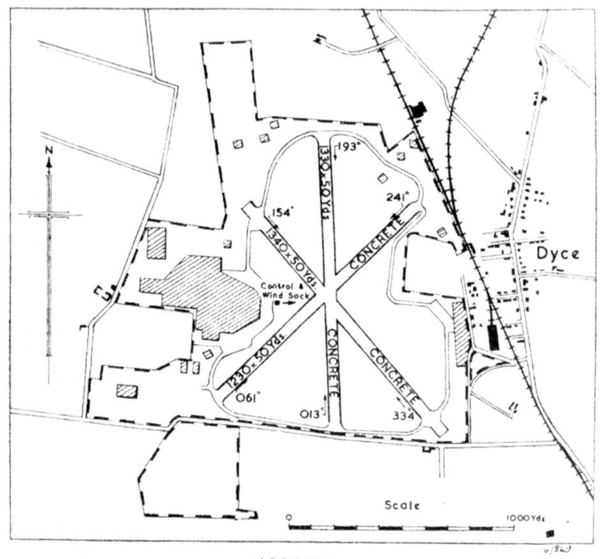

ARRIVALS.

Time	Frequency	Aircraft	From
10.55 a.m.	Weekdays	B.E.A. Rapide	Orkney
11.35 a.m.	Weekdays	B.E.A. Rapide	Shetland
12.20 p.m.	Weekdays	B.E.A. Dakota	London (Northolt)
2.45 p.m.	Weekdays	B.E.A. Rapide	Wick
3.20 p.m.	Weekdays	B.E.A. Rapide	Orkney
5.15 p.m.	Weekdays	B.E.A. Rapide	Wick
5.40 p.m.	Weekdays	B.E.A. Dakota	Orkney
6.40 p.m.	Weekdays	B.E.A. Rapide	Orkney

DEPARTURES.

Time	Frequency	Aircraft	To
8.00 a.m.	Weekdays	B.E.A. Rapide	Orkney
8.50 a.m.	Weekdays	B.E.A. Rapide	Shetland
12.30 p.m.	Weekdays	B.E.A. Dakota	Orkney
12.30 p.m.	Weekdays	B.E.A. Rapide	Wick
1.15 p.m.	Weekdays	B.E.A. Rapide	Orkney
3.00 p.m.	Weekdays	B.E.A. Rapide	Shetland
3.05 p.m.	Weekdays	B.E.A. Rapide	Wick
3.45 p.m.	Weekdays	B.E.A. Rapide	Orkney
6.00 p.m.	Weekdays	B.E.A. Dakota	London (Northolt)

NUTT'S CORNER AIRPORT (BELFAST).

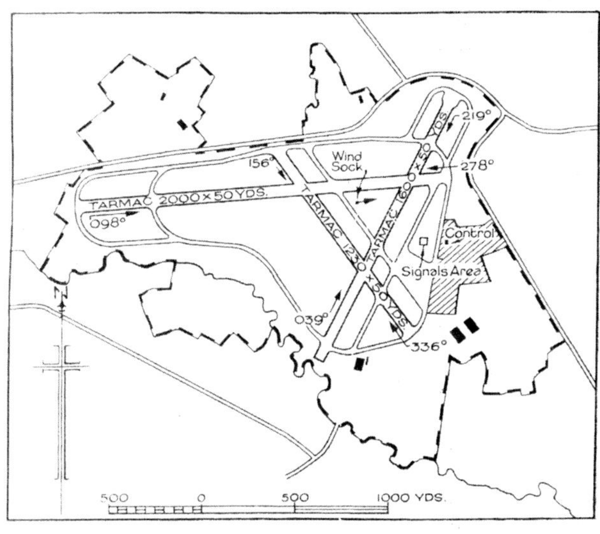

ARRIVALS.

Time	Frequency	Aircraft	From
9.30 a.m.	Weekdays	B.E.A. Dakota	Renfrew (Glasgow)
9.50 a.m.	Weekdays	B.E.A. Dakota	Liverpool
11.40 a.m.	Weekdays	B.E.A. Dakota	Northolt (London)
12.15 noon	Daily	B.E.A. Dakota	Manchester
12.55 noon	Daily	B.E.A. Dakota	Renfrew (Glasgow)
1.25 p.m.	Weekdays	B.E.A. Dakota	Liverpool
4.40 p.m.	Daily	B.E.A. Dakota	Renfrew (Glasgow)
5.40 p.m.	Daily	B.E.A. Dakota	Liverpool
6.16 p.m.	Weekdays	B.E.A. Dakota	Northolt (London)
7.15 p.m.	Weekdays	B.E.A. Dakota	Manchester
7.40 p.m.	Weekdays	B.E.A. Dakota	Renfrew (Glasgow)
8.04 p.m.	Sunday	B.E.A. Dakota	Northolt (London)
9.40 p.m.	Weekdays	B.E.A. Dakota	Northolt (London)

DEPARTURES.

Time	Frequency	Aircraft	To
8.49 a.m.	Weekdays	B.E.A. Dakota	Northolt (London)
10.15 a.m.	Weekdays	B.E.A. Dakota	Liverpool
10.25 a.m.	Weekdays	B.E.A. Dakota	Renfrew (Glasgow)
12.50 noon	Daily	B.E.A. Dakota	Manchester
1.01 p.m.	Weekdays	B.E.A. Dakota	Northolt (London)
2.15 p.m.	Daily	B.E.A. Dakota	Renfrew (Glasgow)

Time	Frequency	Aircraft	To
2.30 p.m.	Daily	B.E.A. Dakota	Liverpool
2.35 p.m.	Sunday	B.E.A. Dakota	Northolt (London)
5.15 p.m.	Daily	B.E.A. Dakota	Renfrew (Glasgow)
6.10 p.m.	Daily	B.E.A. Dakota	Liverpool
7.01 p.m.	Weekdays	B.E.A. Dakota	Northolt (London)
7.45 p.m.	Weekdays	B.E.A. Dakota	Manchester
8.15 p.m.	Weekdays	B.E.A. Dakota	Renfrew (Glasgow)

SQUIRE'S GATE AIRPORT (BLACKPOOL).

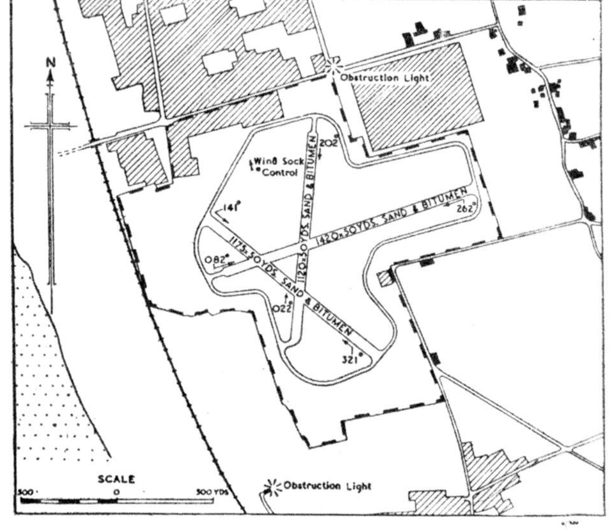

ARRIVALS.

Time	Frequency	Aircraft	From
2.05 p.m.	Daily	B.E.A. Dakota	Isle of Man
6.40 p.m.	Daily	B.E.A. Dakota	Isle of Man

DEPARTURES.

Time	Frequency	Aircraft	To
2.30 p.m.	Daily	B.E.A. Dakota	Isle of Man
7.05 p.m.	Daily	B.E.A. Dakota	Isle of Man

PENGAM MOORS AIRPORT (CARDIFF).

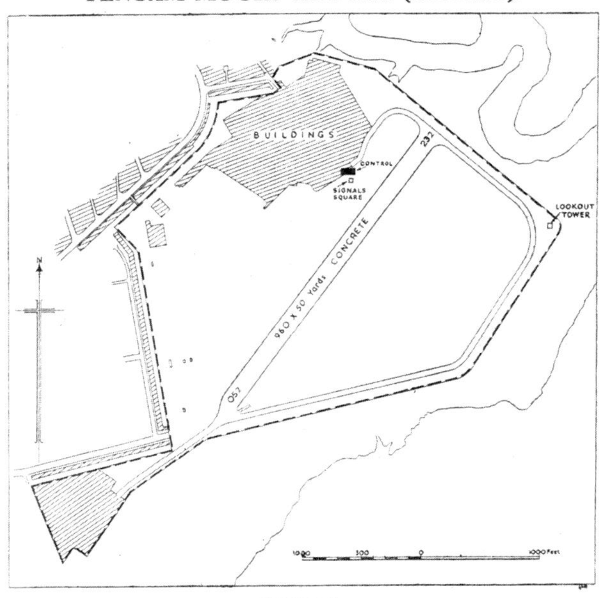

ARRIVALS.

Time	Frequency	Aircraft	From
9.00 a.m.	Daily	Western Airways Anson	Weston
9.45 a.m.	Daily	Cambrian Air Services Rapide	Weston
12.30 noon	Daily	Western Airways Anson	Weston
4.45 p.m.	Daily	Cambrian Air Services Rapide	Weston
6.45 p.m.	Daily	Western Airways Anson	Weston
9.15 p.m.	Daily	Cambrian Air Services Rapide	Weston

DEPARTURES.

Time	Frequency	Aircraft	To
9.00 a.m.	Daily	Cambrian Air Services Rapide	Weston
11.00 a.m.	Daily	Western Airways Anson	Weston
12.45 noon	Daily	Cambrian Air Services Rapide	Weston
3.00 p.m.	Daily	Western Airways Anson	Weston
6.00 p.m.	Daily	Cambrian Air Services Rapide	Weston
9.00 p.m.	Daily	Western Airways Anson	Weston

CROYDON AIRPORT.

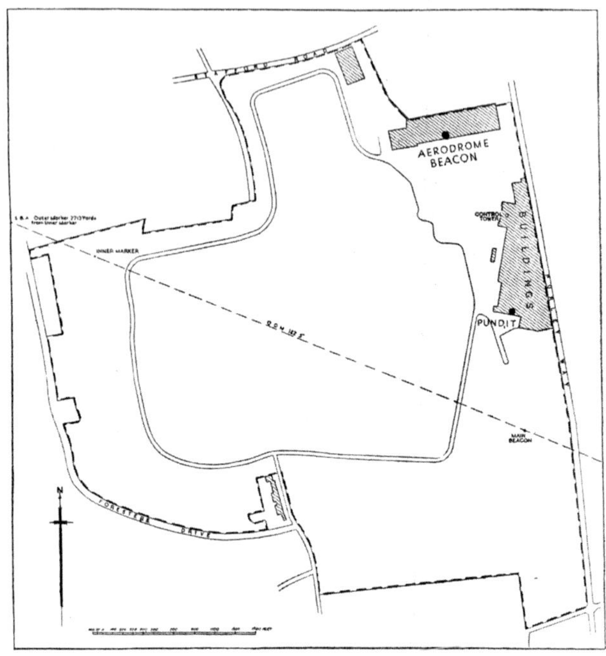

ARRIVALS.

Time	Frequency	Aircraft	From
10.45 a.m.	Weekdays	Air Transport Beechcraft	Deauville
11.05 a.m.	Weekdays	Air Transport Beechcraft	Lille
12.30 noon	Weekdays	Olley Air Service Rapide	Deauville
4.20 p.m.	Daily	Air Transport Beechcraft	Deauville
7.45 p.m.	Daily	Olley Air Service Rapide	Deauville

DEPARTURES.

Time	Frequency	Aircraft	To
10.00 a.m.	Sunday	Olley Air Service Rapide	Deauville
10.00 a.m.	Weekdays	Olley Air Service Rapide	Deauville
11.35 a.m.	Weekdays	Air Transport Beechcraft	Deauville
4.00 p.m.	Weekdays	Olley Air Service Rapide	Deauville
4.40 p.m.	Weekdays	Air Transport Beechcraft	Lille
6.45 p.m.	Daily	Air Transport Beechcraft	Deauville

COLLINSTOWN AIRPORT (DUBLIN).

ARRIVALS.

Time	Frequency	Aircraft	From
9.00 a.m.	Daily	Aer Lingus Dakota	Northolt (London)
10.00 a.m.	Daily	Aer Lingus Dakota	Northolt (London)
10.15 a.m.	Daily	Aer Lingus Dakota	Liverpool
10.25 a.m.	Daily	Aer Lingus Dakota	Renfrew (Glasgow)
10.50 a.m.	Daily	Aer Lingus Dakota	Amsterdam
11.30 a.m.	Daily	Aer Lingus Dakota	Northolt (London)
12.30 noon	Daily	Aer Lingus Dakota	Northolt (London)
1.00 p.m.	Daily	Aer Lingus Dakota	Isle of Man
2.00 p.m.	Daily	Aer Lingus Dakota	Northolt (London)
2.35 p.m.	Daily	Aer Lingus Dakota	Amsterdam
2.55 p.m.	Daily	Aer Lingus Dakota	Renfrew (Glasgow)
3.00 p.m.	Daily	Aer Lingus Dakota	Northolt (London)
4.15 p.m.	Daily	Aer Lingus Dakota	Liverpool
4.20 p.m.	Mon., Wed., Sun.	Aer Lingus Dakota	Paris
4.40 p.m.	Daily	Aer Lingus Dakota	Northolt (London)
5.30 p.m.	Daily	Aer Lingus Dakota	Northolt (London)
6.25 p.m.	Daily	Aer Lingus Dakota	Renfrew (Glasgow)
6.45 p.m.	Daily	Aer Lingus Dakota	Shannon
7.10 p.m.	Daily	Aer Lingus Dakota	Northolt (London)
7.30 p.m.	Daily	Aer Lingus Dakota	Liverpool
7.40 p.m.	Mon., Tues., Sun.	K.L.M. Dakota	Amsterdam
7.40 p.m.	Thur., Fri., Sat.	Aer Lingus Dakota	Amsterdam
8.20 p.m.	Daily	Aer Lingus Dakota	Northolt (London)
8.30 p.m.	Tues, Thurs.	S.A.B.E.N.A. Dakota	Brussels
9.40 p.m.	Daily	Aer Lingus Dakota	Northolt (London)
10.15 p.m.	Sat., Sun.	Aer Lingus Dakota	Isle of Man
10.45 p.m.	Daily	Aer Lingus Dakota	Liverpool
10.50 p.m.	Daily	Aer Lingus Dakota	Northolt (London)

DEPARTURES.

Time	Frequency	Aircraft	To
7.00 a.m.	Daily	Aer Lingus Dakota	Northolt (London)
7.15 a.m.	Mon., Fri., Sat.	Aer Lingus Dakota	Renfrew (Glasgow)
7.30 a.m.	Daily	Aer Lingus Dakota	Liverpool
7.45 a.m.	Daily	Aer Lingus Dakota	Amsterdam
8.00 a.m.	Daily	Aer Lingus Dakota	Northolt (London)
8.15 a.m.	Mon., Wed., Sun.	Aer Lingus Dakota	Paris
8.30 a.m.	Wed., Fri.	S.A.B.E.N.A. Dakota	Brussels
8.40 a.m.	Thurs., Fri., Sat.	Aer Lingus Dakota	Amsterdam
8.40 a.m.	Mon., Tues., Wed.	K.L.M. Dakota	Amsterdam
8.45 a.m.	Daily	Aer Lingus Dakota	Shannon
9.30 a.m.	Daily	Aer Lingus Dakota	Northolt (London)
10.30 a.m.	Daily	Aer Lingus Dakota	Northolt (London)
11.30 a.m.	Daily	Aer Lingus Dakota	Manchester
11.45 a.m.	Daily	Aer Lingus Dakota	Renfrew (Glasgow)
12.10 noon	Daily	Aer Lingus Dakota	Northolt (London)
1.00 p.m.	Daily	Aer Lingus Dakota	Northolt (London)
1.30 p.m.	Daily	Aer Lingus Dakota	Liverpool
2.30 p.m.	Daily	Aer Lingus Dakota	Northolt (London)
3.15 p.m.	Daily	Aer Lingus Dakota	Renfrew (Glasgow)
3.45 p.m.	Daily	Aer Lingus Dakota	Northolt (London)
4.45 p.m.	Daily	Aer Lingus Dakota	Liverpool
5.10 p.m.	Daily	Aer Lingus Dakota	Northolt (London)
6.20 p.m.	Daily	Aer Lingus Dakota	Northolt (London)
7.00 p.m.	Daily	Aer Lingus Dakota	Manchester
7.40 p.m.	Daily	Aer Lingus Dakota	Northolt (London)
8.00 p.m.	Daily	Aer Lingus Dakota	Liverpool
8.15 p.m.	Sat., Sun.	Aer Lingus Dakota	Isle of Man
8.50 p.m.	Daily	Aer Lingus Dakota	Northolt (London)

TURNHOUSE AIRPORT (EDINBURGH).

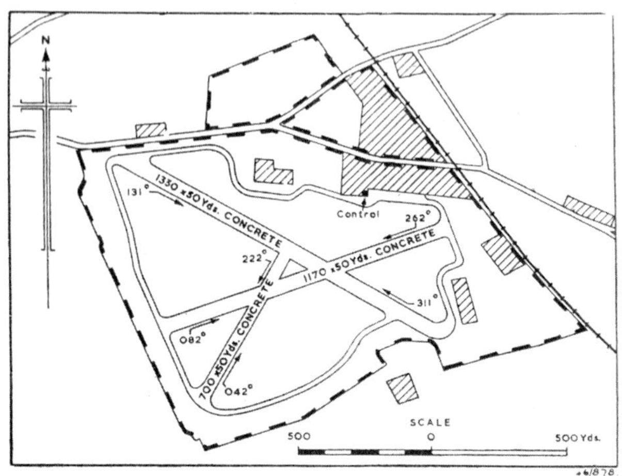

ARRIVALS.

Time	Frequency	Aircraft	From
9.05 a.m.	Weekdays	B.E.A. Dakota	Renfrew (Glasgow)
11.08 a.m.	Weekdays	B.E.A. Dakota	Northolt (London)
6.50 p.m.	Weekdays	B.E.A. Dakota	Orkney
9.23 p.m.	Weekdays	B.E.A. Dakota	Northolt (London)

DEPARTURES.

Time	Frequency	Aircraft	To
9.26 a.m.	Weekdays	B.E.A. Dakota	Northolt (London)
11.30 a.m.	Weekdays	B.E.A. Dakota	Orkney
7.10 p.m.	Weekdays	B.E.A. Dakota	Northolt (London)
9.50 p.m.	Weekdays	B.E.A. Dakota	Renfrew (Glasgow)

GATWICK AIRPORT.

ARRIVALS.

Time	Frequency	Aircraft	From
3.15 p.m.	Saturdays	Air Transport Beechcraft or Bristol 170	Dinard

DEPARTURES.

Time	Frequency	Aircraft	To
12.00 noon	Saturdays	Air Transport Beechcraft or Bristol 170	Dinard

50

SPEKE AIRPORT (LIVERPOOL).

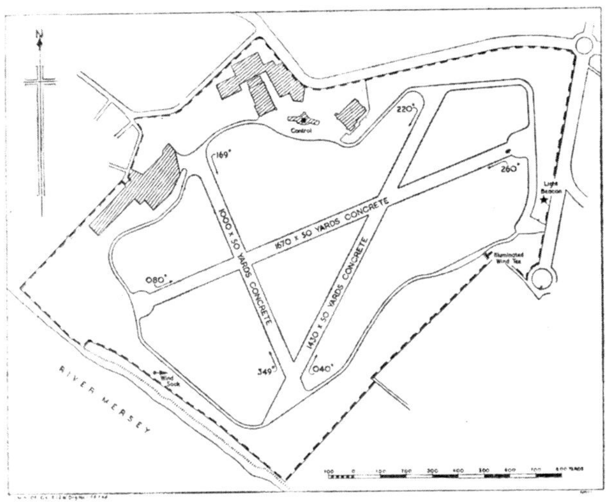

ARRIVALS.

Time	Frequency	Aircraft	From
8.45 a.m.	Weekdays	B.E.A. Dakota	Isle of Man
9.05 a.m.	Daily	Aer Lingus Dakota	Dublin
10.35 a.m.	Daily	B.E.A. Dakota	Isle of Man
11.30 a.m.	Weekdays	B.E.A. Dakota	Belfast
12.35 p.m.	Daily	Aer Lingus Dakota	Dublin
3.00 p.m.	Daily	B.E.A. Dakota	Isle of Man
3.45 p.m.	Daily	B.E.A. Dakota	Belfast
4.05 p.m.	Daily	Aer Lingus Dakota	Dublin
4.45 p.m.	Daily	B.E.A. Dakota	Isle of Man
7.10 p.m.	Mon., Fri., Sat., Sun.	B.E.A. Dakota	Isle of Man
7.50 p.m.	Daily	Aer Lingus Dakota	Dublin
8.00 p.m.	Daily	B.E.A. Dakota	Belfast
8.50 p.m.	Daily	Aer Lingus Dakota	Dublin
9.30 p.m.	Daily	B.E.A. Dakota	Isle of Man

DEPARTURES.

Time	Frequency	Aircraft	To
8.00 a.m.	Weekdays	B.E.A. Dakota	Belfast
9.15 a.m.	Daily	B.E.A. Dakota	Isle of Man
9.45 a.m.	Daily	Aer Lingus Dakota	Dublin
11.50 a.m.	Daily	B.E.A. Dakota	Isle of Man
1.15 p.m.	Daily	Aer Lingus Dakota	Dublin
3.30 p.m.	Daily	B.E.A. Dakota	Isle of Man
4.15 p.m.	Daily	B.E.A. Dakota	Belfast
4.50 p.m.	Daily	Aer Lingus Dakota	Dublin
5.05 p.m.	Daily	B.E.A. Dakota	Isle of Man

43

Time	Frequency	Aircraft	To
7.35 p.m.	Mon., Fri., Sat., Sun.	B.E.A. Dakota	Isle of Man
8.30 p.m.	Daily	Aer Lingus Dakota	Dublin
9.20 p.m.	Daily	Aer Lingus Dakota	Dublin
9.30 p.m.	Daily	B.E.A. Dakota	Isle of Man

LONDON AIRPORT (HEATHROW).

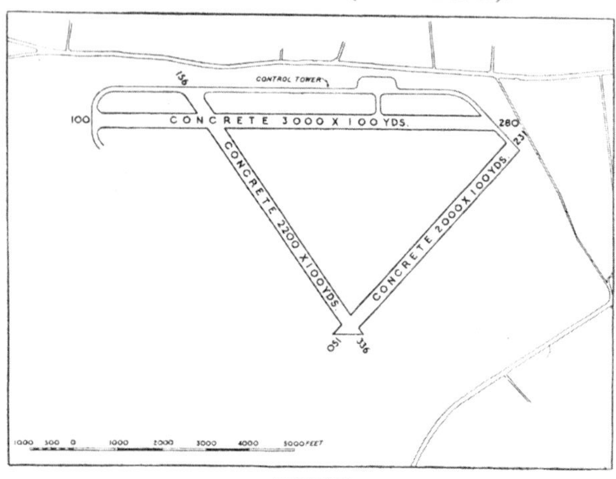

ARRIVALS.

MONDAY

Time	Aircraft	From
00.35 a.m.	Panair Constellation	Buenos Aires
7.45 a.m.	B.O.A.C. York	Calcutta
8.50 a.m.	K.L.M. Skymaster	Amsterdam
8.50 a.m.	Sabena Dakota	Brussels
9.55 a.m.	Air France Languedoc 161	Paris
10.35 a.m.	B.O.A.C. York	Accra (West Africa)
11.10 a.m.	Sabena Dakota	Antwerp
11.20 a.m.	K.L.M. Skymaster	Amsterdam
11.55 a.m.	Air France Languedoc 161	Paris
12.00 noon	Sabena Dakota	Brussels
1.10 p.m.	Sabena Dakota	Brussels
1.20 p.m.	K.L.M. Skymaster	Amsterdam
2.20 p.m.	P.A.A. Constellation	New York
2.35 p.m.	T.C.A. North Star	Montreal
2.55 p.m.	Air France Languedoc 161	Paris
2.55 p.m.	Sabena Dakota	Brussels
3.20 p.m.	K.L.M. Skymaster	Amsterdam
3.35 p.m.	B.S.A.A.C. York	Buenos Aires
4.30 p.m.	A.O.A. Skymaster	Frankfurt
4.55 p.m.	Air France Languedoc 161	Paris

44

Avro Tudor IV G-AHNK *Star Lion* at London Airport. British South American Airways has three Tudor IV airliners in service and other Tudors of a later type on order.

Star Glitter, G-AHFH, one of the ten Avro York Mk. IG airliners on the British South American Airways route to Buenos Aires, via Lisbon, Dakar and Rio de Janeiro.

Avro Lancastrian II *Star Flight* of British South American Airways. Lancastrians now serve mainly for freight duties.

(*Photos: A. S. C. Lumsden*

Upper: Regular visitor to Prestwick and Ringway, the C.O.B.E.T.A. Dakota OO-APC from Brussels.
Lower: C.S.A. (Czech Airlines) Dakota from Prague at Northolt Airport.

(*Photos: A. S. C. Lumsden*

Upper: Douglas Dakota G-AKIK of Cyprus Airways, a new airline company operating as a subsidiary of B.E.A.C. Three Dakotas are in service.
Lower: Avro York LV-AFV of the Argentine airline F.A.M.A. which flies into London Airport on the trunk route from Buenos Aires, calling at Rio, Natal, Dakar, Madrid, Rome and Paris.

Upper: One of F.A.M.A.'s five Douglas DC-4B Skymasters which operate to this country over the same route as the company's three Yorks.
(Photo: A. S. C. Lumsden

Lower: Maid of Athens, a Consolidated Liberator flown into Northolt and Prestwick from Athens by Hellenic Airlines. *(Photo: Scottish Avn.*

(Photos: A. S. C. Lumsden

Upper: The Spanish airline "Iberia" now operates the London-Madrid service with Douglas Skymasters. Illustrated is EC-ACE, one of three aircraft of this type in service.
Lower: K.L.M. Skymaster PH-TLK at London Airport.

Flying Dutchman PH-TDW, one of the twenty-seven Douglas DC-3 Dakota airliners in service with K.L.M. This machine operates the Eindhoven-London schedules.

Luxembourg Airlines Douglas Dakota at Northolt on arrival from Luxembourg. This company is partially owned by Scottish Aviation Ltd.

(Photos: A. S. C. Lumsden

This Pan American World Airways Constellation is a familiar sight at London Airport. *Clipper Challenge* NC 88837 is on the regular Atlantic crossing from New York.

Time	Aircraft	From
5.00 p.m.	Sabena Dakota	Knocke/Le Zoute
5.00 p.m.	B.O.A.C. Dakota	Cairo
5.20 p.m.	C.S.A. Dakota	Prague
5.20 p.m.	K.L.M. Skymaster	Amsterdam
6.35 p.m.	P.A.A. Dakota	Vienna
7.10 p.m.	Sabena Dakota	Brussels
7.20 p.m.	K.L.M. Skymaster	Amsterdam
7.55 p.m.	Air France Languedoc 161	Paris
8.55 p.m.	Air France Languedoc 161	Paris
9.40 p.m.	K.L.M. Dakota	Eindhoven
9.50 p.m.	Air France Languedoc 161	Nice
10.05 p.m.	P.A.A. Constellation	New York
10.20 p.m.	K.L.M. Skymaster	Amsterdam
10.30 p.m.	Sabena Dakota	Prague
10.40 p.m.	Sabena Dakota	Brussels

TUESDAY

Time	Aircraft	From
8.50 a.m.	K.L.M. Skymaster	Amsterdam
8.50 a.m.	Sabena Dakota	Brussels
9.55 a.m.	Air France Languedoc 161	Paris
10.35 a.m.	B.O.A.C. York	Accra (West Africa)
11.10 a.m.	Sabena Dakota	Brussels
11.20 a.m.	K.L.M. Skymaster	Amsterdam
12.00 noon	Sabena Dakota	Brussels
1.10 p.m.	Sabena Dakota	Brussels
1.20 p.m.	K.L.M. Skymaster	Amsterdam
1.25 p.m.	A.O.A. Constellation	New York
2.20 p.m.	P.A.A. Constellation	New York
2.35 p.m.	T.C.A. North Star	Montreal
2.45 p.m.	B.O.A.C. Liberator	Montreal
2.55 p.m.	Air France Languedoc 161	Paris
2.55 p.m.	Sabena Dakota	Brussels
3.15 p.m.	B.O.A.C. Constellation	New York
3.20 p.m.	K.L.M. Skymaster	Amsterdam
4.55 p.m.	Air France Languedoc 161	Paris
5.00 p.m.	B.O.A.C. Dakota	Cairo
5.00 p.m.	Sabena Dakota	Knocke/Le Zoute
5.30 p.m.	K.L.M. Skymaster	Amsterdam
6.30 p.m.	B.O.A.C. Constellation	Montreal
6.35 p.m.	P.A.A. Dakota	Vienna
7.00 p.m.	B.S.A.A.C. Lancastrian	Santiago (Chile)
7.10 p.m.	Sabena Dakota	Brussels
7.10 p.m.	C.S.A. Dakota	Prague
7.20 p.m.	K.L.M. Skymaster	Amsterdam
7.25 p.m.	B.O.A.C. York	Tanganyika
7.55 p.m.	P.A.A. Constellation	Istanbul
7.55 p.m.	Languedoc 161 Air France	Paris
8.15 p.m.	B.O.A.C. Lancastrian Freighter	Johannesburg
8.55 p.m.	Air France Languedoc 161	Paris
9.40 p.m.	K.L.M. Dakota	Eindhoven
10.20 p.m.	K.L.M. Dakota	Prague
10.20 p.m.	K.L.M. Skymaster	Amsterdam
10.40 p.m.	Sabena Dakota	Brussels

WEDNESDAY

Time	Aircraft	From
7.45 a.m.	B.O.A.C. York	Calcutta
8.50 a.m.	K.L.M. Skymaster	Amsterdam
8.50 a.m.	Sabena Dakota	Brussels
9.55 a.m.	Air France Languedoc 161	Paris
10.20 a.m.	South African Skymaster	Johannesburg
11.10 a.m.	Sabena Dakota	Brussels
11.20 a.m.	K.L.M. Skymaster	Amsterdam
11.55 a.m.	Air France Languedoc 161	Paris
12.00 noon	Sabena Dakota	Brussels
1.10 p.m.	Sabena Dakota	Brussels
1.20 p.m.	K.L.M. Skymaster	Amsterdam
1.25 p.m.	A.O.A. Constellation	New York

LONDON AIRPORT—*contd.*

Time	Aircraft	From
2.05 p.m.	P.A.A. Constellation	New York
2.20 p.m.	P.A.A. Constellation	New York
2.35 p.m.	T.C.A. North Star	Montreal
2.55 p.m.	Air France Languedoc 161	Paris
2.55 p.m.	Sabena Dakota	Brussels
3.20 p.m.	K.L.M. Skymaster	Amsterdam
4.30 p.m.	A.O.A. Skymaster	Frankfurt
4.55 p.m.	Air France Languedoc 161	Paris
5.00 p.m.	B.O.A.C. Dakota	Cairo
5.00 p.m.	Sabena Dakota	Brussels
5.20 p.m.	C.S.A. Dakota	Prague
5.20 p.m.	K.L.M. Skymaster	Amsterdam
6.16 p.m.	Qantas Constellation	Sydney (Australia)
6.30 p.m.	P.A.A. Skymaster Freighter	Brussels
6.35 p.m.	P.A.A. Dakota	Vienna
7.10 p.m.	Sabena Dakota	Brussels
7.20 p.m.	K.L.M. Skymaster	Amsterdam
7.25 p.m.	B.O.A.C. York	Nairobi
7.30 p.m.	Air India Constellation	Bombay
7.55 p.m.	P.A.A. Constellation	Calcutta
7.55 p.m.	Air France Languedoc 161	Paris
8.55 p.m.	Air France Languedoc 161	Paris
9.40 p.m.	K.L.M. Dakota	Eindhoven
9.50 p.m.	Air France Languedoc 161	Nice
10.05 p.m.	P.A.A. Constellation	New York
10.20 p.m.	K.L.M. Skymaster	Amsterdam
10.40 p.m.	Sabena Dakota	Brussels

THURSDAY

Time	Aircraft	From
5.30 a.m.	K.L.M. Skymaster	Amsterdam
6.55 a.m.	A.O.A. Constellation	New York
8.50 a.m.	K.L.M. Skymaster	Amsterdam
8.50 a.m.	Sabena Dakota	Brussels
9.55 a.m.	Air France Languedoc 161	Paris
10.05 a.m.	P.A.A. Constellation	New York
10.35 a.m.	B.O.A.C. York	Accra (West Africa)
11.10 a.m.	Sabena Dakota	Brussels
11.20 a.m.	K.L.M. Skymaster	Amsterdam
12.00 noon	Sabena Dakota	Brussels
1.10 p.m.	Sabena Dakota	Brussels
1.20 p.m.	K.L.M. Skymaster	Amsterdam
1.25 p.m.	A.O.A. Constellation	New York
2.20 p.m.	P.A.A. Constellation	New York
2.35 p.m.	T.C.A. North Star	Montreal
2.45 p.m.	B.O.A.C. Liberator	Montreal
2.55 p.m.	Air France Languedoc 161	Paris
2.55 p.m.	Sabena Dakota	Brussels
3.20 p.m.	P.A.A. Dakota	Vienna
3.20 p.m.	K.L.M. Skymaster	Amsterdam
3.35 p.m.	B.S.A.A.C. York	Buenos Aires
4.55 p.m.	Air France Languedoc 161	Paris
5.00 p.m.	B.O.A.C. Dakota	Cairo
5.00 p.m.	Sabena Dakota	Brussels
5.20 p.m.	K.L.M. Skymaster	Amsterdam
6.30 p.m.	B.O.A.C. Constellation	Montreal
7.10 p.m.	Sabena Dakota	Brussels
7.10 p.m.	C.S.A. Dakota	Prague
7.20 p.m.	K.L.M. Skymaster	Amsterdam
7.55 p.m.	Air France Languedoc 161	Paris
8.55 p.m.	Air France Languedoc 161	Paris
9.40 p.m.	K.L.M. Dakota	Eindhoven
10.20 p.m.	K.L.M. Dakota	Prague
10.20 p.m.	K.L.M. Skymaster	Amsterdam
10.40 p.m.	Sabena Dakota	Brussels

FRIDAY

Time	Aircraft	From
7.45 a.m.	B.O.A.C. York	Calcutta

Time	Aircraft	From
8.50 a.m.	K.L.M. Skymaster	Amsterdam
8.50 a.m.	Sabena Dakota	Brussels
9.55 a.m.	Air France Languedoc 161	Paris
10.05 a.m.	P.A.A. Constellation	New York
10.20 a.m.	South African Skymaster	Johannesburg
10.25 a.m.	A.O.A. Skymaster	New York
10.35 a.m.	B.O.A.C. York	Accra (West Africa)
11.10 a.m.	Sabena Dakota	Antwerp
11.20 a.m.	K.L.M. Skymaster	Amsterdam
11.55 a.m.	Air France Languedoc 161	Paris
12.00 noon	Sabena Dakota	Brussels
1.10 p.m.	Sabena Dakota	Brussels
1.20 p.m.	K.L.M. Skymaster	Amsterdam
1.25 p.m.	A.O.A. Constellation	New York
2.20 p.m.	P.A.A. Constellation	New York
2.35 p.m.	T.C.A. North Star	Montreal
2.45 p.m.	B.O.A.C. Liberator	Montreal
2.55 p.m.	Air France Languedoc 161	Paris
2.55 p.m.	Sabena Dakota	Brussels
3.15 p.m.	B.O.A.C. Constellation	New York
3.20 p.m.	K.L.M. Skymaster	Amsterdam
4.30 p.m.	A.O.A. Skymaster	Frankfurt
4.55 p.m.	Air France Languedoc 161	Paris
5.00 p.m.	B.O.A.C. Dakota	Cairo
5.00 p.m.	Sabena Dakota	Knocke/Le Zoute
5.20 p.m.	C.S.A. Dakota	Prague
5.20 p.m.	K.L.M. Skymaster	Amsterdam
6.35 p.m.	P.A.A. Dakota	Vienna
7.10 p.m.	Sabena Dakota	Brussels
7.20 p.m.	K.L.M. Skymaster	Amsterdam
7.25 p.m.	B.O.A.C. York	Nairobi
7.55 p.m.	P.A.A. Constellation	Calcutta
7.55 p.m.	Air France Languedoc 161	Paris
8.55 p.m.	Air France Languedoc 161	Paris
9.40 p.m.	K.L.M. Dakota	Eindhoven
9.50 p.m.	Air France Languedoc 161	Nice
10.05 p.m.	P.A.A. Constellation	New York
10.20 p.m.	K.L.M. Skymaster	Amsterdam
10.30 p.m.	Sabena Dakota	Prague
10.40 p.m.	Sabena Dakota	Brussels

SATURDAY.

Time	Aircraft	From
5.30 a.m.	K.L.M. Skymaster	Amsterdam
7.30 a.m.	B.O.A.C. Lancastrian Freighter	Sydney (Australia)
7.30 a.m.	B.O.A.C.	Colombo
7.45 a.m.	B.O.A.C. York	Delhi
8.50 a.m.	K.L.M. Skymaster	Amsterdam
8.50 a.m.	Sabena Dakota	Brussels
9.55 a.m.	Air France Languedoc 161	Paris
10.35 a.m.	B.O.A.C. York	Accra (West Africa)
11.10 a.m.	Sabena Dakota	Antwerp
11.20 a.m.	K.L.M. Skymaster	Amsterdam
11.55 a.m.	Air France Languedoc 161	Paris
12.00 noon	Sabena Dakota	Brussels
1.10 p.m.	Sabena Dakota	Brussels
1.20 p.m.	K.L.M. Skymaster	Amsterdam
1.25 p.m.	A.O.A. Constellation	Washington
1.40 p.m.	Iberia Skymaster	Madrid
2.05 p.m.	P.A.A. Constellation	New York
2.35 p.m.	T.C.A. North Star	Montreal
2.45 p.m.	B.O.A.C. Constellation	New York
2.55 p.m.	Air France Languedoc 161	Paris
2.55 p.m.	Sabena Dakota	Brussels
3.20 p.m.	P.A.A. Dakota	Vienna
3.20 p.m.	K.L.M. Skymaster	Amsterdam
3.35 p.m.	B.S.A.A.C. York	Buenos Aires
4.35 p.m.	B.O.A.C. Dakota	Teheran
4.55 p.m.	Air France Languedoc 161	Paris

51

Time	Aircraft	From
5.00 p.m.	Sabena Dakota	Knocke/Le Zoute
5.00 p.m.	B.O.A.C. Dakota	Cairo
5.20 p.m.	K.L.M. Skymaster	Amsterdam
5.50 p.m.	P.A.A. Constellation	New York
6.30 p.m.	B.O.A.C. Constellation	Montreal
7.10 p.m.	Sabena Dakota	Brussels
7.10 p.m.	C.S.A. Dakota	Prague
7.20 p.m.	K.L.M. Skymaster	Amsterdam
7.25 p.m.	B.O.A.C. York	Nairobi
7.55 p.m.	Air France Languedoc 161	Paris
8.55 p.m.	Air France Languedoc 161	Paris
9.00 p.m.	B.S.A.A.C. Lancastrian	Havana (Cuba)
9.40 p.m.	K.L.M. Dakota	Eindhoven
9.50 p.m.	Air France Languedoc 161	Nice
10.05 p.m.	P.A.A. Constellation	New York
10.20 p.m.	K.L.M. Dakota	Prague
10.20 p.m.	K.L.M. Skymaster	Amsterdam
10.40 p.m.	Sabena Dakota	Brussels

SUNDAY.

Time	Aircraft	From
7.00 a.m.	Skyways Skymaster	Bahrein
7.30 a.m.	B.O.A.C. York	Colombo
8.40 a.m.	A.O.A. Constellation	New York
8.50 a.m.	K.L.M. Skymaster	Amsterdam
9.55 a.m.	Air France Languedoc 161	Paris
10.20 a.m.	South African Skymaster	Johannesburg
11.20 a.m.	K.L.M. Skymaster	Amsterdam
12.00 noon	Sabena Dakota	Brussels
1.10 p.m.	Sabena Dakota	Brussels
1.20 p.m.	K.L.M. Skymaster	Amsterdam
1.25 p.m.	A.O.A. Constellation	New York
2.20 p.m.	P.A.A. Constellation	New York
2.35 p.m.	T.C.A. North Star	Montreal
2.45 p.m.	F.A.M.A. York or Skymaster	Buenos Aires
2.55 p.m.	Air France Languedoc 161	Paris
2.55 p.m.	Sabena Dakota	Brussels
3.20 p.m.	P.A.A. Dakota	Vienna
3.20 p.m.	K.L.M. Skymaster	Amsterdam
3.35 p.m.	B.S.A.A.C. York	Rio de Janeiro
4.55 p.m.	Air France Languedoc 161	Paris
5.00 p.m.	Sabena Dakota	Knocke/Le Zoute
5.20 p.m.	K.L.M. Skymaster	Amsterdam
5.30 p.m.	B.O.A.C. Dakota	Cairo
7.00 p.m.	B.S.A.A.C. Lancastrian	Nassau (West Indies)
7.10 p.m.	Sabena Dakota	Brussels
7.20 p.m.	K.L.M. Skymaster	Amsterdam
7.25 p.m.	B.O.A.C. York	Tanganyika
7.55 p.m.	Air France Languedoc 161	Paris
8.55 p.m.	Air France Languedoc 161	Paris
10.05 p.m.	P.A.A. Constellation	New York
10.20 p.m.	K.L.M. Dakota	Prague
10.20 p.m.	K.L.M. Skymaster	Amsterdam
10.30 p.m.	P.A.A. Skymaster Freighter	New York
10.30 p.m.	Sabena Dakota	Prague
10.40 p.m.	Sabena Dakota	Brussels

DEPARTURES.

MONDAY

Time	Aircraft	To
7.45 a.m.	Sabena Dakota	Brussels
8.00 a.m.	K.L.M. Dakota	Eindoven
8.15 a.m.	B.O.A.C. York	Nairobi
8.30 a.m.	K.L.M. Skymaster	Amsterdam
9.05 a.m.	Air France Languedoc 161	Paris
10.00 a.m.	B.O.A.C. Dakota	Cairo
10.00 a.m.	Sabena Dakota	Brussels

Time	Aircraft	To
10.25 a.m.	B.S.A.A.C. York	Buenos Aires
10.30 a.m.	P.A.A. Dakota	Vienna
10.30 a.m.	K.L.M. Skymaster	Amsterdam
11.00 a.m.	Panair do Brasil Constellation	Buenos Aires
11.05 a.m.	Air France Languedoc 161	Paris
12.00 noon	South African Skymaster	Johannesburg
12.00 noon	Sabena Dakota	Brussels
12.30 noon	C.S.A. Dakota	Prague
12.30 noon	K.L.M. Skymaster	Amsterdam
12.50 noon	Sabena Dakota	Knocke/Le Zoute
12.55 noon	Air France Languedoc 161	Nice
1.01 p.m.	P.A.A. Constellation	New York
1.45 p.m.	B.O.A.C. York	Accra (West Africa)
2.30 p.m.	Sabena Dakota	Antwerp
2.30 p.m.	K.L.M. Skymaster	Amsterdam
3.45 p.m.	Sabena Dakota	Brussels
4.05 p.m.	Air France Languedoc 161	Paris
4.30 p.m.	K.L.M. Skymaster	Amsterdam
5.55 p.m.	Sabena Dakota	Brussels
6.05 p.m.	Air France Languedoc 161	Paris
6.30 p.m.	A.O.A. Constellation	New York
6.30 p.m.	K.L.M. Skymaster	Amsterdam
7.00 p.m.	B.O.A.C. Constellation	New York
7.45 p.m.	Sabena Dakota	Prague
8.30 p.m.	K.L.M. Skymaster	Amsterdam
8.45 p.m.	P.A.A. Constellation	New York
9.05 p.m.	Air France Languedoc 161	Paris
10.00 p.m.	T.C.A. North Star	Montreal
10.00 p.m.	Sabena Dakota	Antwerp

TUESDAY

Time	Aircraft	To
1.10 a.m.	K.L.M. Skymaster	Amsterdam
7.45 a.m.	Sabena Dakota	Brussels
8.00 a.m.	K.L.M. Dakota	Eindhoven
8.15 a.m.	B.O.A.C. York	Nairobi
8.30 a.m.	B.O.A.C. York	Tanganyika
8.30 a.m.	K.L.M. Skymaster	Amsterdam
8.30 a.m.	K.L.M. Dakota	Prague
9.05 a.m.	Air France Languedoc 161	Paris
10.00 a.m.	B.O.A.C. Dakota	Cairo
10.00 a.m.	Sabena Dakota	Brussels
10.20 a.m.	Air France Languedoc 161	Paris
10.30 a.m.	P.A.A. Dakota	Vienna
10.30 a.m.	K.L.M. Skymaster	Amsterdam
11.05 a.m.	Air France Languedoc 161	Paris
12.00 noon	Sabena Dakota	Brussels
12.30 noon	K.L.M. Skymaster	Amsterdam
12.50 noon	Sabena Dakota	Knocke/Le Zoute
12.55 noon	B.S.A.A.C. Lancastrian	Havana (Cuba)
1.01 p.m.	P.A.A. Constellation	New York
1.45 p.m.	B.O.A.C. York	Accra (West Africa)
2.30 p.m.	Sabena Dakota	Antwerp
2.30 p.m.	K.L.M. Skymaster	Amsterdam
2.30 p.m.	C.S.A. Dakota	Prague
2.45 p.m.	B.O.A.C. York	Delhi
3.45 p.m.	Sabena Dakota	Brussels
4.05 p.m.	Air France Languedoc 161	Paris
4.30 p.m.	K.L.M. Skymaster	Amsterdam
5.30 p.m.	A.O.A. Skymaster	Frankfurt
5.55 p.m.	Sabena Dakota	Brussels
6.05 p.m.	Air France Languedoc 161	Paris
6.30 p.m.	A.O.A. Constellation	New York
6.30 p.m.	K.L.M. Skymaster	Amsterdam
7.00 p.m.	B.O.A.C. Constellation	New York
8.30 p.m.	K.L.M. Skymaster	Amsterdam
8.45 p.m.	P.A.A. Constellation	New York
9.05 p.m.	Air France Languedoc 161	Paris
10.00 p.m.	Sabena Dakota	Brussels

Time	Aircraft	To
10.00 p.m.	P.A.A. Constellation	New York
10.00 p.m.	B.O.A.C. Constellation	Montreal
10.00 p.m.	T.C.A. North Star	Montreal

WEDNESDAY

Time	Aircraft	To
1.10 a.m.	K.L.M. Skymaster	Amsterdam
7.45 a.m.	Sabena Dakota	Brussels
8.00 a.m.	K.L.M. Dakota	Eindhoven
8.30 a.m.	K.L.M. Skymaster	Amsterdam
9.05 a.m.	Air France Languedoc 161	Paris
10.00 a.m.	B.O.A.C. Dakota	Cairo
10.00 a.m.	Sabena Dakota	Brussels
10.25 a.m.	B.S.A.A.C. York	Buenos Aires
10.30 a.m.	P.A.A. Dakota	Vienna
10.30 a.m.	K.L.M. Skymaster	Amsterdam
11.05 a.m.	Air France Languedoc 161	Paris
12.00 noon	Sabena Dakota	Brussels
12.30 noon	C.S.A. Dakota	Prague
12.30 noon	K.L.M. Skymaster	Amsterdam
12.50 noon	Sabena Dakota	Knocke/Le Zoute
12.55 noon	Air France Languedoc 161	Nice
1.00 p.m.	Qantas Constellation	Sydney (Australia)
1.01 p.m.	P.A.A. Constellation	New York
1.45 p.m.	B.O.A.C. York	Accra (West Africa)
2.05 p.m.	P.A.A. Constellation	Calcutta
2.30 p.m.	Sabena Dakota	Antwerp
2.30 p.m.	K.L.M. Skymaster	Amsterdam
2.45 p.m.	B.O.A.C. York	Calcutta
3.45 p.m.	Sabena Dakota	Brussels
4.05 p.m.	Air France Languedoc 161	Paris
4.30 p.m.	K.L.M. Skymaster	Amsterdam
5.00 p.m.	B.O A.C. Liberator	Montreal
5.55 p.m.	Sabena Dakota	Brussels
6.05 p.m.	Air France Languedoc 161	Paris
6.30 p.m.	A.C.A. Constellation	New York
6.30 p.m.	K.L.M. Skymaster	Amsterdam
7.00 p.m.	B.O.A.C. Constellation	New York
7.45 p.m.	P.A.A. Skymaster Freighter	New York
7.55 p.m.	A.O.A. Constellation	Frankfurt
8.30 p.m.	K.L.M. Skymaster	Amsterdam
8.45 p.m.	P.A.A. Constellation	New York
9.05 p.m.	Air France Languedoc 161	Paris
10.00 p.m.	Sabena Dakota	Brussels
10.00 p.m.	T.C.A. North Star	Montreal
10.00 p.m.	P.A.A. Constellation	New York

THURSDAY

Time	Aircraft	To
1.10 a.m.	K.L.M. Skymaster	Amsterdam
7.45 a.m.	Sabena Dakota	Brussels
8.00 a.m.	K.L.M. Dakota	Eindhoven
8.30 a.m.	B.O.A.C. York	Tanganyika
8.30 a.m.	K.L.M. Dakota	Prague
8.30 a.m.	K.L.M. Dakota	Amsterdam
9.05 a.m.	Air France Languedoc 161	Paris
10.00 a.m.	Sabena Dakota	Brussels
10.00 a.m.	B.O.A.C. Dakota	Cairo
10.20 a.m.	Air France Languedoc 161	Paris
10.25 a.m.	B.S.A.A.C. Lancastrian	Nassau (West Indies)
10.30 a.m.	P.A.A. Dakota	Vienna
10.30 a.m.	K.L.M. Skymaster	Amsterdam
11.05 a.m.	Air France Languedoc 161	Paris
12.00 noon	South African Skymaster	Johannesburg
12.00 noon	Sabena Dakota	Brussels
12.30 noon	K.L.M. Skymaster	Amsterdam
12.50 noon	Sabena Dakota	Knocke/Le Zoute
1.01 p.m.	P.A.A. Constellation	New York
2.30 p.m.	Sabena Dakota	Antwerp

54

Time	Aircraft	To
2.30 p.m.	K.L.M. Skymaster	Amsterdam
2.30 p.m.	C.S.A. Dakota	Prague
3.45 p.m.	Sabena Dakota	Brussels
4.05 p.m.	Air France Languedoc 161	Paris
4.30 p.m.	K.L.M. Skymaster	Amsterdam
5.30 p.m.	A.O.A. Skymaster	Frankfurt
5.55 p.m.	Sabena Dakota	Brussels
6.05 p.m.	Air France Languedoc 161	Paris
6.30 p.m.	A.O.A. Constellation	New York
6.30 p.m.	K.L.M. Skymaster	Amsterdam
8.30 p.m.	K.L.M. Skymaster	Amsterdam
8.45 p.m.	P.A.A. Constellation	New York
9.05 p.m.	Air France Languedoc 161	Paris
10.00 p.m.	Sabena Dakota	Brussels
10.00 p.m.	B.O.A.C. Constellation	Montreal
10.00 p.m.	T.C.A. North Star	Montreal

FRIDAY

Time	Aircraft	To
7.45 a.m.	Sabena Dakota	Brussels
8.00 a.m.	K.L.M. Dakota	Eindhoven
8.30 a.m.	K.L.M. Skymaster	Amsterdam
9.05 a.m.	Air France Languedoc 161	Paris
10.00 a.m.	B.O.A.C. Dakota	Cairo
10.00 a.m.	Sabena Dakota	Brussels
10.25 a.m.	B.S.A.A.C. York	Buenos Aires
10.30 a.m.	P.A.A. Dakota	Vienna
10.30 a.m.	K.L.M. Skymaster	Amsterdam
10.45 a.m.	B.O.A.C. Dakota	Cairo
11.05 a.m.	Air France Languedoc 161	Paris
12.00 noon	Sabena Dakota	Brussels
12.30 noon	K.L.M. Skymaster	Amsterdam
12.30 noon	C.S.A. Dakota	Prague
12.50 noon	Sabena Dakota	Knocke/Le Zoute
12.55 noon	Air France Languedoc 161	Nice
1.00 p.m.	Qantas Constellation	Sydney (Australia)
1.01 p.m.	P.A.A. Constellation	New York
1.45 p.m.	B.O.A.C. York	Accra
2.30 p.m.	K.L.M. Skymaster	Amsterdam
2.30 p.m.	Sabena Dakota	Antwerp
2.45 p.m.	B.O.A.C. York	Calcutta
3.45 p.m.	Sabena Dakota	Brussels
4.00 p.m.	Air India Constellation	Bombay
4.05 p.m.	Air France Languedoc 161	Paris
4.30 p.m.	K.L.M. Skymaster	Amsterdam
5.30 p.m.	Skyways Skymaster	Behrein
5.55 p.m.	Sabena, Dakota	Brussels
6.05 p.m.	Air France Languedoc 161	Paris
6.30 p.m.	K.L.M. Skymaster	Amsterdam
6.30 p.m.	A.O.A. Constellation	New York
7.00 p.m.	B.O.A.C. Constellation	New York
7.45 p.m.	Sabena Dakota	Prague
8.30 p.m.	K.L.M. Skymaster	Amsterdam
8.45 p.m.	P.A.A. Constellation	New York
9.05 p.m.	Air France Languedoc 161	Paris
10.00 p.m.	Sabena Dakota	Brussels
10.00 p.m.	A.O.A. Skymaster	New York
10.00 p.m.	T.C.A. North Star	Montreal

SATURDAY

Time	Aircraft	To
7.45 a.m.	Sabena Dakota	Brussels
8.00 a.m.	K.L.M. Dakota	Eindhoven
8.15 a.m.	B.O.A.C. York	Nairobi
8.30 a.m.	K.L.M. Dakota	Prague
8.30 a.m.	K.L.M. Skymaster	Amsterdam
9.05 a.m.	Air France Languedoc 161	Paris
9.40 a.m.	A.O.A. Constellation	Frankfurt
10.00 a.m.	B.O.A.C. Dakota	Cairo
10.00 a.m.	Sabena Dakota	Brussels

55

Time	Aircraft	To
10.25 a.m.	B.S.A.A.C. Lancastrian	Santiago (Chile
10.30 a.m.	P.A.A. Dakota	Vienna
10.30 a.m.	K.L.M. Skymaster	Amsterdam
11.00 a.m.	F.A.M.A. Skymaster or York	Buenos Aires
11.05 a.m.	Air France Languedoc 161	Paris
12.00 noon	Sabena Dakota	Brussels
12.00 noon	South African Skymaster	Johannesburg
12.30 noon	K.L.M. Skymaster	Amsterdam
12.50 noon	Sabena Dakota	Knocke/Le Zoute
12.55 noon	Air France Languedoc 161	Nice
1.01 p.m.	P.A.A. Constellation	New York
1.45 p.m.	B.O.A.C. York	Accra (West Africa)
2.05 p.m.	P.A.A. Constellation	Calcutta
2.30 p.m.	Sabena Dakota	Antwerp
2.30 p.m.	K.L.M. Skymaster	Amsterdam
2.30 p.m.	C.S.A. Dakota	Prague
3.15 p.m.	Iberia Skymaster	Madrid
3.45 p.m.	Sabena Dakota	Brussels
4.05 p.m.	Air France Languedoc 161	Paris
5.00 p.m.	B.O.A.C. Liberator	Montreal
5.15 p.m.	B.O.A.C. York	Colombo
5.55 p.m.	Sabena Dakota	Brussels
6.05 p.m.	Air France Languedoc 161	Paris
6.30 p.m.	K.L.M. Skymaster	Amsterdam
6.30 p.m.	A.O.A. Constellation	New York
7.00 p.m.	B.O.A.C. Constellation	New York
8.30 p.m.	K.L.M. Skymaster	Amsterdam
8.45 p.m.	P.A.A. Constellation	New York
9.05 p.m.	Air France Languedoc 161	Paris
10.00 p.m.	Sabena Dakota	Brussels
10.00 p.m.	B.O.A.C. Constellation	Montreal
10.00 p.m.	T.C.A. North Star	Montreal

SUNDAY

Time	Aircraft	To
7.45 a.m.	Sabena Dakota	Brussels
8.30 a.m.	K.L.M. Skymaster	Amsterdam
8.30 a.m.	K.L.M. Dakota	Prague
9.05 a.m.	Air France Languedoc 161	Paris
9.20 a.m.	B.O.A.C. Dakota	Teheran
10.00 a.m.	B.O.A.C. Dakota	Cairo
10.20 a.m.	Air France Languedoc 161	Paris
10.30 a.m.	K.L.M. Skymaster	Amsterdam
10.30 a.m.	P.A.A. Skymaster Freighter	Brussels
11.05 a.m.	Air France Languedoc 161	Paris
12.30 noon	K.L.M. Skymaster	Amsterdam
12.50 noon	Sabena Dakota	Knocke/Le Zoute
1.01 p.m.	P.A.A. Constellation	New York
2.00 p.m.	Sabena Dakota	Brussels
2.30 p.m.	K.L.M. Skymaster	Amsterdam
2.45 p.m.	B.O.A.C. York	Calcutta
3.45 p.m.	Sabena Dakota	Brussels
4.05 p.m.	Air France Languedoc 161	Paris
4.30 p.m.	K.L.M. Skymaster	Amsterdam
5.00 p.m.	B.O.A.C. Lancastrian Freighter	Johannesburg
5.30 p.m.	A.O.A. Skymaster	Frankfurt
5.55 p.m.	Sabena Dakota	Brussels
6.05 p.m.	Air France Languedoc 161	Paris
6.30 p.m.	K.L.M. Skymaster	Amsterdam
6.30 p.m.	A.O.A. Constellation	New York
7.00 p.m.	B.O.A.C. Constellation	New York
7.45 p.m.	B.O.A.C. Lancastrian Freighter	Sydney (Australia)
7.45 p.m.	Sabena Dakota	Prague
8.30 p.m.	K.L.M. Skymaster	Amsterdam
8.45 p.m.	P.A.A. Constellation	New York
9.05 p.m.	Air France Languedoc 161	Paris
10.00 p.m.	Sabena Dakota	Brussels
10.00 p.m.	P.A.A. Constellation	New York
10.00 p.m.	T.C.A. North Star	Montreal

RINGWAY AIRPORT (MANCHESTER).

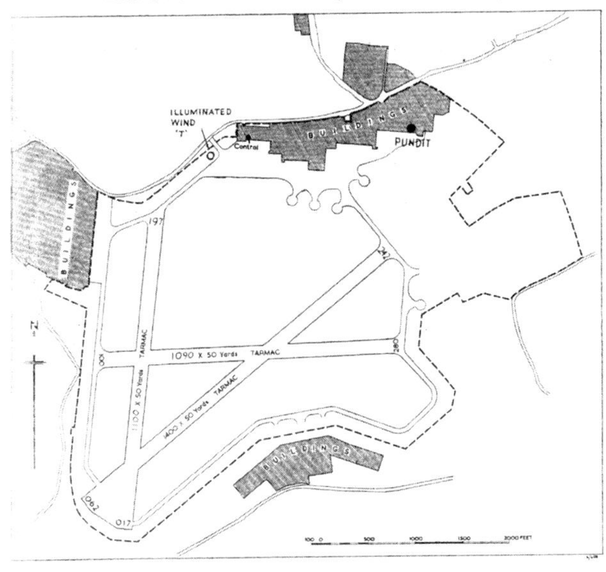

ARRIVALS.

Time	Frequency	Aircraft	From
9.00 a.m.	Daily	Aer Lingus Dakota	Dublin
9.10 a.m.	Tues., Sat.	C.O.B.E.T.A. Dakota	Prestwick (Glasgow)
9.55 a.m.	Mon., Tues., Wed.	K.L.M. Dakota	Dublin
9.55 a.m.	Thur., Fri., Sat.	Aer Lingus Dakota	Dublin
10.25 a.m.	Daily	B.E.A. Dakota	Isle of Man
12.45 p.m.	Daily	Aer Lingus Dakota	Dublin
2.15 p.m.	Daily	B.E.A. Dakota	Belfast
5.10 p.m.	Daily	B.E.A. Dakota	Isle of Man
5.30 p.m.	Mon., Fri.	C.O.B.E.T.A. Dakota	Brussels
5.45 p.m.	Mon., Tues., Sun.	K.L.M. Dakota	Amsterdam
5.45 p.m.	Thur., Fri., Sat.	Aer Lingus Dakota	Amsterdam
8.15 p.m.	Daily	Aer Lingus Dakota	Dublin
9.10 p.m.	Weekdays	B.E.A. Dakota	Belfast
9.35 p.m.	Mon., Tues., Wed., Thur., Fri., Sun.	Air France Languedoc 161	Paris

DEPARTURES.

Time	Frequency	Aircraft	To
8.10 a.m.	Weekdays	B.E.A. Dakota	Isle of Man
9.15 a.m.	Weekdays	Air France Languedoc 161	Paris
9.30 a.m.	Daily	Aer Lingus Dakota	Dublin

Time	Frequency	Aircraft	To
10.00 a.m.	Tues., Sat.	C.O.B.E.T.A. Dakota	Brussels
10.30 a.m.	Mon., Tues., Wed.	K.L.M. Dakota	Amsterdam
10.30 a.m.	Thurs., Fri., Sat.	Aer Lingus Dakota	Amsterdam
10.45 a.m.	Daily	B.E.A. Dakota	Belfast
1.15 p.m.	Daily	Aer Lingus Dakota	Dublin
2.35 p.m.	Weekdays	B.E.A. Dakota	Isle of Man
5.45 p.m.	Weekdays	B.E.A. Dakota	Belfast
6.15 p.m.	Mon., Tues., Sun.	K.L.M. Dakota	Dublin
6.15 p.m.	Thurs., Fri., Sat.	Aer Lingus Dakota	Dublin
8.45 p.m.	Daily	Aer Lingus Dakota	Dublin

NORTHOLT AIRPORT

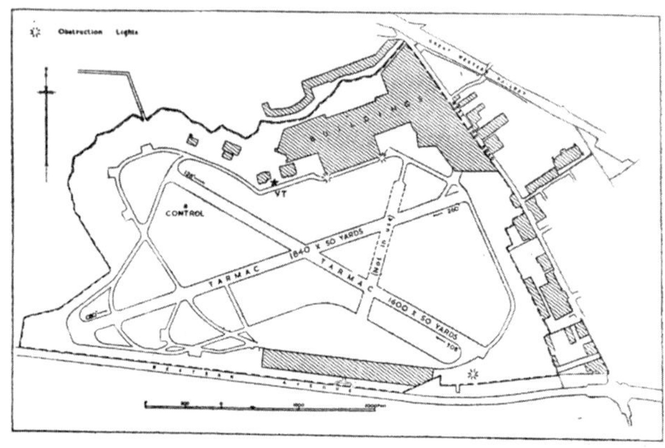

ARRIVALS.

Time	Frequency	Aircraft	From
5.30 a.m.	Wed., Sat.	Hellenic Liberator	Glasgow
8.30 a.m.	Daily	B.E.A. Viking	Amsterdam
9.00 a.m.	Daily	Aer Lingus Dakota	Dublin
9.22 a.m.	Daily	B.E.A. Dakota	Jersey
9.28 a.m.	Daily	B.E.A. Dakota	Guernsey
10.00 a.m.	Daily	Aer Lingus Dakota	Dublin
10.22 a.m.	Daily	B.E.A. Viking	Paris
10.58 a.m.	Weekdays	B.E.A. Viking	Glasgow
11.04 a.m.	Weekdays	B.E.A. Dakota	Belfast
11.16 a.m.	Tues., Sat., Sun.	S.A.S. Viking	Copenhagen
11.22 a.m.	Daily	B.E.A. Dakota	Jersey
11.30 a.m.	Daily	Aer Lingus Dakota	Dublin
11.40 a.m.	Sunday	Swissair Skymaster	Geneva
11.46 a.m.	Weekdays	B.E.A. Viking	Glasgow
11.52 a.m.	Sunday	B.E.A. Viking	Glasgow
11.58 a.m.	Sunday	B.E.A. Dakota	Jersey
12.04 noon	Daily	B.E.A. Viking	Brussels
12.16 noon	Daily	Swissair Skymaster	Zurich
12.22 noon	Mon., Fri., Sat., Sun.	B.E.A. Dakota	Jersey
12.28 noon	Daily	B.E.A. Viking	Paris

Time	Frequency	Aircraft	From
12.30 noon	Daily	Aer Lingus Dakota	Dublin
12.40 noon	Daily	B.E.A. Viking	Copenhagen
12.55 noon	Daily	Aer Lingus Dakota	Shannon
1.04 p.m.	Mon., Wed., Fri.	Swissair Dakota Freighter	Basle
1.22 p.m.	Daily	B.E.A. Dakota	Jersey
1.34 p.m.	Daily	S.A.S. Dakota	Oslo
1.52 p.m.	Tues., Thurs., Sat.	Swissair Dakota	Berne
1.58 p.m.	Weekdays	B.E.A. Viking	Glasgow
2.10 p.m.	Daily	Aer Lingus Dakota	Dublin
2.34 p.m.	Daily	S.A.S. DC-6	Stockholm
2.46 p.m.	Daily	B.E.A. Viking	Stockholm
3.00 p.m.	Daily	Aer Lingus Dakota	Dublin
3.04 p.m.	Tues., Sat.	Alitalia S.M. 95	Rome
3.10 p.m.	Daily	B.E.A. Viking	Paris
3.16 p.m.	Daily	B.E.A. Dakota	Belfast
3.22 p.m.	Daily	B.E.A. Dakota	Jersey
3.28 p.m.	Wednesday	Alitalia S.M. 95	Rome
3.46 p.m.	Mon., Wed., Fri., Sun.	S.A.S. Dakota	Gothenburg
3.52 p.m.	Weekdays	Swissair Dakota	Geneva
4.04 p.m.	Weekdays	B.E.A. Viking	Zurich
4.16 p.m.	Daily	B.E.A. Dakota	Guernsey
4.22 p.m.	Mon., Fri., Sat., Sun.	B.E.A. Dakota	Jersey
4.30 p.m.	Daily	Aer Lingus Dakota	Dublin
4.40 p.m.	Sunday	B.E.A. Dakota	Belfast
4.52 p.m.	Mon., Fri., Sat., Sun.	B.E.A. Dakota	Jersey
5.04 p.m.	Daily	B.E.A. Viking	Paris
5.16 p.m.	Daily	Swissair Dakota	Zurich
5.22 p.m.	Mon., Tues., Thurs., Sat.	C.S.A. Dakota	Prague
5.28 p.m.	Daily	B.E.A. Viking	Brussels
5.30 p.m.	Thurs., Sun.	Hellenic Liberator	Athens
5.34 p.m.	Daily	B.E.A. Dakota	Jersey
5.45 p.m.	Daily	Aer Lingus Dakota	Dublin
6.10 p.m.	Tues., Fri.	B.E.A. Viking	Gibraltar
6.40 p.m.	Weekdays	B.E.A. Dakota	Isle of Man
6.46 p.m.	Mon., Wed., Fri.	B.E.A. Viking	Oslo
6.52 p.m.	Tues., Wed., Thur., Fri., Sat., Sun.	B.E.A. Viking	Berlin
6.58 p.m.	Mon., Wed., Fri.	B.E.A. Viking	Prague
7.10 p.m.	Daily	Aer Lingus Dakota	Dublin
7.16 p.m.	Wed., Sun.	B.E.A. Viking	Malta and Rome
7.28 p.m.	Wed., Sat.	Luxembourg Dakota	Luxembourg
7.40 p.m.	Tues., Thur., Sat.	B.E.A. Viking	Nice
7.52 p.m.	Tues., Thur., Sat.	Swissair Dakota	Zurich
7.58 p.m.	Daily	B.E.A. Dakota	Jersey
8.04 p.m.	Weekdays	B.E.A. Viking	Vienna
8.10 p.m.	Daily	B.E.A. Viking	Paris
8.16 p.m.	Daily	B.E.A. Dakota	Jersey
8.20 p.m.	Daily	Aer Lingus Dakota	Dublin
8.28 p.m.	Weekdays	B.E.A. Viking	Glasgow
8.34 p.m.	Daily	B.E.A. Viking	Geneva
8.46 p.m.	Sunday	B.E.A. Dakota	Guernsey
8.52 p.m.	Mon., Fri., Sat., Sun.	B.E.A. Dakota	Jersey
8.58 p.m.	Mon., Wed., Sat.	B.E.A. Viking	Madrid
9.04 p.m.	Mon., Wed., Fri.	S.A.S. Dakota	Oslo
9.10 p.m.	Daily	B.E.A. Viking	Brussels
9.16 p.m.	Weekdays	B.E.A. Dakota	Belfast
9.28 p.m.	Wed., Sat.	B.E.A. Viking	Istanbul
9.34 p.m.	Weekdays	B.E.A. Dakota	Orkney
9.40 p.m.	Daily	Aer Lingus Dakota	Dublin
10.10 p.m.	Daily	B.E.A. Viking	Paris
10.16 p.m.	Mon., Wed., Thur., Fri., Sun.	B.E.A. Viking	Athens
10.22 p.m.	Mon., Tues., Thurs., Sat., Sun.	B.E.A. Viking	Lisbon
10.50 p.m.	Daily	Aer Lingus Dakota	Dublin

DEPARTURES.

Time	Frequency	Aircraft	To
5.30 a.m.	Daily	B.E.A. Dakota	Guernsey
5.30 a.m.	Daily	B.E.A. Dakota	Jersey
7.00 a.m.	Daily	Aer Lingus Dakota	Dublin
7.00 a.m.	Wed., Sat.	Hellenic Liberator	Athens
7.57 a.m.	Mon., Wed., Sat.	B.E.A. Viking	Madrid
8.00 a.m.	Daily	Aer Lingus Dakota	Dublin
8.00 a.m.	Daily	B.E.A. Dakota	Jersey
8.09 p.m.	Daily	B.E.A. Viking	Brussels
8.12 a.m.	Tues., Sat.	B.E.A. Viking	Rome and Malta
8.15 a.m.	Daily	B.E.A. Viking	Paris
8.21 a.m.	Mon., Tues., Thurs., Fri., Sat.	B.E.A. Viking	Lisbon
8.24 a.m.	Tues., Thur., Fri., Sun.	C.S.A. Dakota	Prague
8.30 a.m.	Daily	B.E.A. Viking	Amsterdam
8.33 a.m.	Sunday	B.E.A. Dakota	Jersey
8.39 a.m.	Tues., Wed., Thurs., Fri., Sat., Sun.	B.E.A. Viking	Berlin
8.45 a.m.	Daily	B.E.A. Viking	Zurich
8.48 a.m.	Weekdays	B.E.A. Dakota	Orkney
8.54 a.m.	Wed., Fri., Sun.	Swissair Dakota	Zurich
9.00 a.m.	Mon., Fri., Sat., Sun.	B.E.A. Dakota	Jersey
9.03 a.m.	Weekdays	B.E.A. Viking	Glasgow
9.15 a.m.	Daily	B.E.A. Dakota	Belfast
9.21 a.m.	Mon., Wed., Fri.	B.E.A. Viking	Oslo
9.30 a.m.	Daily	Aer Lingus Dakota	Dublin
9.30 a.m.	Thurs., Sun.	Luxembourg Dakota	Luxembourg
9.39 a.m.	Mon., Wed., Fri.	B.E.A. Viking	Prague
9.54 a.m.	Tues., Thurs., Sat.	B.E.A. Viking	Nice
9.57 a.m.	Wed. Thurs., Sun.	Alitalia S.M. 95	Rome
10.00 a.m.	Daily	B.E.A. Dakota	Jersey
10.06 a.m.	Daily	B.E.A. Dakota	Guernsey
10.27 a.m.	Tues., Thurs., Sat.	S.A.S. Dakota	Oslo
10.30 a.m.	Daily	Aer Lingus Dakota	Dublin
11.15 a.m.	Daily	B.E.A. Viking	Paris
11.51 a.m.	Daily	B.E.A. Dakota	Isle of Man
12.00 noon	Daily	Aer Lingus Dakota	Dublin
12.00 noon	Daily	B.E.A. Dakota	Jersey
12.33 noon	Tues., Sat., Sun.	S.A.S. Viking	Copenhagen
12.51 noon	Sunday	Swissair Skymaster	Geneva
1.00 p.m.	Daily	Aer Lingus Dakota	Dublin
1.00 p.m.	Mon., Fri., Sat., Sun.	B.E.A. Dakota	Jersey
1.06 p.m.	Daily	B.E.A. Viking	Brussels
1.15 p.m.	Daily	B.E.A. Viking	Paris
1.21 p.m.	Daily	Swissair Skymaster	Zurich
1.27 p.m.	Daily	B.E.A. Viking	Geneva
1.30 p.m.	Mon., Fri., Sat., Sun.	B.E.A. Dakota	Jersey
1.33 p.m.	Daily	B.E.A. Viking	Copenhagen
1.39 p.m.	Daily	B.E.A. Viking	Stockholm
2.10 p.m.	Daily	Aer Lingus Dakota	Shannon
2.12 p.m.	Mon., Wed., Fri., Sun.	Swissair Dakota Freighter	Zurich
2.15 p.m.	Daily	B.E.A. Dakota	Jersey
2.30 p.m.	Daily	S.A.S. Dakota	Oslo
2.39 p.m.	Mon., Wed., Fri.	Swissair Dakota	Berne
2.39 p.m.	Thurs., Sat., Sun.	Swissair Dakota	Basle
2.40 p.m.	Daily	Aer Lingus Dakota	Dublin
3.03 p.m.	Weekdays	B.E.A. Viking	Glasgow
3.09 p.m.	Daily	S.A.S. Viking or Skymaster	Copenhagen
3.30 p.m.	Daily	Aer Lingus Dakota	Dublin
3.51 p.m.	Daily	B.E.A. Dakota	Belfast
4.00 p.m.	Daily	B.E.A. Dakota	Guernsey
4.15 p.m.	Daily	B.E.A. Viking	Paris
4.21 p.m.	Daily	S.A.S. DC-6	Stockholm
4.33 p.m.	Mon., Wed., Fri., Sun.	S.A.S. Dakota	Gothenburg

Time	Frequency	Aircraft	To
4.39 p.m.	Weekdays	Swissair Dakota	Geneva
4.45 p.m.	Daily	B.E.A. Dakota	Jersey
5.03 p.m.	Sunday	B.E.A. Dakota	Guernsey
5.10 p.m.	Daily	Aer Lingus Dakota	Dublin
5.15 p.m.	Daily	B.E.A. Viking	Brussels
5.30 p.m.	Mon., Fri., Sat., Sun.	B.E.A. Dakota	Jersey
5.39 p.m.	Sunday	B.E.A. Dakota	Belfast
6.05 p.m.	Daily	B.E.A. Dakota	Jersey
6.15 p.m.	Daily	B.E.A. Viking	Paris
6.20 p.m.	Daily	Aer Lingus Dakota	Dublin
7.03 p.m.	Weekdays	B.E.A. Dakota	Glasgow (via Edinburgh)
7.09 p.m.	Daily	B.E.A. Viking	Glasgow
7.15 p.m.	Daily	B.E.A. Dakota	Belfast
7.40 p.m.	Daily	Aer Lingus Dakota	Dublin
8.50 p.m.	Daily	Aer Lingus Dakota	Dublin
9.15 p.m.	Daily	B.E.A. Viking	Paris
10.18 p.m.	Tues., Wed., Thurs., Sat., Sun.	B.E.A. Viking	Athens
10.30 p.m.	Thurs., Sun.	Hellenic Liberator	Glasgow
11.57 p.m.	Mon., Thurs.	B.E.A. Viking	Istanbul

PRESTWICK AIRPORT (GLASGOW).

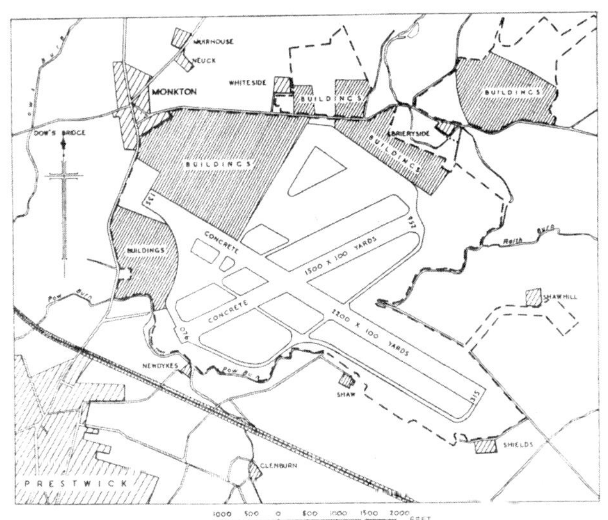

61

ARRIVALS.

MONDAY

Time	Aircraft	From
5.25 a.m.	K.L.M. Constellation	New York
6.40 a.m.	S.A.S. Skymaster or DC-6	New York
9.30 a.m.	K.L.M. Constellation	Curacao (West Indies)
11.20 a.m.	B.O.A.C. Liberator	Montreal
12.00 noon	B.O.A.C. Constellation	New York
3.15 p.m.	B.O.A.C. Constellation	Montreal
7.30 p.m.	C.O.B.E.T.A. Dakota	Brussels
8.10 p.m.	T.C.A. North Star	Montreal
9.45 p.m.	K.L.M. Constellation	Amsterdam
11.45 p.m.	K.L.M. Constellation	Amsterdam
11.50 p.m.	S.A.S. Skymaster or DC-6	Stockholm
12.20 midnight	S.A.S. Skymaster or DC-6	Stockholm

TUESDAY

Time	Aircraft	From
5.25 a.m.	K.L.M. Constellation	New York
6.40 a.m.	S.A.S. Skymaster or DC-6	New York
7.55 a.m.	A.O.A. Skymaster	New York
8.10 p.m.	T.C.A. North Star	Montreal
8.25 p.m.	A.O.A. Skymaster	Copenhagen
8.30 p.m.	Icelandic Liberator	Reykjavik
9.40 p.m.	Air France Languedoc 161	Paris
10.30 p.m.	S.A.S. Dakota	Oslo
10.45 p.m.	B.O.A.C. Constellation	London
11.45 p.m.	B.O.A.C. Constellation	London
11.45 p.m.	K.L.M. Constellation	Amsterdam

WEDNESDAY

Time	Aircraft	From
5.25 a.m.	K.L.M. Constellation	New York
6.40 a.m.	S.A.S. Skymaster or DC-6	New York
11.20 a.m.	B.O.A.C. Liberator	Montreal
3.15 p.m.	B.O.A.C. Constellation	Montreal
6.45 p.m.	B.O.A.C. Liberator	London
8.10 p.m.	T.C.A. North Star	Montreal
11.45 p.m.	K.L.M. Constellation	Amsterdam
12.30 midnight	S.A.S. Skymaster or DC-6	Stockholm

THURSDAY

Time	Aircraft	From
5.25 a.m.	K.L.M. Constellation	New York
6.40 a.m.	S.A.S. Skymaster or DC-6	New York
11.20 a.m.	B.O.A.C. Liberator	Montreal
12.00 noon	B.O.A.C. Constellation	New York
8.25 p.m.	A.O.A. Skymaster	Helsinki
9.40 p.m.	Air France Languedoc 161	Paris
10.30 p.m.	S.A.S. Dakota	Oslo
11.45 p.m.	B.O.A.C. Constellation	London
11.45 p.m.	K.L.M. Constellation	Amsterdam
11.50 p.m.	S.A.S. Skymaster or DC-6	Stockholm
12.20 midnight	S.A.S. Skymaster or DC-6	Stockholm

FRIDAY

Time	Aircraft	From
5.25 a.m.	K.L.M. Constellation	New York
6.40 a.m.	S.A.S. Skymaster-or DC-6	New York
9.30 a.m.	K.L.M. Constellation	Curacao (West Indies)
7.55 a.m.	A.O.A. Skymaster	New York
3.15 p.m.	B.O.A.C. Constellation	Montreal
6.45 p.m.	B.O.A.C. Liberator	London
7.30 p.m.	C.O.B.E.T.A. Dakota	Brussels
8.10 p.m.	T.C.A. North Star	Montreal
10.00 p.m.	A.O.A. Skymaster	London
10.45 p.m.	B.O.A.C. Constellation	London
11.45 p.m.	K.L.M. Constellation	Amsterdam

SATURDAY

Time	Aircraft	From
5.25 a.m.	K.L.M. Constellation	New York
6.40 a.m.	S.A.S. Skymaster or DC-6	New York
12.00 noon	B.O.A.C. Constellation	New York
6.45 p.m.	B.O.A.C. Liberator	London
8.10 p.m.	T.C.A. North Star	Montreal
10.30 p.m.	S.A.S. Dakota	Oslo
11.45 p.m.	K.L.M. Constellation	Amsterdam
11.50 p.m.	S.A.S. Skymaster or DC-6	Stockholm
12.20 midnight	S.A.S. Skymaster or DC-6	Stockholm

SUNDAY

Time	Aircraft	From
5.25 a.m.	K.L.M. Constellation	New York
6.30 a.m.	A.O.A. Constellation	New York
6.40 a.m.	S.A.S. Skymaster or DC-6	New York
8.10 p.m.	T.C.A. North Star	Montreal
9.05 p.m.	A.O.A. Constellation	Frankfurt
9.40 p.m.	Air France Languedoc 161	Paris
10.30 p.m.	S.A.S. Dakota	Oslo
10.45 p.m.	B.O.A.C. Constellation	London
11.45 p.m.	K.L.M. Constellation	Amsterdam

DEPARTURES.

MONDAY

Time	Aircraft	To
1.15 a.m.	K.L.M. Constellation	New York
1.20 a.m.	S.A.S. Skymaster or DC-6	New York
9.10 a.m.	S.A.S. Dakota	Oslo
9.10 a.m.	Air France Languedoc 161	Paris
11.15 a.m.	T.C.A. North Star	Montreal
5.30 p.m.	A.C.A. Skymaster	Frankfurt
11.15 p.m.	K.L.M. Constellation	Curacao (West Indies)

TUESDAY

Time	Aircraft	To
1.15 a.m.	K.L.M. Constellation	New York
1.20 a.m.	S.A.S. Skymaster or DC-6	New York
8.00 a.m.	C.O.B.E.T.A. Dakota	Brussels
8.25 a.m.	A.O.A. Skymaster	Frankfurt
9.30 a.m.	Icelandic Liberator	Reykjavik
11.15 a.m.	T.C.A. North Star	Montreal
12.50 noon	B.O.A.C. Liberator	London
1.30 p.m.	B.O.A.C. Constellation	London
9.10 p.m.	A.O.A. Skymaster	New York
10.45 p.m.	B.O.A.C. Constellation	New York

WEDNESDAY

Time	Aircraft	To
1.15 a.m.	K.L.M. Constellation	New York
1.20 a.m.	S.A.S. Skymaster or DC-6	New York
1.45 a.m.	B.O.A.C. Constellation	Montreal
9.10 a.m.	S.A.S. Dakota	Oslo
9.10 a.m.	Air France Languedoc 161	Paris
11.15 a.m.	T.C.A. North Star	Montreal
3.30 p.m.	Hellenic Liberator	Athens
5.30 p.m.	A.O.A. Skymaster	Frankfurt
8.15 p.m.	B.O.A.C. Liberator	Montreal

THURSDAY

Time	Aircraft	To
1.15 a.m.	K.L.M. Constellation	New York
1.20 a.m.	S.A.S. Skymaster or DC-6	New York
11.15 a.m.	T.C.A. North Star	Montreal
12.50 noon	B.O.A.C. Liberator	London

Time	Aircraft	To
1.30 p.m.	B.O.A.C. Constellation	London
4.45 p.m.	B.O.A.C. Constellation	London
9.10 p.m.	A.O.A. Skymaster	New York
11.15 p.m.	K.L.M. Constellation	Curacao (West Indies)

FRIDAY

Time	Aircraft	To
1.15 a.m.	K.L.M. Constellation	New York
1.20 a.m.	S.A.S. Skymaster or DC-6	New York
1.45 a.m.	B.O.A.C. Constellation	Montreal
8.25 a.m.	A.O.A. Skymaster	London
9.10 a.m.	S.A.S. Dakota	Oslo
9.10 a.m.	Air France Languedoc 161	Paris
11.15 a.m.	T.C.A. North Star	Montrea
12.50 noon	B.O.A.C. Liberator	London
8.15 p.m.	B.O.A.C. Liberator	Montreal
10.30 p.m.	A.O.A. Skymaster	New York
10.45 p.m.	B.O.A.C. Constellation	New York

SATURDAY

Time	Aircraft	To
1.15 a.m.	K.L.M. Constellation	New York
1.20 a.m.	S.A.S. Skymaster or DC-6	New York
8.00 a.m.	C.O.B.E.T.A. Dakota	Brussels
11.15 a.m.	T.C.A. North Star	Montreal
3.30 p.m.	Hellenic Liberator	Athens
4.45 p.m.	B.O.A.C. Constellation	London
8.15 p.m.	B.O.A.C. Liberator	Montreal

SUNDAY

Time	Aircraft	To
1.15 a.m.	K.L.M. Constellation	New York
1.20 a.m.	S.A.S. Skymaster or DC-6	New York
1.45 a.m.	B.O.A.C. Constellation	Montreal
7.40 a.m.	A.O.A. Constellation	Frankfurt
9.10 a.m.	S.A.S. Dakota	Oslo
11.15 a.m.	T.C.A. North Star	Montreal
9.35 p.m.	A.O.A. Constellation	New York
10.45 p.m.	B.O.A.C. Constellation	New York

RENFREW AIRPORT (GLASGOW).

ARRIVALS.

Time	Frequency	Aircraft	From
8.35 a.m.	Mon., Fri., Sat.	Aer Lingus Dakota	Dublin
10.55 a.m.	Weekdays	B.E.A. Rapide	Campbeltown
11.10 a.m.	Weekdays	B.E.A. Rapide	Islay
11.13 a.m.	Weekdays	B.E.A. Viking	Northolt (London)
11.20 a.m.	Weekdays	B.E.A. Dakota	Belfast
1.05 p.m.	Daily	Aer Lingus Dakota	Dublin
3.10 p.m.	Daily	B.E.A. Dakota	Belfast
3.20 p.m.	Weekdays	B.E.A. Rapide	Campbeltown
4.05 p.m.	Weekdays	B.E.A. Dakota	Inverness
4.25 p.m.	Weekdays	B.E.A. Rapide	Benbecula
4.35 p.m.	Weekdays	B.E.A. Rapide	Tiree
4.35 p.m.	Daily	Aer Lingus Dakota	Dublin
5.13 p.m.	Weekdays	B.E.A. Viking	Northolt (London)
6.10 p.m.	Daily	B.E.A. Dakota	Belfast
7.25 p.m.	Weekdays	B.E.A. Rapide	Islay
7.30 p.m.	Weekdays	B.E.A. Dakota	Shetland
7.35 p.m.	Weekdays	B.E.A. Rapide	Campbeltown
9.10 p.m.	Weekdays	B.E.A. Dakota	Belfast
9.19 p.m.	Daily	B.E.A. Viking	Northolt (London)
10.20 p.m.	Weekdays	B.E.A. Dakota	London (via Edinburgh)

Pan American Douglas Skymaster *Clipper Gladiator* NC 88945 at London Airport.

Lockheed Constellation **PP-PDA** of Panair do Brasil, the Brazilian airline. The five Constellations used by Panair do Brasil on the service to London are known as the *Bandeirante* Class.

Qantas Empire Airways Constellation *Lawrence Hargrave* as operated on the London-Australia route at London Airport.   *(Photos: A. S. C. Lumsden*

(Photo: A. S. C. Lumsden

South African Airways Douglas DC-4 Skymaster ZS-BMF *Amatola* at London Airport. S.A.A. employ seven Skymasters on the Johannesburg-London route. The company name appears on the port side of the fuselage in Afrikaans and on the starboard side in English.

(Photo: Sabena

A Douglas DC-6 of the Belgian airline company S.A.B.E.N.A. Belgian DC-6 aircraft call at Shannon Airport on the route from Brussels to New York.

(Photo: A. S. C. Lumsden

Douglas DC-3 Dakota OO-AUQ, as used by S.A.B.E.N.A. on the services from London Airport to Antwerp and Brussels.

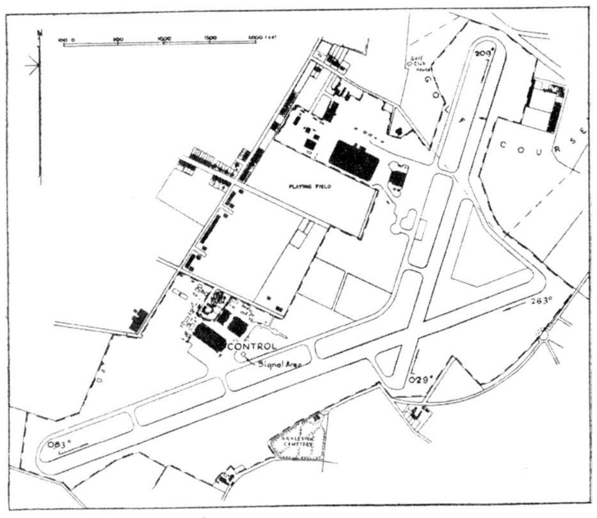

DEPARTURES.

Time	Frequency	Aircraft	To
8.10 a.m.	Weekdays	B.E.A. Dakota	Inverness
8.30 a.m.	Weekdays	B.E.A. Dakota	Belfast
8.35 a.m.	Weekdays	B.E.A. Dakota	London (via Edinburgh)
8.58 a.m.	Weekdays	B.E.A. Viking	Northolt (London)
9.05 a.m.	Weekdays	B.E.A. Rapide	Islay
9.20 a.m.	Weekdays	B.E.A. Rapide	Campbeltown
9.25 a.m.	Weekdays	B.E.A. Rapide	Benbecula
9.52 a.m.	Sunday	B.E.A. Viking	Northolt (London)
11.55 a.m.	Daily	B.E.A. Dakota	Belfast
11.58 a.m.	Weekdays	B.E.A. Viking	Northolt (London)
12.00 noon	Weekdays	B.E.A. Dakota	Shetland
1.35 p.m.	Daily	Aer Lingus Dakota	Dublin
1.45 p.m.	Weekdays	B.E.A. Rapide	Campbeltown
2.05 p.m.	Weekdays	B.E.A. Rapide	Tiree
3.40 p.m.	Daily	B.E.A. Dakota	Belfast
5.05 p.m.	Daily	Aer Lingus Dakota	Dublin
5.15 p.m.	Weekdays	B.E.A. Rapide	Islay
6.00 p.m.	Weekdays	B.E.A. Rapide	Campbeltown
6.28 p.m.	Weekdays	B.E.A. Viking	Northolt (London)
6.05 p.m.	Mon., Fri.	Aer Lingus, Dakota	Dublin
6.40 p.m.	Weekdays	B.E.A. Dakota	Belfast
9.05 p.m.	Mon., Fri., Sat.	Aer Lingus Dakota	Dublin

67

RONALDSWAY AIRPORT (ISLE OF MAN).

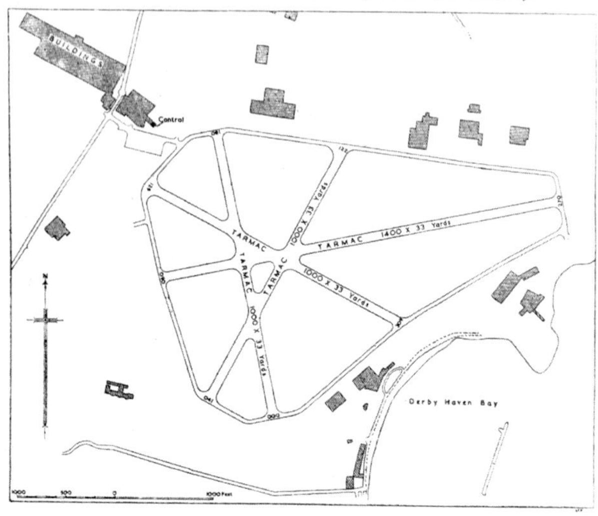

ARRIVALS.

Time	Frequency	Aircraft	From
8.50 a.m.	Weekdays	B.E.A. Dakota	Liverpool
9.10 a.m.	Daily	B.E.A. Dakota	Manchester
9.55 a.m.	Weekdays	B.E.A. Dakota	Renfrew (Glasgow)
10.05 a.m.	Daily	B.E.A. Dakota	Liverpool
10.55 a.m.	Sunday	B.E.A. Dakota	Renfrew (Glasgow)
12.40 noon	Daily	B.E.A. Dakota	Liverpool
1.46 p.m.	Daily	B.E.A. Dakota	Northolt (London)
2.30 p.m.	Sunday	B.E.A. Dakota	Renfrew (Glasgow)
3.10 p.m.	Daily	B.E.A. Dakota	Blackpool
3.35 p.m.	Daily	B.E.A. Dakota	Manchester
4.20 p.m.	Daily	B.E.A. Dakota	Liverpool
5.30 p.m.	Daily	B.E.A. Dakota	Renfrew (Glasgow)
5.55 p.m.	Daily	B.E.A. Dakota	Liverpool
7.45 p.m.	Daily	B.E.A. Dakota	Blackpool
8.25 p.m.	Mon., Fri., Sat., Sun.	B.E.A. Dakota	Liverpool
9.30 p.m.	Daily	B.E.A. Dakota	Liverpool

DEPARTURES.

Time	Frequency	Aircraft	To
8.00 a.m.	Weekdays	B.E.A. Dakota	Liverpool
9.05 a.m.	Weekdays	B.E.A. Dakota	Belfast
9.30 a.m.	Daily	B.E.A. Dakota	Manchester
10.25 a.m.	Weekdays	B.E.A. Dakota	Renfrew (Glasgow)
10.35 a.m.	Daily	B.E.A. Dakota	Liverpool
11.30 a.m.	Sunday	B.E.A. Dakota	Renfrew (Glasgow)
1.25 p.m.	Daily	B.E.A. Dakota	Blackpool

Time	Frequency	Aircraft	To
2.15 p.m.	Daily	B.E.A. Dakota	Liverpool
3.00 p.m.	Sunday	B.E.A. Dakota	Renfrew (Glasgow)
4.00 p.m.	Daily	B.E.A. Dakota	Liverpool
4.15 p.m.	Daily	B.E.A. Dakota	Manchester
6.00 p.m.	Daily	B.E.A. Dakota	Blackpool
6.25 p.m.	Mon., Fri., Sat., Sun.	B.E.A. Dakota	Liverpool
7.15 p.m.	Daily	B.E.A. Dakota	Liverpool
8.30 p.m.	Daily	B.E.A. Dakota	Renfrew (Glasgow)
8.45 p.m.	Daily	B.E.A. Dakota	Liverpool

SHANNON AIRPORT

ARRIVALS.

Time	Frequency	Aircraft	From
00.05 a.m.	Fri., Sun.	T.C.A. North Star	London
00.15 a.m.	Saturday	A.O.A. Skymaster	London
00.20 a.m.	Wednesday	A.O.A. Skymaster	Frankfurt
00.20 a.m.	Mon., Fri., Sun.	A.O.A. Skymaster	Berlin
00.30 a.m.	Alternate Fridays	Swissair Skymaster	Geneva
00.45 a.m.	Mon., Wed., Sat.	Sabena DC-6	Brussels
1.50 a.m.	Tues., Fri.	Air France Constellation	New York
2.50 a.m.	Monday	Air France Constellation	Paris
4.20 a.m.	Friday	A.O.A. Constellation	New York
4.30 a.m.	Wednesday	A.O.A. Constellation	Washington
4.30 a.m.	Mon., Thurs., Sun.	A.O.A. Constellation	New York
5.30 a.m.	Weekdays	A.O.A. Skymaster	New York
5.55 a.m.	Saturday	T.W.A. Constellation or DC-4	Cairo
6.25 a.m.	Mon., Wed., Fri.	T.W.A. Skymaster	Cairo
6.50 a.m.	Mon., Wed., Thurs.	Air France Constellation	New York
9.00 a.m.	Alternate Mondays	Swissair Skymaster	New York
9.15 a.m.	Weekdays	P.A.A. Skymaster	New York
9.30 a.m.	Mon., Tues.	P.A.A. Skymaster	New York
10.25 a.m.	Wednesday	T.W.A. Skymaster Freighter	Cairo
11.00 a.m.	Daily	P.A.A. Constellation	New York
11.30 a.m.	Mon., Wed., Sat.	B.O.A.C. Constellation	New York
12.50 noon	Thursday	Air France Constellation	New York
1.00 p.m.	Wed., Fri.	T.C.A. North Star	Montreal
2.10 p.m.	Sunday	T.W.A. Skymaster Freighter	Washington
3.15 p.m.	Saturday	T.W.A. Constellation	New York
4.50 p.m.	Daily	Aer Lingus Dakota	London
6.20 p.m.	Mon., Tues.	T.W.A. Constellation	Bombay
7.00 p.m.	Sunday	P.A.A. Skymaster Freighter	New York
7.15 p.m.	Tues, Wed., Thurs., Fri., Sat., Sun.	P.A.A. Skymaster	Munich
8.25 p.m.	Mon., Wed., Fri., Sun.	A.O.A. Constellation	London
8.25 p.m.	Sunday	T.W.A. Constellation or DC-4	Chicago
8.35 p.m.	Friday	T.W.A. Constellation	Bombay
8.40 p.m.	Mon., Wed., Thurs., Fri.	T.W.A. Constellation	New York
9.00 p.m.	Mon., Wed., Sat.	B.O.A.C. Constellation	London
9.35 p.m.	Thursday	A.O.A. Constellation	Frankfurt
9.45 p.m.	Tuesday	T.W.A. Constellation	Washington
9.50 p.m.	Daily	Aer Lingus Dakota	Dublin
10.00 p.m.	Wednesday	P.A.A. Skymaster	London
10.45 p.m.	Mon., Fri.	A.O.A. Constellation	Frankfurt
10.50 p.m.	Daily	P.A.A. Constellation	London
11.05 p.m.	Sunday	A.O.A. Constellation	Frankfurt
11.50 p.m.	Weekdays	Air France Constellation	Paris

DEPARTURES.

Time	Frequency	Aircraft	To
00.05 a.m.	Daily	P.A.A. Constellation	New York
00.05 a.m.	Monday	A.O.A. Constellation	New York
1.05 a.m.	Fri., Sun.	T.C.A. North Star	Montreal
1.20 a.m.	Tues., Wed., Thurs., Sat., Sun.	Air France Constellation	New York
1.20 a.m.	Mon., Wed., Fri., Sun.	A.O.A. Skymaster	New York
1.45 a.m.	Saturday	A.O.A. Skymaster	New York
2.00 a.m.	Alternate Fridays	Swissair Skymaster	New York
2.15 a.m.	Mon., Wed., Sat.	Sabena DC-6	New York
4.20 a.m.	Monday	Air France Constellation	New York
4.50 a.m.	Friday	A.O.A. Constellation	Frankfurt
5.00 a.m.	Mon., Wed.	A.O.A. Constellation	Frankfurt
5.05 a.m.	Thurs., Sun.	A.O.A. Constellation	Frankfurt
6.00 a.m.	Mon., Thurs., Sat.	A.O.A. Skymaster	Berlin
6.15 a.m.	Tuesday	A.O.A. Skymaster	Frankfurt
6.15 a.m.	Friday	A.O.A. Skymaster	London
7.55 a.m.	Monday	T.W.A. Constellation	New York
7.55 a.m.	Wednesday	T.W.A. Constellation or DC-4	Chicago
7.55 a.m.	Friday	T.W.A. Constellation or DC-4	Washington
8.05 a.m.	Wed., Fri., Sun.	T.W.A. Skymaster	Paris
8.20 a.m.	Mon., Wed., Fri.	Air France Constellation	Paris
10.00 a.m.	Mon., Tues.	A.O.A. Skymaster	Stockholm
10.00 a.m.	Alternate Mondays	Swissair Skymaster	Geneva
10.20 a.m.	Tues., Fri.	Air France Constellation	Paris
10.25 a.m.	Wednesday	T.W.A. Skymaster Freighter	New York
10.30 a.m.	Weekdays	P.A.A. Skymaster	Prague
10.30 a.m.	Daily	Aer Lingus Dakota	London
11.10 a.m.	Thursday	T.W.A. Skymaster	Paris
12.15 noon	Daily	P.A.A. Constellation	London
12.15 noon	Monday	T.W.A. Skymaster	Paris
12.45 noon	Mon., Wed., Sat.	B.O.A.C. Constellation	London
1.00 p.m.	Thursday	P.A.A. Skymaster	New York
2.00 p.m.	Wed., Fri.	T.C.A. North Star	London
2.20 p.m.	Thursday	Air France Constellation	Paris
3.10 p.m.	Sunday	T.W.A. Constellation or DC-4	Cairo
4.15 p.m.	Saturday	T.W.A. Constellation or DC-4	Cairo
5.45 p.m.	Daily	Aer Lingus Dakota	Dublin
5.55 p.m.	Saturday	T.W.A. Constellation	New York
6.20 p.m.	Tuesday	T.W.A. Constellation	New York
7.50 p.m.	Monday	T.W.A. Constellation or DC-4	New York
8.00 p.m.	Sunday	P.A.A. Skymaster	Brussels
8.30 p.m.	Tues., Wed., Thurs., Fri., Sat., Sun.	P.A.A. Skymaster	New York
9.25 p.m.	Sunday	T.W.A. Skymaster	Cairo
9.25 p.m.	Mon., Wed., Fri.	A.O.A. Constellation	New York
9.25 p.m.	Sunday	A.O.A. Constellation	Washington
9.40 p.m.	Mon., Fri., Thurs.	T.W.A. Constellation	Bombay
9.40 p.m.	Wednesday	T.W.A. Skymaster	Cairo
10.05 p.m.	Friday	T.W.A. Constellation or DC-4	New York
10.35 p.m.	Thursday	A.O.A. Constellation	New York
10.45 p.m.	Mon., Wed., Sat.	B.O.A.C. Constellation	New York
10.45 p.m.	Tuesday	T.W.A. Skymaster	Cairo
11.45 p.m.	Mon., Wed., Fri.	A.O.A. Constellation	New York

70

EASTLEIGH AIRPORT (SOUTHAMPTON).

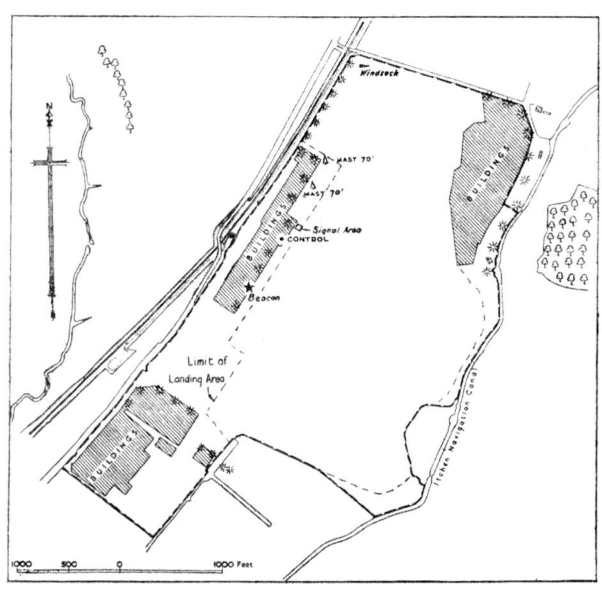

ARRIVALS.

Time	Frequency	Aircraft	From
10.50 a.m.	Daily	B.E.A. Dakota	Jersey
11.40 a.m.	Daily	B.E.A. Rapide	Jersey
12.55 noon	Daily	B.E.A. Dakota	Guernsey
1.55 p.m.	Daily	B.E.A. Dakota	Jersey
3.10 p.m.	Mon., Fri., Sat., Sun.	B.E.A. Rapide	Jersey
5.30 p.m.	Daily	B.E.A. Dakota	Jersey

DEPARTURES.

Time	Frequency	Aircraft	To
11.25 a.m.	Daily	B.E.A. Dakota	Jersey
11.55 a.m.	Daily	B.E.A. Rapide	Jersey
1.25 p.m.	Daily	B.E.A. Dakota	Guernsey
2.25 p.m.	Daily	B.E.A. Dakota	Jersey
3.30 p.m.	Mon., Fri., Sat., Sun.	B.E.A. Rapide	Jersey
6.00 p.m.	Daily	B.E.A. Dakota	Jersey

71

MARINE AIR TERMINAL, BERTH 50, SOUTHAMPTON.

ARRIVALS.

MONDAY

3.00 p.m.	B.O.A.C. " Plymouth " Class from Hong-Kong

WEDNESDAY

1.00 p.m.	B.O.A.C. " Hythe " Class from Karachi
3.30 p.m.	B.O.A.C. " Hythe " Class from Australia

THURSDAY

3.00 p.m.	B.O.A.C. " Plymouth " Class from Tokyo
3.30 p.m.	B.O.A.C. Solent from Johannesburg

FRIDAY

3.30 p.m.	B.O.A.C. " Hythe " Class from Australia

SATURDAY

3.30 p.m.	B.O.A.C. Solent from Johannesburg

SUNDAY

3.30 p.m.	B.O.A.C. " Hythe " Class from Australia
3.30 p.m.	B.O.A.C. Solent from Johannesburg

DEPARTURES.

MONDAY

11.45 a.m.	B.O.A.C. " Hythe " Class to Australia

TUESDAY

11.45 a.m.	B.O.A.C. Solent to Johannesburg
12.30 a.m.	B.O.A.C. " Plymouth " Class to Hong-Kong

WEDNESDAY

11.45 a.m.	B.O.A.C. " Hythe " Class to Australia

THURSDAY

11.45 a.m.	B.O.A.C. " Hythe " Class to Karachi

FRIDAY

11.45 a.m.	B.O.A.C. Solent to Johannesburg
12.30 p.m.	B.O.A.C. " Plymouth " Class to Tokyo

SATURDAY

11.45 a.m.	B.O.A.C. " Hythe " Class to Australia

SUNDAY

11.45 a.m.	B.O.A.C. Solent to Johannesburg

AIRSPEED CONSUL.

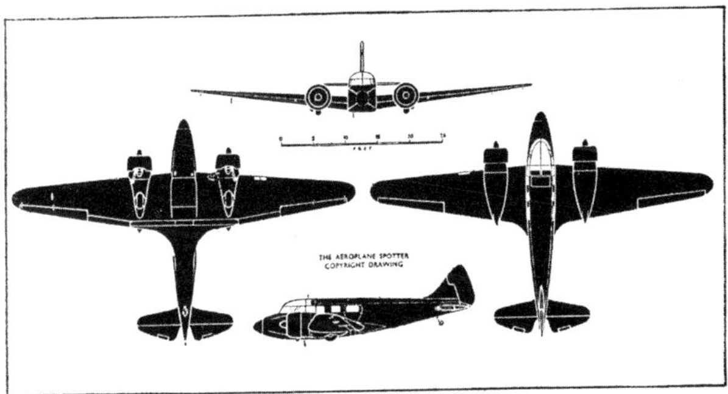

General Description.	Twin-engine low-wing monoplane with single fin and rudder, constructed by Airspeed Ltd., at Portsmouth.
Seating Capacity.	Crew of two and five passengers.
Engines.	Two Armstrong-Siddeley Cheetah X, each of 395 h.p.
Dimensions.	Span : 53 ft. 4 ins. Length : 35 ft. 4 ins.
Performance.	Cruising speed : 150 m.p.h. Range : 900 miles.

First built in 1945, the Consul is a civil conversion of the R.A.F. Oxford navigation trainer, of which nearly 10,000 were built during the war. As the Oxford was in turn derived from the civil Envoy of 1934, the basic design conception of the Consul is thus at least fifteen years old. Production commenced in March, 1946, and the Consul is now one of the most widely-used aircraft in service with charter companies. There are about one hundred Consuls in commercial operation in Britain alone and many more overseas.

AVRO XIX ANSON.

General Description.	Twin-engine low-wing monoplane with single fin and rudder, constructed by A. V. Roe & Co. Ltd. at Yeadon and Manchester.
Seating Capacity.	Crew of two and six or nine passengers.
Engines.	Two Armstrong-Siddeley Cheetah XV, each of 420 h.p.
Dimensions.	Span : 56 fr. 6 ins. Length : 42 ft. 3 ins.
Performance.	Cruising speed : 155 m.p.h. Range : 570 miles.

The Anson has had a very long career and there are several variations of the basic design in service with the charter companies. Some are

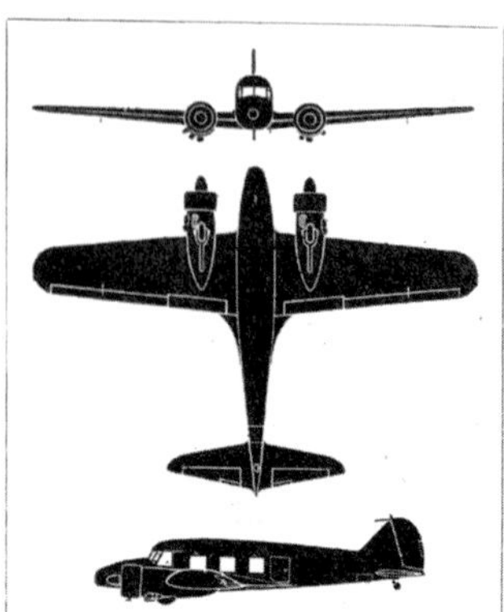

AVRO XIX ANSON—*contd.*

converted ex-R.A.F. trainers, but the majority are of the Avro XIX type which was produced as a civil version of the military Anson XII in 1944. Like the Consul, the Avro XIX derives from a military aircraft which was initially developed itself from a civil design. Military service of the Anson dates back to 1936, and the civil machine from which it was developed was the Avro 652, two of which served with the old Imperial Airways from 1934 onwards. Fundamentally unchanged in outline since 1934, the latest Anson differs in having a tapered all-metal wing.

AVRO LANCASTRIAN.

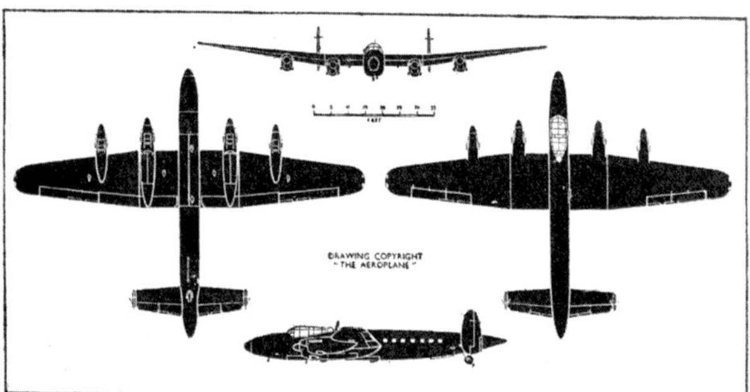

General Description.	Four-engine mid-wing monoplane with twin fins and rudders, constructed by A. V. Roe & Co. Ltd., at Manchester.
Seating Capacity.	Crew of five and thirteen passengers.
Engines.	Four Rolls-Royce Merlin T.24, each of 1,640 h.p.
Dimensions.	Span : 102 ft. 0 ins. Length : 76 ft. 10 ins.
Performance.	Cruising speed : 280 m.p.h. Range : 2,820 miles. With 13 passengers.

One of the several British airliner types derived from war-time bombers for the immediate post-war period, the Lancastrian is a civil version of the renowned Lancaster bomber. First manufactured and used commercially in Canada during 1943, production in Britain for both the R.A.F. and B.O.A.C. began in 1944. Lancastrians pioneered post-war landplane routes to Australia with B.O.A.C. and to South America with B.S.A.A.C. The Lancastrian can boast high speed but restricted cabin capacity reduces its value for commercial operation and it is now being relegated to freighter duties as newer types come into service.

AVRO TUDOR IV.

General Description. Four-engine low-wing monoplane with single fin and rudder, constructed by A. V. Roe & Co. Ltd., at Manchester.

Seating Capacity. Crew of four and thirty-two passengers.

Engines. Four Rolls-Royce Merlin 621, each of 1,752 h.p.

Dimensions. Span : 120 ft. 0 ins. Length: 85 ft. 6 ins.

Performance. Cruising speed : 280 m.p.h. Range : 3,700 miles.

First of the Tudor series to go into regular airline operation, the Tudor IV was grounded by the Ministry of Civil Aviation early in 1948 owing to the unfortunate loss of *Star Tiger* over the South Atlantic. The type is now in operation again, but is provisionally restricted to freight work. Much controversy rages over the technical aspects of this matter, but it is fairly safe to say that the Tudor IV is a promising aircraft and that the temporary withdrawal was merely a reflection of extreme caution. The original Tudor, designed for transatlantic operation, first flew in 1945.

AVRO YORK.

General Description. Four-engine high-wing monoplane with three fins. Constructed by A. V. Roe & Co. Ltd., at Manchester

Seating Capacity. Crew of four and twenty-four passengers.

Engines. Four Rolls-Royce Merlin T.24, each of 1,640 h.p.

Dimensions. Span: 102 ft. 0 ins. Length : 78 ft. 0 ins.

Performance. Cruising speed : 260 m.p.h. Range : 2,700 miles.

Utilizing many Lancaster components to facilitate production, the York was developed in 1942 as a military transport for the R.A.F., the first machine flying in July, 1942. Yorks became the personal transports of a number of high-ranking personages, including Mr. Winston Churchill and Field-Marshal Smuts. Yorks for civil use were in service before the war ended, B.O.A.C. taking delivery of their first York early in 1944. Still a mainstay of B.O.A.C. equipment, the York is also in service with British South American Airways, Skyways Ltd. and the Argentine company F.A.M.A. Production of the York finally ceased in April, 1948.

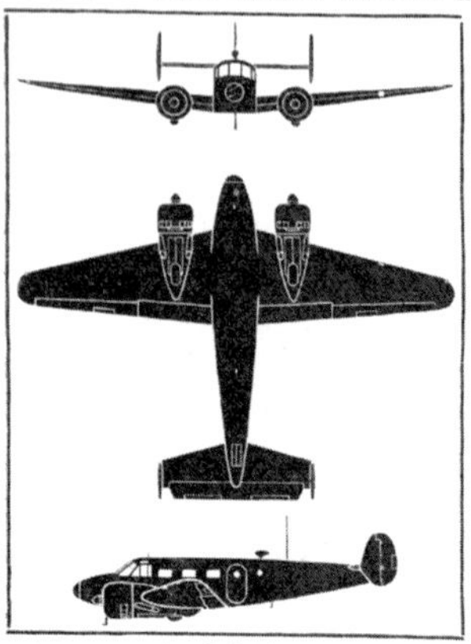

BEECH EXPEDITER.

General Description. Twin-engine low-wing monoplane with twin fins and rudders. Constructed by the Beech Aircraft Corporation, Wichita, Kansas, U.S.A.

Seating Capacity. Crew of two and six passengers.

Engines. Two Pratt and Whitney Wasp Junior, each of 450 h.p.

Dimensions. Span : 47 ft. 8 ins. Length : 34 ft. 3 ins.

Performance. Cruising speed : 220 m.p.h. Range : 900 miles.

Used extensively by the French charter company *Air Transport* on its services to Croydon and Gatwick, the Beech Expediter is a type formerly used by the United States Air Force in Europe during the war. Surplus Beech aircraft have been sold to a number of European airline companies. The Expediter is in much the same category as the British Anson and Consul, but has a rather higher performance. The original version of the Expediter was first flown in 1937.

BOEING STRATOCRUISER.

General Description. Four-engine mid-wing monoplane with single fin and rudder. Constructed by the Boeing Airplane Company, Seattle, Washington, U.S.A.

Seating Capacity. Crew of five and maximum passenger accommodation for one hundred.

Engines. Four Pratt and Whitney Wasp Major, each of 3,500 h.p.

Dimensions. Span : 141 ft. 3 ins. Length 110 ft. 4 ins.

Performance. Cruising speed : 300 m.p.h. Range : 4,100 miles.

Developed concurrently with the Stratofreighter, a similar aircraft for the United States Air Force, the Stratocruiser is nearing the end of its acceptance trials and deliveries to airlines are expected to commence before the end of 1948. Just as the British Tudor airliners employ the same wing design as the Lincoln bomber, so does the Stratocruiser incorporate the same wings as the Superfortress bomber. B.O.A.C. has five Stratocruisers on order to supplement the Constellations on the London-New York route.

BRISTOL FREIGHTER AND WAYFARER.

General Description. Twin-engine high-wing monoplane with single fin and rudder and non-retracting undercarriage. Constructed by the Bristol Aeroplane Company Ltd., Filton, Bristol.

Seating Capacity (*Wayfarer*). Crew of two and thirty-six passengers.

Engines. Two Bristol Hercules 638, each of 1,690 h.p.

Dimensions. Span: 108 ft. 0 ins. Length : 68 ft. 4 ins.

Performance. Cruising speed : 170 m.p.h. Range : 1,100 miles.

The Bristol Type 170 Freighter was originally intended as a troop transport for service in the Far East, but with the end of the war it was decided to place the aircraft on the civil market as a short-haul high-capacity passenger or freight-carrying machine. The passenger version is known as the Wayfarer and both versions are similar externally. Freighters and Wayfarers have sold well in the export market and, amongst the foreign airlines, the French firm Air Transport operates Wayfarers into Gatwick. The latest model of the Freighter has rounded wing-tips, the earlier version having square-cut wings of rather less span.

CANADAIR DC-4M NORTH STAR.

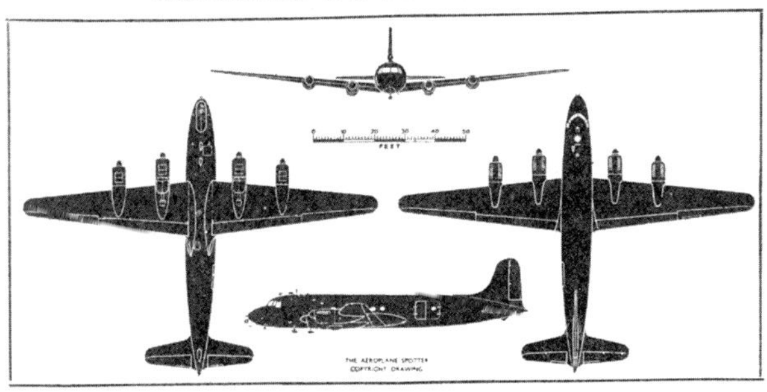

77

85

General Description.	Four-engine low-wing monoplane with single fin and rudder. Constructed by Canadair Ltd., Montreal, Canada.
Seating Capacity.	Crew of four and twenty-four passengers.
Engines.	Four Rolls-Royce Merlin 620, each of 1,780 h.p.
Dimensions.	Span : 117 ft. 6 ins. Length : 93 ft. 5 ins.
Performance.	Cruising speed : 319 m.p.h. Range : 3,065 miles.

Essentially a Douglas DC-4 built under licence in Canada, the Canadair DC-4M differs from its American counterpart in having Rolls-Royce Merlin engines in place of the Twin Wasp radials. First produced in 1943 to meet the requirements of Trans-Canada Airlines, the DC-4M, popularly known as the North Star, incorporates many refinements over the original DC-4, and has many features of the later DC-6. The first six DC-4M aircraft did not have the fully-pressurized passenger cabin of the twenty DC-4M2 versions now in service. B.O.A.C. is to purchase twenty-two DC-4M4 airliners for service on the N. Atlantic and Middle East routes.

CONSOLIDATED LIBERATOR.

General Description. Four-engine high-wing monoplane with twin fins and rudders. Constructed by the Consolidated-Vultee Aircraft Corporation, San Diego, California, U.S.A.

Seating Capacity. Varies with requirements of operator.

Engines. Four Pratt and Whitney Twin Wasp, each of 1,200 h.p.

Dimensions. Span: 110 ft. 0 ins. Length : 66 ft. 4 ins.

Performance. Cruising speed : 220 m.p.h. Range : 2,500 miles.

In company with the Flying Fortress, the Liberator was the standard heavy bomber of the U.S. Air Force during the war and some were also supplied to the R.A.F. under Lend-Lease. A capacious fuselage and exceptional range made the Liberator especially suitable for transport duties and the original machines supplied to the R.A.F. in 1941 were converted for this work. Liberators gave good service on the war-time routes of B.O.A.C., but the type is now obsolescent and carries only freight on the Atlantic services, although Scottish Airlines and its subsidiary Hellenic Airways still use the passenger version. Recently, B.O.A.C. Liberators have been employed on flight refuelling experiments. The original Liberator flew in 1939.

CONVAIR 240.

General Description.	Twin-engine low-wing monoplane with single fin and rudder Constructed by the Consolidated-Vultee Corporation, San Diego California, U.S.A.

78

Seating Capacity. Crew of four and forty passengers.

Engines. Two Pratt and Whitney Double Wasp, each of 2,400 h.p.

Dimensions. Span: 91 ft. 9 ins. Length : 74 ft. 8 ins.

Performance. Cruising speed : 300 m.p.h.   Range : 800 miles.

The American equivalent in performance and capacity of the British Airspeed Ambassador, the Convair 240 is the modern replacement for the evergreen Dakota. Convair Liners are scheduled to replace Dakotas on the European routes of S.A.B.E.N.A., K.L.M. and Swissair. The Convair 240 made its maiden flight in March, 1947, and over 150 are now being built for airlines in the U.S.A., Latin America and Australia, as well as the European companies previously mentioned.

DE HAVILLAND DOVE.

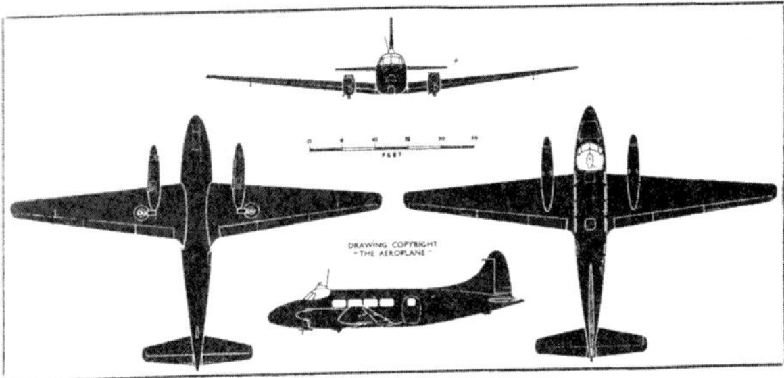

General Description. Twin-engine low-wing monoplane with single fin and rudder. Constructed by the De Havilland Aircraft Company Ltd., Hatfield, Herts.

Seating Capacity. Crew of two and eight passengers.

Engines. Two D.H. Gipsy Queen 70, each of 340 h.p.

Dimensions. Span : 57 ft. 0 ins.   Length : 39 fr. 6 ins.

Performance. Cruising speed : 179 m.p.h.   Range : 780 miles

Enjoying a most healthy sale in the export market, the Dove is a wholly post-war production and continues the De Havilland tradition of success in the light transport field which was established by the Dragon and Dragon Rapide biplanes. Succeeding the Rapide as a light transport and feeder liner with low operating and maintenance costs, the Dove shares with the Miles Aerovan the introduction of the tricycle undercarriage in standard British transport aircraft. Heavier British airliners currently in service employ the older form of tailwheel undercarriage long since abandoned by the American transports. The first Dove flew in September, 1945. A pleasant feature of the Dove is the excellent vision from the passengers' cabin provided by the large windows.

DE HAVILLAND DRAGON RAPIDE.

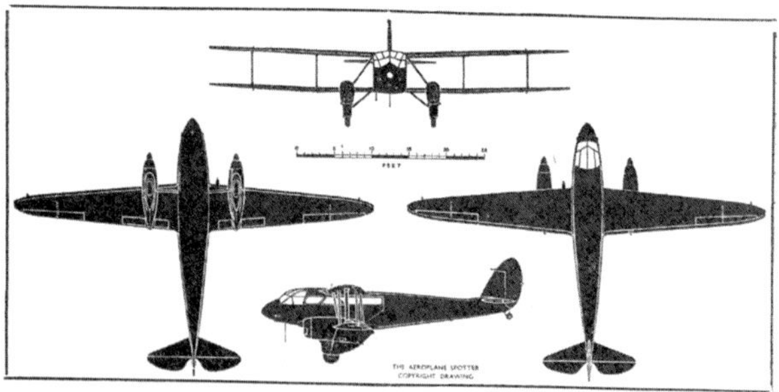

General Description.	Twin-engine biplane with tapered wings, fixed undercarriage and single fin and rudder. Constructed by De Havilland Aircraft Company Ltd., Witney, Oxford, and Brush Coachwork Ltd., Loughborough, Leicester.
Seating Capacity.	Crew of two and six passengers or crew of one and eight passengers.
Engines.	Two D.H. Gipsy Queen III, each of 200 h.p.
Dimensions.	Span : 48 ft. 0 ins. Length : 34 ft. 6 ins.
Performance.	Cruising speed : 123 m.p.h. Range : 495 miles.

Undoubtedly the most popular light airliner ever produced, the economical operating costs of the Dragon Rapide made it the mainstay of internal air routes in the United Kingdom before the war, and indeed made many such routes otherwise impracticable a commercial proposition. Nearly 700 Rapides were built between 1934 and 1946, the type being used during the war as the Dominie wireless and navigation trainer. Now converted once more for civil operation, the Rapide forms part of the fleet of nearly every charter operator in Great Britain. Its ability to operate from small grass aerodromes makes it especially suitable for operation in the Scottish islands, where it is mainly used by British European Airways.

80

One of the fleet of 17 Douglas DC-6 airliners recently placed into operation by S.A.S., and now used on the Copenhagen-Stockholm to London Northolt) route.

Scandinavian Airlines System Vickers Viking *Tormund Viking* OY-DLO. S.A.S. Vikings share the Copenhagen-London route with DC-6s.

(*Photos: A. S. C. Lumsden*

Douglas Dakota SE-BAS of A.B.A. (Swedish Airlines) at Northolt.

Upper: Swissair Douglas DC-4 Skymaster HB-ILA at Northolt Airport.
Lower: A Douglas DC-3 Dakota of Swissair at Northolt. Swissair's Dakotas are scheduled for replacement by Convair 240 Liners.

(Photos: A. S. C. Lumsden

Upper: One of the twenty Canadair North Star II airliners employed on the transatlantic route and home transcontinental routes by Trans-Canada Airlines.
Lower: Lockheed Constellation NC 86505 *Paris Sky Chief* of Trans-World Airline at Shannon Airport. Sabena DC-6s and Air France Constellations also operate through Shannon.

90

DOUGLAS DC.-3 DAKOTA.

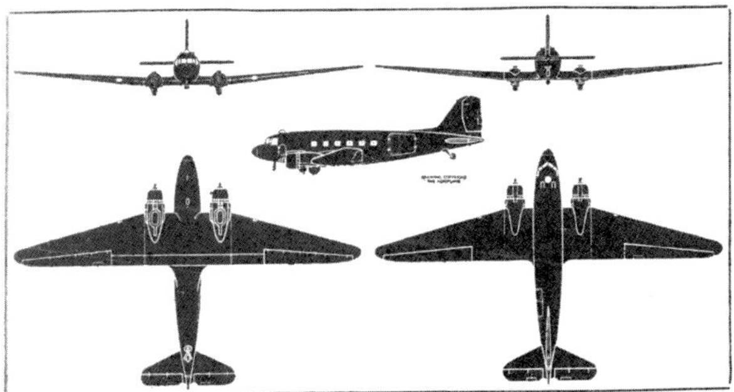

General Description.	Twin-engine low-wing monoplane with single fin and rudder. Constructed by the Douglas Aircraft Company, Santa Monica, California, U.S.A.
Seating Capacity.	Crew of three and from fourteen to twenty-one passengers.
Engines.	Two Pratt and Whitney Twin Wasp, each of 1,200 h.p.
Dimensions.	Span : 95 ft. 0 ins. Length : 64 ft. 5 ins.
Performance.	Cruising speed : 185 m.p.h. Range : 1,500 miles.

Most widely known of all transport aircraft, the Douglas DC-3 was christened the Dakota by the R.A.F. during the war and the name has been retained by the post-war civil airliner conversions. Although first introduced as early as 1936 for American domestic airlines, the DC-3 is to-day the most widely-used airliner type in the world and will probably remain so until at least 1950. Produced in vast quantities during the war for service as a troop-carrier with every Allied air force, there were as a result many surplus Dakotas available for conversion to civil standard with the arrival of peace and these aircraft were eagerly snapped up by those European airline companies which had lost their original fleet due to war action. The popular impression created by the lay press that the Dakota is an accident-prone aircraft is completely fallacious. As the Dakota is used by very nearly every airline in the world, it is obvious that when accidents on regular routes do occur it is frequently a Dakota which is involved. The law of averages would produce similar statistics for any aircraft so widely used as the Dakota.

DOUGLAS DC-4 SKYMASTER.

General Description.	Four-engine low-wing monoplane with single fin and rudder. Constructed by the Douglas Aircraft Company, Santa Monica, California, U.S.A.
Seating Capacity.	Crew of five and forty-four passengers or twenty-two sleeping berths.
Engines.	Four Pratt and Whitney Twin Wasp, each of 1,350 h.p.
Dimensions.	Span : 117 ft. 6 ins. Length : 93 ft. 11 ins.
Performance.	Cruising speed : 239 m.p.h. Range : 3,300 miles.

83

The original DC-4 of 1939 differed considerably from the form in which we now know it as the Skymaster, the early version being larger, with triple fins and rudders. The present model with the single fin first flew in April, 1942, and although originally intended for American domestic airlines the entry of U.S.A. in the war saw the DC-4 taken over by the Army as a troop transport. Consequently, the Skymaster did not see service as a civil airliner until 1945 when Skymasters declared surplus by the U.S. Army were stripped of military equipment and refurnished for service on trunk routes with American, Belgian, Dutch, French and Swedish airlines. Skymasters have been converted to civil requirements by the Glenn Martin and Republic aircraft factories.

DOUGLAS DC-6.

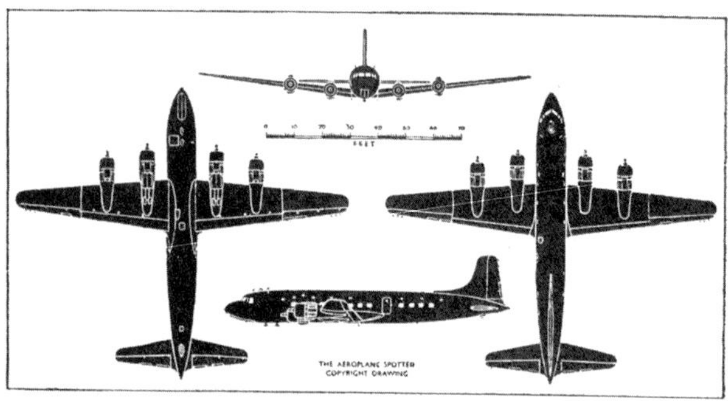

General Description.	Four-engine low-wing monoplane with single fin and rudder. Constructed by the Douglas Aircraft Company, Santa Monica, California, U.S.A.
Seating Capacity.	Crew of six and fifty-two passengers or twenty-six sleeper berths.
Engines.	Four Pratt and Whitney Double Wasp, each of 1,700 h.p.
Dimensions.	Span : 117 ft. 6 ins. Length : 100 ft. 7 ins.
Performance.	Cruising speed : 300 m.p.h. Range : 4,480 miles.

The DC-6 is the latest of the famous Douglas series of airliners in service on world air routes and is a direct development of the DC-4, from which it differs in having a longer, more capacious fuselage, more powerful engines and a cabin pressurized for operation to 19,000 ft. Otherwise the DC-6 and the earlier DC-4 are outwardly similar. The original DC-6 flew in February, 1946, and the first commercial flight was by a United Airlines machine in April, 1947. Now in service with a number of European airlines, including K.L.M. and the Scandinavian Airlines System, the Belgian S.A.B.E.N.A. firm took delivery of the first DC-6 in Europe in July, 1947.

LANGUEDOC 161.

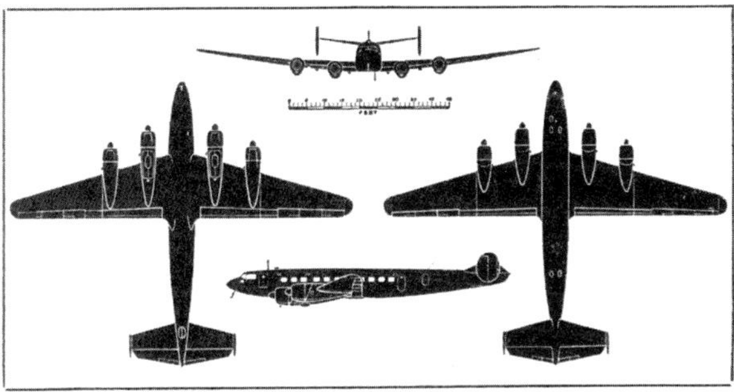

General Description.	Four-engine low-wing monoplane with twin fins and rudders. Constructed by Societe Nationale de Constructions Aeronautiques de Sud-Est, Paris, France.
Seating Capacity.	Crew of five and thirty-three passengers.
Engines.	Four Gnome-Rhone 14N, each of 1,200 h.p.
Dimensions.	Span : 96 ft. 5 ins. Length : 79 ft. 7 ins.
Performance.	Cruising speed : 233 m.p.h. Range : 1,700 miles.

Major type of airliner employed on the European network of Air France, including the London-Paris service, the Languedoc 161 was originally designed as the S.O. (Bloch) 161, a development of the Bloch 160 of 1938, and the first machine flew at Bordeaux in 1939. Outbreak of war delayed further progress and the prototype aircraft, later confiscated by the Germans, did not complete its flight trials until January, 1942. Manufacture of the Languedoc 161 in quantity did not commence until after the liberation of France when the re-constituted Air France ordered forty. The first post-war production aircraft flew in September, 1945 and deliveries to Air France are now completed.

LOCKHEED CONSTELLATION.

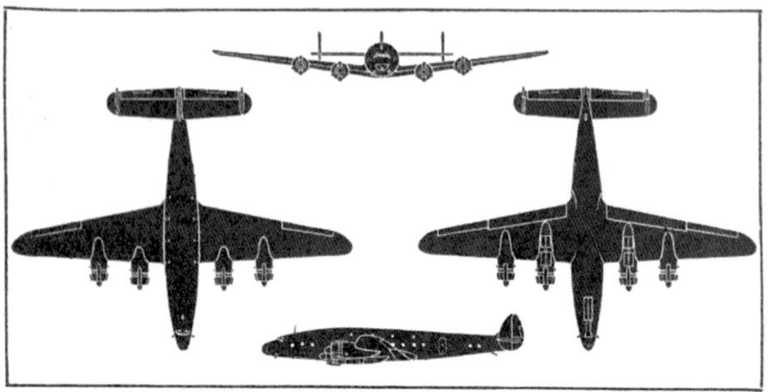

General Description.	Four-engine low-wing monoplane with triple fins and rudders. Constructed by the Lockheed Aircraft Corporation, Burbank, California, U.S.A.
Seating Capacity.	Crew of five and forty-eight passengers or twenty-two sleeper berths.
Engines.	Four Wright Duplex Cyclone, each of 2,500 h.p.
Dimensions.	Span : 123 ft. 0 ins. Length 95 ft. 1 in.
Performance.	Cruising speed : 321 m.p.h. Range : 4,630 miles.

Now the most widely-used type of airliner on the transatlantic route from London to New York, the aesthetically satisfying lines of the Constellation are a common sight at London Airport where " Connies " of B.O.A.C., Pan American and American Overseas Airlines are daily visitors. The Constellation is also used on the North Atlantic crossing by T.W.A. and Air France, operating through Shannon Airport, and by K.L.M. through Prestwick. In the same way as the Skymaster, the Constellation was designed initially for American domestic airlines but overtaken by war and commandeered by the U.S. Air Force. The first Constellation flew in January, 1943. Fifty Constellations laid down for the U.S. Air Force were converted as civil airliners when the war ended and delivered to commercial operators in 1946 as the Model 49. Latest production version, outwardly similar, has additional petrol tanks in the wings and various other refinements and is known as the Model 749.

MILES AEROVAN.

General Description.	Twin-engine high-wing monoplane with triple fins and rudders, tadpole fuselage and tricycle undercarriage. Constructed by Miles Aircraft Ltd. at Reading, Berks.
Seating Capacity.	Crew of one and nine passengers.
Engines.	Two Blackburn Cirrus Major III, each of 155 h.p.
Dimensions.	Span : 50 ft. 0 ins. Length : 34 ft. 4 ins.
Performance.	Cruising speed : 112 m.p.h. Range : 400 miles.

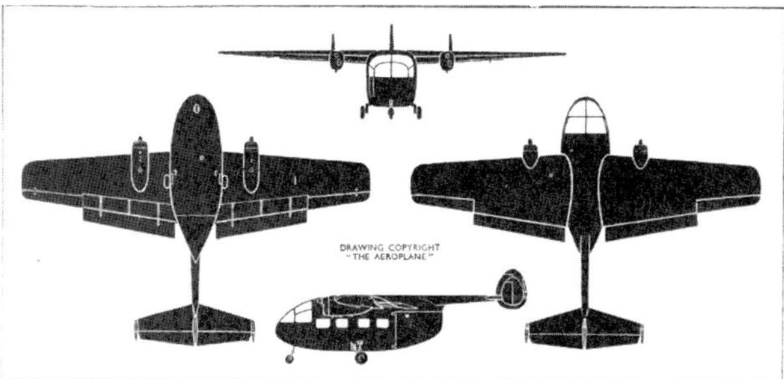

A useful " maid-of-all-work " primarily used by charter companies, the Aerovan serves both as a short-haul passenger aircraft for local services or as a freighter carrying a variety of cargoes, ranging from light cars and race horses to crates of fruit and furniture. Freight is loaded through the hinged rear door, the tail being well clear of the loading van or truck. Aerovans have contributed to the export trade and are used by Belgian, French, Spanish and Swiss charter firms. First flown in January, 1945, the Aerovan has since been delivered in this country to Air Transport (Charter) Ltd. of Jersey ; Culliford Air Lines Ltd. of Blackpool ; East Anglian Flying Services of Southend ; Patrick-Duval Aviation Services of Birmingham ; Sivewright Airways Ltd. of Manchester and Ulster Aviation Ltd. of Belfast.

S.I.A.I. MARCHETTI S.M. 95.

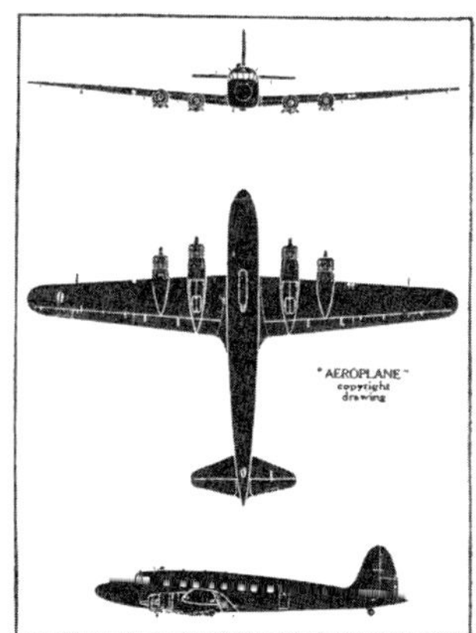

General Description.	Four-engine low-wing monoplane with single fin and rudder. Constructed by Societa Italiana Aeroplani Idrovolanti Marchetti, Sesto Calende, Italy.
Seating Capacity.	Crew of five and eighteen passengers.
Engines.	Four Alfa-Romeo, R.C.10, each of 930 h.p.
Dimensions.	Span: 112 ft. 5 ins. Length: 72 ft. 11 ins.
Performance.	Cruising speed : 186 m.p.h. Range: 2,113 miles.

87

Three-engine Savoia-Marchetti airliners were familiar sights at European airports before the war, being widely employed by the Belgian company S.A.B.E.N.A. as well as the Italian air lines. The S.M. 95 is the first Marchetti product to serve on the post-war Italian air routes. It was designed during the war period and one of the first examples built was seized by the German occupation forces and used by the *Luftwaffe*. After the Allied occupation of Italy another S.M. 95 was taken over by the R.A.F. and eventually used as a military transport aircraft between Great Britain and the Continent during 1945. The first post-war commercial versions of the S.M. 95 are in service with the Anglo-Italian company Alitalia and operate between Northolt Airport and Rome.

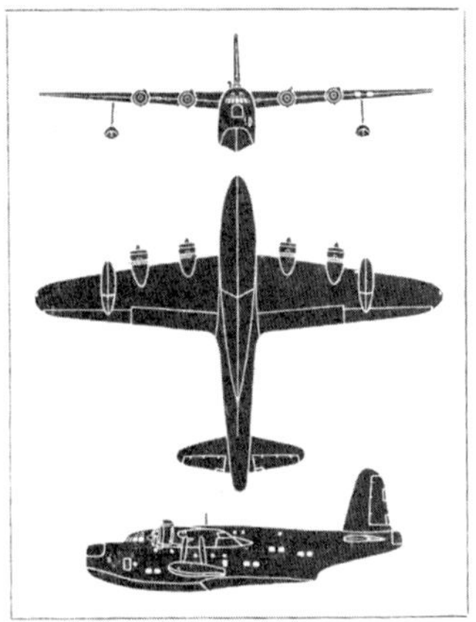

SHORT " HYTHE CLASS " FLYING-BOAT.

General Description. Four-engine high-wing monoplane flying-boat with single fin and rudder. Constructed by Short Brothers and Harland Ltd., Belfast and Rochester.

Seating Capacity. Crew of six and twenty-two passengers or sixteen sleeper berths.

Engines. Four Bristol Pegasus 48, each of 1,000 h.p.

Dimensions. Span : 112 ft. 9 ins. Length : 85 ft. 6 ins.

Performance. Cruising speed : 178 m.p.h. Range : 1,400 miles.

The tradition of using flying-boats on the Empire routes was inherited by B.O.A.C. from Imperial Airways which introduced the fleet of " Empire " flying-boats in 1936. The famous Sunderland flying-boat of the R.A.F. is merely a militarized version of the original " Empire " boats. " Empire " flying-boats served with distinction on the war-time routes of B.O.A.C. but, inevitably, many were lost due to war hazards, and in 1943 it was decided to augment the flying-boat fleet with a number of Sunderland III's originally laid down as transports for the R.A.F. Eventually twenty-four Sunderlands were delivered to B.O.A.C., of which seventeen now remain in service, the name of " Hythe Class " being bestowed in 1946 when extra civilian comforts were added to the internal furnishings. The faired-in turret in the bows of the " Hythe " boats betray their military derivation. B.O.A.C. now plans to dispose of the " Hythe " flying-boats and replace them on the Australian route with the five new Constellation landplanes recently purchased from Ireland. Two " Hythes " have already been sold to a British charter company.

88

SHORT "PLYMOUTH CLASS" FLYING-BOAT.

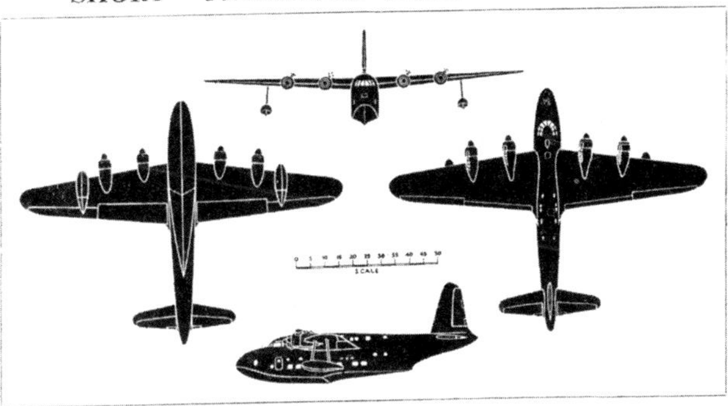

General Description.	Four-engine high-wing flying-boat with single fin and rudder. Constructed by Short Brothers and Harland Ltd., Belfast and Rochester.
Seating Capacity.	Crew of six and twenty-two passengers, or sixteen sleeper berths.
Engines.	Four Bristol Pegasus 38, each of 1,030 h.p.
Dimensions.	Span : 112 ft. 9 ins. Length : 85 ft. 4 ins.
Performance.	Cruising speed : 184 m.p.h. Range : 1,600 miles.

Unlike the " Hythe " boats, the " Plymouth Class " aircraft were designed from the outset as civil airliners. Though fundamentally the same as the Sunderland in construction, the " Plymouths " have luxurious interior accommodation and can be distinguished from the " Hythes " by the streamlined nose and tail in place of the angular, sealed turrets. " Plymouth " is the B.O.A.C. name for the aircraft, the manufacturer's name being Sandringham V. Sandringhams have been sold abroad, and serve with airlines in Norway, New Zealand and South America. The first Sandringham flew in November, 1945. B.O.A.C.'s eight " Plymouth " boats operate from Berth 50, Southampton, on the " Dragon " Route to India, Hong Kong and Japan.

SHORT SOLENT.

General Description.	Four-engine high-wing monoplane flying-boat with single fin and rudder. Constructed by Short Brothers and Harland Ltd., Belfast and Rochester.
Seating Capacity.	Crew of seven and thirty passengers or twenty-four sleeper berths.
Engines.	Four Bristol Hercules 637, each of 1,690 h.p.
Dimensions.	Span : 112 ft. 9 ins. Length : 89 ft. 6 ins.
Performance.	Cruising speed : 240 m.p.h. Range : 2,300 miles.

Latest of the series of Short flying-boats to go into service on British Empire routes, the Solent commenced to replace landplane Yorks on the route to Johannesburg in May, 1948. Yorks had been operating

89

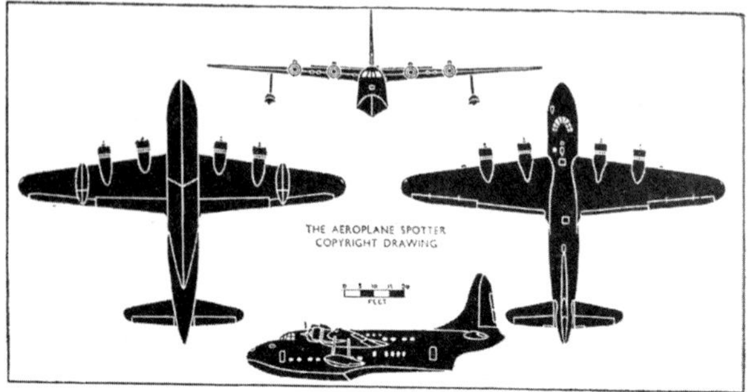

the " Springbok " service since the end of the war, but with the introduction of the Solent this route is once again flown by flying-boats as it was pre-war by " Empire " aircraft. B.O.A.C. is almost alone in world airlines in offering the increased comfort of the flying-boat on trunk routes, though a considerable sacrifice in speed is inevitable. Many contend that the airline traveller wants speed first and foremost and the popularity or otherwise of the new Solent service will prove an interesting test case of this vexed question. Derived from the military Seaford, a development of the Sunderland, the Solent was first launched at Rochester in December, 1946. It can readily be distinguished from the other Short flying-boats by the existence of the curved fairing sweeping down from the fin to the hull.

VICKERS VIKING

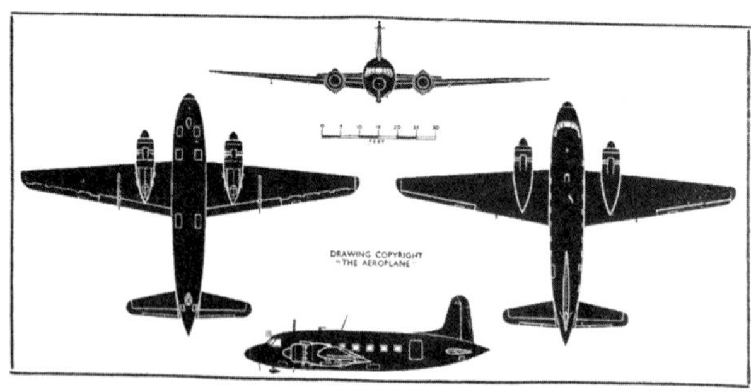

90

Douglas Dakota G-AIWE of Air Contractors Ltd. Air Contractors Ltd. operate three Dakotas from Bovingdon Airport.

Beech Expediter of the French charter company Air Transport at Gatwick Airport.

De Havilland Rapide of Air Enterprises Ltd. at Gatwick Airport.

Avro Anson G-AIXU, one of the aircraft operated by British Air Transport Ltd. on the service to Cowes.

Miles Aerovan of Culliford Air Lines Ltd. visiting Gatwick Airport.

De Havilland Rapide of Island Air Services Ltd.

(Photos:
A. S. C. Lumsden

Morton Air Services Airspeed Consul at Croydon Airport.

De Havilland Dove of Olley Air Service Ltd. Olley operates internal routes to Newmarket and Cowes.

Miles Aerovan G-AJOI of Sivewright Airways Ltd., one of the largest charter operators in the North at Ringway Airport.

Douglas DC-4 Skymaster of Skyways Ltd., Dunsfold, operating to Bahrein under charter to B.O.A.C.

An Avro York of Skyways Ltd., G-AHFI, *Skyway*.

Silver City Airways Lancastrian G-AHBV owned by British Aviation Services.

(*Photos:*
A. S. C. Lumsden
& F. J. Martin

General Description.	Twin-engine mid-wing monoplane with single fin and rudder. Constructed by Vickers-Armstrong Ltd., Weybridge, Surrey.
Seating Capacity.	Crew of four and from twenty-one to twenty-seven passengers.
Engines.	Two Bristol Hercules 634, each of 1,690 h.p.
Dimensions.	Span : 89 ft. 3 ins. Length : 65 ft. 2 ins.
Performance.	Cruising speed : 210 m.p.h. Range : 1,700 miles.

First post-war British civil aircraft to be put into regular airline service, the Vickers Vikings with their red B.E.A. " Speed-Key " insignia are now as familiar on European air routes as were the old Handley-Page Heracles biplanes of Imperial Airways in the 'thirties. Developed initially from the notable Wellington bomber of the R.A.F., the first Viking flew in June, 1945. Produced mainly for British European Airways, the Viking has also been sold to many foreign airlines including the Scandinavian Airlines System, Indian National Airways, Iraqi Airways, Central African Airways and South African Airways. First scheduled flight by a B.E.A. Viking took place on 1st September, 1946, between Northolt and Copenhagen. The first type of Viking in service with B.E.A. was the Mk. 1A which had a noticeably shorter nose than the present model, the Mk. 1B. All the Viking 1A aircraft have now been withdrawn from scheduled services of B.E.A. in favour of the Viking 1B, of which type the Corporation now has its full fleet of thirty-five aircraft.

ASSOCIATE COMPANIES OF BRITISH EUROPEAN AIRWAYS OPERATING INTERNAL ROUTES IN GREAT BRITAIN

Cardiff—Weston-super-Mare	Cambrian Air Services Ltd. Western Airways Ltd.
Carlisle—Isle of Man	Air Navigation & Trading Co. Manx Air Charters Ltd. [Ltd. Scottish Aviation Ltd. West Cumberland Air Services.
Croydon—Cowes	Air Enterprises Ltd. British Air Transport Ltd. Olley Air Services.
Croydon—Newmarket	Olley Air Services.
Birmingham—Isle of Man	Patrick-Duval Aviation Ltd.
Birmingham—Liverpool	Patrick-Duval Aviation Ltd.
Birmingham—Southampton	Patrick-Duval Aviation Ltd.
Newcastle—Isle of Man	Northern Air Charter Ltd.
Prestwick—Blackpool	Scottish Aviation Ltd.
Southampton—Cowes	Air Enterprises Ltd.
Yeadon—Isle of Man	Lancashire Aircraft Corporation

Acclaimed by modellers everywhere as setting a new standard in Model Books

Model Aviation Series

Edited by
Bill Dean and Ron Warring

(Two of Britain's best known writers and designers on aero-modelling subjects)

MODEL PLANES ANNUAL

POWER MODELS

2/6
Per copy

68 large pages ($11'' \times 8\frac{1}{2}''$).
Well written articles,
plans and illustrations.

Obtainable from W. H. Smith & Son, Wyman's and leading booksellers and model shops or direct from the publishers

Ian Allan Ltd

282 VAUXHALL BRIDGE ROAD, LONDON, S.W.1.

Send stamped and addressed envelope for our booklist

39/218/75/1048

ABC
CIVIL
AIRCRAFT
MARKINGS
by J.W.R. Taylor
AN Ian Allan PUBLICATION
2/-

CONTENTS

Introduction 3

Aircraft Nationality Markings 4

Abbreviations 4

BRITISH CIVIL AIRCRAFT REGISTRATIONS (G-) 5

FOREIGN AIR LINERS SERVING THE U.K. ... 58

Canada (CF) 58

Portugal (CS) 58

Spain (EC) 58

Eire (EI) 59

France (F) 59

Switzerland (HB) 60

Italy (I) 61

Norway (LN) 61

Argentine (LV) 61

Luxembourg (LX) 61

U.S.A. (N) 61

Czechoslovakia (OK) 63

Belgium (OO) 63

Denmark (OY) 64

Netherlands (PH) 64

Philippines (PI) 65

Brazil (PP) 66

Sweden (SE) 66

Greece (SX) 66

Iceland (TF) 66

Australia (VH) 66

Ceylon (VP) 67

India (VT) 67

Iraq (YI) 67

South Africa (ZS) 67

Israel (4X) 70

CIVIL AIRCRAFT SPECIFICATIONS 68

MILITARY REGISTRATIONS 70

THE ABC OF CIVIL AIRCRAFT MARKINGS

By JOHN W. R. TAYLOR

LONDON

Ian Allan Ltd

John W. R. Taylor who was responsible for *Civil Aircraft Markings* from the early days until 1978 sadly died on 12 December 1999 aged 77. From the very beginning the March publishing date for the pocket-sized annual was eagerly awaited by enthusiasts at the start of another season. John Taylor ensured that they were not disappointed and the popular book always maintained the same standard through the years. His efforts helped to generate an interest in civil aviation at a time when they were few facilities and even fewer books on the subject. John Taylor will be much missed by his friends and associates but he will not be forgotten.

de Havilland **COMET**

First published 1950
Reprinted 2000

ISBN 0 7110 2759 5

All rights reserved. No part of this book may be reproduced or transmitted in any form or by any means, electronic or mechanical, including photocopying, recording or by any information storage and retrieval system, without permission from the Publisher in writing.

© Ian Allan Publishing Ltd 1950 / 2000

Published by Ian Allan Publishing

an imprint of Ian Allan Publishing Ltd, Terminal House, Station Approach, Shepperton, Surrey TW17 8AS.

Printed by Ian Allan Printing Ltd, Riverdene Business Park, Hersham, Surrey KT12 4RG.

Code: 0005/A

Introduction

MOST of us were aircraft " spotters " to some degree or other during the last war, from the Royal Observer Corps expert who could report a speck in the sky as a "Spitfire at 10,000ft. flying S.W." to the housewife who happily identified it by instinct as " one of ours."

The life and death urgency of wartime plane spotting has passed, but it kindled the spark of a fascinating hobby which is helping to fill public enclosures at our airports every fine Summer day with thousands of people, who want to know not merely that a Stratocruiser has four engines, but that the particular Stratocruiser in front of them belongs to B.O.A.C. and has just come over from America with 70 passengers, including film star Aurora Borealis, the " Alaskan Bombshell."

We do not claim that this book will tell you all that, but it *will* tell you the type of aircraft that you are looking at, who owns it and quite a lot about it. Furthermore, it is not intended just for the lucky few who can get to London Airport or Northolt, as it will be equally helpful to the many who look up as an aeroplane passes over their homes and think " What is it?" Many who use it will devise their own methods of recording in it which registrations they have seen.

Every aircraft carries registration markings on its wings and fuselage, which distinguish it readily from all others, and this A.B.C. lists the markings of virtually every civil aircraft normally seen in British skies, including all foreign air liners which serve this country regularly. In this it is more comprehensive than its popular predecessor—the *A.B.C. of British Aircraft Markings*—as well as being, of course, bang up-to-date. It has also profited from criticism, both kind and otherwise, of the earlier book ; in particular, the British civil markings are arranged alphabetically instead of under the aircraft type names.

Anthony Fokker, the great Dutch aircraft designer, once said that " Flying will be here to stay only when it ceases to be an adventure." For thousands of people today, flying is just another means of getting from A to B quickly and comfortably. But there must always be adventure in a form of transport that can bring men and women from the furthermost ends of the earth in a matter of hours, over deserts, mountains, oceans and jungles rich in history and romance. If this little book helps just a few people to share more fully in this great adventure of flying it will have been very worth-while.

J.W.R.T.

AIRCRAFT NATIONALITY MARKINGS

AP	Pakistan	**OE**	Austria	**TC**	Turkey
CC	Chile	**OH**	Finland	**TF**	Iceland
CF	Canada	**OK**	Czecho-Slovakia	**URSS**	Russia
CS	Portugal	**OO**	Belgium	**VH**	Australia
EC	Spain	**OY**	Denmark	**VP**	E. & W. Africa
EI	Eire	**PH**	Netherlands	**VP-C**	Ceylon
EP	Iran	**PI**	Philippines	**VQ-C**	Cyprus
ET	Ethiopia	**PJ**	Neth. W. Indies	**VR-G**	Gibraltar
F	France	**PK**	Neth. E. Indies	**VR-H**	Hong Kong
G	Great Britain	**PP**	Brazil	**VT**	India
HA	Hungary	**PT**	Brazil	**XT**	China
HB	Switzerland	**RX**	Panama	**XY**	Burma
HS	Siam	**SA**	Saudi Arabia	**YI**	Iraq
I	Italy	**SE**	Sweden	**YR**	Roumania
LN	Norway	**SN**	Sudan	**YU**	Yugo-Slavia
LV	Argentina	**SP**	Poland	**YV**	Venezuela
LX	Luxembourg	**SR**	Syria	**ZK**	New Zealand
LZ	Bulgaria	**SU**	Egypt	**ZS**	South Africa
NC	U.S.A.	**SX**	Greece	**4X**	Israel

ABBREVIATIONS
used in this book

A.O.A.	American Overseas Airlines
Assoc.	Association
B.E.A.C.	British European Airways Corporation
B.O.A.C.	British Overseas Airways Corporation
C. I.	Channel Islands
Corp.	Corporation
D.H.	de Havilland
F.A.M.A.	Flota Aerea Mercante Argentina (Argentine Air Lines)
I.o.M.	Isle of Man
K.L.M.	Royal Dutch Airlines
M.C.A.	Ministry of Civil Aviation
M.o.S.	Ministry of Supply
P.A.A.	Pan American World Airways
U.L.A.A.	Ultra Light Aircraft Association
U.L.A.C.	Ultra Light Aero Club

4

British Civil Aircraft Registrations

(Correct to mid-June, 1950)

in alphabetical order

Registration	Type	Owner or Operator
G–EBKY	Sopwith Pup	Shuttleworth Trust
G–EBMB	Hawker Cygnet	Hawker Aircraft Co.
G–EBRN	Widgeon 3	N. C. Anderson
G–EBWD	D.H.60X Moth	Shuttleworth Trust
G–AAHW	Klemm L–25–1A	G. R. Lush
G–AAPZ	Desoutter	Shuttleworth Trust
G–AAWO	D.H.60 Moth	T. H. Marshall
G–AAYX	Southern Martlet	U.L.A.A.
G–AAZP	Puss Moth	Autowork (Winchester)
G–ABAG	D.H.60 Moth	P.M.A. Hull
G–ABDF	Puss Moth	J. M. Banks
G–ABEE	Avian 4M	H. R. A. Edwards
G–ABJJ	D.H. 60 Moth	Universal Flying Services
G–ABMB	Hawker Cygnet	Hawker Aircraft
G–ABMR	Hart 2	Hawker Aircraft
G–ABUS	Comper Swift	A. L. Cole
G–ABUU	Comper Swift	P/O Baneudale
G–ABWP	Arrow	Shuttleworth Trust
G–ABYA	D.H.60 Moth	M. C. Harley
G–ACCB	Fox Moth	Giro Aviation Co.
G–ACDI	Tiger Moth	Air Service Training
G–ACEJ	Fox Moth	Giro Aviation Co.
G–ACHP	Club Cadet	Saunders-Roe
G–ACIT	Dragon	Airways Aero Assoc.
G–ACKE	Avian 4m	H. M. Woodhams
G–ACLD	Blackburn B–2	Blackburn Aircraft
G–ACLL	Leopard Moth	C. P. L. Godsal
G–ACMA	Leopard Moth	de Havilland Aircraft Co.
G–ACMN	Leopard Moth	de Havilland Aircraft Co.
G–ACPP	Dragon Rapide	Yellow Air Taxis
G–ACRW	Leopard Moth	F. T. Bingham
G–ACTF	Swift	R. E. Clear
G–ACTJ	Leopard Moth	A. R. Frogley
G–ACUU	Cierva C.30A	Cierva Autogiro Co.
G–ACYE	Cierva C.30A	M. Maxwell-Channell
G–ACYO	Hawk Major	B. C. Barton & Son
G–ACYR	Dragon Rapide	Reid & Sigrist
G–ACZP	D.H.86B	Bowmaker
G–ADAB	Hawk Major	C. N. Cooper
G–ADAH	Dragon Rapide	E. L. Gander-Dower
G–ADBE	Pitcairn PA–19	
G–ADCV	Hawk Major	B. S. St. A. H. Hurle-Hobbs
G–ADDI	Dragon	Air Charter
G–ADFD	Cadet	
G–ADFH	Falcon	D. E. Bianchi

"

Registration	Type	Owner or Operator
G–ADGP	Hawk Speed Six	R. R. Paine
G–ADHE	Moth Major	S. H. Wood
G–ADIA	Tiger Moth	Brooklands Aviation
G–ADIH	Tiger Moth	L. D. Trappitt
G–ADIJ	Tiger Moth	Brooklands Aviation
G–ADJV	Hornet Moth	J. J. Lister
G–ADKC	Hornet Moth	J. H. Minet & Co.
G–ADKK	Hornet Moth	C. B. Mills
G–ADKM	Hornet Moth	Mrs. M. K. Wilberforce
G–ADLI	Falcon	L. T. E. Bradley
G–ADLY	Hornet Moth	Viscountess Mairi Bury
G–ADMJ	Hornet Moth	L. H. Ridell
G–ADMT	Hornet Moth	London Aero Club
G–ADMW	Hawk Major	T. Shipside
G–ADNB	Hornet Moth	West London Aero Services
G–ADND	Hornet Moth	W. D. Macpherson
G–ADNE	Hornet Moth	West London Aero Services
G–ADNL	Sparrowhawk	C. G. M. Alington
G–ADOK	Tiger Moth	Inter-City Air Services
G–ADOT	Hornet Moth	Herts & Essex Aero Club
G–ADPR	Gull	Percival Aircraft
G–ADPS	Swallow 2	Walker & Thompson
G–ADSK	Hornet Moth	E. D. Wynn
G–ADTD	Falcon	R. S. Turner
G–ADUF	D.H.86B	J. A. W. Hill
G–ADUH	D.H.86B	Bond Air Services
G–ADUR	Hornet Moth	London Aeroplane Club
G–ADVJ	D.H.86B	Bond Air Services
G–ADWT	Hawk Major	T. Shipside Ltd.
G–ADYS	Aeronca C.3	
G–ADZL	Falcon	Fairey Aviation Co.
G–AEAI	Cessna C.34	R. E. Dewhurst
G–AEAL	Dragon Rapide	Hunting Aerosurveys
G–AEBJ	Blackburn B.2	Blackburn Aircraft
G–AECC	Falcon Six	J. Rush
G–AECN	Burgoyne Stirling Dicer	
G–AEET	Hornet Moth	London Aero Club
G–AEGI	Heck 2C	J. Crammond
G–AEGN	Swallow 2	T. C. Sparrow
G–AEGO	Eagle 2	Wing Cdr. F. S. Cotton
G–AEKY	Hornet Moth	West London Aero Services
G–AELG	Swallow 2	Swansea & District Flying Club
G–AELO	Hornet Moth	Airborne Taxi Services
G–AELX	Aeronca C.3	R. R. Ward
G–AEMH	Dragon Rapide	G. Clifton
G–AEML	Dragon Rapide	Sir W. G. Armstrong Whitworth Aircraft
G–AEMW	Swallow 2	L. F. P. Walters
G–AENU	Wicko I	S./Ldr. J. T. Shaw.
G–AEOA	Puss Moth	Airways Aero Assoc.
G–AERN	Dragon Rapide	Gibraltar Airways
G–AERV	Whitney Straight	H. W. H. Moore
G–AESE	Hornet Moth	Goodhew Aviation
G–AESP	Aeronca 100	Airways Aero Assoc.
G–AESR	Dragon Rapide	Airwork
G–AESV	Phoenix	A. R. Pilgrim
G–AESZ	Chilton D.W.I	L. W. Taylor

Registration	Type	Owner or Operator
G–AEUT	Praga	Flt. Lt. F. Bosworth
G–AEUZ	Whitney Straight	H. Tempest
G–AEVA	Whitney Straight	J. C. Rice
G–AEVG	Whitney Straight	Air Service Training
G–AEVL	Whitney Straight	Lady M. F. A. Vane-Tempest Stewart.
G–AEVS	Aeronca 100	Airways Aero Assoc.
G–AEVT	Aeronca 100	P. Simpson
G–AEWA	Whitney Straight	S. J. Burt
G–AEWI	Swallow 2	D. A. Doughty
G–AEWL	Dragon Rapide	Air Kruise (Kent)
G–AEWU	Aeronca 100	T. S. Gooch
G–AEWV	Aeronca 100	F. Gill
G–AEWY	Hornet Moth	G. & A. Morgan Trust
G–AEWZ	Dragonfly	V. H. Bellamy
G–AEXD	Aeronca 100	Airways Aero Assoc.
G–AEXY	Taylor Cub	F. R. Evans
G–AEYC	Vega Gull	Lambskin Exports
G–AEYE	Percival Q.6	C. G. M. Alington
G–AEZF	Scion Junior	S. S. Caro
G–AEZG	Hornet Moth	Flightways
G–AEZM	Swallow 2	D. Kirk
G–AFAY	Falcon	Hawker Aircraft
G–AFBC	Vega Gull	Lady Sherborne
G–AFBF	Falcon	Cunliffe-Owen Aircraft
G–AFBY	Cessna C.34	W. Jaworski
G–AFCI	Short S.26	Buchan Marine Services
G–AFCL	Swallow 2	G. H. Forsaith
G–AFCR	Monarch	Air Schools
G–AFDT	Hornet Moth	Cardiff Aero Club
G–AFEA	Vega Gull	D. F. Little
G–AFEH	Vega Gull	Lancashire Aircraft Corp.
G–AFEN	Dragon Rapide	W. A. Rollason
G–AFEZ	Dragon Rapide	B.E.A.C.
G–AFFB	Dragon Rapide	Air Transport (Charter) (C.I.)
G–AFFD	Percival Q.6	R. H. Braime
G–AFFH	Taylor Cub	E. Brett
G–AFFJ	Piper Cub	Airways Aero Assoc.
G–AFGC	Swallow 2	H. Pain
G–AFGE	Swallow 2	G. C. Taylor
G–AFGH	Chilton D.W.1	J. M. Bickerton
G–AFGI	Chilton D. W.1	J. S. Sproule
G–AFGK	Whitney Straight	E. H. Thiery
G–AFGV	Swallow 2	I. H. Cameron
G–AFHC	Swallow 2	B. Arden
G–AFHH	Swallow 2	F. L. Haigh
G–AFHS	Swallow 2	J. Heath
G–AFIH	Dragon Rapide	Air Charter
G–AFIR	Luton Minor	A. W. Orde-Hume
G–AFJA	Watkinson Dingbat	
G–AFJB	Wicko	Miss M. Bennet
G–AFJC	Aeronca Chief	K. C. Millican
G–AFJO	Taylorcraft A	Rotol Flying Club
G–AFJP	Taylorcraft A	South Hants U.L.A.C.
G–AFJR	Tipsy Trainer	Tattersall's Garages
G–AFJS	Tipsy Trainer	Cardiff U.L.A.C.
G–AFJT	Tipsy Trainer	K. C. Millican
G–AFJU	Monarch	A. R. Pilgrim
G–AFKP	Tipsy Trainer	H. C. N. M. Oulton

Registration	Type	Owner or Operator
G-AFLT	Gemini 1A	Iliffe & Sons
G-AFLW	Monarch	Rolls-Royce Ltd.
G-AFMF	Dragon Rapide	J. W. Adamson
G-AFMJ	Dragon Rapide	Air Enterprises
G-AFMS	Moss M.A.2	W. H. Moss
G-AFNF	Moth Minor	E. I. H. Ward
G-AFNG	Moth Minor	S. J. Burt
G-AFNH	Moth Minor	G. S. Meek
G-AFNI	Moth Minor	H. W. J. Bethall
G-AFNJ	Moth Minor	J. Cooper
G-AFOB	Moth Minor	J. R. McConnell
G-AFOI	Dragon Rapide	Gibraltar Airways
G-AFOZ	Moth Minor	R.A.F. Flying Club
G-AFPD	Moth Minor	Airways Aero Assoc.
G-AFPH	Moth Minor	G. H. Forsaith
G-AFPM	Moth Minor	G. Whyte
G-AFPN	Moth Minor	J. N. & R. H. B. Enterprises
G-AFPO	Moth Minor	M. W. Woodard
G-AFPP	Piper Cub	W. Smyth
G-AFPR	Moth Minor	Miss J. L. Bird
G-AFRE	Hornet Moth	H. J. Aldington
G-AFRK	Dragon Rapide	B.E.A.C.
G-AFRR	Moth Minor	H. H. E. M. Winch
G-AFRU	Tipsy Trainer	L. D. Birkett
G-AFRV	Tipsy Trainer	J. H. Reed
G-AFRW	Gunton Special	R. Bracewell
G-AFRY	Moth Minor	G. S. Meek
G-AFSC	Tipsy Trainer	Mrs. E. F. Slade
G-AFSV	Chilton D.W.1A	A. R. Ward
G-AFSZ	J-4A Cub	Aero Hire
G-AFTA	Tom-tit	N. F. Duke
G-AFTN	Taylorcraft C.2	H. Pain
G-AFUA	Taylorcraft C	R. M. Smith
G-AFUB	Taylorcraft D	Southern Aircraft (Gatwick)
G-AFVN	Tipsy Trainer	I. H. Cameron
G-AFVR	Cygnet 2	T. F. W. Gunton
G-AFVT	Reliant	Fairey Aviation Co.
G-AFWM	Taylorcraft C.2	Earl of Cardigan
G-AFWO	Taylorcraft D	H. Sullivan
G-AFWS	J-4A Cub	S. Colley & Ptns.
G-AFWT	Tipsy Trainer	W. R. Trounson
G-AFXS	J-4A Cub	C. M. Newton
G-AFYH	Flamingo	British Air Transport
G-AFZI	Taylorcraft D	S. M. Cox
G-AFZP	Fokker F.22	Scottish Aviation
G-AFZY	Whitney Straight	Lord P. W. S. G. Calthorpe
G-AGAK	Hirtenberg H.S.9A	J. H. Davies
G-AGAX	Cygnet 2	L. V. Scarah
G-AGBD	Douglas DC-3	Skyways *Sky Hawk*
G-AGBG	Lockheed 14	North Sea Air Transport
G-AGBN	Cygnet 2	A. Costella
G-AGDL	Sparrowhawk	T. Shipside
G-AGDM	Dragon Rapide	Sivewright Airways
G-AGDP	Dragon Rapide	Modern Transport Ltd.
G-AGDT	Lockheed 12A	North Sea Air Transport
G-AGEE	Dragon Rapide	Gibraltar Airways
G-AGER	Sunderland 3	Aquila Airways
G-AGEU	Sunderland 3	Aquila Airways

112

Registration	Type	Owner or Operator
G–AGFU	Dragon Rapide	Air Charter Ltd.
G–AGHF	Dakota 3	North-West Airlines (I.o.M.)
G–AGHI	Dragon Rapide	C. L. Burton
G–AGHJ	Dakota 3	B.E.A.C.
G–AGHL	Dakota 3	B.E.A.C.
G–AGHM	Dakota 3	Skyways *Sky Monitor*
G–AGHO	Dakota 3	North-West Airlines (I.o.M.)
G–AGHP	Dakota 3	Field Aircraft Services
G–AGHS	Dakota 3	B.E.A.C.
G–AGIA	Sunderland 3	Aquila Airways
G–AGIF	Dragon Rapide	Ulster Aviation
G–AGIP	Dakota 3	B.E.A.C.
G–AGIS	Dakota 3	B.E.A.C.
G–AGIU	Dakota 3	B.E.A.C.
G–AGIW	Dakota 3	B.E.A.C.
G–AGIZ	Dakota 3	B.E.A.C.
G–AGJA	York I	B.O.A.C. *Kingston*
G–AGJB	York I	B.O.A.C. *Marathon*
G–AGJC	York I	B.O.A.C. *Malmesbury*
G–AGJD	York I	B.O.A.C. *Mansfield*
G–AGJE	York I	B.O.A.C. *Panama*
G–AGJG	Dragon Rapide	Mediterranean Air Services
G–AGJL	Sunderland 3	Aquila Airways
G–AGJP	Liberator	B.O.A.C.
G–AGJV	Dakota 3	B.E.A.C.
G–AGJW	Dakota 3	B.E.A.C.
G–AGJZ	Dakota 3	B.E.A.C.
G–AGKB	Dakota 4	B.O.A.C.
G–AGKC	Dakota 4	Airwork Ltd.
G–AGKV	Sunderland 3	Short Bros. & Harland
G–AGKW	Sunderland 3	Short Bros. & Harland
G–AGKX	Sandringham I	Aquila Airways
G–AGKY	Sunderland 3	Aquila Airways
G–AGLE	Dragon Rapide	C. L. Burton
G–AGLJ	Proctor 3	M.C.A.
G–AGLK	Auster 5	M.C.A.
G–AGLP	Dragon Rapide	C. L. Burton
G–AGLR	Dragon Rapide	Lees Hill Aviation
G–AGLS	Lancastrian I	B.O.A.C. *Nelson*
G–AGLW	Lancastrian I	B.O.A.C. *Northampton*
G–AGLY	Lancastrian I	B.O.A.C. *Norfolk*
G–AGMA	Lancastrian I	B.O.A.C. *Newport*
G–AGMG	Lancastrian I	B.O.A.C. *Nicosia*
G–AGMJ	Lancastrian I	B.O.A.C. *Naseby*
G–AGMK	Lancastrian I	B.O.A.C. *Newbury*
G–AGNG	Dakota 4	Eagle Aviation
G–AGNH	Dragon Rapide	M.C.A.
G–AGNK	Dakota 4	Sivewright Airways
G–AGNL	York I	B.O.A.C. *Mersey*
G–AGNM	York I	Eagle Aviation
G–AGNN	York I	B.O.A.C. *Atlantic Trader*
G–AGNO	York I	B.O.A.C. *Manton*
G–AGNP	York I	B.O.A.C. *Manchester*
G–AGNS	York I	B.O.A.C. *Pacific Trader*
G–AGNT	York I	B.O.A.C. *Mandalay*
G–AGNU	York I	B.O.A.C. *Nassau*
G–AGNV	York I	B.O.A.C. *Morville*
G–AGNW	York I	B.O.A.C. *Caribbean Trader*

Registration	Type	Owner or Operator
G–AGNX	York I	B.O.A.C. *Lima*
G–AGNY	York I	Eagle Aviation
G–AGNZ	York I	Eagle Aviation
G–AGOA	York I	B.O.A.C. *Montrose*
G–AGOB	York I	B.O.A.C. *Milford*
G–AGOD	York I	B.O.A.C. *Midlothian*
G–AGOE	York I	B.O.A.C. *Medway*
G–AGOF	York I	B.O.A.C. *McDuff*
G–AGOG	Proctor 3	M.C.A.
G–AGOH	Autocrat	Blackburn Aircraft
G–AGOJ	Dragon Rapide	Lancashire Aircraft Corp.
G–AGOR	Dragon Rapide	Iraq Petroleum Transport Co.
G–AGOS	Desford	Reid & Sigrist
G–AGOY	Messenger 3	Uniformity Shoes
G–AGPB	Avro 19	M.C.A.
G–AGPG	Avro 19	A. V. Roe & Co.
G–AGPH	Dragon Rapide	B.E.A.C.
G–AGPJ	Dove	M.o.S.
G–AGPU	Avro 19	Secretary of State for Air
G–AGPW	Brabazon I	M.o.S.
G–AGPX	Messenger 3	North Sea Air Transport Ltd.
G–AGRA	Tiger Moth	M.C.A.
G–AGRB	Tiger Moth	M.C.A.
G–AGRC	Tudor 4C	M.o.S. *Star Troilus*
G–AGRD	Tudor I	M.o.S. *Star Cymbeline*
G–AGRF	Tudor 4B	M.o.S. *Elizabeth of England*
G–AGRG	Tudor 4C	M.o.S. *Star Cresida*
G–AGRH	Tudor Freighter I	M.C.A. *Star Ceres*
G–AGRI	Tudor 4C	M.C.A. *Star Oberon*
G–AGRJ	Tudor Freighter I	M.C.A. *Star Celia*
G–AGRK	Tudor 4C	M.o.S. *Star Prospero*
G–AGRL	Tudor 4C	M.o.S. *Star Proteus*
G–AGRP	Viking IA	Sale & Co.
G–AGRR	Viking IA	M.o.S.
G–AGRV	Viking IA	Sale & Co.
G–AGRW	Viking IA	Sale & Co.
G–AGRY	Tudor 2	D. C. T. Bennett
G–AGSH	Dragon Rapide	B.E.A.C.
G–AGSI	Dragon Rapide	Olley Air Service
G–AGSK	Dragon Rapide	B.E.A.C.
G–AGSL	York I	B.O.A.C. *Morley*
G–AGSM	York I	B.O.A.C. *Malvern*
G–AGSN	York I	B.O.A.C. *Marlow*
G–AGSO	York I	B.O.A.C. *Manston*
G–AGSP	York I	B.O.A.C. *Santiago*
G–AGSR	Be 550 Bibi	H. Clive-Smith
G–AGSV	Avro 711A	M.o.S.
G–AGSX	Proctor 5	Hunting Air Travel
G–AGTC	Proctor 5	Percival Aircraft
G–AGTE	Proctor 5	Butlin's Ltd.
G–AGTF	Proctor 5	Cambridge University Gliding Club
G–AGTG	Aerocar	Portsmouth Aviation
G–AGTH	Proctor 3	B.O.A.C. *Star Pixie*
G–AGTL	Lockheed 12A	F. S. Cotton
G–AGTM	Dragon Rapide	Iraq Petroleum Transport Co.
G–AGTN	Dragon Rapide	Iraq Petroleum Transport Co.
G–AGTO	Autocrat	T. W. Shipside
G–AGTP	Autocrat	T. Carlyle

10

Registration	Type	Owner or Operator
G–AGTR	Autocrat	R. H. Braime
G–AGTT	Autocrat	Inter-City Air Services
G–AGTV	Autocrat	G. S. Pine
G–AGTW	Autocrat	Anglo-Continental Air Services
G–AGTX	Autocrat	W. Nadin
G–AGTY	Autocrat	T. Shipside Ltd.
G–AGUA	Ambassador	M.o.S.
G–AGUB	Hermes 2	M.o.S.
G–AGUD	Avro 19	M.C.A.
G–AGUF	Dragon Rapide	J. A. R. Helps
G–AGUG	Dragon Rapide	Lancashire Aircraft Corp.
G–AGUH	Avro 19	Hawker Aircraft
G–AGUP	Dragon Rapide	B.E.A.C.
G–AGUR	Dragon Rapide	B.E.A.C.
G–AGUS	Gemini 2	Walter Instruments
G–AGUU	Dragon Rapide	B.E.A.C.
G–AGUV	Dragon Rapide	B.E.A.C.
G–AGUX	Avro 19	Fairey Aviation Co.
G–AGVA	Avro 19	M.C.A.
G–AGVB	Wayfarer 21	Bowmaker Ltd.
G–AGVC	Freighter 21	Bristol Aeroplane Co.
G–AGVD	Shetland 2	M.o.S.
G–AGVF	Autocrat	Loxhams Flying Service
G–AGVG	Autocrat	R. W. Braime
G–AGVH	Autocrat	R. W. Kerry
G–AGVI	Autocrat	Bidgood & Catton Taxi-Planes
G–AGVJ	Autocrat	British Air Transport
G–AGVK	Autocrat	M. C. D. Wilson
G–AGVL	Autocrat	Bembridge and Sandown Aero Club
G–AGVM	Autocrat	Bristol & Wessex Aero Club
G–AGVN	Autocrat	R. A. Walley
G–AGVO	Autocrat	E. L. Sprayson
G–AGVP	Autocrat	Wiltshire School of Flying
G–AGVR	Autocrat	British Salmson Aero Engines
G–AGVU	Autocrat	J. H. Watts
G–AGVX	Mercury 4	W. S. Shackleton
G–AGVZ	Lockheed 12A	
G–AGWA	Avro 19	M.C.A.
G–AGWB	Proctor 3	Secretary of State for Air
G–AGWC	Dragon Rapide	Air Transport (Charter) (C.I.)
G–AGWE	Avro 19	M.C.A.
G–AGWF	Avro 19/1	M.C.A.
G–AGWI	Lancastrian 3	Flight Refuelling
G–AGWL	Lancastrian 3	Flight Refuelling
G–AGWN	Lockheed 12A	Skyways Ltd.
G–AGWP	Dragon Rapide	Morton Air Services
G–AGWR	Dragon Rapide	Morton Air Services
G–AGWS	Dakota	Scottish Aviation
G–AGWT	Nighthawk	R. Crewdson
G–AGWV	Proctor 1	G. M. Tonge
G–AGWY	Autocrat	T. Carlyle
G–AGXB	Autocrat	Lt. Col. J. J. Dykes
G–AGXC	Autocrat	D. H. Eastwood
G–AGXD	Autocrat	Lancashire Aircraft Corp.
G–AGXF	Autocrat	H. Mitchell
G–AGXG	Autocrat	A. J. Linnel
G–AGXH	Autocrat	Hunting Aerosurveys
G–AGXJ	Autocrat	United Services Flying Club
G–AGXK	Autocrat	Midland Aero Club

Registration	Type	Owner or Operator
G–AGXM	Autocrat	R. G. Parker
G–AGXN	Autocrat	G. Brady
G–AGXO	Autocrat	S. W. Freestone
G–AGXP	Autocrat	Private Flying (Ipswich) Ltd.
G–AGXS	Autocrat	M. A. Crouch
G–AGXT	Autocrat	United Services Flying Club
G–AGXU	Autocrat	Fairey Aviation Co.
G–AGXV	Autocrat	R. G. Presland, W. H. Wetton
G–AGXX	Autocrat	Marshalls' Flying Schools
G–AGYA	Proctor I	R. J. Jones
G–AGYB	Proctor I	J. Drennan
G–AGYC	Proctor I	W. A. Rollason
G–AGYD	Autocrat	J. C. H. Wildbore
G–AGYF	Autocrat	Hastings & East Sussex Air Service
G–AGYH	Autocrat	Coventry (Civil) Aviation
G–AGYI	Autocrat	Royal Artillery Aero Club
G–AGYJ	Autocrat	R. G. Banks
G–AGYK	Autocrat	R. J. Bowes
G–AGYL	Autocrat	W. A. Munro
G–AGYM	Autocrat	W. M. B. May
G–AGYN	Autocrat	London Aero Club
G–AGYO	Autocrat	Airways Aero Assoc.
G–AGYP	Autocrat	J. L. Shaw
G–AGYR	Autocrat	R. P. Alder
G–AGYT	Autocrat	J. H. Watts
G–AGYU	Autocrat	Marshalls' Flying Schools
G–AGYX	Dakota 3	B.E.A.C.
G–AGYZ	Dakota 3	B.E.A.C.
G–AGZB	Dakota 3	B.E.A.C.
G–AGZC	Dakota 3	B.E.A.C.
G–AGZD	Dakota 3	B.E.A.C.
G–AGZF	Dakota 3	Scottish Aviation Ltd.
G–AGZG	Dakota 3	Scottish Aviation Ltd.
G–AGZJ	Dragon Rapide	J. H. Watts
G–AGZK	Dragon Rapide	Iraq Petroleum Co., Ltd.
G–AGZM	Proctor I	Herts & Essex Aero Club
G–AGZO	Dragon Rapide	Marshalls' Flying Schools
G–AGZS	Avro 19	M.C.A.
G–AGZT	Avro 19	M.C.A.
G–AGZU	Dragon Rapide	Herts & Essex Aero Club
G–AGZW	Voyager	Southampton Air Services
G–AHAA	Mercury 6	K. E. Millard & Co., Ltd.
G–AHAB	Proctor I	C. E. Berens
G–AHAC	Envoy 3	Private Charter Ltd.
G–AHAD	Taylorcraft D	A. Rees
G–AHAE	Taylorcraft D	Newcastle-on-Tyne Aero Club
G–AHAG	Dragon Rapide	North Sea Air Transport
G–AHAI	Taylorcraft D	Denham Flying Club
G–AHAK	Taylorcraft D	Air Taxis (Croydon)
G–AHAL	Autocrat	A. Christian
G–AHAM	Autocrat	T. E. Dalton
G–AHAO	Autocrat	Air Schools
G–AHAP	Autocrat	Kennings Ltd.
G–AHAR	Autocrat	A. M. Ashery
G–AHAT	Autocrat	Congo Charter Air Services
G–AHAU	Autocrat	Col. C. W. D. Rowe
G–AHAV	Autocrat	J. S. Bancroft
G–AHAW	Autocrat	Lawson's Aerial Photographs

Registration	Type	Owner or Operator
G–AHAX	Autocrat	J. D. H. Radford
G–AHAY	Autocrat	Fairey Aviation Co.
G–AHBA	Proctor 5	Dunlop Rubber Co.
G–AHBC	Proctor 5	Donaldson Bros.
G–AHBD	Proctor 5	Sir W. G. Armstrong-Whitworth Aircraft
G–AHBH	Proctor 5	Western Airways
G–AHBI	Proctor 5	Goodhew Aviation Co.
G–AHBJ	Proctor 5	Yellow Air Taxis
G–AHBL	Hornet Moth	West London Aero Club
G–AHBM	Hornet Moth	West London Aero Club
G–AHBO	Taylorcraft D	H. E. Scrope
G–AHBS	Proctor 1	L. H. B. Roper
G–AHBT	Lancastrian 3	Skyways *Sky Ranger*
G–AHBV	Lancastrian 3	Skyways
G–AHCC	Lancastrian 3	Skyways *Sky Chieftain*
G–AHCG	Taylorcraft D	Boston Air Transport
G–AHCI	Taylorcraft D	Brooklands Aviation
G–AHCK	Autocrat	British Air Transport
G–AHCL	Autocrat	United Services Flying Club
G–AHCM	Autocrat	G. & A. Morgan Trust
G–AHCN	Autocrat	Bristol & Wessex Aero Club
G–AHCO	Autocrat	Lockwood's Flying Services
G–AHCR	Taylorcraft D	Wiltshire School of Flying
G–AHCT	Dakota 3	B.E.A.C.
G–AHCU	Dakota 3	B.E.A.C.
G–AHCV	Dakota 3	B.E.A.C.
G–AHCX	Dakota 3	B.E.A.C.
G–AHCZ	Dakota 3	B.E.A.C.
G–AHDD	Tiger Moth	Wiltshire School of Flying
G–AHDH	Proctor 1	Newman Aircraft
G–AHDI	Proctor 1	S. Caliendi
G–AHDJ	Proctor 1	Newman Aircraft
G–AHDM	Halton 1	Westminster Airways
G–AHDN	Halton 1	Aviation Traders
G–AHDO	Halton 1	Bond Air Services
G–AHDS	Halton 1	Bond Air Services
G–AHDU	Halton 1	Aviation Traders
G–AHDV	Halton 1	Westminster Airways
G–AHDW	Halton 1	Aviation Traders
G–AHDY	Liberator 3	Scottish Aviation
G–AHDZ	Oxford 2	Scottish Aviation
G–AHEA	Dragon Rapide	Lancashire Aircraft Corp.
G–AHED	Dragon Rapide	Marshall's Flying School
G–AHEE	Proctor 1	Hunting Flying Clubs
G–AHEF	Consul	Airspeed Ltd.
G–AHEH	Consul	G. C. S. Pearson
G–AHEI	Taylorcraft D	R.A.F. Flying Club
G–AHEJ	Constellation	B.O.A.C. *Bristol II*
G–AHEK	Constellation	B.O.A.C. *Berwick II*
G–AHEL	Constellation	B.O.A.C. *Bangor II*
G–AHEM	Constellation	B.O.A.C. *Balmoral*
G–AHEN	Constellation	B.O.A.C. *Baltimore*
G–AHER	Sunderland 3	Aquila Airways
G–AHES	Proctor 1	Silver City Airways
G–AHET	Vega Gull	Essex Aero Ltd.
G–AHEU	Proctor 1	J. H. Watts
G–AHEV	Proctor 1	J. H. Watts

13

Registration	Type	Owner or Operator
G–AHEY	York	B.O.A.C. *Star Quest*
G–AHFA	York	B.O.A.C. *Star Dale*
G–AHFB	York	B.O.A.C. *Star Stream*
G–AHFC	York	B.O.A.C. *Star Dew*
G–AHFD	York	B.O.A.C. *Star Mist*
G–AHFE	York	B.O.A.C. *Star Vista*
G–AHFF	York	B.O.A.C. *Star Gleam*
G–AHFG	York	B.O.A.C. *Star Haze*
G–AHFH	York	B.O.A.C. *Star Glitter*
G–AHFK	Proctor 3	Kelvin & Hughes
G–AHFL	Walrus I	United Whalers
G–AHFM	Walrus I	United Whalers
G–AHFN	Walrus I	C. Mauritzen Ltd.
G–AHFO	Walrus I	United Whalers
G–AHFP	Messenger 4	Airwork
G–AHFR	Proctor 5	Rolls-Royce Ltd.
G–AHFS	Consul	British Air Transport
G–AHFT	Consul	Morton Air Services
G–AHFU	Proctor I	Chartair
G–AHFW	Proctor I	S. G. Newport
G–AHFY	Proctor I	L. G. S. Payne
G–AHGA	Proctor I	Stewart Smith & Co.
G–AHGC	Dragon Rapide	Hawker Aircraft
G–AHGD	Dragon Rapide	North Sea Air Transport
G–AHGF	Dragon Rapide	F. A. Hill
G–AHGG	Dragon Rapide	Olley Air Service
G–AHGH	Dragon Rapide	Patrick Motors
G–AHGI	Dragon Rapide	Patrick Motors
G–AHGJ	Proctor 5	B. N. White & Spencer Ltd.
G–AHGL	Proctor 5	E. S. Davis
G–AHGM	Proctor 5	Hunting Air Travel
G–AHGN	Proctor 5	M.C.A.
G–AHGR	Proctor 5	D. J. Bennett
G–AHGS	Proctor 5	Patrick Motors
G–AHGT	Proctor 5	Helliwells
G–AHGU	Oxford	Bristol Aeroplane Co.
G–AHGX	Taylorcraft D	Wiltshire School of Flying
G–AHGY	Taylorcraft D	Wycombe Flying Club
G–AHGZ	Taylorcraft D	Carlight Trailers
G–AHHB	Taylorcraft D	Light Planes (Lancs.)
G–AHHC	Taylorcraft D	Inter-City Airways
G–AHHH	Autocrat	Anglo-Continental Air Services
G–AHHK	Autocrat	J. M. S. Chipperfield
G–AHHL	Autocrat	Yellow Air Taxis
G–AHHM	Autocrat	Weston Webb
G–AHHN	Autocrat	F. B. Austin
G–AHHO	Autocrat	G. S. Pine
G–AHHP	Autocrat	E. E. Kimbell
G–AHHR	Autocrat	M. W. B. May
G–AHHS	Autocrat	G. G. Plank & Co.
G–AHHT	Autocrat	F. H. W. Wheaton
G–AHHU	Autocrat	Colt Ventilation
G–AHHW	Autocrat	J. C. Hoyland
G–AHHX	Autocrat	Light Planes (Lancs.)
G–AHHY	Taylorcraft D	Sivewright Airways
G–AHHZ	Taylorcraft D	G. C. Mawer
G–AHIA	Dragon Rapide	Skyways
G–AHIB	Avro 19	Thorne Aviation

Registration	Type	Owner or Operator
G-AHIC	Avro 19	M.C.A.
G-AHID	Avro 19	M.C.A.
G-AHIE	Avro 19	Thorne Aviation
G-AHIF	Avro 19	F. A. Laker
G-AHIG	Avro 19	M.C.A.
G-AHIH	Avro 19	M.C.A.
G-AHII	Avro 19	Starways
G-AHIJ	Avro 19	M.C.A.
G-AHIK	Avro 19	Starways
G-AHIL	Solent 2	M.C.A. *City of Salisbury*
G-AHIM	Solent 2	M.C.A. *Scarborough*
G-AHIN	Solent 2	M.C.A. *Southampton*
G-AHIO	Solent 2	M.C.A. *Somerset*
G-AHIR	Solent 2	M.C.A. *Sark*
G-AHIS	Solent 2	M.C.A. *City of York*
G-AHIT	Solent 2	M.C.A. *Severn*
G-AHIU	Solent 2	M.C.A. *Solway*
G-AHIV	Solent 2	M.C.A. *Salcombe*
G-AHIW	Solent 2	M.C.A. *Stornoway*
G-AHIY	Solent 2	M.C.A. *Southsea*
G-AHIZ	Tiger Moth	London Aero Club
G-AHJA	Dragon Rapide	Vickers-Armstrongs Ltd.
G-AHJD	Wayfarer 21	Airwork
G-AHJS	Dragon Rapide	Fairey Aviation Co.
G-AHJU	Lancaster 1	Flight Refuelling
G-AHJX	Consul	Morton Air Services
G-AHJY	Consul	N. H. Teakle
G-AHJZ	Consul	De Havilland Aircraft Co.
G-AHKA	Dragon Rapide	De Havilland Aircraft Co.
G-AHKB	Dragon Rapide	Vickers-Armstrongs Ltd.
G-AHKH	Anson 1	British Air Transport
G-AHKK	Halifax 8	
G-AHKL	Gemini 1A	Smithfield Refrigerator Co.
G-AHKO	Taylorcraft D	F. R. J. Britten
G-AHKP	Hawk Trainer 3	Wiltshire School of Flying
G-AHKS	Dragon Rapide	B.E.A.C.
G-AHKT	Dragon Rapide	B.E.A.C.
G-AHKU	Dragon Rapide	B.E.A.C.
G-AHKV	Dragon Rapide	B.E.A.C.
G-AHKX	Avro 19	Smiths Aircraft Instruments
G-AHKY	Miles M.18/2	H. B. Iles
G-AHKZ	Tiger Moth	Coventry (Civil) Aviation
G-AHLA	Tiger Moth	Helliwells Ltd.
G-AHLB	Tiger Moth	Midland Bank Flying Club
G-AHLD	Tiger Moth	Midland Bank Flying Club
G-AHLF	Dragon Rapide	Westland Aircraft
G-AHLH	Lockheed 12A	Earl of Granard
G-AHLI	Auster 3	Vickers-Armstrongs Ltd.
G-AHLJ	Taylorcraft Plus D	Vickers-Armstrongs Ltd.
G-AHLK	Auster 3	Vickers-Armstrongs Ltd.
G-AHLL	Dragon Rapide	B.E.A.C.
G-AHLM	Dragon Rapide	Marshall's Flying School
G-AHLN	Dragon Rapide	Ulster Aviation
G-AHLO	Puss Moth	Autowork (Winchester)
G-AHLR	Tiger Moth	Goodhew Aviation
G-AHLT	Tiger Moth	Walker & Thompson
G-AHLV	York 1	Skyways *Sky Courier*
G-AHMD	Consul	Lancashire Aircraft Corp.

15

Registration	Type	Owner or Operator
G-AHME	Tiger Moth	J. W. Tomkins
G-AHML	Tiger Moth	Brooklands Aviation
G-AHMM	Tiger Moth	Brooklands Aviation
G-AHMN	Tiger Moth	Brooklands Aviation
G-AHMP	Proctor 1	de Havilland Engine Co.
G-AHMR	Proctor 1	Barnet Instruments
G-AHMT	Proctor 1	Scottish Aviation
G-AHMV	Proctor 1	Field Aircraft Services
G-AHNA	Proctor 1	A. S. K. Paine
G-AHNB	Proctor 2	Cinque Ports Flying Club
G-AHNC	Tiger Moth	Light Planes (Lancs.)
G-AHND	Tiger Moth	Air Navigation and Trading Co.
G-AHNE	Hawk Trainer 3	Air Navigation and Trading Co.
G-AHNG	Taylorcraft D	T. J. S. Kidner
G-AHNH	Tudor 4C	M.o.S. *Star Ophelia*
G-AHNI	Tudor Freighter 4B	M.C.A. *Star Olivia*
G-AHNJ	Tudor 4	B.O.A.C. *Star Lion*
G-AHNK	Tudor 4	B.O.A.C. *Star Panther*
G-AHNL	Tudor Freighter 4B	M.C.A.
G-AHNM	Tudor Freighter 4B	M.C.A. *Star Cluster*
G-AHNN	Tudor 4	B.O.A.C. *Star Leopard*
G-AHNO	Tudor 4B	M.C.A. *Star Titania*
G-AHNR	Tudor 4C	M.o.S. *Star Theseus*
G-AHNS	Anson 1	Air Service Training
G-AHNT	Anson 1	Air Service Training
G-AHNU	Hawk Trainer 3	Wolverhampton Flying School
G-AHNV	Hawk Trainer 3	Wolverhampton Flying School
G-AHNW	Hawk Trainer 3	H. T. Ryan
G-AHNZ	Taylorcraft D	A. Walmesley
G-AHOB	Master 2	
G-AHOM	Percival Q/6	Ductile Steels
G-AHON	Viking 1A	A. J. Gaul
G-AHOP	Viking 1A	British Nederland Airservices
G-AHOR	Viking 1A	Sale & Co.
G-AHOT	Viking 1A	A. J. Gaul
G-AHOV	Viking 1A	Sale & Co.
G-AHOW	Viking 1A	Sale & Co.
G-AHOY	Viking 1	Hunting Air Travel
G-AHPB	Viking 1	Hunting Air Travel
G-AHPC	Viking 1	Hunting Air Travel
G-AHPD	Viking 1	Hunting Air Travel
G-AHPH	Viking 1A	B.E.A.C.
G-AHPI	Viking 1A	Hunting Air Travel
G-AHPJ	Viking 1A	Hunting Air Travel
G-AHPL	Viking 1B	B.E.A.C. *Verdant*
G-AHPM	Viking 1B	B.E.A.C. *Verderer*
G-AHPN	Viking 1B	B.E.A.C. *Ventnor*
G-AHPO	Viking 1B	B.E.A.C. *Venture*
G-AHPP	Viking 1B	B.E.A.C. *Venus*
G-AHPR	Viking 1B	B.E.A.C. *Verily*
G-AHPS	Viking 1B	B.E.A.C. *Verity*
G-AHPT	Dragon Rapide	Island Air Charters
G-AHPU	Dragon Rapide 2	J. E. Steel
G-AHRB	Dove 1	Skyways *Sky Maid*
G-AHRC	Tiger Moth	J. C. Rice
G-AHRF	Viscount	M.o.S.
G-AHRG	Viscount	M.o.S.

120

Registration	Type	Owner or Operator
G–AHRH	Dragon Rapide	Gloster Aircraft Co.
G–AHRI	Dove	Iraq Petroleum Transport Co.
G–AHRK	Consul	Silver City Airways
G–AHRL	Tiger Moth	Blackburn Aircraft Co.
G–AHRM	Tiger Moth	Blackburn & General Aircraft
G–AHRN	Tiger Moth	Blackburn & General Aircraft
G–AHRR	Tiger Moth	Inter City Airways
G–AHRV	Tiger Moth	E. S. Morrell
G–AHRX	Tiger Moth	Goodhew Aviation Co.
G–AHRY	Proctor 3	Hunting Aerosurveys
G–AHSA	Tutor	J. Neasham
G–AHSB	Taylorcraft D	W. Greenlalgh
G–AHSD	Taylorcraft D	Lockwood's Flying Services
G–AHSG	Taylorcraft D	A. R. Julian
G–AHSH	Autocrat	R. A. Young
G–AHSI	Autocrat	Longford Engineering Co.
G–AHSJ	Taylorcraft D	J. S. Swansea
G–AHSK	Taylorcraft D	I. H. Cameron
G–AHSM	Autocrat	A. J. Pickering
G–AHSN	Autocrat	R.N. Flying Club
G–AHSO	Autocrat	Universal Flying Services
G–AHSP	Autocrat	J. G. Robertson & Co.
G–AHSR	Autocrat	R. W. Ward
G–AHSS	Autocrat	Loxham's Flying Services
G–AHST	Autocrat	D. Everall
G–AHSW	Autocrat	C. G. Wheatley
G–AHSX	Autocrat	Barton Motors (Preston)
G–AHTE	Proctor 5	C. G. Wheatley
G–AHTF	Proctor 5	Western Airways
G–AHTG	Proctor 5	Dawn Hire
G–AHTI	Proctor 5	Fairway Engineering Co.
G–AHTK	Proctor 5	Willis Hole Aviation
G–AHTL	Proctor 5	Dennis Aviation
G–AHTM	Proctor 5	P. M. Bennett & Co.
G–AHTN	Proctor 1	Aerial Medical Service
G–AHTR	Dragon Rapide	Anglo-Iranian Oil Co.
G–AHTT	Dragon Rapide	Anglo-Iranian Oil Co.
G–AHTV	Proctor 1	Air Service Training
G–AHTW	Oxford 1	Boulton Paul Aircraft
G–AHTX	Aerovan 3	S. G. Newport
G–AHTY	Dragon Rapide	North Sea Air Transport
G–AHTZ	Cierva C.30A	Rota Towels
G–AHUB	Tiger Moth	London Aero Club
G–AHUE	Tiger Moth	Airwork
G–AHUG	Taylorcraft D	G. F. K. Donaldsoh
G–AHUI	Messenger 2A	Derek Crouch (Contractors)
G–AHUJ	Hawk Trainer 3	J. McDonald & Sons
G–AHUL	Hawk Trainer 3	Home Counties Aero Club
G–AHUM	Taylorcraft D	T. H. Marshall
G–AHUN	Tiger Moth	Hampshire School of Flying
G–AHUO	Tiger Moth	Hampshire School of Flying
G–AHUT	Tiger Moth	Universal Flying Services
G–AHUU	Globe Swift	Helliwells Ltd.
G–AHUV	Tiger Moth	Airwork
G–AHUX	Proctor 1	J. Oliver
G–AHUZ	Proctor 1	N. W. Charlton

Registration	Type	Owner or Operator
G–AHVA	Proctor I	Extractors (Hull)
G–AHVB	Proctor I	Air Couriers
G–AHVC	Proctor I	Air Couriers
G–AHVG	Proctor I	Blackburn & General Aircraft
G–AHVK	Proctor I	Air Kruise (Kent)
G–AHVN	Lancaster I	Flight Refuelling
G–AHVO	Avro 626	A. G. Harding
G–AHVP	Taylorcraft D	Midland Aero Club
G–AHVR	Taylorcraft D	Midland Aero Club
G–AHVS	Taylorcraft D	Midland Aero Club
G–AHVU	Tiger Moth	Cardiff Aero Club
G–AHVV	Tiger Moth	Plymouth & District Aero Club
G–AHVW	Tiger Moth	J. MacDonald & Sons
G–AHVX	Tiger Moth	Air Service Training
G–AHVY	Tiger Moth	Air Service Training
G–AHWA	Tiger Moth	Air Service Training
G–AHWB	Tiger Moth	Air Service Training
G–AHWC	Tiger Moth	Air Service Training
G–AHWD	Taylorcraft D	Newcastle-upon-Tyne Aero Club
G–AHWE	Tiger Moth	Weston Aero Club
G–AHWF	Dragon Rapide	Iraq Petroleum Transport Co.
G–AHWH	Globe Swift	C. G. Wheatley
G–AHWI	Taylorcraft D	Bristol & Wessex Aero Club
G–AHWJ	Taylorcraft D	Bristol & Wessex Aero Club
G–AHWK	Taylorcraft D	Bristol & Wessex Aero Club
G–AHWN	Halifax 8	Lancashire Aircraft Corp.
G–AHWO	Proctor 5	Gerald C. Judd Ltd.
G–AHWR	Proctor 5	North Sea Air Transport
G–AHWS	Proctor 5	Yorkshire Aeroplane Club
G–AHWT	Proctor 5	L. M. Cooper
G–AHWU	Proctor 5	Shell Refining & Marketing Co.
G–AHWV	Proctor 5	D. Napier & Sons
G–AHWW	Proctor 5	A. J. Bradshaw
G–AHWZ	Proctor 5	Colnbrook Trading Co.
G–AHXB	Tiger Moth	London Aero Club
G–AHXC	Tiger Moth	London Aero Club
G–AHXE	Taylorcraft D	R. A. McMurtrie
G–AHXF	Taylorcraft D	W. S. Shackleton
G–AHXG	Taylorcraft D	H. W. Ayre
G–AHXH	Aerovan 4	S. G. Newport
G–AHXI	Cierva C.30A	Southern Aircraft (Gatwick)
G–AHXK	Avro 19	Sivewright Airways
G–AHXL	Avro 19	B.E.A.C.
G–AHXM	Avro 19	B.E.A.C.
G–AHXN	Tiger Moth	Marshall's Flying School
G–AHXR	Messenger 2A	Hon. J. B. Fermor-Hesketh
G–AHXS	Anson I	Fairey Aviation Co.
G–AHXU	Marathon 2	M.o.S.
G–AHXW	Dragon Rapide	B.E.A.C.
G–AHXX	Dragon Rapide	B.E.A.C.
G–AHXZ	Dragon Rapide	B.E.A.C.
G–AHYB	Liberator	B.O.A.C.
G–AHYD	Liberator	B.O.A.C.
G–AHYF	Liberator	B.O.A.C.
G–AHYG	Liberator	B.O.A.C.
G–AHYL	Hawk Trainer 3	Fairey Aviation Co.
G–AHYM	Hawk Trainer 3	Fairey Aviation Co.
G–AHYN	Avro 19	Sivewright Airways

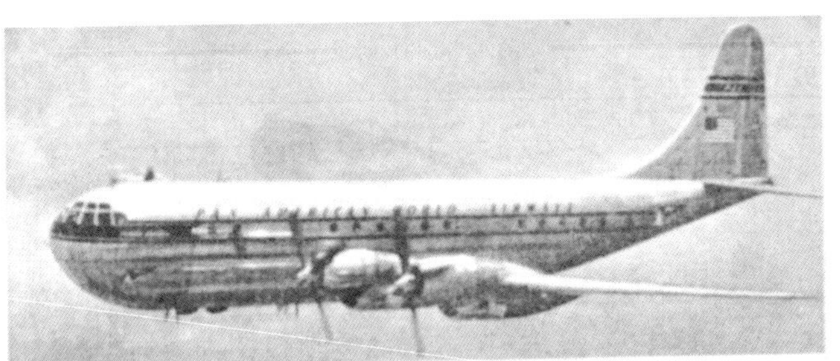

Above : Boeing STRATO-CRUISER. Biggest air liner in regular service. Operated into London Airport by B.O.A.C., P.A.A. and A.O.A.

Right : Bristol BRABA-ZON I. Designed to fly direct from London to New York with 100 passengers. G–AGPW has eight Centaurus piston-engines. Brabazon 2 (G–AIML) will have eight Proteus " propjets."

Below : Douglas DC–6. Successor to the famous Dakota and Skymaster, the DC–6 is here seen in S.A.S. markings.

Left : Avro YORK. Developed from the Lancaster bomber and mainstay of the R.A.F.'s contribution *to* the Berlin Air Lift in 1948–9. (*F.A.M.A. photo.*)

Above : *Lockheed* CONSTELLATION. More than 210 "Connies" are in service with 14 major world airlines. VT–DAR is flown between Bombay and London by Air India International.

Left : *Canadair* DC–4M2. The Canadair Four, 22 of which constitute B.O.A.C.'s *Argonaut* Class, is a Canadian-built development of the DC–4 with Merlin engines and DC–6 type cabin pressurisation. The aircraft illustrated is one of T.C.A.'s 20 *North Stars.*

Registration	Type	Owner or Operator
G–AHYP	Tiger Moth	Aikman Airways
G–AHYY	Sandringham 5	B.O.A.C. *Portsmouth*
G–AHZA	Sandringham 5	B.O.A.C. *Penzance*
G–AHZC	Sandringham 5	B.O.A.C. *Pembroke*
G–AHZD	Sandringham 5	B.O.A.C. *Portmarnock*
G–AHZE	Sandringham 5	B.O.A.C. *Portsea*
G–AHZF	Sandringham 5	B.O.A.C. *Poole*
G–AHZG	Sandringham 5	B.O.A.C. *Pevensey*
G–AHZH	Tiger Moth	Hampshire School of Flying
G–AHZS	Messenger 2A	H. C. Kennard
G–AHZT	Messenger 2A	H. Deterding
G–AHZU	Messenger 2A	Tractor Spares Ltd.
G–AHZV	Consul	Lancashire Aircraft Corp.
G–AHZW	Consul	Lancashire Aircraft Corp.
G–AHZY	Proctor 5	Anglo-American Oil Co.
G–AIAA	Proctor 5	T. Wayman-Hales
G–AIAE	Proctor 5	A. G. D. Mackenzie
G–AIAF	Proctor 5	T. W. Dupree
G–AIAG	Proctor 5	W. J. Twitchell
G–AIAH	Consul	Morton Air Services
G–AIAI	Hawk Trainer	Airways Aero Assoc.
G–AIAJ	Messenger 2A	Major Hubert Blount
G–AIAP	Halifax 8	Eagle Aviation
G–AIAR	Halifax 8	Chartair
G–AIAT	Oxford I	B.O.A.C.
G–AIAU	Oxford I	B.O.A.C.
G–AIAV	Oxford I	B.O.A.C.
G–AIAW	Oxford I	B.O.A.C.
G–AIAX	Oxford I	B.O.A.C.
G–AIBB	Dragon Rapide	Patrick Motors
G–AIBC	Consul	F. C. Wilmer
G–AIBD	Messenger 2A	T. Carlyle
G–AIBE	Fulmar 2	Fairey Aviation Co.
G–AIBF	Consul	Silver City Airways
G–AIBH	Autocrat	M. M. Mallorie
G–AIBL	Autocrat	Machine Tools Ltd.
G–AIBM	Autocrat	Mr. & Mrs. R. E. O. Velten
G–AIBN	Tiger Moth	Marshall's Flying School
G–AIBP	Autocrat	P. O. Bennie
G–AIBR	Autocrat	Brooklands Aviation
G–AIBS	Autocrat	G. & A. Morgan Trust
G–AIBT	Autocrat	Sykes & Robinson
G–AIBW	Autocrat	Air Schools
G–AIBX	Autocrat	East Riding Flying Club
G–AIBY	Autocrat	J. D. H. Radford
G–AIBZ	Autocrat	Wright Aviation
G–AICA	Arrow	Auster Aircraft
G–AICD	Hawk Trainer 3	Bournemouth Flying Club
G–AICE	Hawk Trainer 3	Bournemouth Flying Club
G–AICM	Freighter I	M.C.A. (Hunting Aerosurveys)
G–AICT	Wayfarer 2A	Bristol Aeroplane Co.
G–AICY	Dove I	Iraq Petroleum Transport Co.
G–AIDB	Tiger Moth	Wiltshire School of Flying
G–AIDD	Tiger Moth	Brooklands Aviation
G–AIDE	Monarch	B. G. Heron
G–AIDF	Hawk Trainer	Hunting Flying Club
G–AIDH	Messenger 2A	Mrs. L. K. King
G–AIDI	Aerovan 3	S. G. Newport

Registration	Type	Owner or Operator
G AIDK	Messenger 2A	Wallis & Linnell
G AIDL	Tiger Moth	E. C. Gander-Dower
G AIDN	Spitfire Tr. 8	Vickers-Armstrongs
G-AIDO	Gemini 1A	E. G. Hayes
G-AIDR	Tiger Moth	Herts & Essex Aero Club
G-AIDS	Tiger Moth	Herts & Essex Aero Club
G-AIDT	Tiger Moth	Herts & Essex Aero Club
G-AIDV	Tiger Moth	Herts & Essex Aero Club
G-AIDW	Consul	Dexford Motors
G-AIDX	Consul	Anglo-American Oil Co.
G-AIDZ	Consul	British Air Transport
G-AIEA	Consul	British Air Transport
G-AIEB	Proctor 1	W./Cdr. R. L. Bowes
G-AIED	Proctor 1	Shell Mex & B.P.
G-AIEE	Proctor 1	P. Lennox
G-AIEG	Proctor 2	W. Graham & M. J. Edwards
G-AIEH	Proctor 2	R. F. Martin
G-AIEK	Messenger 2A	A. J. Linnell
G-AIEL	Tiger Moth	R. H. Braime
G-AIEN	Proctor 5	Kearsley Airways
G-AIEP	Proctor 5	Hornton Airways
G-AIER	Proctor 5	Blue Line Airways
G-AIES	Proctor 5	D. H. L. McCowen
G-AIET	Proctor 5	Vivian Van Damm
G-AIEV	Proctor 5	N. King
G-AIEX	Proctor 1	Yorkshire Aeroplane Club
G-AIEY	Proctor 1	Vosper Ltd.
G-AIFD	Anson 1	Straight Aviation Training Weston Airways
G-AIFE	Proctor 2	E. G. Davis
G-AIFV	Freighter 21	Bristol Aeroplane Co.
G-AIFZ	Autocrat	L. Youngs
G-AIGC	Autocrat	Wiltshire School of Flying
G-AIGD	Autocrat	Loxhams Flying Services
G-AIGE	Autocrat	Southend Municipal Council
G-AIGF	Autocrat	F. J. R. Elliott
G-AIGG	Autocrat	H. Whitaker
G-AIGH	Autocrat	W. H. Binns
G-AIGI	Autocrat	Hunting Aerosurveys
G-AIGK	Autocrat	D. E. Harrington
G-AIGL	Autocrat	East Anglian Flying Services
G-AIGM	Autocrat	Eagle Aviation
G-AIGO	Autocrat	C. W. Blankley
G-AIGP	Autocrat	G. C. Wright
G-AIGR	Autocrat	Wolverhampton Aviation
G-AIGS	Autocrat	W. H. Byars
G-AIGT	Autocrat	H. N. R. Dale
G-AIGU	Autocrat	H. Mitchell
G-AIGV	Autocrat	G. C. Wright
G-AIGX	Autocrat	T. C. Fooks
G-AIGY	Autocrat	J. H. Watts & Ptns.
G-AIGZ	Auster J/4	H. F. Fulford
G-AIHB	Proctor 2	W. Vinter
G-AIHD	Proctor 3	Lancashire Aircraft Corp.
G-AIHE	Proctor 1	J. C. Hyland
G-AIHF	Proctor 1	Lancashire Aircraft Corp.
G-AIHG	Proctor 1	Air Enterprises
G-AIHH	Proctor 1	Lancashire Aircraft Corp.

22

Registration	Type	Owner or Operator
G–AIHK	Aerovan 3	S. G. Newport
G–AIHM	Gemini 1A	Ulster Aviation
G–AIHN	Dragon Rapide	Gibraltar Airways
G–AIHO	Tiger Moth	Coventry Aeroplane Club
G–AIHV	Halifax 8	Lancashire Aircraft Corp.
G–AIHX	Halifax 8	Lancashire Aircraft Corp.
G–AIIF	Gemini 1A	Cambridge University Flying Club
G–AIIG	Aerovan 3	Bowmaker Ltd.
G–AIIH	J–3C Cub	A. C. Cox
G–AIII	Proctor 1	Darlington & Dist. Aero Club
G–AIIK	Proctor 1	Field Aircraft Services
G–AIIL	Proctor 3	Olley Air Service
G–AIIP	Proctor 2	A. T. Leaning
G–AIIR	Proctor 1	Southend-on-Sea Flying Services
G–AIIS	Consul	International Airways
G–AIIT	Vega Gull	St. Christopher Travelways
G–AIIU	Taylorcraft D	Airways Aero Assoc.
G–AIIW	Proctor 1	Reid & Sigrist
G–AIIZ	Tiger Moth	L. T. (Central Buses) Sports Assoc.
G–AIJA	Tiger Moth	L.T. (Central Buses) Sports Assoc.
G–AIJD	Dakota 3	S. Rubin
G–AIJE	Viking 1	M.o.S. (B.E.A.C.)
G–AIJG	Autocrat	Cardiff Aeroplane Club
G–AIJH	Autocrat	R. E. Clive
G–AIJI	Autocrat	Britavia
G–AIJK	Auster J/4	Warwickshire Aero Club
G–AIJL	Auster J/4	R. H. Braime
G–AIJM	Auster J/4	P. Parry
G–AIJN	Auster J/4	H. Gadsby
G–AIJO	Auster J/4	Miss G. Pendleton
G–AIJP	Auster J/4	Skyfreight
G–AIJR	Auster J/4	Loxhams Flying Services
G–AIJS	Auster J/4	Auster Aircraft
G–AIJT	Auster J/4	Spa & Warwick Timber Co.
G–AIJW	Autocrat	Ten-Sixty-Six Products
G–AIJZ	Autocrat	Leek Hill Aviation (Birmingham)
G–AIKA	Auster 5	T. Shipside Ltd.
G–AIKC	Auster 5	J. H. Reyner
G–AIKE	Auster 5	J. Moore
G–AIKG	Proctor 1	C. G. Blanter
G–AIKI	Proctor 1	Brooklands Aviation
G–AIKJ	Proctor 3	Brooklands Aviation
G–AIKK	Proctor 1	Reid & Sigrist
G–AIKO	Consul	Chartair
G–AIKR	Consul	Airwork
G–AIKS	Consul	Bowmaker Ltd.
G–AIKT	Consul	Wirral Airways
G–AIKU	Consul	Butlins Ltd.
G–AIKX	Consul	Samuel Hodge & Sons
G–AIKZ	Consul	Bowmaker Ltd.
G–AILF	Aerovan 4	Western Manufacturing Estate
G–AILG	Gemini 1A	Neptune Continental Merchants
G–AILH	Marathon 1	M.o.S.
G–AILI	Messenger 2A	W. G. Breen-Turner
G–AILL	Messenger 2A	Air Schools Ltd.
G–AILM	Aerovan 4	Western Manufacturing Estate
G–AILN	Proctor 1	Field Aircraft Services

23

Registration	Type	Owner or Operator
G-AILO	Halifax 8	Lancashire Aircraft Corp.
G-AILP	Proctor I	Miss R. Rees
G-AILS	Tiger Moth	Herts & Essex Aero Club
G-AILT	Tiger Moth	Herts & Essex Aero Club
G-AIME	Freighter 21E	Bristol Aeroplane Co.
G-AIML	Brabazon 2	M.o.S.
G-AINY	Tiger Moth	Southend Municipal Council
G-AINZ	Anson I	Straight Aviation Training Weston Airways
G-AIOA	Anson I	Straight Aviation Training Weston Airways
G-AIOB	Anson I	Straight Aviation Training Weston Airways
G-AIOC	Cierva C.30A	G. S. Baker
G-AIOK	Hawk Trainer 3	Derby Aero Club
G-AIOP	Consul	Transair
G-AIOS	Consul	Morton Air Services
G-AIOT	Consul	Air Enterprises
G-AIOV	Consul	Air Enterprises
G-AIOW	Consul	Morton Air Services
G-AIOX	Consul	Flyaway
G-AIOY	Consul	Solar Air Services
G-AIPA	Anson I	College of Aeronautics
G-AIPB	Anson I	College of Aeronautics
G-AIPC	Anson I	College of Aeronautics
G-AIPD	Anson I	College of Aeronautics
G-AIPE	Auster 5	C. L. Bendall
G-AIPF	Auster 5	N. B. Williams & J. B. Hall
G-AIPG	Auster J/4	B. F. Francis
G-AIPH	Auster J/4	Wright Aviation
G-AIPI	Auster J/4	T. Shipside Ltd.
G-AIPJ	Auster J/4	T. Shipside Ltd.
G-AIPK	Auster J/4	Warwickshire Aero Club
G-AIPL	Auster J/4	Inter-City Airways
G-AIPM	Auster J/4	C. W. Blankley
G-AIPN	Auster 5	N. D. Roughsedge
G-AIPO	Auster 5	Fred Mellor (Wolverhampton)
G-AIPR	Auster J/4	H. C. N. Goodhart
G-AIPS	Auster J/4	Miss E. I. Kidner
G-AIPU	Autocrat	Aerial Spraying Contractors
G-AIPV	Autocrat	J. C. Wilson
G-AIPW	Autocrat	Miss R. H. Reeves
G-AIPY	Autocrat	Mrs. F. G. Myland
G-AIPZ	Autocrat	C. V. Young
G-AIRA	Autocrat	P. W. Scotney
G-AIRB	Autocrat	Inter-City Airways
G-AIRC	Autocrat	W. S. Shackleton
G-AIRD	Auster J/4	Boston Air Transport
G-AIRE	Taylorcraft D	R. J. Bowers
G-AIRI	Tiger Moth	West London Aero Club
G-AIRJ	Tiger Moth	West London Aero Club
G-AIRK	Tiger Moth	West London Aero Club
G-AIRM	Anson I	Aero & Engineering (Merseyside)
G-AIRN	Anson I	Aero & Engineering (Merseyside)
G-AIRP	Consul	Brevet Flying Club
G-AIRR	Tiger Moth	Short Bros. & Harland
G-AIRS	Gemini IA	M.C.A.
G-AIRW	Anson I	Airwork

Registration	Type	Owner or Operator
G–AIRX	Anson 1	North Sea Air Transport
G–AIRY	Messenger 4	British Aviation Insurance Co.
G–AIRZ	Oxford 1	B.O.A.C.
G–AISA	Tipsy B	R.N. Flying Club
G–AISB	Tipsy B	R.N. Flying Club
G–AISC	Tipsy B	Fairey Aviation Co.
G–AISE	Aerovan 4	British Nederland Airservices
G–AISF	Aerovan 4	T. C. Pick
G–AISI	Aerovan 4	Aviation Traders
G–AISK	Gemini 1A	Sir Clifford Paterson
G–AISL	Messenger 2A	C. H. Simpson
G–AISM	Gemini 1A	A. W. Sawyer
G–AISN	Gemini 1A	J. Brockhouse & Co.
G–AISP	J–3C Cub	G. Reid-Walker
G–AISR	Tiger Moth	Hampshire School of Flying
G–AISU	Spitfire 5B	A. H. Wheeler
G–AISX	J–3C Cub	F. Smith
G–AITB	Oxford 1	Air Service Training
G–AITD	Tiger Moth	Lockwoods Flying Services
G–AITE	Tiger Moth	D. Heaton
G–AITF	Oxford 1	Air Service Training
G–AITI	Tiger Moth	Airwork Flying Club
G–AITJ	Anson 1	Whitney Straight Ltd.
G–AITL	Anson 1	Barclays International Airways
G–AITN	Hawk Trainer 3	Woodward & Son (Derby)
G–AITO	Hawk Trainer 3	East Riding Flying Club
G–AITS	Hawk Trainer 3	T. F. W. Gunton
G–AITZ	Hawk Trainer 3	H. V. Behar
G–AIUA	Hawk Trainer 3	R. H. Young
G–AIUB	Hawk Trainer 3	Universal Flying Services
G–AIUE	Hawk Trainer 3	T. C. Sparrow
G–AIUG	Hawk Trainer 3	R. G. Forbes-Bassett
G–AIUH	Oxford 1	Reid & Sigrist
G–AIUK	Dragon Rapide	Air Schools
G–AIUL	Dragon Rapide	Air Transport (Charter) (C.I.)
G–AIUM	Dragon Rapide	Hunting Flying Clubs
G–AIUN	Dragon Rapide	Mayfair Air Services
G–AIUO	Dragon Rapide	Hornton Airways
G–AIUU	Consul	Thomas Barclay Ltd.
G–AIUW	Consul	Transair
G–AIUX	Consul	B.O.A.C. *Star Master*
G–AIUY	Consul	Olley Air Service
G–AIVA	Consul	Transair
G–AIVB	Viking 1B	B.E.A.C. *Vernal*
G–AIVC	Viking 1B	B.E.A.C. *Vernon*
G–AIVD	Viking 1B	B.E.A.C. *Veteran*
G–AIVF	Viking 1B	B.E.A.C. *Vibrant*
G–AIVG	Viking 1B	B.E.A.C. *Viceroy*
G–AIVH	Viking 1B	B.E.A.C. *Vicinity*
G–AIVI	Viking 1B	B.E.A.C. *Victor*
G–AIVJ	Viking 1B	B.E.A.C. *Victoria*
G–AIVK	Viking 1B	B.E.A.C. *Victory*
G–AIVL	Viking 1B	B.E.A.C. *Vigilant*
G–AIVM	Viking 1B	B.E.A.C. *Vigorous*
G–AIVN	Viking 1B	B.E.A.C. *Violent*
G–AIVO	Viking 1B	B.E.A.C. *Villain*
G–AIVV	Tiger Moth	Newcastle Aero Club
G–AIVW	Tiger Moth	Newcastle Aero Club

25

Registration	Type	Owner or Operator
G-AIVX	Sealand 1	Short Bros. & Harland
G-AIVY	Oxford 1	B.O.A.C. *Star Mentor*
G-AIVZ	Tiger Moth	T. Shipside Ltd.
G-AIWA	Proctor 1	W. J. Twitchell
G-AIWC	Dakota 3	Skyways *Sky Dispatch*
G-AIWD	Dakota 3	Skyways *Sky Warrior*
G-AIWE	Dakota 3	Skyways *Sky Lancer*
G-AIWF	Dove 2	Silver City Airways
G-AIWN	Halifax 8	Payloads
G-AIWS	Gemini 1A	Mayfair Air Service
G-AIWT	Halifax 8	Payloads
G-AIWU	Walrus 2	Sir C. A. C. Hampson
G-AIWV	Anson 1	British Air Transport
G-AIWX	Anson 1	British Air Transport
G-AIXA	Taylorcraft D	Cotswold Aero Club
G-AIXB	Taylorcraft D	Denham Flying Club
G-AIXC	Argus 1	F. Bosworth
G-AIXD	Tiger Moth	D. Lloyd
G-AIXG	Tiger Moth	College of Aeronautics
G-AIXI	Tiger Moth	College of Aeronautics
G-AIXJ	Tiger Moth	College of Aeronautics
G-AIXL	Tiger Moth	Universal Flying Services
G-AIXM	Argus 2	J. J. Mackersey
G-AIXN	M-1C Sokol	G. Shaw
G-AIXO	Anson 1	Culliford Air Lines
G-AIXR	Viking 1B	Airwork
G-AIXS	Viking 1B	Airwork
G-AIXU	Anson 1	Gulf Aviation
G-AIXV	Anson 1	Tangiers Transport (London
G-AIXZ	Anson 1	Dennis Aviation
G-AIYA	Tudor Freighter 3	M.C.A.
G-AIYB	Hawk Trainer 3	Redhill Flying Club
G-AIYC	Hawk Trainer 3	Redhill Flying Club
G-AIYD	Hawk Trainer 3	Redhill Flying Club
G-AIYE	Dragon Rapide	Olley Air Services
G-AIYH	Proctor 1	Hunting Flying Clubs
G-AIYK	Avro 19/2	Hunting Air Travel
G-AIYL	Hawk Trainer 3	J. Neasham
G-AIYM	Tutor	A. P. Fraser
G-AIYN	Apollo	M.o.S.
G-AIYO	Argus 1	Womens Junior Air Corps.
G-AIYP	Dragon Rapide	V. H. Bellamy
G-AIYR	Dragon Rapide	Reid & Sigrist
G-AIYS	Leopard Moth	H. F. Buckmaster
G-AIYU	J-3C Cub	Community Flying Club
G-AIYV	J-3C Cub	A. J. Walter
G-AIYX	J-3C Cub	Denham Air Services
G-AIYY	Dragon Rapide	Reid & Sigrist
G-AIZA	Proctor 3	D. Stansfield
G-AIZB	Proctor 5	East Hull Press
G-AIZC	Proctor 5	Flyaway
G-AIZE	Argus 1	B. R. Companini
G-AIZF	Tiger Moth	Midland Bank Flying Club
G-AIZI	Dragon Rapide	Reid & Sigrist
G-AIZK	Hawk Trainer 3	J. P. Gunner
G-AIZL	Hawk Trainer 3	J. V. Green
G-AIZU	Autocrat	R. A. Davies (Birmingham)
G-AIZV	Autocrat	Herts & Essex Aero Club

130

Registration	Type	Owner or Operator
G-AIZW	Autocrat	Wiltshire School of Flying
G-AIZY	Autocrat	Hastings & East Sussex Air Service
G-AIZZ	Autocrat	Air Kruise (Kent)
G-AJAB	Autocrat	R. P. Sayer
G-AJAC	Autocrat	R. L. Hutchins
G-AJAE	Autocrat	Royal Artillery Aero Club
G-AJAG	Autocrat	Inter-City Air Services
G-AJAH	Autocrat	G. Hadman
G-AJAI	Autocrat	Fen Drains & Excavations
G-AJAJ	Autocrat	McVitie Price
G-AJAK	Auster 5	Eagle Aerophotos
G-AJAM	Arrow	B. Hynes
G-AJAN	Auster 5	E. P. Jenks Ltd.
G-AJAR	Autocrat	R. A. Pateman
G-AJAS	Autocrat	Hunting Flying Clubs
G-AJAT	Argus 1	J. J. Hofer
G-AJAV	Dakota 3	Silver City Airways
G-AJAW	Lodestar	Silver City Airways
G-AJBF	Argus 1	J. R. Grice (Thorne Aviation)
G-AJBH	Dakota 3	Lamberts Trust
G-AJBI	Dove 1	Morton Air Services
G-AJBJ	Dragon Rapide	Birkett Air Service
G-AJBM	Viking 1B	B.E.A.C. *Vincent*
G-AJBN	Viking 1B	B.E.A.C. *Vindictive*
G-AJBO	Viking 1B	B.E.A.C. *Vintage*
G-AJBP	Viking 1B	B.E.A.C. *Vintner*
G-AJBR	Viking 1B	B.E.A.C. *Virginia*
G-AJBS	Viking 1B	B.E.A.C. *Virgo*
G-AJBT	Viking 1B	B.E.A.C. *Viper*
G-AJBU	Viking 1B	B.E.A.C. *Virtue*
G-AJBV	Viking 1B	B.E.A.C. *Viscount*
G-AJBW	Viking 1B	B.E.A.C. *Vista*
G-AJBX	Viking 1B	B.E.A.C. *Vital*
G-AJBY	Viking 1B	B.E.A.C. *Vitality*
G-AJCA	Viking 1B	B.E.A.C. *Vixen*
G-AJCD	Viking 1B	B.E.A.C. *Vizor*
G-AJCE	Viking 1B	B.E.A.C. *Vivacious*
G-AJCK	Heath Parasol	Airways Aero Association
G-AJCL	Dragon Rapide	Allgood Manufacturing Co.
G-AJCM	Hawk Trainer 3	
G-AJCN	Proctor 3	A. Andrew
G-AJCO	Anson 1	
G-AJCP	Anson 1	
G-AJCR	Anson 1	
G-AJCS	Anson 1	
G-AJCT	Anson 1	
G-AJCU	Proctor 3	F. J. R. Elliott
G-AJCV	Proctor 3	
G-AJCW	Proctor 3	
G-AJCX	Proctor 3	L. C. Hazard
G-AJCY	Proctor 3	M. Dumont
G-AJCZ	Proctor 3	J. R. Brittain
G-AJDA	Proctor 3	
G-AJDB	Proctor 3	
G-AJDC	Argus	
G-AJDF	Messenger 4A	N. B. Williams
G-AJDH	Avro 19	Secretary of State for Air
G-AJDI	Viking 1B	B.E.A.C. *Volatile*

27

Registration	Type	Owner or Operator
G–AJDJ	Viking 1B	B.E.A.C. *Volley*
G–AJDK	Viking 1B	B.E.A.C. *Volunteer*
G–AJDL	Viking 1B	B.E.A.C. *Vortex*
G–AJDM	Messenger 2A	Boston Air Transport
G–AJDN	Dragon Rapide	Birkett Air Service
G–AJDO	Argus 1	H. Molt-Bignell
G–AJDP	Dove 1	Hunting Air Travel
G–AJDR	Hawk Trainer 3	
G–AJDS	J–3C Cub	A. J. Walter
G–AJDT	Argus	R. B. Pursey
G–AJDV	Autocrat	Universal Flying Services
G–AJDW	Autocrat	Brooklands Aviation
G–AJDY	Autocrat	P. J. S. Dredge
G–AJDZ	Autocrat	A. F. Johnson
G–AJEA	Autocrat	F. J. R. Elliott
G–AJEB	Autocrat	Hunting Aerosurveys
G–AJEC	Autocrat	Fen Drains & Excavations
G–AJED	Autocrat	Redhill Flying Club
G–AJEE	Autocrat	W. S. Shackleton
G–AJEF	Autocrat	British Air Transport
G–AJEH	Autocrat	Redhill Flying Club
G–AJEK	Autocrat	J. N. Williamson
G–AJEN	Autocrat	Loxhams Flying Service
G–AJEO	Autocrat	Southend Municipal Council
G–AJEP	Autocrat	Airwork
G–AJEU	Autocrat	G. A. Whittaker
G–AJEW	Autocrat	A. W. Bingham
G–AJEX	Gemini 1A	Modern Houses (Jersey)
G–AJEY	Messenger 2A	Thomas Carlyle
G–AJFC	Messenger 2A	T. Shipside Ltd.
G–AJFD	Gemini 1A	Bees Flight Ltd.
G–AJFE	Mercury 4C	J. F. Schumaker
G–AJFF	Messenger 2A	G. Clifton
G–AJFH	Messenger 2A	Ulster Aviation
G–AJFJ	Dragon Rapide	C. W. J. Allen
G–AJFK	Dragon Rapide	Island Air Charters
G–AJFR	Viking 1B	Airwork
G–AJFS	Viking 1B	Airwork
G–AJFT	Viking 1B	Airwork
G–AJFU	Sea Otter	British Aviation Services
G–AJFW	Sea Otter	British Aviation Services
G–AJFX	Anson 1	Blue Line Airways
G–AJGA	Consul	Lancashire Aircraft Corp.
G–AJGB	Consul	Barclays International Airways
G–AJGG	Consul	Chartair
G–AJGH	Consul	Air Charter
G–AJGJ	Auster 5	Walker & Thomson
G–AJGM	Hawk Trainer 3	Airways Aero Assoc.
G–AJGO	Proctor 1	Southern Aircraft (Gatwick)
G–AJGP	Hawk Trainer 3	M. W. R. Philp
G–AJGR	Oxford 1	Hunting Aerosurveys
G–AJGS	Dragon Rapide	Miss C. Brunning
G–AJGT	Dove 2	Airlinks
G–AJGU	Bristol 171	Bristol Aeroplane Co.
G–AJGV	Dragon Rapide	Manx Air Charter
G–AJGW	Argus 1	Aviation Traders
G–AJGY	Super Cruiser	C. G. Reid-Walker
G–AJHA	Hawk Trainer 3	E. D. Harris
G–AJHB	Hawk Trainer 3	Darlington & District Aero Club
G–AJHC	Hawk Trainer 3	J. Neasham

Registration	Type	Owner or Operator
G-AJHD	Hawk Trainer 3	J. Neasham
G-AJHG	Hawk Trainer 3	David C. Black & Co.
G-AJHI	Tiger Moth	Edinburgh Flying Club
G-AJHJ	Auster 5	Bertram Arden & Co.
G-AJHM	K.Z. Lark	Guernsey Salvage Co.
G-AJHO	Dragon Rapide	Brooklands Aviation
G-AJHP	Dragon Rapide	Brooklands Aviation
G-AJHR	Tiger Moth	Scottish Aviation
G-AJHS	Tiger Moth	Reid & Sigrist
G-AJHT	Tiger Moth	Reid & Sigrist
G-AJHU	Tiger Moth	Reid & Sigrist
G-AJHW	Sikorsky S–51	B.E.A.C.
G-AJHX	Dove I	Anglo-Iranian Oil Co.
G-AJHY	Dakota 3	B.E.A.C.
G-AJHZ	Dakota 3	B.E.A.C.
G-AJIA	Dakota 3	B.E.A.C.
G-AJIB	Dakota 3	B.E.A.C.
G-AJIC	Dakota 3	B.E.A.C.
G-AJID	Autocrat	A. C. Kingham
G-AJIE	Autocrat	A. L. Williams
G-AJIG	Autocrat	East Riding Flying Club
G-AJIH	Autocrat	Light Planes (Lancs)
G-AJII	Auster 5	F. C. Griffiths
G-AJIK	Auster 5	S. G. Newport
G-AJIN	Autocrat	East Riding Flying Club
G-AJIO	Autocrat	G. W. Barker
G-AJIP	Autocrat	Edinburgh Flying Club
G-AJIR	Autocrat	Mrs. D. B. Walker
G-AJIS	Autocrat	Russel Gunton
G-AJIT	Autocrat	Weston Aero Club
G-AJIU	Autocrat	G. Clifton & C. H. Wellband
G-AJIV	Autocrat	G. N. Drake
G-AJIW	Autocrat	W. H. & J. Rogers (Engineers)
G-AJIX	Autocrat	A. & Mrs. J. A. Bailey
G-AJIY	Autocrat	J. R. Ratcliffe
G-AJIZ	Autocrat J.I.A.	Auster Aircraft
G-AJJB	Auster 5	Bristol & Wessex Aero Club
G-AJJE	Beech D–17–S	David Brown and Sons (Huddersfield)
G-AJJF	Dove I	Iraq Petroleum Transport Co.
G-AJJG	Auster 5	T. W. Hayhow
G-AJJH	Auster 5A	F. M. J. H. de Malet-Rocquefort
G-AJJI	Hawk Trainer 3	R. N. H. Courtney
G-AJJJ	Beech 17	A. R. Pilgrim
G-AJJN	Viking 1B	B.E.A.C. *Vulcan*
G-AJJP	Gyrodyne	Fairey Aviation Co.
G-AJJR	Auster 5	O. Hill & F. E. A. Mitchell
G-AJKC	Tudor Freighter 3	M.C.A.
G-AJKD	Tiger Moth	Midland Aero Club
G-AJKE	Dragon Rapide	W. A. Rollason Ltd.
G-AJKG	Messenger 2A	N. B. Williams
G-AJKH	Dragon Rapide	Anglo-Iranian Oil Co.
G-AJKI	Dragon Rapide	Anglo-Iranian Oil Co.
G-AJKK	Messenger 2A	Westfield Transport
G-AJKL	Messenger 2A	J. Fusco
G-AJKP	Aerovan 4	Patrick Motors
G-AJKR	Gemini 1A	W. Stevens
G-AJKS	Gemini 1A	British Aviation Insurance
G-AJKT	Messenger 2A	G. O. Lawford

Registration	Type	Owner or Operator
G–AJKU	Aerovan 4	Ulster Aviation
G–AJKV	Gemini 1A	A. Ercolani
G–AJKW	Dragon Rapide	Lancashire Aircraft Corp.
G–AJKX	Dragon Rapide	Lancashire Aircraft Corp.
G–AJKY	Dragon Rapide	Lancashire Aircraft Corp.
G–AJLE	Auster 5	Lancashire Aircraft Corp.
G–AJLG	Auster 4	Lancashire Aircraft Corp.
G–AJLH	Consul	Lancashire Aircraft Corp.
G–AJLI	Consul	Fairflight
G–AJLK	Consul	J. Patient
G–AJLM	Consul	J. T. Donaldson
G–AJLN	Consul	English Electric Co.
G–AJLP	Consul	Flyaway Ltd.
G–AJLR	Consul	Olley Air Services
G–AJLS	Proctor 1	D. C. T. Bennett
G–AJLT	Sea Otter	B.O.A.C.
G–AJLU	Sea Otter	B.O.A.C.
G–AJLV	Dove 1	M.C.A.
G–AJLW	Dove 2	De Havilland Aircraft Co.
G–AJLX	Dakota 3	Scottish Aviation
G–AJMA	Dove 1	M.C.A.
G–AJMH	Proctor 4	E. Williams
G–AJMI	Proctor 4	Whitehouse Industries
G–AJMK	Proctor 4	Field Aircraft Services
G–AJMP	Proctor 4	G. C. S. Whyman
G–AJMV	Proctor 4	British Syphon Co.
G–AJMW	Proctor 4	Short Bros. & Harland
G–AJMX	Proctor 4	Short Bros. & Harland
G–AJMY	Dragon Rapide	Sivewright Airways
G–AJMZ	Sandringham 5	B.O.A.C. *Perth*
G–AJNC	Oxford	Fairey Aviation Co.
G–AJNE	Consul	Air Enterprises
G–AJNG	Consul	Chartair
G–AJNN	Argus 1	F. A. Laker
G–AJNO	Walrus 1	Scottish Aviation
G–AJNP	Walrus 1	Scottish Aviation
G–AJNT	Halifax 8	Payloads
G–AJNV	Halifax 8	Payloads
G–AJNW	Halifax 8	Westminster Airways
G–AJOA	Tiger Moth	Short Bros. & Harland
G–AJOB	Aerovan 4	Ulster Aviation
G–AJOC	Messenger 2A	C. E. Hickman
G–AJOD	Messenger 2A	Claremont Shipping Co.
G–AJOE	Messenger 2A	Reproducers & Amplifiers
G–AJOF	Aerovan 4	Patrick Motors
G–AJOG	Aerovan 4	North Sea Air Transport
G–AJOH	Gemini 1A	J. R. A. Stroyan
G–AJOI	Aerovan 4	Sivewright Airways
G–AJOJ	Gemini 1A	Loxhams Flying Services
G–AJOK	Gemini 1A	Fairey Aviation Co.
G–AJOM	Gemini 1A	Sir Alexander Gibb
G–AJOO	Sikorsky S–51	Pest Control
G–AJOP	Sikorsky S–51	
G–AJOR	Sikorsky S–51	B.E.A.C.
G–AJOT	Dove 1	Olley Air Services
G–AJOV	Sikorsky S–51	B.E.A.C.
G–AJOW	Argus	P. MacKisray
G–AJOX	Argus 1	J. G. Crampton

Registration	Type	Owner or Operator
G-AJOZ	Argus 1	Weston Aero Club
G-AJPA	Argus 1	Weston Aero Club
G-AJPC	Argus 1	G. Clifton
G-AJPD	Argus 1	Weston Aero Club
G-AJPE	Argus	Aviation Traders
G-AJPF	Dakota 3	Trent Valley Aviation
G-AJPH	Viking (Nene)	M.o.S.
G-AJPI	Argus 1	West London Aero Club
G-AJPR	Dove 1	B.O.A.C.
G-AJPS	Arrow	Somerton Airways
G-AJPU	Arrow	J. M. Rollo
G-AJPW	Autocrat	Duncan Smith & Co.
G-AJPX	Autocrat	W. Midlands Erection Co.
G-AJPY	Autocrat	T. Shipside Ltd.
G-AJRB	Autocrat	Brooklands Aviation
G-AJRC	Autocrat	Lancashire Aircraft Corp.
G-AJRE	Autocrat	W. Hutchinson
G-AJRF	Autocrat	Aero Industries
G-AJRG	Autocrat	Mrs. E. F. Slade
G-AJRH	Autocrat	Auster Aircraft
G-AJRK	Autocrat	N. West
G-AJRN	Autocrat	Auster Aircraft
G-AJRO	Autocrat	Auster Aircraft
G-AJRP	Autocrat	H. A. Sissons
G-AJRR	Arrow	Auster Aircraft
G-AJRS	Hawk Trainer 3	British Air Transport
G-AJRT	Hawk Trainer 3	British Air Transport
G-AJRU	Hawk Trainer 3	British Air Transport
G-AJRV	Hawk Trainer 3	Darlington & District Aero Club
G-AJRZ	Argus 1	West London Aero Club
G-AJSE	Anson 1	E. E. McIlree
G-AJSF	Hawk Trainer 3	W. Holderness
G-AJSG	Argus 1	L. D. Hawthorn
G-AJSH	Argus 1	L. D. Hawthorn
G-AJSK	Dragon Rapide	B.E.A.C.
G-AJSL	Dragon Rapide	Trent Valley Aviation
G-AJSN	Argus 1	Hon. B. L. Bathurst
G-AJSO	Argus 1	West London Aero Club
G-AJSP	Argus 1	J. J. Hofer
G-AJSR	Argus 1	Pasolds
G-AJSS	Argus 1	Suffolk Trust
G-AJSZ	Halifax 8	Lancashire Aircraft Corp.
G-AJTB	Gemini 1A	C. F. L. Hersee
G-AJTC	Aerovan 4	Western Manufacturing Estate
G-AJTG	Gemini 1B	Hon. Max Aitken
G-AJTK	Aerovan 4	British Nederland Airservices
G-AJTL	Gemini 1A	A.B.C. Motor Co.
G-AJTM	Auster 5	Wiltshire School of Flying
G-AJTN	Auster 5	Wiltshire School of Flying
G-AJTO	Dakota 3	Zinc Corporation
G-AJTP	Proctor 4	Newman Aircraft
G-AJTR	Argus 1	Taylor Electrical Instruments
G-AJTV	Auster 5	G. Bukley
G-AJTW	Tiger Moth	Short Bros. & Harland
G-AJUC	Autocrat	
G-AJUD	Autocrat	Auster Aircraft
G-AJUE	Autocrat	Darlington & District Aero Club
G-AJUF	Autocrat	Auster Aircraft

Registration	Type	Owner or Operator
G–AJUH	Autocrat	C. H. Webb
G–AJUJ	Autocrat	Weston Aero Club
G–AJUK	Autocrat	Southend Municipal Council
G–AJUL	Autocrat	Loxhams Flying Services
G–AJUM	Autocrat	Weston Aero Club
G–AJUN	Autocrat	W. Petrie-Hay
G–AJUO	Autocrat	Weston Aero Club
G–AJUP	Autocrat	Southend Municipal Council
G–AJUR	Autocrat	J. E. Coxon
G–AJUW	Aiglet J/1B	Ariel Spraying Contractors
G–AJUY	Autocrat	Auster Aircraft
G–AJUZ	Autocrat	Miss M. Kelly
G–AJVA	Dragon Rapide	Iraq Petroleum Transport Co.
G–AJVB	Dragon Rapide	Iraq Petroleum Transport Co.
G–AJVC	Messenger 2A	Lionel Sage & Co.
G–AJVD	Chipmunk	de Havilland Aircraft Co.
G–AJVE	Tiger Moth	
G–AJVF	Tiger Moth	McDonald Aircraft
G–AJVI	Argus I	S. K. Davies
G–AJVM	Argus	West London Aero Club
G–AJVN	Auster 5	J. J. Mackersey
G–AJVT	Auster 5	Anglo-Continental Air Services
G–AJVU	Auster 5	L. W. Watkins
G–AJVV	Auster 5	Birmingham Aero Club
G–AJVY	Dakota 3	London Express Newspapers
G–AJVZ	Dakota 3	Lambert Bros.
G–AJWA	Gemini IA	J. J. Hofer
G–AJWB	Messenger 2A	Wiltshire School of Flying
G–AJWC	Gemini IA	Derek Crouch (Contractors)
G–AJWD	Aerovan 4	Western Manufacturing Estate
G–AJWE	Gemini IA	Scaffolding (G.B.)
G–AJWF	Gemini IA	Guernsey Salvage Co.
G–AJWG	Gemini IA	J. W. Adamson
G–AJWH	Gemini IA	R. J. B. Pearse
G–AJWI	Aerovan 4	Mayfair Air Services
G–AJWL	Gemini IA	Air Charter
G–AJXA	Argus I	D. B. Munro
G–AJXB	Dragon Rapide	B.E.A.C.
G–AJXC	Auster 5	A. H. Warminger
G–AJXE	Consul	M.C.A.
G–AJXF	Consul	M.C.A.
G–AJXG	Consul	M.C.A.
G–AJXH	Consul	M.C.A.
G–AJXI	Consul	M.C.A.
G–AJXO	Autocrat	R. K. Dundas
G–AJXS	Autocrat	Westland Aircraft
G–AJXX	Auster 5	T. W. Hayhow
G–AJXY	Auster 5	T. W. Leadbetter
G–AJXZ	Arrow	A. S. Mackenzie-Lowe
G–AJYB	Auster 5	J. G. Crampton
G–AJYD	Auster 5	Le Bryan Group Products
G–AJYG	Auster J/5	Auster Aircraft
G–AJYI	Auster 5	F. L. de Rosnay
G–AJYK	Autocar	Airviews
G–AJYL	Auster J/5	Auster Aircraft
G–AJYN	Autocar	J. V. Henz-Smith
G–AJYP	Auster 4	R. Pointer
G–AJYS	Avis 2	Auster Aircraft

Top : Short SOLENT. Largest of the supremely comfortable and reliable Short flying boats used by B.O.A.C., the Solents were used on the *Springbok* route to South Africa.

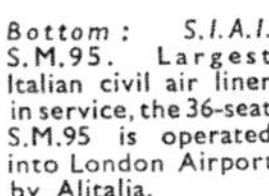

Centre : Handley Page HERMES V. This version of the Hermes, powered by four Theseus "propjets," is basically similar to the Hercules-engined Mark IV, twenty-five of which will be operated by B.O.A.C.

Bottom : S.I.A.I. S.M.95. Largest Italian civil air liner in service, the 36-seat S.M.95 is operated into London Airport by Alitalia.
(B.E.A. photo.)

Left : Bristol FREIGHTER Designed as a "utility" cargo-carrying aircraft without any frills, the Freighter set a new fashion with its large sideways-opening nose doors and capacious fuselage. G—AICM, shown here in Iran, is used by Hunting Aerosurveys for aerial photography.

Below : Vickers VISCOUNT· World's first "prop-jet"-powered air liner, the Viscount is in production for B.E.A. It will bring Rome within four hours of London, by cruising at up to 300 m.p.h.

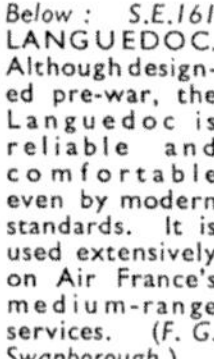

Below : S.E.161 LANGUEDOC. Although designed pre-war, the Languedoc is reliable and comfortable even by modern standards. It is used extensively on Air France's medium-range services. (F. G. Swanborough.)

Right : *Iliushin* IL–12
The IL–12. operated
by Czech Airlines, is
the only modern
Russian aeroplane
seen in this country
since the war.
(*F. G. Swanborough.*)

Left : *de Havilland*
DOVE. More than
300 of these little
8–11 seat air liners
are in service all over
the world.

Right : CONVAIR-
LINER. This 40-
passenger "twin"
is America's most
popular post-war
replacement for the
veteran Dakota.
(*K.L.M. photo.*)

Left : *Vickers*
VIKING. Mainstay of
B.E.A.'s fleet since
the war. The Viking
shown here is one of
four belonging to the
King's Flight.

Above : Short SEALAND. One of the most versatile aircraft flying, the little Sealand can be used as a passenger air liner, freighter or air ambulance, from land or water bases. (*Flight photo.*)

Below : Avro XIX. Developed from the R.A.F.'s Anson, and sharing that aircraft's superb tradition of safety and reliability, the Avro XIX is widely used by British charter companies.

Below: RAPIDE. popular lig built, the giving fine routes an 'plane. (B

Above : *Percival* PRINCE.
Designed as a light air liner
the Prince is used also as a
" flying class-room " by the
Royal Navy and, with modified nose, as shown here, for
air survey work.

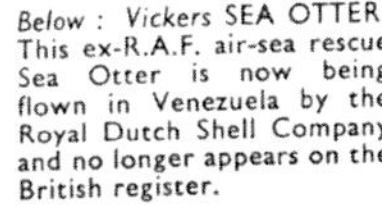

Below : *Vickers* SEA OTTER.
This ex-R.A.F. air-sea rescue
Sea Otter is now being
flown in Venezuela by the
Royal Dutch Shell Company
and no longer appears on the
British register.

Left: Douglas DC–3. World's most famous air liner, the DC–3 Dakota is still in large-scale service in every continent. Altogether, more than 10,000 of these aircraft were built, mostly during the war, when they were standard transport equipment of the Allied airborne armies. (*K.L.M. photo.*)

Right : Handley Page MARATHON I. Soon to go into service on B.E.A.'s shorter routes. G–ALVW is one of the more recent aircraft on register.

Below : Airspeed AMBASSADOR. Twenty of these graceful 49-seat air liners are on order for B.E.A.

Right : Auster AUTO-
CAR. Latest of the
well-known Auster
series of light 'planes,
the Autocar is
Britain's lowest-
priced four-seater.

Below : Chrislea
SUPER ACE. Tricycle
undercarriage and
twin fins and rudders
characterize the
Super Ace, many of
which have been ex-
ported since the war.
(John W. R. Taylor.)

Below : Miles MART-
LET and GEMINI.
First aircraft built by
F. G. Miles, the
biplane Martlet of
1929 is here seen in
flight with a twin-
engine Gemini, one
of the last and most
popular of the Miles
civil types. A Gemini
won the first post-
war race for the
King's Cup in 1949.

Above : *Auster* AUTOCRAT.
Most widely-used British light 'plane. The aircraft shown here is specially equipped with public address loud speakers and castering wheels, which enable it to land safely cross-wind.

Left : *Fairey* PRIMER.
Developed from a pre-war design of the Belgian Avions Fairey Company, the Primer has an unusual hood arrangement, giving an exceptional view from the rear cockpit.

Below : *Tipsy* TRAINER.
Another Avions Fairey design the Tipsy side-by-side two-seat Trainer is used by the Royal Naval Flying Club and several British private owners.

Registration	Type	Owner or Operator
G-AJZD	Dakota 3	British Nederland Airservices
G-AJZG	Aerovan 4	Culliford Airlines
G-AJZH	Hawk Trainer 3	P. J. McNamara
G-AJZJ	Gemini 1A	Air Schools
G-AJZL	Gemini 1A	M.C.A.
G-AJZN	Aerovan 4	Air Schools
G-AJZO	Gemini 1A	Whitbread & Co.
G-AJZS	Gemini 1A	J. J. Hofer
G-AJZT	Dove 2	H.H. Prince Aly Khan
G-AJZW	Viscount	Vickers-Armstrongs Ltd.
G-AJZX	Dakota 3	British Nederland Airservices
G-AJZY	Halifax 8	Lancashire Aircraft Corp.
G-AKAA	J-3C Cub	Airborne Taxi Services
G-AKAI	Messenger 2A	Harben Aviation
G-AKAJ	Lancaster I	Flight Refuelling
G-AKAK	Lancaster I	Flight Refuelling
G-AKAL	Lancaster I	Flight Refuelling
G-AKAM	Lancaster I	Flight Refuelling
G-AKAN	Messenger 2A	G. McLean
G-AKAO	Messenger 2A	E. G. Lamb
G-AKAP	Halifax 6	
G-AKAR	Dakota 4	Kearsley Airways
G-AKAS	Hawk Trainer 3	Essex Aero
G-AKAT	Hawk Trainer 3	Essex Aero
G-AKAU	Hawk Trainer 3	Essex Aero
G-AKAV	Messenger 2A	W. H. Byars
G-AKAX	Bucker Bu 181	O. F. Maclaren
G-AKAY	Dakota 3	Sivewright Airways
G-AKBE	Concordia I	Cunliffe-Owen Aircraft
G-AKBF	Prestwick Pioneer 2	Scottish Aviation
G-AKBG	Viking 1B	B.E.A.C. *Votary*
G-AKBH	Viking 1B	B.E.A.C. *Voyager*
G-AKBI	Halifax 3	Lancashire Aircraft Corp.
G-AKBK	Halifax 8	Lancashire Aircraft Corp.
G-AKBM	Messenger 2A	Plymouth & District Aero Club
G-AKBN	Messenger 2A	W. P. Bowles
G-AKBO	Messenger 2A	Air Schools
G-AKBR	Halifax 8	Eagle Aviation
G-AKBV	J-3C Cub	A. J. Walter
G-AKBZ	Tudor 5	B.O.A.C. *Star Falcon*
G-AKCA	Tudor 5	B.O.A.C. *Star Hawk*
G-AKCB	Tudor 5	B.O.A.C. *Star Kestrel*
G-AKCC	Tudor 5	William Dempster *President Kruger*
G-AKCD	Tudor 5	B.O.A.C. *Star Eagle*
G-AKCE	Constellation	B.O.A.C. *Bedford*
G-AKCF	Dove	B.O.A.C.
G-AKCG	Tiger Moth	Airwork
G-AKCH	Tiger Moth	Scottish Flying Club
G-AKCI	Tiger Moth	Scottish Flying Club
G-AKCJ	Argus I	Air Navigation & Trading Co.
G-AKCM	Tiger Moth	Airwork
G-AKCN	Messenger 2A	T. Shipside Ltd.
G-AKCO	Sandringham 7	B.O.A.C. *St. George*
G-AKCP	Sandringham 7	B.O.A.C. *St. David*
G-AKCR	Sandringham 7	B.O.A.C. *St. Andrew*
G-AKCS	Chipmunk	Loxhams Flying Services
G-AKCZ	Beech C/18-S	Britavia
G-AKDA	Gemini 1A	Patrick Duval Aviation

41

Registration	Type	Owner or Operator
G–AKDB	Gemini 1A	McCowan & Cross
G–AKDC	Gemini 3	J. N. Somers
G–AKDD	Gemini 1A	M.C.A.
G–AKDE	Gemini 1A	L. Roper
G–AKDF	Messenger 2A	Longford Engineering Co.
G–AKDG	Gemini 1A	S. E. Norman
G–AKDH	Gemini 1A	Field Aircraft Services
G–AKDI	Gemini 1A	P. P. Bradley
G–AKDJ	Gemini 1A	Hornton Airways
G–AKDK	Gemini 1A	W/Cdr. H. C. Kennard
G–AKDL	Gemini 1A	N. R. L. Urquhart
G–AKDM	Super Cruiser	E. C. S. Harper
G–AKDN	Chipmunk	de Havilland Aircraft Co.
G–AKDO	Lancastrian 4	⎫
G–AKDR	Lancastrian 4	⎬ Flight Refuelling
G–AKDS	Lancastrian 4	⎭
G–AKDT	Dakota 4	Kearsley Airways
G–AKDU	Avro 19	Secretary of State for Colonies
G–AKDV	Avro 19	Secretary of State for Colonies
G–AKDW	Dragon Rapide	Short Bros. & Harland
G–AKDX	Dragon Rapide	World Evangelisation Trust
G–AKDZ	Proctor 5	W. Stevens
G–AKEA	Proctor 5	N. King
G–AKEB	Proctor 5	William Wilson & Son
G–AKEC	Halifax 8	Lancashire Aircraft Corp.
G–AKED	Dragon Rapide	W. M. Andrews
G–AKEF	Proctor 4	E. R. Pyatt
G–AKEG	Gemini 1A	S. G. Newport
G–AKEH	Gemini 1A	H. H. E. M. Winch
G–AKEI	Gemini 1A	North Sea Air Transport
G–AKEJ	Gemini 1A	Ulster Aviation
G–AKEK	Gemini 1A	M. H. P. McAlpine
G–AKEL	Gemini 1A	D. Macartney-Filgate
G–AKEM	Gemini 1A	N. Rodnight
G–AKEN	Gemini 1A	C. R. Mauritzen
G–AKEP	Gemini 1A	Mayfair Air Services
G–AKER	Gemini 1A	Wallis & Linnell
G–AKES	Gemini 1A	T. Carlyle
G–AKET	Dove 1	Mrs. P. Churchill
G–AKEU	Dragon Rapide	Iraq Petroleum Transport Co.
G–AKEV	Chipmunk	de Havilland Aircraft Co.
G–AKEX	Proctor 1	H. C. V. Hext
G–AKEY	Slingsby T.29A	Slingsby Sailplanes
G–AKEZ	Messenger 2A	M. & H. Mining Contractors
G–AKFA	Bell 47 B3	B.E.A.C.
G–AKFB	Bell 47 B3	B.E.A.C.
G–AKFE	Avro 19/2	Secretary of State for Air
G–AKFF	Lancastrian 4	Flight Refuelling
G–AKFG	Lancastrian 4	Flight Refuelling
G–AKFK	Anson 1	Olds Discount Co.
G–AKFM	Anson 1	Finglands Airways
G–AKFN	Argus 2	L. D. Hawthorn
G–AKFO	Dragon Rapide	Southern Aircraft (Gatwick)
G–AKFP	Hermes 4	B.O.A.C. *Hamilcar*
G–AKFR	Proctor 4	Lancashire Aircraft Corp.
G–AKFS	Proctor 4	Lancashire Aircraft Corp.
G–AKFT	Proctor 4	Lancashire Aircraft Corp.
G–AKFU	Gemini 1A	West Midlands Erection Co.

146

Registration	Type	Owner or Operator
G–AKFX	Gemini IA	Western Manufacturing Estate
G–AKFY	Gemini IA	H. V. Kennedy
G–AKGA	Gemini IA	Air Charter
G–AKGC	Gemini IA	T. Shipside Ltd.
G–AKGD	Gemini IA	Sivewright Airways
G–AKGE	Gemini IA	Goodyear Tyre & Rubber Co. (G B.)
G–AKGF	Tiger Moth	London Transport (Central Buses) Sports Assoc.
G–AKGG	Tiger Moth	W. A. Rollason
G–AKGH	Stratocruiser	B.O.A.C. *Caledonia*
G–AKGI	Stratocruiser	B.O.A.C. *Caribou*
G–AKGJ	Stratocruiser	B.O.A.C. *Cambria*
G–AKGK	Stratocruiser	B.O.A.C. *Canopus*
G–AKGL	Stratocruiser	B.O.A.C. *Cabot*
G–AKGM	Stratocruiser	B.O.A.C. *Caster*
G–AKGN	Halifax 8	Chartair Ltd.
G–AKGO	Halifax 8	Airtech
G–AKGR	Hawk Trainer 3	Bournemouth Flying Club
G–AKGS	Hawk Trainer 3	Bournemouth Flying Club
G–AKGV	Dragon Rapide	William Dempster
G–AKGW	Argus	E. J. Farrow
G–AKGX	Dakota 3	Cyprus Airways
G–AKGY	Dragon Rapide	Manx Air Charters
G–AKHB	Gemini IA	R. E. Bibby
G–AKHC	Gemini IA	K. A. Hogan
G–AKHE	Gemini IA	W. Hutchinson
G–AKHF	Aerovan 6	Avia Britannia Corporation
G–AKHG	Aerovan 4	S. G. Newport
G–AKHJ	Gemini IA	Field Aircraft Services
G–AKHK	Gemini IA	Loxhams Flying Services
G–AKHP	Gemini IA	C. S. Thomas
G–AKHS	Gemini IA	Mrs. A. Leadbetter
G–AKHV	Gemini IA	W. T. Franklin
G–AKHW	Gemini IA	B.O.A.C.
G–AKHX	Gemini IA	Brooklands Aviation
G–AKHY	Gemini IA	Hon. M. A. R. Cayzer
G–AKHZ	Gemini IA	Pasolds
G–AKIA	Walrus 2	Ciro's Aviation
G–AKIC	Sea Otter	Ciro s Aviation
G–AKID	Sea Otter	Ciro's Aviation
G–AKIF	Dragon Rapide	Manx Air Charters
G–AKIG	Tiger Moth	D. Goldstein
G–AKIH	Proctor 5	Hon. E. H. K. Digby
G–AKII	Dakota 3	Cyprus Airways
G–AKIJ	Dakota 3	Cyprus Airways
G–AKIK	Dakota 3	Cyprus Airways
G–AKIL	Dakota 3	Air Transport (Charter) (C.I.)
G–AKIM	Messenger 2A	C. Screen
G–AKIN	Messenger 2A	A. J. Spiller
G–AKIO	Messenger 2A	Bidgood & Catton Taxi Planes
G–AKIR	Messenger 2A	P. Blamire
G–AKIS	Messenger 2A	Porter Spiers (Leicester)
G–AKIU	Proctor 5	Rolls-Royce
G–AKIW	Proctor 5	N. S. Norway
G–AKIX	Proctor 5	Shell Co. of Egypt
G–AKIY	Tiger Moth	Scottish Flying Club
G–AKIZ	Argus I	A. J. Walter
G–AKJA	Argus I	R. L. Whyham

43

Registration	Type	Owner or Operator
G–AKJD	Martin Hearn TQX–I	
G–AKJE	Walrus	Ciro's Aviation
G–AKJG	Dove 2	Silver City Airways
G–AKJH	Dakota 3	H.H. the Maharaja of Baroda
G–AKJL	Argus I	R. G. Kellett
G–AKJM	Argus I	W. S. Shackleton
G–AKJN	Dakota 3	Ciro's Aviation
G–AKJP	Dove 2	Silver City Airways
G–AKJR	Dove 2	Olley Air Service
G–AKJS	Dragon Rapide	Fairey Aviation Co.
G–AKJT	Auster 5	Wiltshire School of Flying
G–AKJU	Auster 5	Wiltshire School of Flying
G–AKJV	Hawk Trainer 3	Short Bros. & Harland
G–AKJX	Hawk Trainer 3	H. C. Kennard
G–AKJY	Dragon Rapide	Brooklands Aviation
G–AKJZ	Dragon Rapide	East Anglian Flying Services
G–AKKB	Gemini IA	F. Dunkerley
G–AKKC	Messenger 2A	J. M. Wilkinson
G–AKKF	Gemini IA	D. Ross
G–AKKG	Messenger 4A	Shell Mex & B.P.
G–AKKH	Gemini IA	S. Bourne & Co.
G–AKKI	Messenger 2A	J. Patson
G–AKKJ	Aerovan 4	
G–AKKK	Messenger 2A	Boston Air Transport
G–AKKL	Messenger 2A	Godfrey Holmes Ltd.
G–AKKN	Messenger 2A	P. S. Murphey
G–AKKO	Messenger 2A	T. Shipside Ltd.
G–AKKP	Halifax 9	Aviation Traders
G–AKKR	Hawk Trainer 3	
G–AKKS	Hawk Trainer 3	Airways Aero Assoc.
G–AKKU	Halifax 9	Aviation Traders
G–AKKV	Hawk Trainer 3	Airways Aero Assoc.
G–AKKW	Hawk Trainer 3	Airways Aero Assoc.
G–AKKX	Hawk Trainer 3	Airways Aero Assoc.
G–AKKY	Hawk Trainer 3	Airways Aero Assoc.
G–AKKZ	Hawk Trainer 3	Airways Aero Assoc.
G–AKLA	Dragon Rapide	Lancashire Aircraft Corp.
G–AKLB	Proctor 4	Lancashire Aircraft Corp
G–AKLD	Proctor 4	Lancashire Aircraft Corp
G–AKLG	Prentice I	Percival Aircraft
G–AKLL	Dakota 3	Hornton Airways
G–AKLN	Sealand I	Short Bros. & Harland
G–AKLO	Sealand	Short Bros. & Harland
G–AKLR	Sealand	Short Bros. & Harland
G–AKLS	Sealand	Short Bros. & Harland
G–AKLT	Sealand	Short Bros. & Harland
G–AKLU	Sealand	Short Bros. & Harland
G–AKLV	Sealand	Short Bros. & Harland
G–AKLW	Sealand	Short Bros. & Harland
G–AKLX	Sealand	Short Bros. & Harland
G–AKLZ	Sealand	Short Bros. & Harland
G–AKMA	Sealand	Short Bros. & Harland
G–AKMB	Auster 5	W. Brazier
G–AKMC	Auster 5	W. S. Shackleton
G–AKMD	Dragon Rapide	Aviation Traders
G–AKME	Dragon Rapide	Tyne Taxis
G–AKMF	Dragon Rapide	Mayfair Air Services
G–AKMG	Dragon Rapide	Sivewright Airways

Registration	Type	Owner or Operator
G-AKMH	Dragon Rapide	I.o.W. Flying Club
G-AKMI	Auster 5	P. L. Chadwick
G-AKMJ	Hawk Trainer 3	J. E. Tomlinson
G-AKMN	Hawk Trainer 3	L. D. Trappitt
G-AKMR	Hawk Trainer 3	L. D. Trappitt
G-AKMU	Hawk Trainer 3	C. J. de Vere
G-AKMV	Anson I	Airwork
G-AKMW	Lancastrian 2	Skyways
G-AKMX	Tiger Moth	Herts & Essex Aero Club
G-AKMY	Hawk Trainer 3	Herts & Essex Aero Club
G-AKMZ	Hawk Trainer 3	Herts & Essex Aero Club
G-AKNA	Hawk Trainer 3	Herts & Essex Aero Club
G-AKNE	Dragon Rapide	M. L. Thomas
G-AKNF	Dragon Rapide	Airlines (Jersey)
G-AKNG	Halifax 6	Lancashire Aircraft Corp.
G-AKNH	Halifax 6	Lancashire Aircraft Corp.
G-AKNI	Halifax 6	Lancashire Aircraft Corp.
G-AKNK	Halifax 6	Lancashire Aircraft Corp.
G-AKNL	Halifax 6	Lancashire Aircraft Corp.
G-AKNM	Dakota 4	Scottish Aviation
G-AKNN	Dragon Rapide	Astral Aviation
G-AKNO	Solent 3	M.C.A. *City of London*
G-AKNP	Solent 3	M.C.A. *City of Cardiff*
G-AKNR	Solent 3	M.C.A. *City of Belfast*
G-AKNS	Solent 3	M.C.A. *City of Liverpool*
G-AKNT	Solent 3	M.C.A.
G-AKNU	Solent 3	M.C.A.
G-AKNV	Dragon Rapide	Lancashire Aircraft Corp.
G-AKNW	Dragon Rapide	R. L. Whyham
G-AKNX	Dragon Rapide	Patrick Motors
G-AKNY	Dragon Rapide	Patrick Motors
G-AKOA	Dragon Rapide	Patrick Motors
G-AKOB	Dragon Rapide	Air Enterprises
G-AKOD	Dragon Rapide	Lancashire Aircraft Corp.
G-AKOE	Dragon Rapide	Lancashire Aircraft Corp.
G-AKOF	Dragon Rapide	Mannin Airways
G-AKOG	Dragon Rapide	Aviation Traders
G-AKOH	Dragon Rapide	Mannin Airways
G-AKOK	Dragon Rapide	Mannin Airways
G-AKOL	Hawk Trainer 3	S. R. C. Partridge
G-AKOM	Dragon Rapide	Southern Aircraft (Gatwick)
G-AKOO	Dragon Rapide	Southern Aircraft (Gatwick)
G-AKOR	Dragon Rapide	Morton Air Services
G-AKOT	Auster 5	A. D. Daly
G-AKOU	Auster 5	C. F. Westley
G-AKOV	Dragon Rapide	Inter-City Air Services
G-AKOW	Auster 5	J. Small
G-AKOX	Auster 5	N. C. Anderson
G-AKOY	Dragon Rapide	Lancashire Aircraft Corp.
G-AKOZ	Dakota 4	Kearsley Airways
G-AKPA	Dragon Rapide	Newman Aircraft Co.
G-AKPE	Hawk Trainer 3	D. C. Jennett
G-AKPF	Hawk Trainer 3	Wards Motolympia
G-AKPG	Hawk Trainer 3	Wolverhampton Flying School
G-AKPH	Auster 5	N. B. Ewing
G-AKPI	Auster 5	J. F. Onions
G-AKPJ	Auster 5	D. Everall
G-AKPL	Hawk Trainer 3	Eagle Aviation

45

Registration	Type	Owner or Operator
G-AKPM	Hawk Trainer 3	W/Cmdr. H. C. Kennard
G-AKPX	Argus	R. L. Whyham
G-AKRC	Auster 5	J. Nicholson
G-AKRD	Ambassador	M.o.S.
G-AKRF	Sea Otter	R. L. Whyham
G-AKRG	Sea Otter	R. L. Whyham
G-AKRH	Hawk Trainer 3	S. J. Bartlam
G-AKRM	Hawk Trainer 3	B. A. G. Woodwards
G-AKRN	Dragon Rapide	East Anglian Flying Services
G-AKRO	Dragon Rapide	Inter-City Air Services
G-AKRP	Dragon Rapide	Short Bros. & Harland
G-AKRR	Dragon Rapide	Short Bros. & Harland
G-AKRS	Dragon Rapide	Air Enterprises
G-AKRT	Hawk Trainer 3	Short Bros. & Harland
G-AKRU	Hawk Trainer 3	Short Bros. & Harland
G-AKRV	Hawk Trainer 3	E. Day
G-AKRW	Hawk Trainer 3	Short Bros. & Harland
G-AKRX	Sea Otter	B.O.A.C.
G-AKSC	Dragon Rapide	Demolition & Construction
G-AKSD	Dragon Rapide	Windmill Theatre Transport Co.
G-AKSE	Dragon Rapide	Manx Air Charter
G-AKSG	Dragon Rapide	R. L. Whyham
G-AKSH	Dragon Rapide	Brooklands Aviation
G-AKSI	Auster 5	British Air Transport
G-AKSJ	Auster 5	
G-AKSK	Dove 1	Olley Air Services
G-AKSL	Dragon Rapide	Goodhew Aviation
G-AKSM	Dakota 3	Sivewright Airways
G-AKSN	Lancastrian 2	Skyways *Sky Consort*
G-AKSO	Lancastrian 2	Skyways *Sky Kingdom*
G-AKSS	Dove 1	British Air Transport
G-AKST	Dove 1	Skyways
G-AKSV	Dove 1	de Havilland Aircraft Co.
G-AKSW	Dove 2	Enfield Rolling Mills
G-AKSY	Auster 5	P. H. I. Jones
G-AKSZ	Auster 5	A. Robinson
G-AKTA	Auster 5	J. D. Hamilton
G-AKTB	Lancastrian 2	Flight Refuelling
G-AKTD	Dragon Rapide	Air Couriers
G-AKTF	Auster 5	Lancashire Aircraft Corp.
G-AKTU	Viking 1B	Airwork
G-AKTV	Viking 1B	Airwork
G-AKTW	Westland S-51	Westland Aircraft
G-AKTX	Dragon Rapide	Mayfair Air Services
G-AKTY	Dragon Rapide	Herts & Essex Aero Club
G-AKTZ	Dragon Rapide	Airwork
G-AKUA	Hawk Trainer 3	Fairey Aviation Co.
G-AKUB	Dragon Rapide	J. H. Watts & Ptns.
G-AKUC	Dragon Rapide	S. K. Davies
G-AKUD	Avro 19	M.o.S.
G-AKUS	Dragon Rapide	Mayfair Air Services
G-AKUV	Super Ace	Chrislea Aircraft Co.
G-AKUW	Super Ace	F. G. Ford (Estates)
G-AKUX	Super Ace	Enterprise Aviation Services
G-AKVA	Super Ace	Autowork (Winchester)

Registration	Type	Owner or Operator
G-AKVB	Super Ace	Chrislea Aircraft Co.
G-AKVC	Super Ace	Chrislea Aircraft Co.
G-AKVD	Super Ace	Autocars (Worcs.)
G-AKVE	Super Ace	Chrislea Aircraft Co.
G-AKVF	Super Ace	Chrislea Aircraft Co.
G-AKVG	Super Ace	Chrislea Aircraft Co.
G-AKVH	Super Ace	Chrislea Aircraft Co.
G-AKVI	Super Ace	Chrislea Aircraft Co.
G-AKVJ	Super Ace	Chrislea Aircraft Co.
G-AKVK	Super Ace	Chrislea Aircraft Co.
G-AKVL	Super Ace	Chrislea Aircraft Co.
G-AKVM	Super Ace	Chrislea Aircraft Co.
G-AKVN	Super Ace	Chrislea Aircraft Co.
G-AKVO	Super Ace	Chrislea Aircraft Co.
G-AKVP	Super Ace	Chrislea Aircraft Co.
G-AKVR	Super Ace	Chrislea Aircraft Co.
G-AKVS	Skyjeep	Chrislea Aircraft Co.
G-AKVT	Super Ace	Chrislea Aircra't Co.
G-AKVU	Dragon Rapide	Patrick Motors
G-AKVV	Proctor 1	D. Goldstein
G-AKVW	Anson 1	British Air Transport
G-AKVZ	Messenger 4A	Thomas Ratcliffe & Co.
G-AKWA	Sea Otter 2	B.O.A.C.
G-AKWE	Proctor 3	C. M. Chown
G-AKWF	Proctor 3	Morton Air Services
G-AKWH	Auster 5	Miss B. L. Duthy
G-AKWI	Auster 5	British Air Transport
G-AKWJ	Proctor 3	A. L. McLeod
G-AKWK	Auster 5	Furze Hill Laboratories
G-AKWL	Proctor 4	Southend Municipal Council
G-AKWM	Proctor 3	Aikman Airways
G-AKWN	Proctor 3	Aikman Airways
G-AKWO	Proctor 3	Lord Malcolm Douglas-Hamilton
G-AKWP	Proctor 3	Aikman Airways
G-AKWR	Proctor 3	Aikman Airways
G-AKWS	Auster 5	R. G. Banks
G-AKWT	Auster 5	V. G. Manton
G-AKWU	Proctor 3	International Air Exports
G-AKWV	Proctor 3	J. P. Crowther
G-AKWY	Tiger Moth	Isle of Wight Flying Club
G-AKXC	Tiger Moth	B. J. Doyle
G-AKXD	Tiger Moth	Mrs. L. K. King
G-AKXG	Tiger Moth	W. A. Rollason
G-AKXH	Tiger Moth	Surrey Financial Trust
G-AKXI	Proctor 3	G. M. Bowles-Evans
G-AKXJ	Proctor 3	E. R. Hill
G-AKXK	Proctor 3	Inter-City Air Services
G-AKXL	Proctor 3	Surrey Financial Trust
G-AKXO	Tiger Moth	Midland Aero Club
G-AKXP	Auster 5	Air Service Training
G-AKXR	Auster 5	Air Service Training
G-AKXS	Tiger Moth	Air Service Training
G-AKXT	Halifax 8	Lancashire Aircraft Corp.
G-AKXU	Tiger Moth	Air Service Training
G-AKXV	Tiger Moth	Air Service Training
G-AKXW	Anson 1	Air Service Training
G-AKXZ	Proctor 3	P. W. Bayliss
G-AKYA	Proctor 5	Percival Aircraft

Registration	Type	Owner or Operator
G-AKYB	Proctor 5	Lancashire Aircraft Corp.
G-AKYC	Proctor 5	L. S. Dawson
G-AKYD	Proctor 5	Gloster Aircraft Co.
G-AKYG	Proctor 3	R. L. Whyham
G-AKYH	Sea Otter	R. L. Whyham
G-AKYJ	Proctor 4	Lancashire Aircraft Corp.
G-AKYK	Proctor 4	Lancashire Aircraft Corp.
G-AKYL	Tiger Moth	Scottish Flying Club
G-AKYM	Tiger Moth	Scottish Flying Club
G-AKYN	Tiger Moth	Adie Aviation
G-AKYP	Tiger Moth	Adie Aviation
G-AKYR	Tiger Moth	Cardiff Aeroplane Club
G-AKYS	Dove 2	David Brown & Sons (Huddersfield)
G-AKYT	Auster 5	C. G. Wheatley
G-AKYU	Auster 5	H. Mitchell
G-AKZB	Dragon Rapide	B.E.A.C.
G-AKZC	Messenger 4A	Wolverhampton Aviation
G-AKZD	Proctor 3	
G-AKZE	Proctor 3	R. L. Whyham
G-AKZF	Proctor 3	R. L. Whyham
G-AKZG	Proctor 3	D. E. Barton
G-AKZH	Dragon Rapide	Herts & Essex Aero Club
G-AKZI	Dragon Rapide	Mayfai rAir Services
G-AKZJ	Dragon Rapide	Mediterranean Air Services
G-AKZK	Tiger Moth	Air Service Training
G-AKZL	Tiger Moth	Air Service Training
G-AKZM	Tiger Moth	Air Service Training
G-AKZN	Proctor 3	Air Service Training
G-AKZO	Dragon Rapide	J. Nesbit-Evans & Co.
G-AKZP	Dragon Rapide	E. Holden
G-AKZR	Proctor 3	Hyland Ltd.
G-AKZS	Proctor 3	Hyland Ltd.
G-AKZT	Dragon Rapide	R. L. Whyham
G-AKZU	Messenger 4A	Morgan Aviation
G-AKZW	Dragon Rapide	H. A. E. Towle
G-AKZX	Messenger 4A	N. M. Browning
G-AKZY	Me 108 D–I	Air Couriers
G-AKZZ	Messenger 4A	N. M. Browning
G-ALAA	Proctor 5	Percival Aircraft
G-ALAB	Proctor 5	Percival Aircraft
G-ALAC	Proctor 5	Percival Aircraft
G-ALAD	Proctor 5	Percival Aircraft
G-ALAE	Messenger 4A	E. W. Wagner
G-ALAF	Messenger 4A	E. J. Morton
G-ALAG	Messenger 4A	J. C. Rice
G-ALAH	Messenger 4A	E. P. Jenks
G-ALAI	Messenger 4A	L. W. Hamp
G-ALAJ	Messenger 4A	L. W. Farrer
G-ALAK	Constellation	B.O.A.C. *Brentford*
G-ALAL	Constellation	B.O.A.C. *Banbury*
G-ALAM	Constellation	B.O.A.C. *Belfast*
G-ALAN	Constellation	B.O.A.C. *Beaufort*
G-ALAO	Constellation	B.O.A.C. *Braemar*
G-ALAP	Messenger 4A	Porter Spiers (Leics.)
G-ALAR	Messenger 4A	T. W. Leadbetter
G-ALAT	Dragon Rapide	J. H. Watts & Ptns.
G-ALAV	Messenger 4A	N. B. Neaum
G-ALAW	Messenger 4A	Skegness Steam Laundry Co.

Registration	Type	Owner or Operator
G–ALAX	Dragon Rapide	Saunders-Roe
G–ALBA	Dragon Rapide	R. A. Gunton
G–ALBB	Dragon Rapide	E. A. Taylor
G–ALBC	Dragon Rapide	M. H. D. McAlpine
G–ALBD	Tiger Moth	College of Aeronautics
G–ALBE	Messenger 4A	E. W. Westbrook
G–ALBF	Dove I	Iraq Petroleum Transport Co.
G–ALBH	Dragon Rapide	Scottish Aviation
G–ALBJ	Auster 5	V. G. Manton
G–ALBK	Auster 5	V. G. Manton
G–ALBL	Primer	Fairey Aviation Co.
G–ALBM	Dove I	de Havilland Aircraft Co.
G–ALBN	Bristol 173	M.o.S.
G–ALBO	Bristol 175	Bristol Aeroplane Co.
G–ALBP	Messenger 4A	J. E. Nicholson
G–ALBS	Halifax 8	Hyland Automobiles
G–ALBT	Halifax 8	Hyland Automobiles
G–ALBU	Halifax 8	Hyland Automobiles
G–ALBV	Halifax 8	Hyland Automobiles
G–ALBW	Auster 5	Photoflight
G–ALCB	Dakota 3	B.E.A.C.
G–ALCC	Dakota 3	B.E.A.C.
G–ALCD	Dakota 3	
G–ALCH	Proctor 3	Lancashire Aircraft Corp.
G–ALCJ	Proctor 3	Lancashire Aircraft Corp.
G–ALCK	Proctor 3	Lancashire Aircraft Corp.
G–ALCL	Proctor 3	W. Jamison
G–ALCM	Prince I	Percival Aircraft
G–ALCN	Proctor 3	R. Watson
G–ALCO	Proctor 3	
G–ALCP	Proctor 3	
G–ALCR	Proctor 3	C. W. J. Allen
G–ALCS	Gemini 3A	Claremont Shipping Co.
G–ALCT	Auster 5	
G–ALCU	Dove 2	E. P. Jenks Ltd.
G–ALCW	Air Horse	M.o.S.
G–ALCX	Halifax 8	Lancashire Aircraft Corp.
G–ALCY	Halifax 3	
G–ALCZ	Halifax 3	
G–ALDA	Hermes 4	B.O.A.C. *Hecuba*
G–ALDB	Hermes 4	B.O.A.C. *Hebe*
G–ALDC	Hermes 4	B.O.A.C. *Hermione*
G–ALDD	Hermes 4	B.O.A.C. *Hannibal*
G–ALDE	Hermes 4	B.O.A.C. *Hanno*
G–ALDF	Hermes 4	B.O.A.C. *Hadrian*
G–ALDG	Hermes 4	B.O.A.C. *Horsa*
G–ALDH	Hermes 4	B.O.A.C. *Heracles*
G–ALDI	Hermes 4	B.O.A.C. *Horatius*
G–ALDJ	Hermes 4	B.O.A.C. *Hengist*
G–ALDK	Hermes 4	B.O.A.C. *Helena*
G–ALDL	Hermes 4	B.O.A.C. *Hector*
G–ALDM	Hermes 4	B.O.A.C. *Hero*
G–ALDN	Hermes 4	B.O.A.C. *Horus*
G–ALDO	Hermes 4	B.O.A.C. *Heron*
G–ALDP	Hermes 4	B.O.A.C. *Homer*
G–ALDR	Hermes 4	B.O.A.C. *Herodotus*
G–ALDS	Hermes 4	B.O.A.C. *Hesperides*
G–ALDT	Hermes 4	B.O.A.C. *Hesta*

49

Registration	Type	Owner or Operator
G-ALDU	Hermes 4	B.O.A.C. *Halcyone*
G-ALDV	Hermes 4	B.O.A.C. *Hera*
G-ALDW	Hermes 4	B.O.A.C. *Helios*
G-ALDX	Hermes 4	B.O.A.C. *Hyperion*
G-ALDY	Hermes 4	B.O.A.C. *Honor*
G-ALDZ	Halifax 3	
G-ALEA	Halifax 3	
G-ALEB	Halifax 3	
G-ALEC	Halifax 3	
G-ALED	Halifax 3	
G-ALEE	Halifax 3	
G-ALEF	Halifax 8	Eagle Aviation
G-ALEG	Westland S.51/1A	Pest Control
G-ALEI	Westland S.51/1	Pest Control
G-ALEJ	Dragon Rapide	Lancashire Aircraft Corp.
G-ALEM	Anson 1	
G-ALEN	Anson 1	
G-ALEO	Proctor 4	
G-ALEP	Skymaster	Mining & Exploration Air Services
G-ALER	Proctor 3	R. C. Preston
G-ALES	Proctor 3	
G-ALET	Dragon Rapide	Mannin Airways
G-ALEU	Hermes 5	M.o.S.
G-ALEV	Hermes 5	M.o.S.
G-ALEX	Proctor 4	
G-ALEY	Auster 5	J. M. Sykes
G-ALEZ	Dakota	
G-ALFA	Auster 5	A. Harrison
G-ALFB	Proctor 3	Silver City Airways
G-ALFC	Proctor 3	
G-ALFD	Anson	
G-ALFE	Hawk Trainer 3	H. J. C. Turner
G-ALFF	Proctor 3	G. Cribb
G-ALFG	Tiger Moth	Short Bros. & Harland
G-ALFH	Hawk Trainer 3	Airways Aero Assoc.
G-ALFI	Hawk Trainer 3	Airways Aero Assoc.
G-ALFK	Proctor 3	C. M. Chown
G-ALFN	Avro 19/2	Secretary of State for Air
G-ALFO	Dakota 3	The Zinc Corporation
G-ALFP	Anson 1	Finglands Airways
G-ALFR	Ambassador	Airspeed Ltd.
G-ALFS	Proctor 3	B. H. Hurle-Hobbs
G-ALFT	Dove 2	M.C.A.
G-ALFU	Dove 2	M.C.A.
G-ALFV	Proctor 3	
G-ALFW	Proctor 3	
G-ALFX	Proctor 3	Autocars (Worcs.)
G-ALFY	Proctor 3	
G-ALFZ	Prince 1	Percival Aircraft
G-ALGA	Kirby Kitten	Airways Aero Assoc.
G-ALGB	Dragon Rapide 2	R. H. Braime & Ptns.
G-ALGC	Dragon Rapide 2	A. R. Pilgrim
G-ALGE	Dragon Rapide 2	Melba Airways
G-ALGG	Proctor 3	
G-ALGH	J-3C Cub	H. Tinsley

Registration	Type	Owner or Operator
G-ALGI	Dragon Rapide 2	W. Westoby
G-ALGJ	Hawk Trainer 3	W. L. Foster
G-ALGK	Hawk Trainer 3	Short Bros. & Harland
G-ALGL	Proctor 4	R. L. Whyham
G-ALGM	Dragon Rapide	Adie Aviation
G-ALGN	Dragon Rapide	Adie Aviation
G-ALGO	Dragon Rapide	Anglo-Iranian Oil Co.
G-ALGP	Proctor 3	Adie Aviation
G-ALGR	Proctor 3	Adie Aviation
G-ALGS	Proctor 3	G. P. Reece
G-ALGT	Spitfire 14	Rolls-Royce
G-ALGU	Mosquito 19	Flight Refuelling
G-ALGV	Mosquito 19	Flight Refuelling
G-ALGW	Auster 6	K. V. Nelson
G-ALGX	Tiger Moth	H. B. Showell
G-ALGY	Proctor 3	T. G. Henderson
G-ALGZ	Hawk Trainer 3	Sqdn. Ldr. Nalson
G-ALHA	Hawk Trainer 3	Sqdn. Ldr. Nalson
G-ALHB	Hawk Trainer 3	Sqdn. Ldr. Nalson
G-ALHC	Canadair Four	B.O.A.C. Ariadne
G-ALHD	Canadair Four	B.O.A.C. Ajax
G-ALHE	Canadair Four	B.O.A.C. Argo
G-ALHF	Canadair Four	B.O.A.C. Atlas
G-ALHG	Canadair Four	B.O.A.C. Aurora
G-ALHH	Canadair Four	B.O.A.C. Attica
G-ALHI	Canadair Four	B.O.A.C. Antares
G-ALHJ	Canadair Four	B.O.A.C. Arcturus
G-ALHK	Canadair Four	B.O.A.C. Atalanta
G-ALHL	Canadair Four	B.O.A.C. Altair
G-ALHM	Canadair Four	B.O.A.C. Antaeus
G-ALHN	Canadair Four	B.O.A.C. Argosy
G-ALHO	Canadair Four	B.O.A.C. Amazon
G-ALHP	Canadair Four	B.O.A.C. Aethra
G-ALHR	Canadair Four	B.O.A.C. Antiope
G-ALHS	Canadair Four	B.O.A.C. Astra
G-ALHT	Canadair Four	B.O.A.C. Athena
G-ALHU	Canadair Four	B.O.A.C. Artemis
G-ALHV	Canadair Four	B.O.A.C. Adonis
G-ALHW	Canadair Four	B.O.A.C. Aeolus
G-ALHX	Canadair Four	B.O.A.C. Astroea
G-ALHY	Canadair Four	B.O.A.C. Arion
G-ALHZ	Anson 10	R. L. Whyham
G-ALIA	Anson 10	R. L. Whyham
G-ALIB	Anson 10	R. L. Whyham
G-ALIC	Anson 10	R. L. Whyham
G-ALID	Anson 11	R. L. Whyham
G-ALIE	Anson 11	R. L. Whyham
G-ALIF	Anson 11	R. L. Whyham
G-ALIG	Anson 11	R. L. Whyham
G-ALIH	Anson 11	R. L. Whyham
G-ALII	Anson 11	R. L. Whyham
G-ALIJ	Seaford	R. L. Whyham
G-ALIK	Westland S.51/1A	Westland Aircraft
G-ALIM	Hawk Trainer 3	Short Bros. & Harland
G-ALIN	Hawk Trainer 3	Short Bros. & Harland
G-ALIO	Hawk Trainer 3	Maj. Gen. J. E. C. McCandlish
G-ALIP	Hawk Trainer 3	Short Bros. & Harland
G-ALIR	Halifax 9	Aviation Traders

Registration	Type	Owner or Operator
G–ALIS	Proctor 3	W. A. Stuart
G–ALIT	Proctor 3	B. C. Barton & Son
G–ALIU	Tiger Moth	Wolverhampton Flying Club
G–ALIV	Tiger Moth	Wolverhampton Flying Club
G–ALIX	Tiger Moth	London Aeroplane Club
G–ALIY	Tiger Moth	Derby Aviation
G–ALJA	Prince 1	Percival Aircraft
G–ALJB	Auster 5	A. E. Morris
G–ALJC	Auster 5	Darlington & District Aero Club
G–ALJD	Auster 5	Darlington & District Aero Club
G–ALJE	Auster 4	Darlington & District Aero Club
G–ALJF	Proctor 3	Darlington & District Aero Club
G–ALJH	Proctor 3	S. N. Dennis
G–ALJI	Proctor 3	Central Aeronautical Bureau
G–ALJJ	Beech Model 18S	
G–ALJK	Proctor 3	L. K. Jackson
G–ALJL	Tiger Moth	Air Service Training
G–ALKA	Auster	
G–ALKB	Auster	
G–ALKC	Auster	
G–ALKD	Auster	
G–ALKE	Auster	
G–ALKF	Auster	
G–ALKG	Auster	
G–ALKH	Auster	
G–ALKI	Auster 5C	A. H. Wheeler
G–ALKK	Auster 5	
G–ALKL	Westland S–51	Westland Aircraft
G–ALLI	Dakota 3	B.E.A.C.
G–ALLK	Drover	de Havilland Aircraft Co.
G–ALMA	J–3C Cub	E. N. Haywood
G–ALMB	Westland S–51	Westland Aircraft
G–ALMC	Westland S–51	Westland Aircraft
G–ALMD	Westland S–51	Westland Aircraft
G–ALMR	Dove 2	de Havilland Aircraft Co.
G–ALMS	Proctor 3	T. A. Menzies
G–ALNA	Tiger Moth	Bembridge and Sandown Aero Club
G–ALND	Tiger Moth	Air Service Training
G–ALNS	Dragon Rapide	W. Hutchinson
G–ALNT	Dragon Rapide	W. Hutchinson
G–ALNU	Auster 5	
G–ALNV	Auster 5	Tattersalls Garages
G–ALNW	Auster 5	
G–ALNX	Hawk Trainer 3	R. A. Short
G–ALNY	Hawk Trainer 3	R. A. Short
G–ALNZ	Hawk Trainer 3	R. A. Short
G–ALOA	Hawk Trainer 3	R. A. Short
G–ALOB	Hawk Trainer 3	R. A. Short
G–ALOC	Hawk Trainer 3	R. A. Short
G–ALOE	Hawk Trainer 3	R. A. Short
G–ALOF	Hawk Trainer 3	R. A. Short
G–ALOG	Hawk Trainer 3	D. M. Brown
G–ALOH	Hawk Trainer 3	
G–ALOI	Satellite	Planet Aircraft
G–ALOJ	Proctor	
G–ALOK	Proctor 3	Miss B. John
G–ALOL	Proctor	
G–ALOM	Halifax 6	Aviation Traders

Above : *Percival* PROCTOR. Best-known of the excellent Percival sporting and touring 'planes, the Proctor is a comfortable, high-performance four-seater, widely used both privately and by the R.A.F.

Right : *Aeronca* 100. One of the smallest British aircraft, the ultra-light Aeronca 100 is powered by a 36 h.p. J.A.P. engine (*John W. R. Taylor.*)

Below : *Vickers* SPITFIRE TRAINER. Two-seat training version of the famous Spitfire fighter. G–AIDN is Vickers' demonstration model. (*F. G. Swanborough.*)

Top : Sopwith PUP. Oldest aircraft on the register, this Sopwith Pup, built in 1916, is still used in aerobatic displays.

Centre : de Havilland TIGER MOTH. Most of the R.A.F.'s wartime pilots completed their early training on "Tigers," which are still used extensively for sporting and club flying.

Bottom : Miles MESSENGER. Single-engined counterpart of the Gemini, which was developed from the Messenger. Both aircraft feature prominent high-lift wing flaps, which enable them to land and take off in restricted spaces.

Registration	Type	Owner or Operator
G–ALON	Halifax 9	Aviation Traders
G–ALOS	Halifax 9	Aviation Traders
G–ALOU	Bristol 171/1	M.o.S.
G–ALOV	Dragon Rapide	Short Bros. & Harland
G–ALOW	Beaver	de Havilland Aircraft Co.
G–ALOX	Tiger Moth	Airways Aero. Assoc.
G–ALPF	Lincoln 2	Airtech
G–ALPK	Dragon Rapide	Lancashire Aircraft Corp.
G–ALPM	Douglas DC–3	
G–ALPN	Douglas DC–3	
G–ALRW	Dragon Rapide	Cambrian Air Services
G–ALRX	Bristol 175	Bristol Aeroplane Co.
G–ALRY	Prince P.54	Hunting Aerosurveys
G–ALSA	Stratocruiser	B.O.A.C. *Cathay*
G–ALSB	Stratocruiser	B.O.A.C. *Champion*
G–ALSC	Stratocruiser	B.O.A.C. *Centaurus*
G–ALSD	Stratocruiser	B.O.A.C. *Cassiopeia*
G–ALSH	Tiger Moth	Wiltshire School of Flying
G–ALSK	Halifax 9	Aviation Traders
G–ALSL	Halifax 9	Aviation Traders
G–ALSM	Proctor 3	L. W. Watkins
G–ALSP	Bristol 171/3	Bristol Aeroplane Co
G–ALSR	Bristol 171/3	Bristol Aeroplane Co.
G–ALSS	Bristol 171/3	Bristol Aeroplane Co.
G–ALST	Bristol 171/3	Bristol Aeroplane Co.
G–ALSU	Bristol 171/3	Bristol Aeroplane Co.
G–ALSV	Bristol 171/3	Bristol Aeroplane Co.
G–ALSW	Bristol 171/3	Bristol Aeroplane Co.
G–ALSX	Bristol 171/3	Bristol Aeroplane Co.
G–ALSY	Bristol 171/3	Bristol Aeroplane Co.
G–ALSZ	Bristol 171/3	Bristol Aeroplane Co.
G–ALTA	Bristol 171/3	Bristol Aeroplane Co.
G–ALTB	Bristol 171/3	Bristol Aeroplane Co.
G–ALTC	Bristol 171/3	Bristol Aeroplane Co.
G–ALTD	Bristol 171/3	Bristol Aeroplane Co.
G–ALTE	Bristol 171/3	Bristol Aeroplane Co.
G–ALTF	Proctor 3	
G–ALTG	Proctor 3	
G–ALTM	Dove 2	B.O.A.C.
G–ALTP	Oxford I	Air Service Training
G–ALTR	Oxford I	Air Service Training
G–ALTT	Dakota 3	B.E.A.C.
G–ALTW	Tiger Moth	F. B. Scott
G–ALTX	Sea Otter	
G–ALTZ	Consul	B.O.A.C. *Star Monitor*
G–ALUA	Zaunkoenig	U.L.A.A.
G–ALUB	Marathon I	Handley Page (Reading)
G–ALUC	Tiger Moth	W. A. Webb
G–ALUE	Autocrat	J. M. Heathcoty
G–ALUF	Skeeter 2	Cierva Autogiro Co.
G–ALUG	Gemini IA	J. P. G. Daly
G–ALUI	Proctor 3	
G–ALUJ	Proctor 3	
G–ALUK	Proctor 3	
G–ALUM	Anson I	Transair
G–ALUN	Princess	M.o.S.
G–ALUO	Princess	M.o.S.
G–ALUP	Princess	M.o.S.

Registration	Type	Owner or Operator
G-ALUR	Anson 1	Aviation Traders
G-ALUS	Anson 1	Aviation Traders
G-ALUT	Halifax 9	Aviation Traders
G-ALUU	Halifax 9	Aviation Traders
G-ALUV	Halifax 9	Aviation Traders
G-ALUW	Hawk Trainer 3	W. A. Rollason
G-ALUX	Hawk Trainer 3	W. A. Rollason
G-ALUY	Proctor 3	
G-ALUZ	Luton Minor	
G-ALVA	Proctor 3	
G-ALVC	Lancaster 7	Eagle Aviation
G-ALVD	Dove 2	Dunlop Rubber Co.
G-ALVE	Proctor 3	
G-ALVF	Lodestar	
G-ALVG	Comet	M.o.S.
G-ALVP	Tiger Moth	R. Pointer
G-ALVR	J–3C Cub	A. J. Walter
G-ALVS	Dove 2	M.C.A.
G-ALVT	Dove 2	M.C.A.
G-ALVU	Dragon Rapide	C. G. S. Whyham
G-ALVV	Auster 5	C. G. S. Whyham
G-ALVW	Marathon 1	Handley Page (Reading)
G-ALVX	Marathon 1	Handley Page (Reading)
G-ALVY	Marathon 1	Handley Page (Reading)
G-ALVZ	Dakota	Crewsair
G-ALWA	Athena 2	M.o.S.
G-ALWB	Chipmunk	de Havilland Aircraft Co.
G-ALWC	Dakota 3	Airtech
G-ALWD	Dakota 3	Airtech
G-ALWE	Viscount	Vickers-Armstrongs
G-ALWF	Viscount	Vickers-Armstrongs
G-ALWI	Dragon Rapide	Short Bros. & Harland
G-ALWJ	Dragon Rapide	Short Bros. & Harland
G-ALWK	Dragon Rapide	R. C. Cox
G-ALWL	Dragon Rapide	V. H. Bellamy
G-ALWM	Dragon Rapide	V. H. Bellamy
G-ALWN	Dragon Rapide	V. H. Bellamy
G-ALWO	Dragon Rapide	Wealey & Nash
G-ALWP	Dragon Rapide	Allen Aircraft Services
G-ALWR	Proctor 1	Air Service Training
G-ALWS	Tiger Moth	Air Service Training
G-ALWT	Tiger Moth	Air Service Training
G-ALWU	Tiger Moth	Air Service Training
G-ALWV	Tiger Moth	Air Service Training
G-ALWW	Tiger Moth	Air Service Training
G-ALWX	Anson	Air Enterprises
G-ALWY	Dragon Rapide	Air Enterprises
G-ALXA	Dragon Rapide	Darlington & Dist. Aero Club
G-ALXB	Anson 1	Transair
G-ALXC	Anson 1	Transair
G-ALXD	Anson 1	Transair
G-ALXE	Anson 1	Transair
G-ALXF	Anson 1	Mrs. D. Whyham
G-ALXG	Anson 1	Mrs. D. Whyham
G-ALXH	Anson 1	Mrs. D. Whyham

160

Registration	Type	Owner or Operator
G–ALXI	Dragon Rapide	Mrs. D. Whyham
G–ALXJ	Dragon Rapide	Mrs. D Whyham
G–ALXK	Dakota 4	B.E.A.C.
G–ALXL	Dakota 4	B.E.A.C.
G–ALXM	Dakota 4	B.E.A.C.
G–ALXN } G–ALXO	Dakota 3	Scottish Aviation
G–ALXP	Firth Helicopter	Firth Helicopters
G–ALXR	Marathon I	Handley Page (Reading)
G–ALXS	Dragon Rapide	R. A. Short
G–ALXT	Dragon Rapide	A. R. Frogley
G–ALXU	Dragon Rapide	R. A. Short
G–ALXX	Oxford	Lancashire Aircraft Corp.
G–ALXY	Oxford	Lancashire Aircraft Corp.
G–ALXZ	Auster 5	S. J. Cooper
G–ALYA	Herald	Hants & Sussex Aviation
G–ALYB	Auster 5	L .R. Vandome
G–ALYC	Proctor I	D. E. Bianchi
G–ALYD	Auster 5	D. G. S. Cotter
G–ALYE	Anson I	Transair
G–ALYF	Dakota 3	Scottish Aviation
G–ALYG		
G–ALYH	Auster 5	T. H. Marshall
G–ALYO	Devon 1	Secretary of State for Air
G–ALZE	Britten-Norman B.N.—F.1.	
G–ALZF	Dragon Rapide	
G–ALZG	Gemini IA	P. Blamire
G–ALZH	Dragon Rapide	W. J. E. Lee
G–ALZJ	Dragon Rapide	Cambrian Air Services
G–ALZK	Comet	M.o.S.
G–ALZL	Heron	de Havilland Aircraft Co.
G–AMAI	Dragon Rapide	
G–AMAJ	Tiger Moth	
G–AMAK	Westland S.51	
G–AMAL	Proctor I	
G–AMAM	Dragon Rapide	
G–AMAN	Proctor I	
G–AMAO	Auster 5	
G–AMAP	Auster 5	J. Green
G–AMAR	Tiger Moth	
G–AMAU	Hurricane 2c	Hawker Aircraft Ltd.
G–AMBE	Anson I	
G–AMBF	Anson I	
G–AMBG	Anson I	
G–AMBH	Gemini IA	E. G. Hayes
G–AMBI	Tiger Moth	
G–AMBJ	Tiger Moth	
G–AMBK	Tiger Moth	
G–AMBS	Proctor 3	
G–AMBT	Consul	Airspeed
G–AMBU	Consul	Airspeed
G–AMBW	Dakota 3	Airwork
G–AMBX	Halifax 9	
G–AMCA	Dakota	
G–AMCF	Halifax 9	
G–AMCG	Halifax 9	

57

Foreign Air Liners
Serving the U.K.

In alphabetical order

CANADA (CF)

Registration	Type	Owner or Operator
CF–TFA	North Star	Trans-Canada Air Lines
CF–TFB	" "	" " " "
CF–TFC	" "	" " " "
CF–TFD	" "	" " " "
CF–TFE	" "	" " " "
CF–TFF	" "	" " " "
CF–TFG	" "	" " " "
CF–TFH	" "	" " " "
CF–TFI	" "	" " " "
CF–TFJ	" "	" " " "
CF–TFK	" "	" " " "
CF–TFL	" "	" " " "
CF–TFM	" "	" " " "
CF–TFN	" "	" " " "
CF–TFO	" "	" " " "
CF–TFP	" "	" " " "
CF–TFQ	" "	" " " "
CF–TFR	" "	" " " "
CF–TFS	" "	" " " "
CF–TFT	" "	" " " "

PORTUGAL (CS)

Registration	Type	Owner or Operator
CS–TSA	Douglas DC–4	Transportes Aereos Portugueses
CS–TSB	" "	" " "
CS–TSD	" "	" " "

SPAIN (EC)

Registration	Type	Owner or Operator
EC–ACD	Douglas DC–4	Iberia
EC–ACE	" "	"
EC–ACF	" "	"
EC–AEK	" "	"
EC–AEO	" "	"
EC–AEP	" "	"

162

EIRE (EI)

Registration	Type	Owner or Operator
EI-ACD	Douglas C-47	Aer Lingus St. Patrick
EI-ACE	Douglas DC-3D	,, ,, St. Colmcille
EI-ACF	Douglas DC-3D	,, ,, St. Kieran
EI-ACG	Douglas C-47	,, ,, St. Malachy
EI-ACH	Douglas C-47A	,, ,, St. Brigid
EI-ACI	Douglas C-47	,, ,, St. Aidan
EI-ACK	Douglas C-47A	,, ,, St. Albert
EI-ACL	Douglas C-47	,, ,, St. Declan
EI-ACM	Douglas C-47	,, ,, St. Fintan
EI-ACT	Douglas C-47A	,, ,, St. Colman
EI-AFA.	Douglas C-47A	,, ,, St. Kevin
EI-AFB	Douglas C-47A	,, ,, St. Brendan
EI-AFC	Douglas DC-3F	,, ,, St. Enda

FRANCE (F)

Registration	Type	Owner or Operator
F-BATA	Languedoc	Air France
F-BATB	,,	,, ,,
F-BATC	,,	,, ,,
F-BATD	,,	,, ,,
F-BATE	,,	,, ,,
F-BATG	,,	,, ,,
F-BATH	,,	,, ,,
F-BATI	,,	,, ,,
F-BATJ	,,	,, ,,
F-BATK	,,	,, ,,
F-BATL	,,	,, ,,
F-BATN	,,	,, ,,
F-BATO	,,	,, ,,
F-BATP	,,	,, ,,
F-BATQ	,,	,, ,,
F-BATR	,,	,, ,,
F-BATS	,,	,, ,,
F-BATT	,,	,, ,,
F-BATU	,,	,, ,,
F-BATV	,,	,, ,,
F-BATW	,,	,, ,,
F-BATX	,,	,, ,,
F-BATY	,,	,, ,,
F-BATZ	,,	,, ,,
F-BBDA	Douglas DC-4	,, ,, Ciel de Bretagne
F-BBDB	,, ,,	,, ,, Ciel de Touraine
F-BBDD	,, ,,	,, ,, Ciel de Bourgogne
F-BBDE	,, ,,	,, ,, Ciel de Picardie
F-BBDF	,, ,,	,, ,, Ciel de Artois
F-BBDG	,, ,,	,, ,, Ciel de Champagne
F-BBDH	,, ,,	,, ,, Ciel de Bearn
F-BBDI	,, ,,	,, ,, Ciel de Provence
F-BBDJ	,, ,,	,, ,, Ciel Ile de France
F-BBDK	,, ,,	,, ,, Ciel de Normandie

Registration	Type	Owner or Operator
F–BBDL	Douglas DC–4	Air France *Ciel de Alsace*
F–BBDM	,, ,,	,, ,, *Ciel de Gascogne*
F–BBDN	,, ,,	,, ,, *Ciel de Lorraine*
F–BBDO	,, ,,	,, ,, *Ciel de Savoie*
F–BBDP	,, ,,	,, ,,
F–BBDQ	,, ,,	,, ,,
F–BBDR	,, ,,	,, ,,
F–BCUA	Languedoc	,, ,,
F–BCUB	,,	,, ,,
F–BCUE	,,	,, ,,
F–BCUF	,,	,, ,,
F–BCUG	,,	,, ,,
F–BCUH	,,	,, ,,
F–BCUI	,,	,, ,,
F–BCUJ	,,	,, ,,
F–BCUK	,,	,, ,,
F–BCUL	,,	,, ,,
F–BCUM	,,	,, ,,
F–BCUN	,,	,, ,,
F–BCUO	,,	,, ,,
F–BCUP	,,	,, ,,
F–BCUR	,,	,, ,,
F–BCUS	,,	,, ,,
F–BELC	Douglas DC–4	,, ,,
F–BELD	,, ,,	,, ,,
F–BELE	,, ,,	,, ,,
F–BELF	,, ,,	,, ,,
F–BELI	,, ,,	,, ,,
F–BELJ	,, ,,	,, ,,
F–BELK	,, ,,	,, ,,
F–BELL	,, ,,	,, ,,
F–BELM	,, ,,	,, ,,
F–BELN	,, ,,	,, ,,

SWITZERLAND (HB)

Registration	Type	Owner or Operator
HB–ILA	Douglas DC–4	Swissair *Geneve*
HB–ILE	,, ,,	,,
HB–ILI	,, ,,	,, *Basel*
HB–ILO	,, ,,	,,
HB–IRA	Douglas DC–3	,,
HB–IRB	,, ,,	,,
HB–IRC	,, ,,	,,
HB–IRD	,, ,,	,,
HB–IRE	,, ,,	,,
HB–IRF	,, ,,	,,
HB–IRG	,, ,,	,,
HB–IRI	,, ,,	,,
HB–IRK	,, ,,	,,
HB–IRL	,, ,,	,,
HB–IRM	,, ,,	,,
HB–IRN	,, ,,	,,
HB–IRO	,, ,,	,,

Registration	Type	Owner or Operator
HB–IRP	Convair-Liner	Swissair
HB–IRS	,, ,,	,,
HB–IRT	,, ,,	,,
HB–IRV	,, ,,	,,
HB–IRX	Douglas DC–3	,,

ITALY (I)

Registration	Type	Owner or Operator
I–DALJ	S.I.A.I. Marchetti S.M.95	Alitalia *Christoforo Colombo*
I–DALK	,, ,, ,,	,, *Amerigo Vespucci*
I–DALL	,, ,, ,,	,, *Marco Polo*
I–DALN	,, ,, ,,	,, *Sebastiano Caboto*
I–DALO	,, ,, ,,	,, *Ugo Vivaldi*

NORWAY (LN)

Registration	Type	Owner or Operator
LN–LAG	Douglas DC–6	Scandinavian Airlines System *Sverre*
LN–LAH	,, ,,	,, ,, ,, *Harald*

N.B. Scandinavian Airlines System aircraft names are suffixed " **Viking** "

ARGENTINA (LV)

Registration	Type	Owner or Operator
LV–AFV	York	F.A.M.A.
LV–AFY	York	,,
LV–AFZ	York	,,

LUXEMBOURG (LX)

Registration	Type	Owner or Operator
LX–LAA	Douglas C–47	Luxembourg Airlines *Echternach*
LX–LAC	Dragon Rapide	,, ,,
LX–LAD	,, ,,	,, ,,

U.S.A. (N)

Registration	Type	Owner or Operator
N1027V	Stratocruiser	P.A.A. *America*
N1028V	,,	,, *Flyin Cloud*

Registration	Type	Owner or Operator
N1031V	Stratocruiser	P.A.A. Mayflower
N1032V	,,	,, United States
N1033V	,,	,, Seven Seas
N1034V	,,	,, Westward Ho !
N1035V	,,	,, Flying Eagle
N1036V	,,	,, Washington
N1041V	,,	,,
N	,,	,,
N	,,	,,
N25686	Douglas DC–3	A.O.A. Helsinki
N88832	Constellation	P.A.A. Flora Temple
N88833	,,	,, Robin Hood
N88836	,,	,, Yankee Ranger
N88837	,,	,, Challenge
N88838	,,	,, Donald McKay
N88846	,,	,, Great Republic
N88847	,,	,, Hotspur
N88850	,,	,, Intrepid
N88855	,,	,, Undaunted
N88856	,,	,, Paul Jones
N88857	,,	,, Flying Mist
N88859	,,	,, Talisman
N88861	,,	,, Winged Arrow
N88868	,,	,, Golden Fleece
N88919	Douglas DC–4	,, Panama
N88922	,, ,,	,, Radiant
N88923	,, ,,	,, West Wind
N88926	,, ,,	,, Twilight
N88927	,, ,,	,, Skylark
N88933	,, ,,	,, Winged Racer
N88934	,, ,,	,, Pride of America
N88942	,, ,,	,, Bostonian
N88945	,, ,,	,, Gladiator
N88955	,, ,,	,, Nonpareil
N88958	,, ,,	,, Derby
N88959	,, ,,	,, Live Yankee
N90902	,, ,,	A.O.A. Frankfurt
N90905	,, ,,	,, Berlin
N90908	Douglas DC–3	,, Nairobi
N90913	Douglas DC–4	P.A.A.
N90921	Constellation	A.O.A. London
N90922	,,	,, Oslo
N90923	,,	,, Stockholm
N90924	,,	,, Shannon
N90925	,,	,, Copenhagen
N90926	,,	,, Amsterdam
N90927	,,	,, Glasgow
N90941	Stratocruiser	,, Europe
N90942	,,	,, Great Britain
N90943	,,	,, Holland
N90944	,,	,, Ireland
N90945	,,	,, Norway
N90946	,,	,, Sweden
N90947	,,	,, Denmark
N90948	,,	,, Scotland

N.B. P.A.A. aircraft names are prefixed **Clipper**
A.O.A. ,, ,, ,, ,, **Flagship**

CZECHOSLOVAKIA (OK)

Registration	Type	Owner or Operator
OK–CBA	Ilyushin II 12	Cs Statni Aerolinie
OK–CBB	,, ,, ,,	,, ,, ,,
OK–CBC	,, ,, ,,	,, ,, ,,
OK–CBD	,, ,, ,,	,, ,, ,,
OK–CBE	,, ,, ,,	,, ,, ,,
OK–CBF	,, ,, ,,	,, ,, ,,
OK–CBG	,, ,, ,,	,, ,, ,,
OK–CBH	,, ,, ,,	,, ,, ,,
OK–CBJ	,, ,, ,,	,, ,, ,,
OK–CBK	,, ,, ,,	,, ,, ,,
OK–WAA	Douglas DC–3	,, ,, ,,
OK–WAP	,, ,,	,, ,, ,,
OK–WAX	,, ,,	,, ,, ,,
OK–WCN	,, ,,	,, ,, ,,
OK–WCO	,, ,,	,, ,, ,,
OK–WCP	,, ,,	,, ,, ,,
OK–WCR	,, ,,	,, ,, ,,
OK–WCS	,, ,,	,, ,, ,,
OK–WCT	Douglas C–47	,, ,, ,,
OK–WDA	,, ,,	,, ,, ,,
OK–WDC	,, ,,	,, ,, ,,
OK–WDD	,, ,,	,, ,, ,,
OK–WDE	,, ,,	,, ,, ,,
OK–WDF	,, ,,	,, ,, ,,
OK–WDG	,, ,,	,, ,, ,,
OK–WDH	,, ,,	,, ,, ,,
OK–WDI	,, ,,	,, ,, ,,
OK–WDJ	,, ,,	,, ,, ,,
OK–WDK	,, ,,	,, ,, ,,
OK–WDL	,, ,,	,, ,, ,,
OK–WDN	,, ,,	,, ,, ,,
OK–WDO	,, ,,	,, ,, ,,
OK–WDP	,, ,,	,, ,, ,,
OK–WDQ	,, ,,	,, ,, ,,
OK–WDR	,, ,,	,, ,, ,,
OK–WDS	,, ,,	,, ,, ,,
OK–WDT	,, ,,	,, ,, ,,
OK–WDU	,, ,,	,, ,, ,,
OK–WDV	,, ,,	,, ,, ,,
OK–WDW	,, ,,	,, ,, ,,
OK–WDY	,, ,,	,, ,, ,,
OK–WDZ	,, ,,	,, ,, ,,
OK–XDG	,, ,,	,, ,, ,,
OK–XDH	,, ,,	,, ,, ,,
OK–XDN	,, ,,	,, ,, ,,

BELGIUM (OO)

Registration	Type	Owner or Operator
OO–APC	Douglas C–47	Cobelsa
OO–APG	Avro 19	,,
OO–API	Hudson	,,

Registration	Type	Owner or Operator
OO–AUL	Douglas DC–3	Sabena
OO–AUM	" "	"
OO–AUN	" "	"
OO–AUO	" "	"
OO–AUP	" "	"
OO–AUV	" "	"
OO–AUW	Douglas C–47	"
OO–AUX	" DC–3	"
OO–AUY	" "	"
OO–AUZ	" "	"
OO–AWA	" DC–6	"
OO–AWB	" "	"
OO–AWC	" "	"
OO–AWF	" C–47	"
OO–AWG	" DC–3	"
OO–AWJ	" C–47	"
OO–AWK	" "	"
OO–AWL	" DC–3	"
OO–AWM	" C–47	"
OO–AWO	Convair-Liner	"
OO–AWP	" "	"
OO–AWQ	" "	"
OO–AWR	" "	"
OO–AWS	" "	"
OO–AWT	" "	"
OO–CBA	Douglas DC–3	"
OO–CBB	" "	"
OO–CBC	" "	"
OO–CBN	Douglas C–47	"
OO–SBC	" DC–3	"
OO–SBD	" "	"
OO–UBJ	" "	"
OO–UBT	" C–47	"

DENMARK (OY)

Registration	Type	Owner or Operator
OY–AAE	Douglas DC–6	Scandinavian Airlines System *Skjalm*
OY–AAF	" "	" " " *Skiold*
OY–DFI	" DC–4	" " " *Dan*
OY–DFO	" "	" " " *Rolf*

N.B.—Scandinavian Airlines System aircraft names are all suffixed Viking

NETHERLANDS (PH)

Registration	Type	Owner or Operator
PH–TAU	Constellation L49	K.L.M. *Utrecht*
PH–TAV	" "	" *Venlo*
PH–TAY	Douglas C–47A	"
PH–TAZ	" "	"
PH–TBH	" "	"
PH–TBI	" "	"

Registration	Type	Owner or Operator
PH–TBK	Douglas C–47A	K.L.M.
PH–TBL	,, ,,	,,
PH–TBM	,, ,,	,,
PH–TBP	,, ,,	,,
PH–TBY	,, ,,	,,
PH–TBZ	,, ,,	,,
PH–TCB	,, ,,	,,
PH–TCE	Douglas DC–4	,, Edam
PH–TCI	,, C–47A	,,
PH–TCK	,, ,,	,,
PH–TCL	,, ,,	,,
PH–TCS	,, ,,	,,
PH–TCT	,, ,,	,,
PH–TCU	,, ,,	,,
PH–TCY	,, ,,	,,
PH–TDA	Constellation L–49	,, Arnhem
PH–TDB	Constellation L749	,, Walcheren
PH–TDC	,, ,,	,, Curacao
PH–TDD	,, ,,	,, Delft
PH–TDE	,, ,,	,, Eindhoven
PH–TDG	,, ,,	,, Gouda
PH–TDH	,, ,,	,, Holland
PH–TDI	,, ,,	,, Enschede
PH–TDK	,, ,,	,, Amsterdam
PH–TDL	Douglas C–54B	,, Groningen
PH–TDM	,, ,,	,, Aalsmeer
PH–TDN	Constellation L–749A	,, Vlaardingen
PH–TDO	,, ,,	,, Maastricht
PH–TDU	Douglas C–47A	,,
PH–TDV	,, ,,	,,
PH–TDW	,, ,,	,,
PH–TDZ	,, ,,	,,
PH–TEA	Convair-Liner	,, Adriaan van Ostade
PH–TEB	,, ,,	,, Rembrandt
PH–TEC	,, ,,	,, Albert Cuyp
PH–TED	,, ,,	,, Gerard Terboch
PH–TEE	,, ,,	,, Jan Steen
PH–TEF	,, ,,	,, Frans Hals
PH–TEG	,, ,,	,, Jan van Goyen
PH–TEH	,, ,,	,, Pieter de Hooch
PH–TEI	,, ,,	,, Paulus Potter
PH–TEK	,, ,,	,, Johannes Vermeer
PH–TEL	,, ,,	,, Jacob van Ruisdael
PH–TEM	,, ,,	,, Meindert Hobbema
PH–TEP	Constellation L–749	,, Pontianak
PH–TES	,, ,,	,, Soerabaja
PH–TET	,, ,,	,, Tilburg
PH–TEY	Douglas C–54B	,, Limburg
PH–TEZ	,, ,,	,, Zeeland

PHILIPPINES (PI)

Registration	Type	Owner or Operator
PI–C290	Douglas DC–6	Philippine Air Lines Bataan
PI–C291	,, ,,	,, ,, ,, Layte
PI–C292	,, ,,	,, ,, ,, Lingayen
PI–C293	,, ,,	,, ,, ,, Manila
PI–C294	,, ,,	,, ,, ,, Mindoro

169

BRAZIL (PP)

Registration	Type	Owner or Operator
PP–PCB	Constellation	Panair do Brasil
PP–PCF	,,	,, ,, ,,
PP–PCG	,,	,, ,, ,,
PP–PCR	,,	,, ,, ,,
PP–PDA	,,	,, ,, ,,

SWEDEN (SE)

Registration	Type	Owner or Operator	
SE–BBA	Douglas DC–4	Scandinavian Airlines System	Sigtrygg
SE–BBC	,, ,,	,, ,, ,,	Sigvard
SE–BBD	,, ,,	,, ,, ,,	Sigmund
SE–BBE	,, ,,	,, ,, ,,	Svavar
SE–BBF	,, ,,	,, ,, ,,	Sverker
SE–BDB	Douglas DC–6	,, ,, ,,	Agne
SE–BDC	,, ,,	,, ,, ,,	Alf
SE–BDD	,, ,,	,, ,, ,,	Algaut
SE–BDE	,, ,,	,, ,, ,,	Alrek
SE–BDF	,, ,,	,, ,, ,,	Alvar
SE–BDL	,, ,,	,, ,, ,,	Asmund
SE–BDM	,, ,,	,, ,, ,,	Anund
SE–BDO	,, ,,	,, ,, ,,	Arngrim

N.B.—Scandinavian Airlines System aircraft names are suffixed Viking

GREECE (SX)

Registration	Type	Owner or Operator
SX–DAA	Liberator	Hellenic Airlines *Maid of Athens*
SX–DAB	,,	,, ,,

ICELAND (TF)

Registration	Type	Owner or Operator
TF–ISE	Douglas C–54	Flugfelag Islands H.F. *Gullfaxi*
TF–RVC	,, ,,	Loftleidir H.F. *Geysir*
TF–RVH	,, ,,	,, ,, *Hekla*

AUSTRALIA (VH)

Registration	Type	Owner or Operator
VH–EAA	Constellation	Qantas Empire Airways *Ross Smith*
VH–EAB	,,	,, ,, ,, *Lawrence Hargrave*

Registration	Type	Owner or Operator
VH–EAC	Constellation	Qantas Empire Airways *Harry Hawker*
VH–EAD	,,	,, ,, ,, *Charles Kingsford Smith*
VH–	,,	,, ,, ,,
VH–EBK	Douglas C–54	,, ,, ,,
VH–EBL	,, ,,	,, ,, ,,
VH–EBM	,, ,,	,, ,, ,,

CEYLON (VP)

Registration	Type	Owner or Operator
VP–CBD	Douglas C–54	Air Ceylon *Laxapana*
VP–CBE	,, ,,	,, *Ratmalana*

INDIA (VT)

Registration	Type	Owner or Operator
VT–CQP	Constellation	Air India International *Malabar*
VT–CQS	,,	,, ,, ,, *Moghul*
VT–DAR	,,	,, ,, ,, *Maratha*
VT–DAS	,,	,, ,, ,, *Himalayan*

N.B.—Air India International Constellations are suffixed Princess

IRAQ (YI)

Registration	Type	Owner or Operator
YI–ABP	Viking IB	Iraqi Airways *Al Mahfoutah*
YI–ABQ	,, ,,	,, ,, *Al Maanounah*
YI–ABR	,, ,,	,, ,, *Al Mamica*

SOUTH AFRICA (ZS)

Registration	Type	Owner or Operator
ZS–AUA	Douglas DC–4	South African Airways *Tafelberg*
ZS–AUB	,, ,,	,, ,, ,, *Outeniqua*
ZS–AUC	,, ,,	,, ,, ,, *Drakensberg*
ZS–BMF	,, ,,	,, ,, ,, *Amatola*
ZS–BMG	,, ,,	,, ,, ,, *Magaliesberg*
ZS–BMH	,, ,,	,, ,, ,, *Lebombo*
ZS–BWN	,, ,,	,, ,, ,, *Swartberg*
ZS–	Constellation	,, ,, ,,
ZS–	,,	,, ,, ,,
ZS–	,,	,, ,, ,,
ZS–	,,	,, ,, ,,

(Concluded on page 70

CIVIL AIRCRAFT SPECIFICATIONS

AIRCRAFT	MANUFACTURER	ENGINES	SEATS	SPAN	Loaded Wt.: (lb.)	Cruising Speed M.P.H.
Aeronca 100	Aeronca (G.B.)	1 × 36 J.A.P.	2	36'	1,005	70
Aerovan	Miles (G.B.)	2 × 155 Cirrus Major	9/Freight	50'	5,800	110
Air Horse Hel.	Cierva (G.B.)	1 × 1,620 Merlin	24	95'	17,500	95
Ambassador	Airspeed (G.B.)	2 × 2,700 Centaurus	49	115'	52,000	245
Anson 1	A.V. Roe (G.B.)	2 × 320 Cheetah	9	56' 6"	7,663	158
Apollo	Armst. Whit. (G.B.)	4 × 1,000 + 320 lb. Mamba	24-41	92'	43,000	276
Argus	Fairchild (U.S.A.)	1 × 165 Super Scarab	4	36' 4"	2,801	104
Arrow	Auster (G.B.)	1 × 75 Continental	2	36'	1,450	87
Auster 5	" "	1 × 130 Lycoming	2-3	36'	1,920	112
Auster J/4	" "	1 × 90 Cirrus	2	36'	1,600	92
Autocar	" "	1 × 130 Gipsy Major	4			106
Autocrat	" "	1 × 100 Cirrus Minor	3	36'	1,850	100
Avro XIX	A.V. Roe (G.B.)	2 × 420 Cheetah	6-9	56' 6"	10,400	155
Beaver	De Havilland (Canada)	1 × 450 Wasp Junior	4-7	48'	4,500	146
Brabazon 1	Bristol (G.B.)	8 × 2,650 Centaurus	101	230'	290,000	250
Bristol Type 170	" "	2 × 1,780 Hercules	36/Freight	108'	40,000	162
Bristol Type 171 Hel.	" "	1 × 550 Leonides	4	48' 7" Dia.	5,200	
C.30 A Autogiro	Cierva (G.B.)	1 × 140 Genet Major	2	37'	1,900	85
Canadair Four	Canadair (Canada)	4 × 1,760 Merlin	40	117' 6"	82,300	302
Chipmunk	De Havilland (G.B.)	1 × 140 Gipsy Major	2	34' 4"	1,900	113
Comet	" "	4 × 5,000 lb. Ghost	36-48	115'	105,000	490
Constellation 749A	Lockheed (U.S.A.)	4 × 2,500 Cyclone	44-64	123'	107,000	309
Consul	Airspeed (G.B.)	2 × 395 Cheetah	5-6	53' 4"	8,250	156
Convair-Liner	Consolidated (U.S.A.)	2 × 2,400 P & W R-2800	40	91' 9"	40,500	291
Cub	Piper (U.S.A.)	1 × 65 Continental	2	35' 2"	1,220	75
DC-3 Dakota	Douglas (U.S.A.)	2 × 1,200 P & W R-1830	21-32	95'	25,200	207
DC-4 Skymaster	" "	4 × 1,350 P & W R-2000	36-47	117' 6"	73,000	231
DC-6	" "	4 × 2,150 P & W R-2800	52-68	117' 6"	93,200	285
Dove	De Havilland (G.B.)	2 × 345 Gipsy Queen	8-11	57'	8,500	179
Gemini	Miles (G.B.)	2 × 100 Cirrus Minor	4	36' 2"	3,000	135
Halifax	Handley Page (G.B.)	4 × 1,650 Hercules	11/Freight	104'	65,000	270
Hawk Major	Miles (G.B.)	1 × 130 Gipsy Major	2	33'	1,800	135
Hawk Trainer 3	" "	1 × 130 Gipsy Major	2	33' 10"	1,900	120
Hermes 4	Handley Page (G.B.)	4 × 2,100 Hercules	40-74	113'	82,000	252

Hermes 5	Handley Page (G.B.)	4×2,430 Theseus	40-74	113'	86,000	343
Hornet Moth	De Havilland (G.B.)	1×130 Gipsy Major	2	31' 11"	2,000	105
IL-12	Ilyushin (Russia)	2×1,800 Ash-82	27-32	104'	38,000	217
Lancastrian	A.V. Roe (G.B.)	4×1,280 Merlin	9/Freight	102'	65,000	285
Languedoc	S.N.C.A.S.E. (France)	4×1,220 Gnome-Rhone	12-33	96' 5"	45,364	233
Liberator	Consolidated (U.S.A.)	4×1,200 P & W R-1830	16-20/F.	110'	56,000	215
Lodestar	Lockheed (U.S.A.)	2×1,200 Cyclone	14	65' 8"	18,500	200
M-18	Miles (G.B.)	1×150 Gipsy Major	2	31'	1,918	120
Marathon 1	Handley Page (G.B.)	4×330 Gipsy Queen	14-20	65'	18,000	209
Marathon 2	" "	2×1,270+384 lb. Mamba	14-20	65'		256
Messenger	Miles (G.B.)	1×155 Cirrus Major	3-4	36' 2"	2,400	112
Moth Minor	De Havilland (G.B.)	1×90 Gipsy Minor	2	36' 7"	1,550	100
Primer	Fairey (G.B.)	1×135 Gipsy Major	2	32' 10"	1,960	122
Prince	Percival (G.B.)	2×520 Leonides	8-10	56'	10,650	179
Proctor 5	"	1×208 Gipsy Queen	4	39' 6"	3,500	140
Pup	Sopwith (G.B.)	1×80 Le Rhone	1	26' 6"	1,225	100
Q-6	Percival (G.B.)	2×205 Gipsy Six	6	46' 8"	5,550	181
Rapide	De Havilland (G.B.)	2×200 Gipsy Six	5-8	48'	5,550	132
Sandringham 5	Short (G.B.)	4×1,200 P & W R-1830	22	112' 9"	56,000	204
Sealand	" "	2×350 Gipsy Queen	5-8	59'	9,100	181
Sea Otter	Vickers (G.B.)	1×805 Mercury	5	46'	10,000	100
Sikorsky S-51 Hel.	Westland (G.B.)	1×505 Leonides	4	48' Dia.	5,374	85
Skeeter Hel.	Cierva (G.B.)	1×145 Gipsy Major	2	32' Dia.	1,800	73
Sky Jeep	Chrislea (G.B.)	1×155 Cirrus Major	4	36'	2,400	110
SM. 95	SIAI-Marchetti (Italy)	4×1,215 Twin Wasp	30-38	112' 5"	47,600	215
Solent	Short (G.B.)	4×1,795 Hercules	24-39	112' 9"	78,000	236
Spitfire Trainer	Vickers (G.B.)	1×1,325 Merlin	2	36' 10"	7,400	232
Stratocruiser	Boeing (U.S.A.)	4×3,500 P & W R-4360	55-80	141' 3"	142,000	340
Sunderland 3	Short (G.B.)	4×1,065 Pegasus	22	112' 9"	55,000	115
Super Ace 2	Chrislea (G.B.)	1×145 Gipsy Major	4	36'	2,350	112
Swallow	British Aircraft (G.B.)	1×20 Cataract	2	42' 8"	1,500	92
Swift	Comper (G.B.)	1×80 Pobjoy 8	1	24'	985	110
Taylorcraft D	Taylorcraft (G.B.)	1×90 Cirrus Minor	2	36'	1,400	107
Tiger Moth	De Havilland (G.B.)	1×130 Gipsy Major	2	29' 4"	1,825	94
Tipsy Trainer	Tipsy (G.B.)	1×52 Mikron	2	31' 2"	1,200	100
Tudor 5	A.V. Roe (G.B.)	4×1,740 Merlin	44	120'	80,000	285
Vega Gull	Percival (G.B.)	1×200 Gipsy Six	4	39' 6"	3,250	170
Viking	Vickers (G.B.)	2×1,690 Hercules	27	89' 3"	34,000	210
Viscount 700	" "	4×1,420+325 lb. Dart	40-53	94'	48,000	326
Whitney Straight	Miles (G.B.)	1×130 Gipsy Major	2	35' 8"	1,896	130
York	A.V. Roe (G.B.)	4×1,280 Merlin	12-56	102'	68,597	255

Registration	Type	Owner or Operator
4X–ACC	Douglas DC–4	El Al Rechovoth
4X–ACD	,, ,,	,, ,, Herzel

MILITARY REGISTRATIONS

MILITARY aircraft, like their civil counterparts, all carry some kind of identification markings, and these " serial numbers," as they are usually called, form the basis of a fascinating but complicated study. Although they are really outside the scope of this book, the following notes are included to help readers to understand how military serial numbers are allocated and how they can be distinguished from civil registrations.

Serial numbers for aircraft operated by the Royal Air Force and the Air Branch of the Royal Navy are allocated by a department of the Ministry of Supply in a co-ordinated system. Each serial consists of a five-symbol group, made up of either one letter followed by four digits or, more recently, two letters followed by three digits. Through the years, they have run progressively, starting with the prefix A, then B, C, etc., through to Z, which was followed by the AA prefix, then AB, etc., up to WF, which is in use as this book goes to press.

The serial number on R.A.F. and R.N. aircraft is displayed on each side of the rear fuselage and beneath each wing, in addition to the national red, white and blue roundels. Such a serial number is, therefore, readily distinguishable and can be ignored by those using this book as a means of identifying civil aircraft types.

The Ministry of Supply, in its capacity of foster-mother to many of the civil prototypes developed in this country since the war, has allocated military-type serials to most of these prototypes for the period of their testing by its test pilots. These same aircraft also receive normal civil registrations, however, and these are included in the appropriate section of this book.

Military aircraft of other countries also can be seen flying over the United Kingdom. The identification systems of these various countries are too diverse to be dealt with here, but, as a rule, military aircraft can be quickly identified by national insignia on their wings and fuselage. Furthermore, an identification marking which does not fit into the scheme of national civil markings as laid down in this book can be assumed to be a military serial.

70

Left : Comper SWIFT. Although the oldest 'plane in the 1949 King's Cup race and flown by the youngest pilot, G–ABUS gained third place. (*F.G. Swanborough.*)

Right : B.A. SWALLOW. Based on the old German Klemm design, the Swallow was one of the lowest priced pre-war two-seaters. (*F. G. Swanborough.*)

Left: de Havilland HORNET MOTH Last of the famous de Havilland Moth biplanes, the Hornet Moth is a cabin two-seater. (*F. G. Swanborough.*)

Right : Miles M-18. A development of the better - known Magister (Hawk Trainer 3), only a few M-18's were built.

Above : *Cierva* AIR HORSE. World's largest helicopter, the Air Horse was designed to carry 24 passengers or 3 tons of freight. (*John W. R. Taylor.*)

Left : *Cierva* C.30A. Autogiros of this type were used during the war for radar calibration work. (*John W. R. Taylor.*)

Below : *Sikorsky* S–51. G–ALEI has been specially fitted out with crop-spraying equipment by Pest Control Ltd. Other S–51's are used by B.E.A. for passenger and mail carrying.

*One of the
most popular sports of today.*

BRITISH ROAD RACING

by John Dudley

2/-

magnificently illustrated

AN Ian Allan PUBLICATION

*Available from W. H. Smith & Son, Wymans
and leading booksellers everywhere.*

Ian Allan
abc
Civil Aircraft
Recognition
SHELL
A A
B
C
G-AEXF
2/6

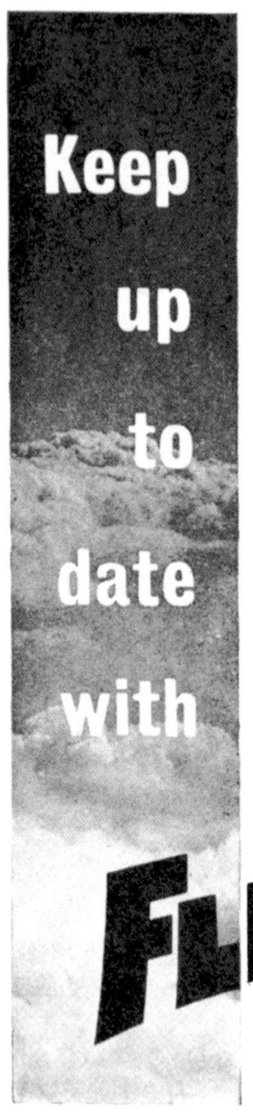

FLIGHT provides the highest possible standard of information on everything to do with aviation, and is read throughout the world. Its contents include — reviews of the work and equipment of the R.A.F., Fleet Air Arm and air forces of other nations; commercial and club aviation news, and information on the latest developments in military, civil and research aircraft throughout the world. Its descriptions, photographs and sectional drawings of aircraft and their power units are the finest anywhere. FLIGHT is also a particularly valuable source of information for those interested in aircraft performance and recognition.

Every Friday 1s. 6d.
Annual Subscription £4   10s. 0d.

FLIGHT

● FRIDAYS • 1s. 6d.

THE WORLD'S FOREMOST AERONAUTICAL] JOURNAL

abc

CIVIL AIRCRAFT RECOGNITION

1955

BY

John W. R. Taylor

LONDON :

Ian Allan Ltd

Contents

	Page
ADVENTURER	10
AERONCA 100	57
AEROVAN	64
AIGLET (J/1B)	8
AIGLET TRAINER (J/8L etc.)	8
AMBASSADOR	5
ARGONAUT	19
ARGUS	61
ARIES	43
ARROW (J/2)	57
AUSTER 4 & 5	7
AUSTER J/4	57
AUSTER J/5	10
AUTOCAR (J/5G etc.)	9
AUTOCRAT (J/1)	10
AVRO 19	11
BALLIOL	59
BEAVER	23
BELL 47	58
BLACKBURN B-2	59
BRISTOL 170	16
BRISTOL 171	17
BRITANNIA	18
CANADAIR FOUR	19
CHIPMUNK	24
CLUB CADET	58
COMET	25
COMMANDO	22
COMPER SWIFT	59
CONSTELLATION L-749	41
CONSTELLATION L-1049	42
CONSUL	6
CONVAIR-LINER 240	20
CONVAIR-LINER 340	21
CUB	48
CYGNET (G.A.L.)	62
CYGNET (HAWKER)	62
DAKOTA	33
DC-3	33
DC-4	34
DC-6, 6A, 6B & 6C	35
DC-7	36
DEUX PONTS	15
DISCOVERY	54
DOVE	26
DRAGON	60
DRAGON RAPIDE	27
DRAGONFLY	60
DRONE	58
ELIZABETHAN	5
FALCON MAJOR	64
FALCON SIX	64
FOX MOTH	60
FREIGHTER	16
GEMINI	43
GLADIATOR	62
HART	63
HAWK SPEED SIX	65
HAWK TRAINER 3	44
HERALD	38
HERMES	37
HERON	28
HILLER 360	63
HORNET MOTH	29
HURRICANE	63
HYTHE	50
JUNIOR	61
KITTEN	60
LEOPARD MOTH	31
M-28	65
MESSENGER	45
METEOR	62
MOTH	61
MOTH MINOR	30
NORECRIN	65
OTTER	61
OXFORD	6
PIONAIR	33
PIONEER	66
PIPER CUB	48
PRINCE	39
PRINCESS	66
PROCTOR	40
PROVOST	64
PUSS MOTH	31
Q.6	64
SAFIR	65
SEALAND	66
SEVEN SEAS	36
SIKORSKY S-51	55
SIKORSKY S-55	56
SKEETER	66
SKYJEEP	59
SKYMASTER	34
SOLENT	50
SPARROWJET	46
STRATOCRUISER	14
SUPER ACE	59
SUPER CONSTELLATION L-1049	42
SUPERFREIGHTER	16
SWALLOW	58
SWIFT (COMPER)	59
TAYLORCRAFT PLUS D	51
TIGER MOTH	32
TIPSY TRAINER	52
TOMTIT	63
TUDOR	12
TWIN PIONEER	49
VEGA GULL	40
VIKING	53
VISCOUNT	54
WAYFARER	16
WHITNEY STRAIGHT	47
YORK	13

Introduction

THIS new edition of *ABC of Civil Aircraft Recognition gives* details of virtually all British and foreign civil aeroplanes likely to be seen in the U.K. It follows the same format as last year's edition; except that the aircraft are now arranged in the alphabetical order of their makers' names. All data has been revised and brought up-to-date. In addition, 50 of the 52 photographs in the main section of the book are new, as are more than half of the 39 pictures of minor types at the back.

The series of Ian Allan Aircraft ABCs will include also this year completely new 1955 editions of the well-established *ABCs of Civil Aircraft Markings, British Military Aircraft, Continental Military Aircraft* and *Helicopters*, plus the new *ABC of U.S. and Canadian Military Aircraft*. The complete set will form the most up-to-date and handy collection of data and photographs of current aircraft types in the world, at a price that everyone can afford.

Our sincere thanks are due once more to Barry Jones, who drew the new silhouettes for this book; to A. J. Jackson for photographs of some rarer types; to " *Flight* " and the Controller of H.M. Stationery Office for permission to reproduce copyright photographs and silhouettes; and to many other friends who have supplied data and photographs to ensure the accuracy and value of this new edition.

April, 1955   J.W.R.T.

B.O.A.C. luxury Stratocruiser

Look how **B·O·A·C** takes good care of you!

BEHIND THIS SCENE—35 YEARS OF LOOKING AFTER PASSENGERS!

Throughout your journey by B.O.A.C., the steward and stewardess are always at your service without tips or extras! Delicious complimentary meals, mealtime drinks.   Enjoy this service yourself . . . on any one of B.O.A.C's world-wide routes to 51 countries on all 6 continents!

Consult your local B.O.A.C. Appointed Agent or B.O.A.C., Airways Terminal, S.W.1 (VIC 2323), 75 Regent Street, W.1 (MAY 6611) or offices in Glasgow. Manchester, Birmingham and Liverpool.

FLY ➤ B·O·A·C

B R I T I S H   O V E R S E A S   A I R W A Y S   C O R P O R A T I O N

AMBASSADOR 2 (ELIZABETHAN)

AIRSPEED DIVISION OF DE HAVILLAND AIRCRAFT CO. LTD.

TYPE: Medium-range air liner.
ACCOMMODATION: 5 crew + 40-49 passengers.
POWERED BY: 2 × 2,625 h.p. Bristol Centaurus 661 piston-engines.
SPAN: 115 ft.
LENGTH: 82 ft.
LOADED WEIGHT: 52,500 lb.
MAX. SPEED: 312 m.p.h.
CEILING: 28,500 ft.
TYPICAL RANGE: 550 miles at 268 m.p.h. at 20,000 ft. with 11,650 lb. payload.

RECOGNITION FEATURES

Graceful, streamlined fuselage, rather like Constellation (page 41), with three fins of distinctive shape. Long narrow tapered wings with engines and fuselage underslung. Engines project beyond wing trailing edge.

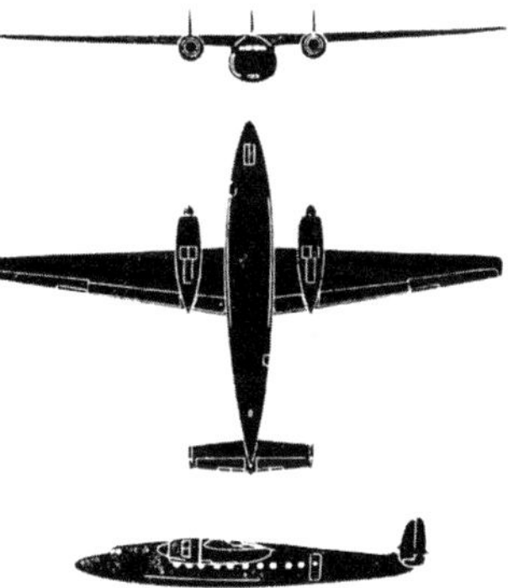

REMARKS

20 *Elizabethan* class Ambassadors are in service with B.E.A., on the Corporation's medium-range European routes. A prototype (G-AKRD) has been fitted experimentally with Proteus 705 turboprops by Bristol's Engine Division and another (G-ALFR) will be flying with Napier Eland turboprops during 1955.

5

CONSUL
(AND OXFORD)
AIRSPEED LTD.

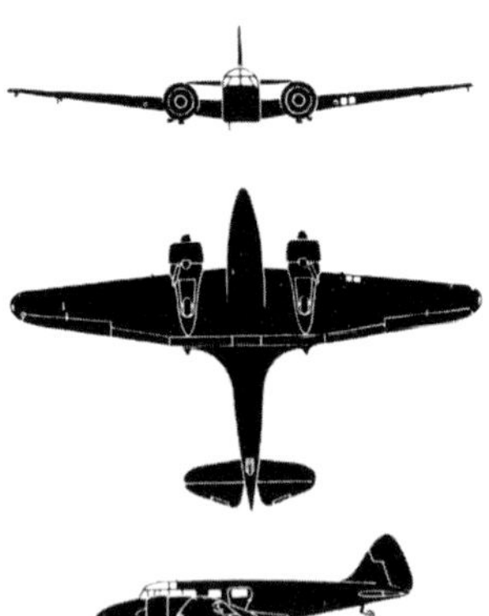

TYPE: Light passenger transport.

ACCOMMODATION: 2 crew+5-6 passengers.

POWERED BY: 2×395 h.p. A.S. Cheetah 10 piston-engines.

SPAN: 53 ft. 4 in.

LENGTH: 35 ft. 4 in.

LOADED WEIGHT: 8,250 lb.

MAX. SPEED: 190 m.p.h.

MAX. RANGE: 900 miles at 156 m.p.h.

RECOGNITION FEATURES

Compared with Avro 19 (page 11), the Consul has sleeker nose; more pointed fin and rudder; broader and more rounded tailplane. Its engine nacelles do not project so far forward of wing, but end in points behind trailing edge.

REMARKS

Civil conversion of the R.A.F.'s wartime Oxford trainer, used by several British charter companies. Standard Oxfords, with small transparent panel under nose, may also be seen in civil markings.

TYPE: Light aircraft.

ACCOMMODATION: 2-3.

POWERED BY: 130 h.p. Lycoming O-290-3/1 piston engine.

SPAN: 36 ft.

LENGTH: 22 ft. 5 in.

LOADED WEIGHT: 1,850 lb.

MAX. SPEED: 130 m.p.h.

CEILING: 15,100 ft.

TYPICAL RANGE: 220 miles at 112 m.p.h. at 1,000 ft.

RECOGNITION FEATURES

Similar to Aiglet Trainer (page 8), but longer-span wings and broader ▽ shaped engine cowling.

REMARKS

Successive development of the Auster 1 (see page 51) during the War led to the Lycoming-engined Mks. 4 and 5, many of which are still used by private owners, clubs, etc. Mk. 4 has small trimming surface under tailplane. Variants include 4-seat Mk. 5A; Gipsy Major-engined Mk. 5C and 5D, the latter with larger fin and rudder; and Mk. 5M with neon tube signs under wings.

AUSTER 4 and 5

AUSTER AIRCRAFT LTD.

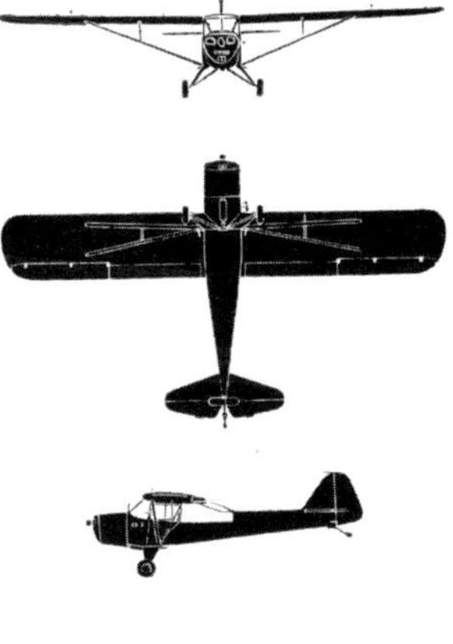

AIGLET TRAINER (J/8L)

AUSTER AIRCRAFT LTD.

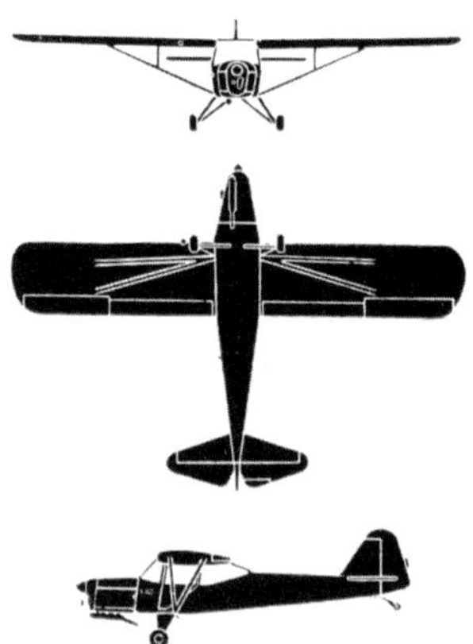

TYPE: Light trainer.
ACCOMMODATION: 2-3.
POWERED BY: 145 h.p. D.H. Gipsy Major 10 piston-engine.
SPAN: 32 ft. LENGTH: 23 ft. $2\frac{1}{2}$ in.
LOADED WEIGHT: 2,200 lb.
MAX. SPEED: 129 m.p.h.
CEILING: 10,500 ft.
TYPICAL RANGE: 450 miles with 2 up and 100 lb. baggage.

RECOGNITION FEATURES

Typical high-wing light monoplane with two V-bracing struts, square-section fuselage and big cockpit " glass house ". Longer, deeper nose than Piper Cub, without projecting cylinders, and no shock-absorbing rubber on ↓ undercarriage bracings between wheels. Exhaust pipe under engine.

REMARKS

The Aiglet Trainer was developed from the standard J/1B Aiglet by reducing the span to increase the rate of roll. Initial production versions were the J/5F with Gipsy Major 1, J/5K with Cirrus Major 3 and J/5L with Gipsy Major 10. The new J/8 series has minor internal improvements.

TYPE: Light aircraft.
ACCOMMODATION: 4.
POWERED BY: 155 h.p. Cirrus Major 3 piston-engine.
SPAN: 36 ft.
LENGTH: 23 ft. 2 in.
LOADED WEIGHT: 2,400 lb.
MAX. SPEED: 116 m.p.h.
CEILING: 11,000 ft.
TYPICAL RANGE: 500 miles at 100 m.p.h. at 1,000 ft.

AUTOCAR (J/5G)
AUSTER AIRCRAFT LTD.

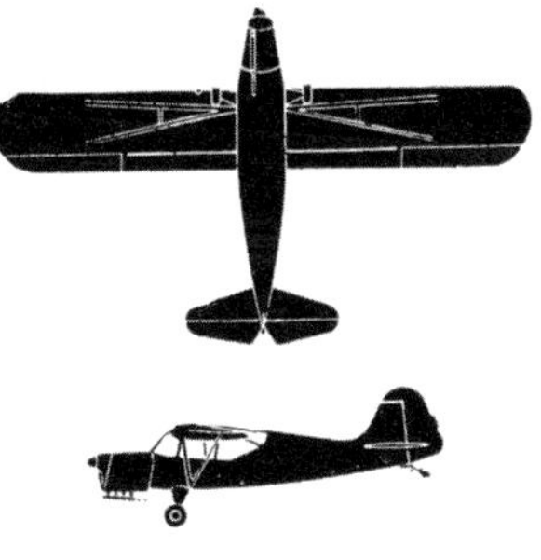

RECOGNITION FEATURES

Similar to Aiglet Trainer (page 8), but longer-span wings and wider, less square-section fuselage. Exhaust pipe under engine.

REMARKS

A four-seat development of the Autocrat (page 10), with wider fuselage and more powerful engine. The first version was the J/5B with 130 h.p. Gipsy Major 1 engine, now superseded by the J/5G with Cirrus Major 3 engine. Other versions are J/5H with 145 h.p. Cirrus Major 2 and J/5P with Gipsy Major 10. One J/5G has flown with Saro hydro-skis.

[John W. R. Taylor

AUTOCRAT (J/1)

AUSTER AIRCRAFT LTD.

TYPE: Light aircraft.
ACCOMMODATION: 3-4.
POWERED BY: 90 h.p. Blackburn Cirrus Minor 2 piston-engine.

SPAN: 36 ft.
LENGTH: 23 ft. 5 in.
LOADED WEIGHT: 1,850 lb.
MAX. SPEED: 120 m.p.h.
CEILING: 15,000 ft.
TYPICAL RANGE: 600 miles at 100 m.p.h. with long-range tank.

RECOGNITION FEATURES

Similar to Aiglet Trainer (page 8) but with longer-span wings and no exhaust pipe silencer under engine. Can carry a small flush-fitting fuel tank under its fuselage.

REMARKS

Original post-war civil development of the military Auster Mk. 5. The J/1 is the basic three-seater; the J/1A was a four-seater. From the Autocrat was developed the Auster J/5, with 130 h.p. Gipsy Major 1 engine, for the Australian and New Zealand market, where the 3-seat version is known as the Autocrat and the 4-seater as the Adventurer. Later developments were the J/1B Aiglet (distinguishable by horn-balanced rudder), J/2 Arrow (page 57), J/4 (page 57), J/5B Autocar (page 9) and J/5F series Aiglet Trainer (page 8).

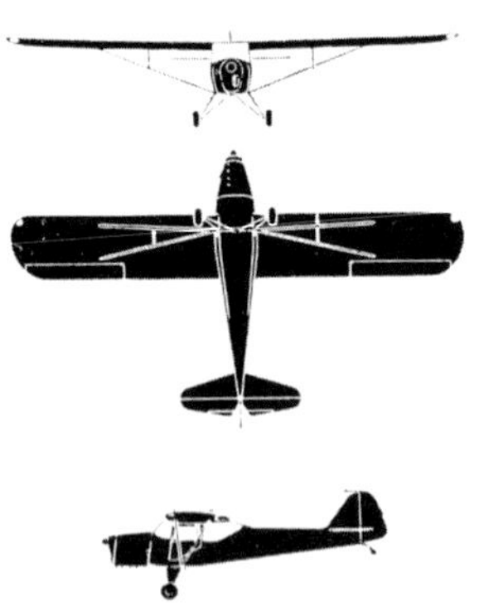

190

[*"The Aeroplane"*

TYPE: Light transport.

ACCOMMODATION: 6-9.

POWERED BY: 2 × 420 h.p. A.S. Cheetah 15 or 17 piston-engines.

SPAN: 56 ft. 6 in.

LENGTH: 42 ft. 3 in.

LOADED WEIGHT: 10,400 lb.

MAX SPEED: 190 m.p.h.

CEILING: 19,000 ft.

TYPICAL RANGE: 610 miles at 155 m.p.h. at 3,000 ft. with five passengers.

RECOGNITION FEATURES

Can be distinguished from Consul (page 6) by long " needle " nose, low-set diamond-shaped tailplane; broader, less pointed rudder; and longer engine nacelles forward of wing.

REMARKS

Civil version of the wartime Anson. Some are used for experimental purposes, including one with cloud and collision warning radar in a nose radome.

AVRO 19
A. V. ROE AND CO. LTD.

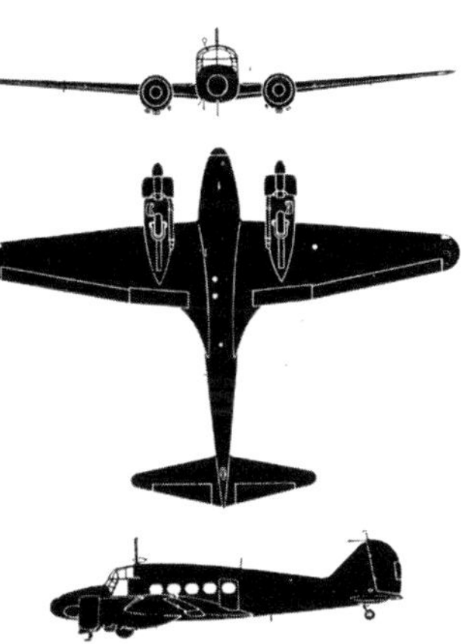

AVRO TUDOR 4

A. V. ROE AND CO. LTD.

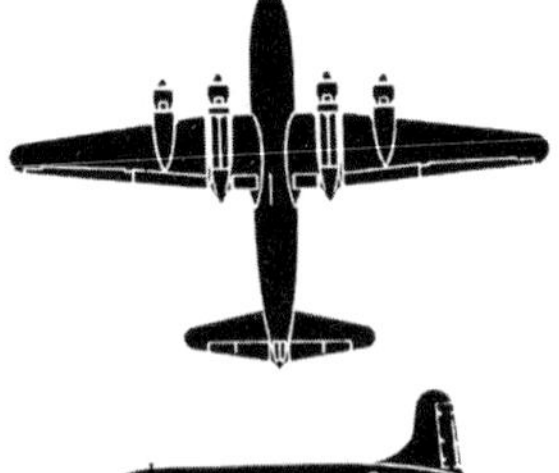

TYPE: Passenger and freight transport.

ACCOMMODATION: 3 crew + 45 passengers.

POWERED BY: 4 × 1,740 h.p. Rolls-Royce Merlin 621 piston-engines.

SPAN: 120 ft.

LENGTH: 85 ft. 6 in.

LOADED WEIGHT: 80,000 lb.

MAX. SPEED: 345 m.p.h.

TYPICAL RANGE: 3,900 miles at 230 m.p.h.

RECOGNITION FEATURES

Fairly orthodox low-wing monoplane. Very like Hermes in some aspects; but with very tall, oddly-shaped fin and rudder, tapered tailplane and in-line engines, the inboard pair of which project behind wing trailing edge. Mk. 2 has a much longer (106 ft. 7 in.) fuselage.

REMARKS

A number of Tudors of various Marks are used by Air Charter Ltd. for passenger and freight charters. The Super Trader is a version of the Tudor 4 with special freight-loading doors.

TYPE: Passenger and freight transport.
ACCOMMODATION: 4-5 crew + 17-32 passengers.
POWERED BY: 4 × 1,620 h.p. Rolls-Royce Merlin 24 or 500 piston-engines.
SPAN: 102 ft.
LENGTH: 78 ft.
LOADED WEIGHT: 71,000 lb.
MAX. SPEED: 306 m.p.h.
CEILING: 23,000 ft.
TYPICAL RANGE: 2,700 miles at 255 m.p.h. at 10,500 ft. with 21 passengers and baggage.

RECOGNITION FEATURES

Tapered wing with four in-line engines and a big square-section fuselage slung underneath it. Short nose. High-mounted tailplane with three fins. Dihedral only outboard of inner engines.

REMARKS

Designed to R.A.F. transport requirements 1942-43 as a Lancaster derivative, using same wing and tail. Adopted as stop-gap passenger transport by B.O.A.C. 1946; now mostly used (including surplus R.A.F. aircraft) for charter flights and freighting.

AVRO YORK

A. V. ROE AND CO. LTD.

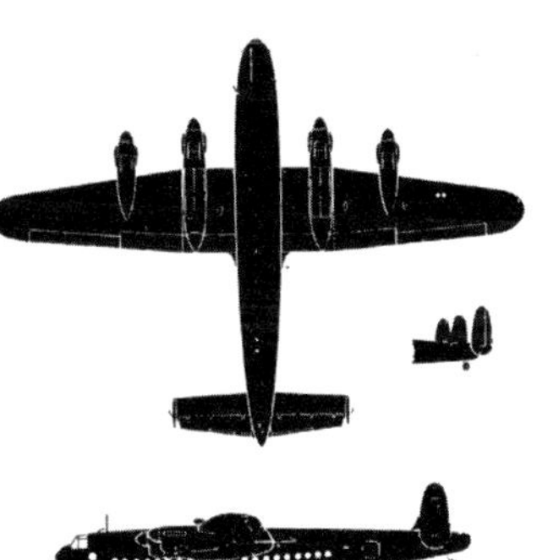

13

STRATOCRUISER

BOEING AIRPLANE CO. (U.S.A.)

TYPE: Long-range passenger transport.
ACCOMMODATION: 7 crew + up to 100 passengers.
POWERED BY: 4 × 3,500 h.p. P. & W. R-4360 piston-engines.
SPAN: 141 ft. 3 in.
LENGTH: 110 ft. 4 in.
LOADED WEIGHT: 145,800 lb.
MAX. SPEED: 375 m.p.h.
CEILING: 32,000 ft.
MAX. RANGE: 4,600 miles.

RECOGNITION FEATURES

Deep, blunt-nosed "figure 8" fuselage carried on long, narrow tapered wings, with four engines in big nacelles which project beyond the trailing edge. Sharply upswept rear fuselage, surmounted by huge fin and rudder.

REMARKS

Passenger transport development of B-29/B-50 Superfortress (via C-97 Stratofreighter) with new fuselage and power plants. Used by major U.S. airlines and B.O.A.C. Military versions used by U.S. Military Air Transport Service for passenger, freight and casualty transport, and by U.S.A.F. for flight refuelling duties.

TYPE: Heavy passenger or freight transport.
ACCOMMODATION: 3 crew+up to 107 passengers.
POWERED BY: 4×2,400 h.p. P. & W. R-2800 CA 18 piston-engines.
SPAN: 140 ft. 5 in.
LENGTH: 94 ft. 11 in.
LOADED WEIGHT: 113,800 lb.
MAX. CRUISING SPEED: 231 m.p.h.
TYPICAL RANGE: 1,430 miles at 210 m.p.h. at 10,000 ft. with full load.

RECOGNITION FEATURES

Unmistakable massive double-deck fuselage, with squat centre fin, and very narrow outboard fins and rudders. Mid-wing, with parallel chord centre-section and marked sweepback on leading edge of outer panels.

REMARKS

Twelve Breguet Type 763 Deux-Ponts transports are used by Air France for high density passenger and freight services, and occasionally visit the U.K. Usually, 59 tourist-class passengers are carried on the upper deck and 48 second-class passengers on the lower deck.

DEUX-PONTS

SOCIETE ANONYME DES AVIONS LOUIS BREGUET (FRANCE)

SUPERFREIGHTER Mk. 32

FREIGHTER and SUPERFREIGHTER Mk. 32 (BRISTOL 170)

BRISTOL AEROPLANE CO. LTD.

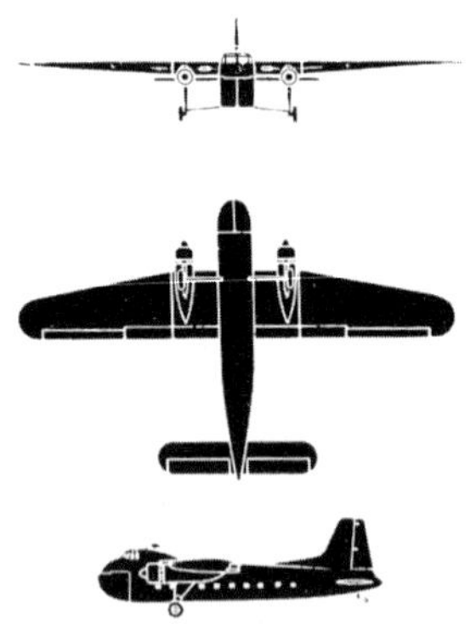

Mk. 31

TYPE: Medium-range transport.

ACCOMMODATION: 3 crew+12-20 passengers and 3 motor cars.

POWERED BY: 2×2,000 h.p. Bristol Hercules 734 piston-engines.

SPAN: 108 ft.   LENGTH: 73 ft. 4 in.

LOADED WEIGHT: 44,000 lb.

MAX. SPEED: 230 m.p.h.

CEILING: 24,500 ft.

TYPICAL RANGE: 1,270 miles at 164 m.p.h. with 8,000 lb. payload.

RECOGNITION FEATURES

Boxcar-type, bull-nosed fuselage with big loading doors at the front and large tail. Massive wing, with swept-back outer panels, underslung engines and fixed, braced undercarriage. Mk. 32 has longer nose than earlier versions and taller fin.

REMARKS

Utility post-war passenger and freight transport, designed for economical operation in all climates with minimum servicing. Long-nosed Mk. 32, illustrated above, is used by Air Charter and by Silver City Airways on their cross-channel car ferry services, together with Mk. 21 aircraft similar to silhouette but without dorsal fin. Mk. 31 is used by Aer Lingus and other operators. Data applies to Superfreighter Mk. 32.

Mk. 3A

TYPE: Taxi and general purpose helicopter.
ACCOMMODATION: 4-5.
POWERED BY: 550 h.p. Alvis Leonides LE23HM piston-engine.
ROTOR DIAMETER: 48 ft. 7 in.
FUSELAGE LENGTH: 43 ft. 8½ in.
LOADED WEIGHT: 5,300 lb.
MAX. SPEED: 141 m.p.h.
CEILING: 16,000 ft.
TYPICAL RANGE: 270 miles at 90 m.p.h. at 1,000 ft.

RECOGNITION FEATURES

Tadpole-shaped fuselage, with short well-rounded cabin section and long cranked tail-boom. Rotor is much closer to top of cabin than that of Westland-Sikorsky S-51 (page 55).

REMARKS

First British-designed helicopter to gain C. of A. Two Mk. 1 prototypes had 450 h.p. Wasp Junior engines. Mk. 2 was the Leonides-engined prototype for the initial production batch of Mk. 3 aircraft. Two Mk. 3A are used by B.E.A. for regular passenger and freight-carrying services. The current production version for civil and military duties is the Mk. 4, to which the above data applies.

BRISTOL TYPE 171

BRISTOL AEROPLANE CO. LTD.

BRITANNIA Mk.100 (BRISTOL TYPE 175)

BRISTOL AEROPLANE CO. LTD.

TYPE: Long-range transport.
ACCOMMODATION: 5 crew+50-104 passengers.

POWERED BY: 4×3,780 e.h.p. Bristol Proteus 705 propeller-turbines.
SPAN: 140 ft.   LENGTH: 114 ft.
LOADED WEIGHT: 140,000 lb.
MAX. SPEED: 400 m.p.h.
RANGE: 3,000 miles at 350 m.p.h. at 30,000 ft. with maximum payload, with fuel reserves.

RECOGNITION FEATURES

Long cylindrical fuselage with pointed nose and big "Welsh hat" fin and rudder, with long dorsal fin. Low-set straight tapered tailplane. Long straight tapered wings with sweptback leading edge and dihedral along whole length. Engines centrally mounted in long nacelles which project well beyond wing trailing edge.

REMARKS

The Mk. 100 will be followed by a longer-fuselage version with Proteus 755 engines. This version will be built as the Series 300 passenger transport, the Series 300 L.R., with increased fuel tankage, and Series 250 mixed passenger/freight aircraft. B.O.A.C. have ordered 15 Mk. 100's, 8 Mk. 300's and 10 Mk. 300 L.R.'s. Some 300's and 300 L.R.'s will be re-engined later with BE.25 turboprops. El Al have ordered 3 Mk. 300 L.R.'s and the Government some Mk. 250 L.R.'s.

TYPE: Passenger and freight transport.
ACCOMMODATION: 6 crew+40-55 passengers.
POWERED BY: 4×1,760 h.p. Rolls-Royce Merlin 626 piston-engines.
SPAN: 117 ft. 6 in.
LENGTH: 93 ft. 7½ in.
LOADED WEIGHT: 82,300 lb.
MAX. SPEED: 353 m.p.h.
CEILING: 29,500 ft.
TYPICAL RANGE: 3,500 miles at 302 m.p.h.

CANADAIR FOUR (ARGONAUT)

CANADAIR LTD. (CANADA)

RECOGNITION FEATURES

Basically similar to DC-4 (page 34), but with "in-line" engines and broken line of square windows down each side of cabin. Compare also with Hermes.

REMARKS

Developed version of DC-4, built under licence in Canada. 24 unpressurised C-54GM military transports supplied to R.C.A.F. and 20 pressurised DC-4M2's to Trans-Canada Air Lines. B.O.A.C.'s 22 Canadair Fours (*Argonaut*-class) are basically similar to DC-4M2.

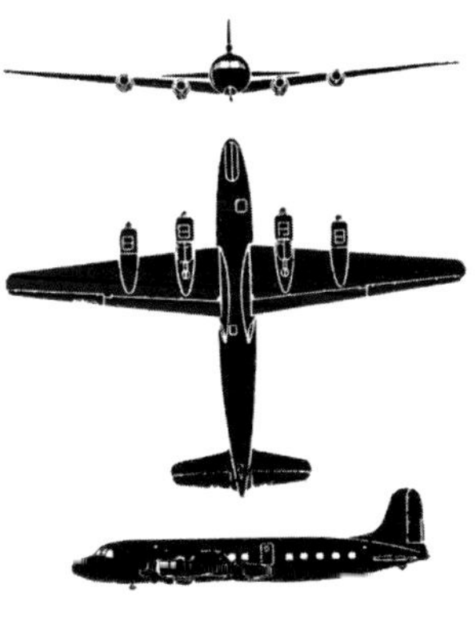

[John W. R. Taylor

CONVAIR-LINER 240

CONVAIR DIVISION OF GENERAL DYNAMICS CORP. (U.S.A.)

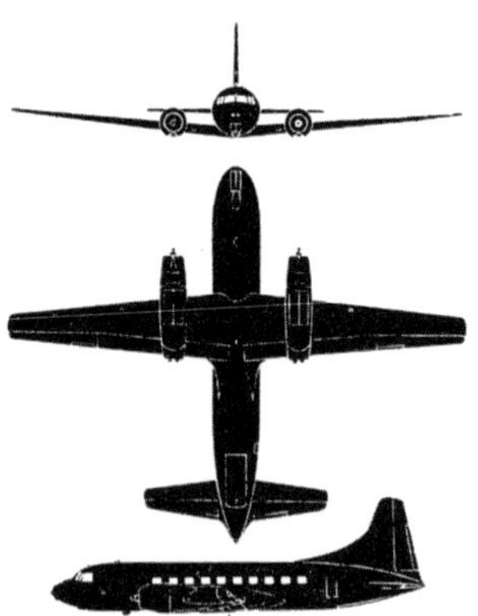

TYPE: Medium-range passenger transport.

ACCOMMODATION: 3-4 crew + 40 passengers.

POWERED BY: 2 × 2,400 h.p. P. & W. R-2800-CA18 piston-engines.

SPAN: 91 ft. 9 in.

LENGTH: 74 ft. 8 in.

LOADED WEIGHT: 41,790 lb.

MAX. SPEED: 347 m.p.h.

CEILING: 30,000 ft.

TYPICAL RANGE: 1,800 miles at 270 m.p.h. at 16,000 ft.

RECOGNITION FEATURES

Cylindrical fuselage with smooth rounded nose and very large dorsal fin forward of its square-cut fin and rudder. Long, tapered low wing carrying high-mounted engines, each with two big exhaust pipes which project distinctively above wing trailing edge. Compare with longer Convair-Liner 340 (opposite).

REMARKS

Standard medium-range air liner used by K.L.M., Sabena and Swissair on services to U.K. From it has been developed the Convair-Liner 340.

TYPE: Medium-range passenger transport.

ACCOMMODATION: 3-4 crew+44 passengers.

POWERED BY: 2×2,400 h.p. P. & W. R-2800-CB16 piston-engines.

SPAN: 105 ft. 4 in.

LENGTH: 79 ft. 2 in.

LOADED WEIGHT: 47,000 lb.

MAX. SPEED: 314 m.p.h.

CEILING: 26,000 ft.

TYPICAL RANGE: 1,040 miles at 284 m.p.h. at 18,000 ft. with fuel reserves

RECOGNITION FEATURES

Basically same as Convair-Liner 240 (opposite), but with bigger wing span and longer fuselage.

REMARKS

Developed from the earlier Model 240, the Convair-Liner 340 is one of the most popular air liners built post-war, and can be seen in Britain in the insignia of Alitalia, Finnair, Lufthansa and K.L.M. One Convair 340 has been purchased by Napiers, who are fitting two Eland turbo-props for demonstration flying later in 1955.

CONVAIR-LINER 340

CONVAIR DIVISION OF GENERAL DYNAMICS CORP. (U.S.A.)

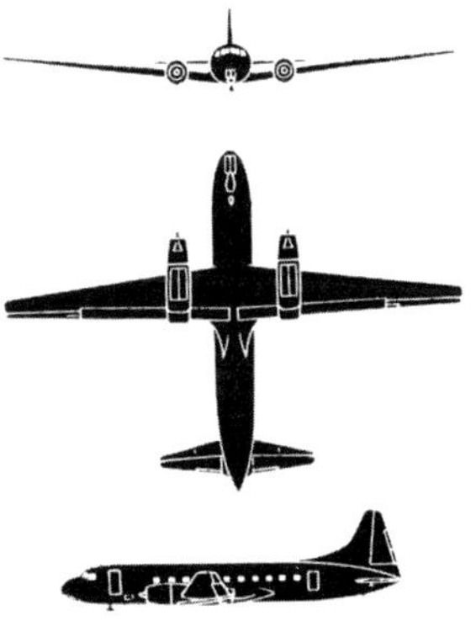

C-46 COMMANDO

THE CURTISS-WRIGHT CORP.
(U.S.A.)

TYPE: Passenger and freight transport.
ACCOMMODATION: 4 crew+36 passengers or freight.
POWERED BY: 2×2,000 h.p. P. & W. R-2800-51 piston-engines.
SPAN: 108 ft. 1 in. LENGTH: 76 ft. 4 in.
LOADED WEIGHT: 45,000 lb.
MAX. SPEED: 265 m.p.h.
CEILING: 24,500 ft.
RANGE: 1,600 miles at 195 m.p.h.

RECOGNITION FEATURES

Although often referred to as a "Double-bubble Dak", the Commando is quite distinctive. Its bulky figure-8 section fuselage has no cockpit "step" at the front, and a well-rounded fin and rudder. The wings are more evenly-tapered on their leading and trailing edges than are the Dakota's wings.

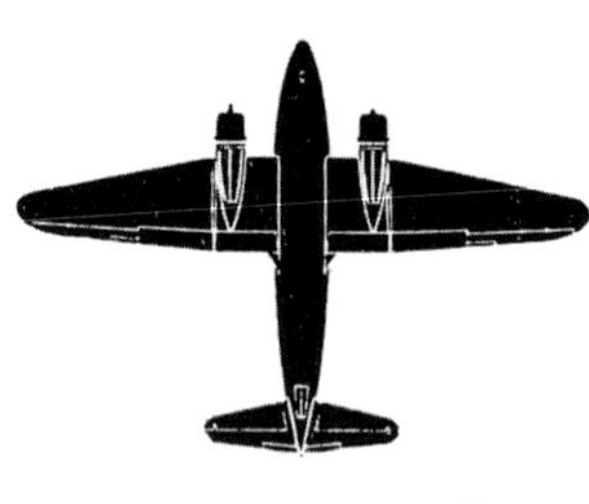

REMARKS

Ex-U.S.A.F. Commandos are used by many airlines throughout the world. El Al, the Israeli airline, fly them on regular freight services to the United Kingdom.

22

TYPE: Light passenger/freight transport.
ACCOMMODATION: 7.
POWERED BY: 570 h.p. Alvis Leonides 502/4 piston-engine.
SPAN: 48 ft. 8 in.   LENGTH: 31 ft. 9 in.
LOADED WEIGHT: 5,100 lb.
MAX. SPEED: 172 m.p.h.
CEILING: 21,300 ft.
MAX. RANGE: 1,000 miles at 155 m.p.h. at 10,000 ft.

RECOGNITION FEATURES

Rugged, practical design with few frills. Orthodox square-section fuselage, with large triangular fin and rudder. Fixed cantilever undercarriage. Long, narrow, plank-like wings, braced with a single strut each side.

REMARKS

The aircraft illustrated is used as a demonstration machine and runabout by the parent de Havilland company in England. Series 1 Beavers (silhouette) may also be seen in the U.K., both in civil markings and in the insignia of the U.S.A.F. and U.S. Army. They have 450 h.p. R-985 Wasp Junior engines and different-shaped fin and rudder.

BEAVER
Series 2

DE HAVILLAND AIRCRAFT OF CANADA LTD.

['Flight'']

CHIPMUNK 21

DE HAVILLAND AIRCRAFT CO. LTD.

TYPE: Light trainer and private aircraft.

ACCOMMODATION: 2.

POWERED BY: 145 h.p. D.H. Gipsy Major 10-2 piston-engine.

SPAN: 34 ft 4 in.

LENGTH: 25 ft. 8 in.

LOADED WEIGHT: 2,000 lb.

MAX. SPEED: 138 m.p.h.

CEILING: 16,000 ft.

TYPICAL RANGE: 292 miles at 124 m.p.h. at 5,000 ft.

RECOGNITION FEATURES

Neat little monoplane with long narrow wings, in-line engine, slender rear fuselage and spindly fixed undercarriage. Typical de Havilland elliptical fin and rudder (see Dove, Rapide, etc.).

REMARKS

Designed by de Havilland Aircraft of Canada Ltd., the Chipmunk has also been built in quantity by the parent company in the U.K. for the R.A.F. and overseas air forces, and for civil operators. It is flying in small numbers with clubs and training organisations.

DATA APPLIES TO COMET 3
TYPE: Medium-range air liner.
ACCOMMODATION: 4 crew + 58-76 passengers.
POWERED BY: 4 × 10,000 lb. thrust Rolls-Royce Avon turbojets.
SPAN: 115 ft.   LENGTH: 111 ft. 6 in.
LOADED WEIGHT: 150,000 lb.
RANGE: 2,600 miles at 500 m.p.h. at 40,000 ft.

RECOGNITION FEATURES
Cylindrical fuselage with down-swept nose containing cockpit and upswept tail. Small straight-tapered fin and rudder ; straight-tapered dihedral tailplane; broad, gracefully sweptback low wings with cranked trailing edge and engines buried in long blisters at roots. Series 3 has leading edge fuel tanks as shown in illustrations.

REMARKS
Temporarily withdrawn from service, the Comet is under active development for future passenger operations. First to go into service again will be modified Series 2 aircraft, which will be used by R.A.F. Transport Command. B.O.A.C. will have 20 Series 4's, which will be developments of the Series 3, with later Avons and more fuel.

COMET Series 2 & 3

DE HAVILLAND AIRCRAFT CO. LTD.

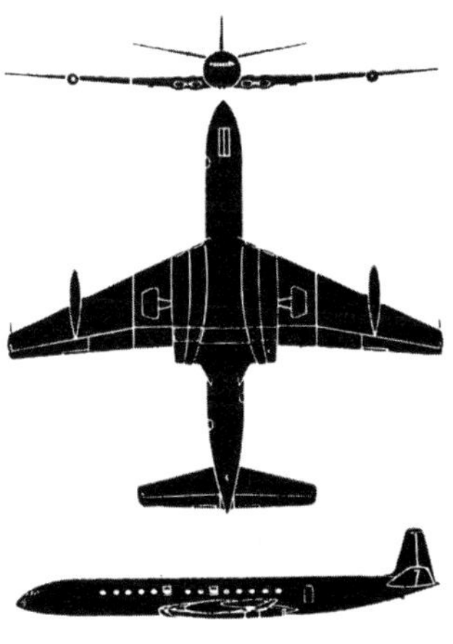

Comet 3

205

DOVE Series 6
DE HAVILLAND AIRCRAFT CO. LTD.

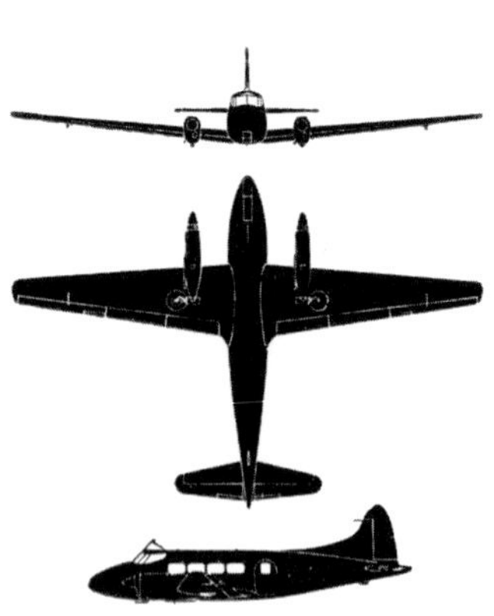

TYPE: Light transport.

ACCOMMODATION: 2 crew+8-11 passengers.

POWERED BY: 2×380 h.p. D.H. Gipsy Queen 70 Mk.2 piston-engines.

SPAN: 57 ft.

LENGTH: 39 ft. 6 in.

LOADED WEIGHT: 8,800 lb.

MAX. SPEED: 210 m.p.h.

CEILING: 20,000 ft.

TYPICAL RANGE: 850 miles at 179 m.p.h. at 8,000 ft. with 1,500 lb. payload.

RECOGNITION FEATURES

Low-wing monoplane with long tapered wings, and engines in slim nacelles close to fuselage. Distinctive blister on cockpit hood and typical de Havilland elliptical fin and rudder (see Chipmunk, Rapide, etc.), with dorsal fairing. Conical rear fuselage.

REMARKS

Popular post-war light transport. In service with R.A.F. as the Devon and with the F.A.A. as the Sea Devon. Dove Series 1 is standard with 340 h.p. Gipsy Queen 70 engines and 8,500 lb. all-up weight; Dove Series 2 is executive version; Dove Series 5 and 6 respectively standard and executive transports.

TYPE: Pre-war light transport.
ACCOMMODATION: 1 crew+6-8 passengers.
POWERED BY: 2×205 h.p. D.H. Gipsy Six III or Gipsy Queen III piston-engines.
SPAN: 48 ft.
LENGTH: 34 ft. 6 in.
LOADED WEIGHT: 5,750 lb.
MAX. SPEED: 157 m.p.h.
CEILING: 16,700 ft.
RANGE: 556 miles at 117 m.p.h. at 2,000 ft. with normal load.

RECOGNITION FEATURES

Twin-engined biplane, with narrow, pointed wings and slab-sided fuselage with typical de Havilland elliptical fin and rudder. Non-retractable wheels under engines, enclosed in " trouser " fairings.

REMARKS

The D.H.89A Dragon Rapide was one of the last de Havilland aircraft produced before the War. Hundreds were built 1939-45 for R.A.F. training and communications as the Dominie, and many of these, plus a few pre-war models, are used by charter companies, clubs, private owners, and B.E.A.

DRAGON RAPIDE

DE HAVILLAND AIRCRAFT CO. LTD.

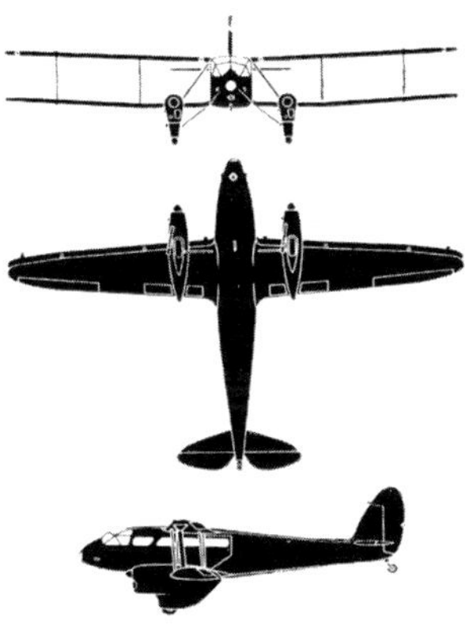

HERON Series 2

DE HAVILLAND AIRCRAFT CO. LTD.

SERIES I

TYPE: Feeder-line transport.

ACCOMMODATION: 2 crew + 14-17 passengers.

POWERED BY: 4 × 250 h.p. D.H. Gipsy Queen 30 Mk.2 piston-engines.

SPAN: 71 ft. 6 in.

LENGTH: 48 ft. 6 in.

LOADED WEIGHT: 13,000 lb.

CEILING: 18,500 ft.

TYPICAL RANGE: 460 miles at 183 m.p.h. at 8,000 ft. with capacity payload.

RECOGNITION FEATURES

Fuselage and wing very like elongated Dove. Dihedral tailplane and four engines in long slim nacelles. Series 1 has fixed undercarriage (silhouette).

REMARKS

Enlarged, four-engined version of the Dove (page 26), with which many components are interchangeable. In service with B.E.A. on Northern Scottish services, Jersey Airlines, and several overseas local airlines. Series 1 and 2 are generally similar except for the retractable undercarriage fitted to the latter. Data applies to Series 2.

208

["*Flight*"]

HORNET MOTH

DE HAVILLAND AIRCRAFT CO. LTD.

TYPE: Pre-war light aircraft.

ACCOMMODATION: 2.

POWERED BY: 130 h.p. D.H. Gipsy Major I piston-engine.

SPAN: 31 ft. 11 in.

LENGTH: 24 ft. $11\frac{1}{2}$ in.

LOADED WEIGHT: 1,950 lb.

MAX. SPEED: 124 m.p.h.

CEILING: 14,300 ft.

TYPICAL RANGE: 623 miles at 105 m.p.h. at 1,000 ft.

RECOGNITION FEATURES

Biplane version of Leopard and Puss Moth (page 31), with square-cut wings, enclosed cabin, fixed, strutted undercarriage and typical de Havilland elliptical tailplane, fin and rudder. Compare with Tiger Moth (page 32), and Fox Moth (page 60).

REMARKS

A popular private owner cabin type before the war, used in numbers on communication duties through the war. First version had elliptical wing tips, but none of these are now flying in this country.

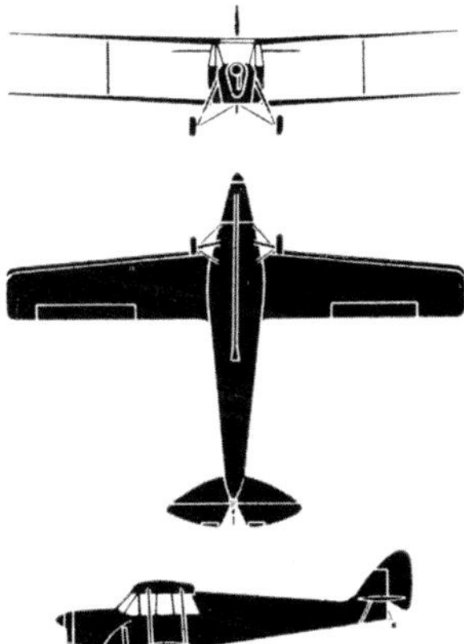

MOTH MINOR

DE HAVILLAND AIRCRAFT CO. LTD.

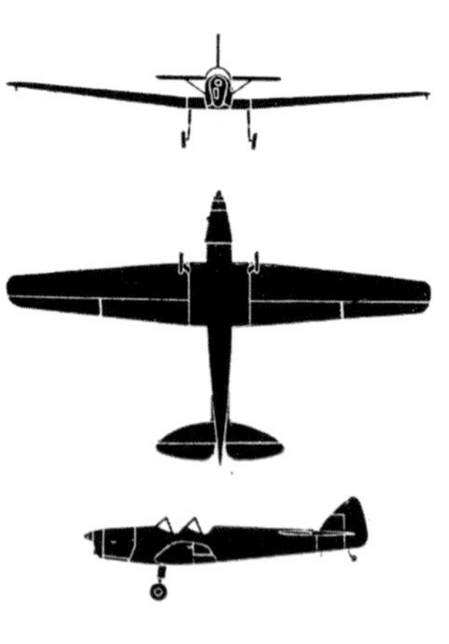

TYPE: Pre-war light aircraft.

ACCOMMODATION: 2.

POWERED BY: 90 h.p. D.H. Gipsy Minor piston-engine.

SPAN: 36 ft. 7 in.

LENGTH: 24 ft. 5 in.

LOADED WEIGHT: 1,550 lb.

MAX. SPEED: 120 m.p.h.

CEILING: 16,600 ft.

TYPICAL RANGE: 300 miles at 100 m.p.h

RECOGNITION FEATURES

Slim fuselage with two open cockpits and typical de Havilland elliptical tail. Long-span tapered wings. Fixed, cantilever undercarriage. Compare with more "boxy" Swallow (page 58).

REMARKS

De Havilland's last pre-war light aircraft, intended to reduce private flying and training costs to a minimum, without sacrificing performance. Several survived war and are still giving good service. At least one coupé version is still flying, with enclosed cabin.

PUSS MOTH

TYPE: Pre-war light aircraft.

ACCOMMODATION: 2.

POWERED BY: 120 h.p. D.H. Gipsy III piston-engine.

SPAN: 36 ft. 9 in.

LENGTH: 25 ft.

LOADED WEIGHT: 2,050 lb.

MAX. SPEED: 128 m.p.h.

CEILING: 17,500 ft.

TYPICAL RANGE: 710 miles.

RECOGNITION FEATURES

Compared with Auster series, the Puss and Leopard Moths have less plank-like wings with cutaway centre section; typical de Havilland elliptical tail and much-strutted undercarriage. Photograph shows Puss Moth; silhouette shows Leopard Moth.

REMARKS

Famous de Havilland high wing private-owner monoplanes, best distinguished by their main undercarriage struts, which continue to the top of the cabin in the Puss Moth. A few examples of each still fly. Data refers to Puss Moth.

PUSS MOTH (and LEOPARD MOTH)

DE HAVILLAND AIRCRAFT CO. LTD.

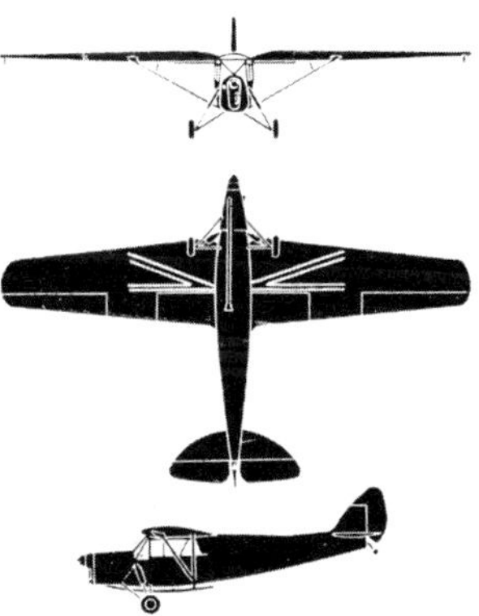

LEOPARD MOTH

TIGER MOTH

DE HAVILLAND AIRCRAFT CO., LTD.

TYPE: Pre-war trainer and light aircraft.

ACCOMMODATION: 2.

POWERED BY: 130 h.p. de Havilland Gipsy Major I piston-engine.

SPAN: 29 ft. 4 in.

LENGTH: 23 ft. 11 in.

LOADED WEIGHT: 1,770 lb.

MAX. SPEED: 109 m.p.h.

CEILING: 13,600 ft.

TYPICAL RANGE: 300 miles at 94 m.p.h.

RECOGNITION FEATURES

Orthodox light biplane. Compared with Club Cadet (page 58) has more sweptback wings, typical de Havilland elliptical tail (see Rapide) and fairing forward of tailplane.

REMARKS

Few aeroplanes are more famous. Built before the war for clubs and the R.A.F., and produced in vast quantities during war in U.K., Australia and Canada as standard primary R.A.F. trainer. Many still used by clubs and private owners, mostly ex-R.A.F. aircraft.

212

TYPE: Medium-range passenger and freight transport.

ACCOMMODATION: 3 crew + 32 passengers. LOADED WEIGHT: 28,000 lb.

POWERED BY: 2 × 1,200 h.p. P. & W. R-1830-92 piston-engines.

SPAN: 95 ft.   LENGTH: 64 ft. 5 in.

MAX. SPEED: 230 m.p.h.

CEILING: 23,200 ft.

TYPICAL RANGE: 1,510 miles at 167 m.p.h. at 5,000 ft.

RECOGNITION FEATURES

Low-wing monoplane, with distinctive dihedral and sweep-back on leading edges of wing, and engines mounted close to fuselage. Wheels do not retract fully in flight. Typical Douglas fin and rudder.

REMARKS

World's best-known air liner, seen over Britain in the colours of many overseas airlines and British independent companies, as well as B.E.A., who have 38 improved versions known as Pionairs, eight Pionair Leopard convertible passenger/freighters and two Pionair Freighters. Most are converted C-47 military transports, of

DC-3, DAKOTA and PIONAIR
DOUGLAS AIRCRAFT CO. INC.
(U.S.A.)

which 10,123 were built. Data applies to Pionair.

213

DC-4 SKYMASTER

DOUGLAS AIRCRAFT CO. INC.
(U.S.A.)

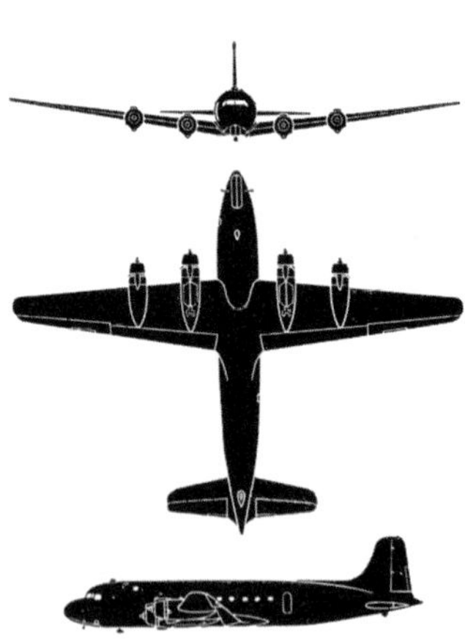

TYPE: Passenger and freight transport.
ACCOMMODATION: 5 crew + 44 passengers.
POWERED BY: 4×1,450 h.p. P. & W. Twin-Wasp R-2000 piston-engines.
SPAN: 117 ft 6 in.
LENGTH: 93 ft. 11 in.
LOADED WEIGHT: 73,000 lb.
MAX. SPEED: 280 m.p.h.
CEILING: 22,300 ft.
TYPICAL RANGE: 1,500 miles at 220 m.p.h. at 10,000 ft. with 16,500 lb. cargo.

RECOGNITION FEATURES

Circular fuselage with Dakota-type nose and typical Douglas tail. Sharply tapered wings. Note especially the big wing dihedral and four mid-set engines with no propeller spinners. Unbroken line of 10 circular windows each side of cabin. Compare with DC-6, Canadair Four and Hermes.

REMARKS

Civil counterpart of the C-54 military transport. 74 built post-war to supplement several hundred C-54's civilianised for airline service throughout the world.

DC-6B

TYPE: Passenger and freight transport.
ACCOMMODATION: 5 crew + 54-92 passengers.
POWERED BY: 4×2,500 h.p. P. & W. Double-Wasp R-2800-CB17.
SPAN: 117½ ft.   LENGTH: 105 ft. 7 in.
LOADED WEIGHT: 106,000 lb.
MAX. SPEED: 360 m.p.h.
TYPICAL RANGE: 3,860 miles at 311 m.p.h. at 20,600 ft. at 100,000 lb. all-up weight.

RECOGNITION FEATURES

Basically similar to DC-4 (page 34), but longer fuselage with square windows and more square top to fin and rudder.

REMARKS

The DC-6 (length 100 ft. 7 in.) is a larger and slightly more powerful development of the DC-4, carrying 48-58 passengers. The 5 ft. longer DC-6A Liftmaster is a specially-developed freight version of the standard DC-6. The DC-6B is a passenger version of the DC-6A, in service with many airlines, and the DC-6C is a convertible passenger-freighter with a loaded weight of 107,000 lb. and accommodation for 76 passengers. Data refers to DC-6B.

DC-6, DC-6A and DC-6B

DOUGLAS AIRCRAFT CO. INC.
(U.S.A.)

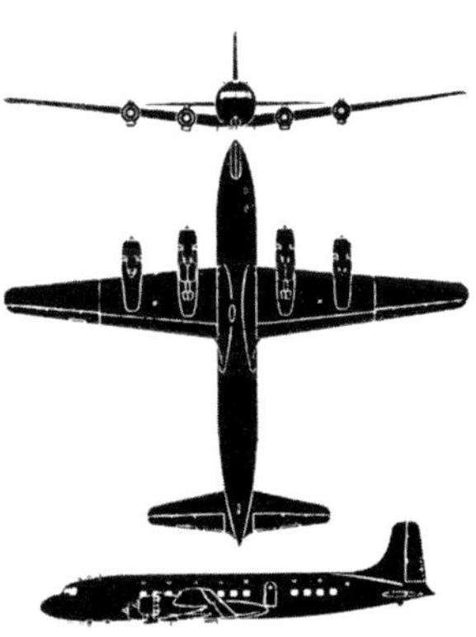

DC-6

215

DC-7

DOUGLAS AIRCRAFT CO. INC.
(U.S.A.)

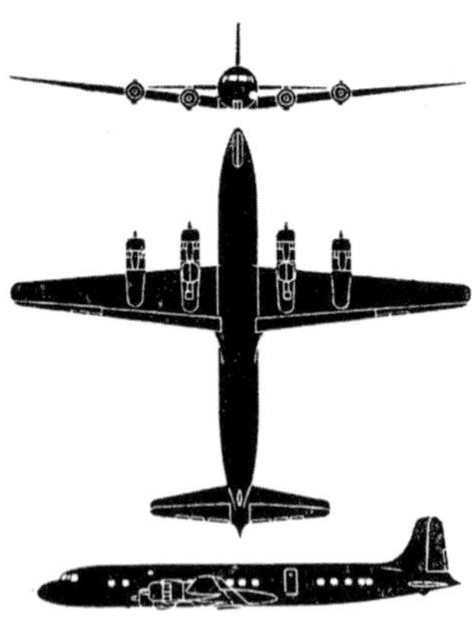

TYPE: Long-range passenger transport.
ACCOMMODATION: 7+66-95 passengers.
POWERED BY: 4×3,250 h.p. Wright R-3350-18DA1 Turbo Compound engines.
SPAN: 117 ft. 6 in.
LENGTH: 108 ft. 11 in.
LOADED WEIGHT: 122,200 lb.
MAX. SPEED: 410 m.p.h.
CEILING: 27,900 ft.
TYPICAL RANGE: 4,430 miles with 5,512 gallons of fuel.

RECOGNITION FEATURES

Slightly longer fuselage than DC-6 series (page 35), but almost indistinguishable from them.

REMARKS

Progressive development of the DC-6, with longer fuselage and more powerful engines. Later version will be the DC-7C " Seven Seas ", ordered by B.O.A.C., Scandinavian Airlines System, Pan American and other airlines, for service on the North Atlantic and similar long-distance routes. With an all-up weight of 137,000 lb., it will carry 38 first class or 76 tourist passengers for 3,450 miles at 320 m.p.h.

TYPE: Passenger transport.
ACCOMMODATION: 5 crew+40-74 passengers.
POWERED BY: 4×2,100 h.p. Bristol Hercules 773 piston-engines.
SPAN: 113 ft.
LENGTH: 96 ft. 10 in.
LOADED WEIGHT: 86,000 lb.
MAX. SPEED: 355 m.p.h.
TYPICAL RANGE: 2,000 miles at 276 m.p.h. at 20,000 ft. with 14,400 lb. payload.

RECOGNITION FEATURES

Compared with Skymaster (page 34) and Canadair Four (page 19), Hermes has a more pointed nose, " straight" wing centre-section, less dihedral and straight elevator trailing edge. The top of its fin slopes back: fins of other two slope forward. Propeller spinners are fitted and the engines appear more underslung.

REMARKS

Civil counterpart of the R.A.F.'s Hastings transport, in service with Airwork, Britavia and Skyways, and used largely for trooping duties.

HERMES 4A

HANDLEY PAGE LTD.

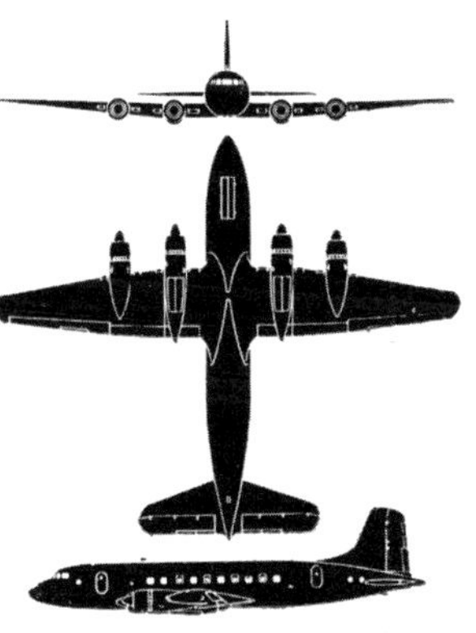

HPR-3 HERALD

HANDLEY PAGE (READING) LTD.

TYPE: Medium-range passenger/freight transport.

ACCOMMODATION: 2 crew + 36-44 passengers.

POWERED BY: 4 × 870 h.p. Alvis Leonides Major piston-engines.

SPAN: 95 ft.   LENGTH: 70 ft. 3 in.

LOADED WEIGHT: 34,000 lb.

CEILING: 24,500 ft.

TYPICAL RANGE: 1,4!7 miles at 231 m.p.h. at 13,500 ft. with 6,930 lb. payload.

RECOGNITION FEATURES

Fuselage reminiscent of Viscount, but with big squarish fin and rudder. Straight-tapered high wings, with four underslung radial engines.

REMARKS

The prototype of this new British feeder-line and general purpose transport is due to fly in the summer of 1955. Intended as a Dakota replacement, 29 have been ordered by airlines in Australia and South America.

218

TYPE: Light transport.
ACCOMMODATION: 2 crew+8-12 passengers.
POWERED BY: 2 × 550 h.p. Alvis Leonides 502/4 piston-engines.
SPAN: 56 ft.   LENGTH: 42 ft. 10 in.
LOADED WEIGHT: 11,000 lb.
MAX. SPEED: 232½ m.p.h.
CEILING: 23,400 ft.
TYPICAL RANGE: 853 miles at 178 m.p.h. at 10,000 ft. with 1,280 lb. payload.

RECOGNITION FEATURES

Long, straight tapered wings with square tips. Underslung engines, projecting behind wing trailing edges. Big, square-section fuselage slung under wing, with egg-shaped fin and rudder. Unusual bump-down under fuselage at tail. Noses of varying length, according to duty.

REMARKS

Many types of Prince have been built for civil and military use. Prince Series III (P.50), shown in silhouette, is basic 8-11 passenger transport; Series IIIA and IIID (P.54) are air survey versions with lengthened, glazed nose. Series IIIB (P.54 Mk. IV), with lengthened, " solid " nose, as shown in photograph, is used by M.C.A. for

PRINCE Series III

HUNTING PERCIVAL AIRCRAFT LTD.

airport radio calibration and other duties. Prince Series V is a projected 10-12 passenger counterpart of the R.A.F. Pembroke, with increased wing span (64ft. 6 in.) and weight (12,500 lb.)

PROCTOR
(and VEGA GULL)

HUNTING PERCIVAL AIRCRAFT LTD.

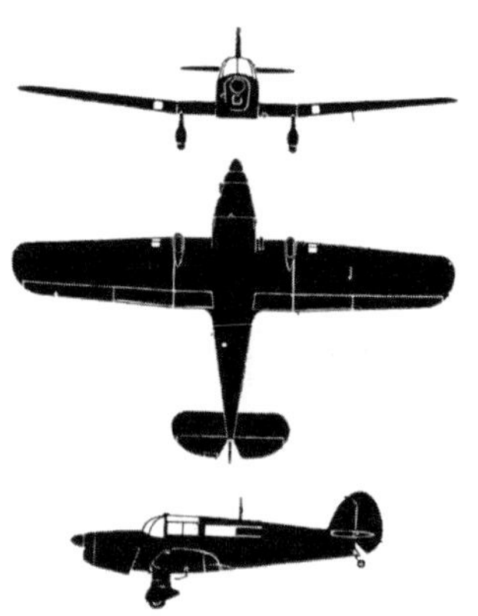

TYPE: Light aircraft.
ACCOMMODATION: 4.
POWERED BY: 208 h.p. D.H. Gipsy Queen II piston-engine.
SPAN: 39 ft. 6 in.
LENGTH: 28 ft. 2 in.
LOADED WEIGHT: 3,500 lb.
MAX. SPEED: 160 m.p.h.
CEILING: 14,000 ft.
TYPICAL RANGE: 500 miles at 146 m.p.h. at 6,000 ft.

RECOGNITION FEATURES

Compared with the Miles series of light cabin monoplanes, Proctor has more tapered wings, more rounded fin, rudder and tailplane, with a distinctive "bite" out of base of rudder. Compare with Whitney Straight (page 47).

REMARKS

Proctors 1-4 were used by R.A.F. and R.N. during war for training and communications; they were basically similar to pre-war Vega Gull light plane. Examples of all R.A.F. marks have been civilianised, and the civil Proctor 5 has been built in numbers for private owners and charter operation since 1946.

TYPE: Long-range passenger transport
ACCOMMODATION: 6 crew+44-68 passengers.
POWERED BY: 4×2,500 h.p. Wright Cyclone, GR-3350-BDI piston-engines.
SPAN: 123 ft.
LENGTH: 95 ft. I in.
LOADED WEIGHT: 107,000 lb.
MAX. SPEED: over 350 m.p.h.
CEILING: 27,300 ft.
TYPICAL RANGE: 3,000 miles at 298 m.p.h. at 20,000 ft.

CONSTELLATION L-749A

LOCKHEED AIRCRAFT CORP. (U.S.A.)

RECOGNITION FEATURES

Long circular section fuselage, appearing to slope down at nose and up at tail, with three fins and rudders. Long pointed wings set well back along fuselage, with marked dihedral. Compare with longer Super Constellation (page 42).

REMARKS

Standard long-range air liner with many airlines serving U.K., including B.O.A.C., who use it largely for low-fare tourist-class services. From it has been developed the Model 1049 Super Constellation (page 42).

SUPER CONSTELLATION L-1049C

LOCKHEED AIRCRAFT CORP.
(U.S.A.)

TYPE: Long-range passenger transport.
ACCOMMODATION: 6 crew+43-81 passengers.

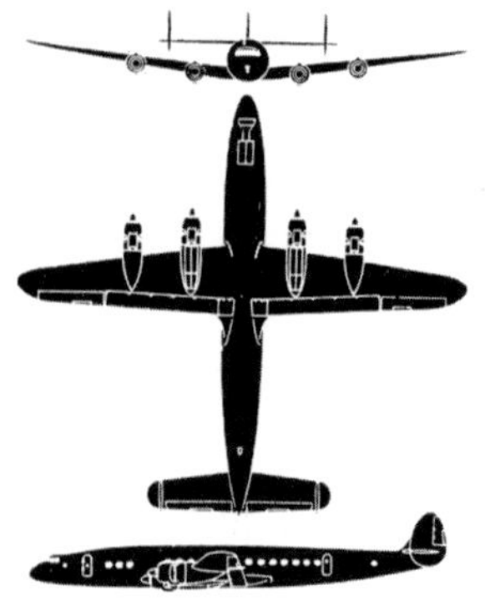

POWERED BY: 4×3,250 h.p. Wright 972C-18 DA1 Turbo Compound engines.
SPAN: 123 ft.
LENGTH: 113 ft. 7 in.
LOADED WEIGHT: 133,000 lb.
MAX. SPEED: 376 m.p.h.
CEILING: 27,600 ft.
TYPICAL RANGE: 2,450 miles at 310 m.p.h.

RECOGNITION FEATURES

Basically similar to Model 749 Constellation (page 41), with fuselage lengthened by 18 ft. 6 in. and more powerful engines. " S " shaped fuselage less noticeable than before.

REMARKS

Development of the L-749 Constellation, with increased accommodation and improved performance. Original Model 1049 had 2,700 h.p. R3350-C18-CA1 engines and carried 92 passengers. This model is used by T.W.A. and other airlines. Model 1049B is freighter equivalent of L-1049C, with Turbo Compound engines. L-1049C's can be seen over U.K. in colours of Pakistan International, K.L.M., Air France, T.C.A., Qantas and other airlines.

[*Blackburn & General Aircraft Ltd.*

TYPE: Light aircraft.

ACCOMMODATION: 4.

POWERED BY: 2 × 100 h.p. Cirrus Minor
  II piston-engines.

SPAN: 36 ft. 2 in.

LENGTH: 22 ft. 3 in.

LOADED WEIGHT: 3,000 lb.

MAX. SPEED: 150 m.p.h.

TYPICAL RANGE: 520 miles at 135 m.p.h.

GEMINI 1A
(and ARIES)

MILES AIRCRAFT LTD.

RECOGNITION FEATURES

In the air gives impression of engines and cockpit all bunched together. Typical broad Miles wing with distinctive trailing-edge flaps and underslung engines in long nacalles. Short fuselage nose. Twin fins and rudders.

REMARKS

Twin-engined development of the Messenger (page 45). Many still in service as private-owner and taxi aircraft. Gemini 3A has Gipsy Major 10-1 in bigger nacelles. A further development of the type by F. G. Miles Ltd. is the M.75 Aries, with Cirrus Major 3 engines and larger fins and rudders.

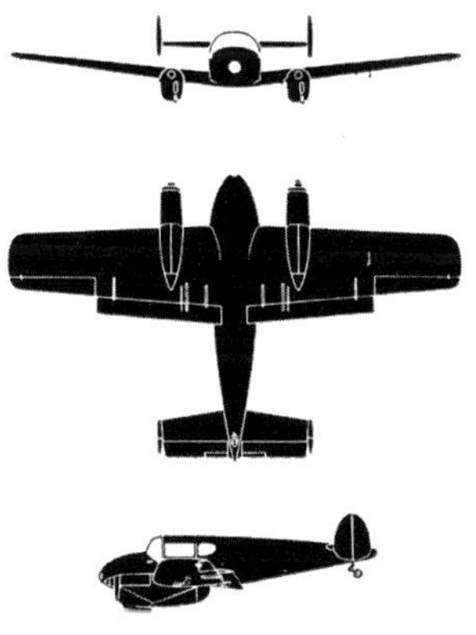

HAWK TRAINER 3

MILES AIRCRAFT LTD.

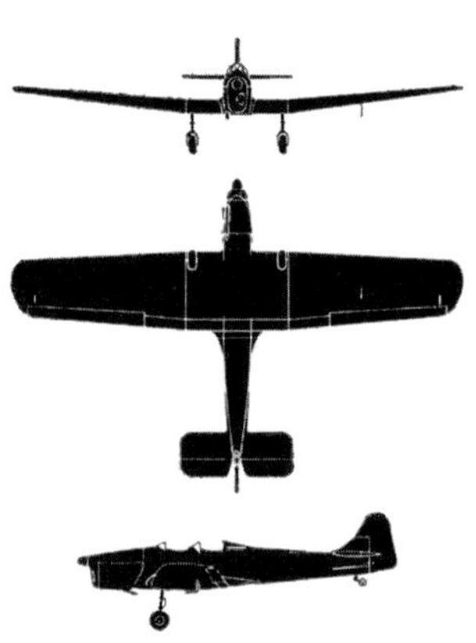

TYPE: Light aircraft.

ACCOMMODATION: 2.

POWERED BY: 130 h.p. D.H. Gipsy Major I piston-engine.

SPAN: 33 ft. 10 in.

LENGTH: 25 ft. 3 in.

LOADED WEIGHT: 1,900 lb.

MAX. SPEED: 145 m.p.h.

CEILING: 18,000 ft.

RECOGNITION FEATURES

Low-wing monoplane with fixed spatted undercarriage, typical Miles broad wing, rectangular tailplane and triangular fin and rudder. Two open cockpits. Anti-spin fairing forward of tailplane. Compare with Moth Minor (page 30).

REMARKS

As the Magister, was a standard R.A.F. wartime primary trainer. Many civilianised post-war, and used extensively by flying clubs as basic trainers.

TYPE: Light aircraft.

ACCOMMODATION: 3-4.

POWERED BY: 155 h.p. Blackburn Cirrus Major III or 145 h.p. D.H. Gipsy Major 10 piston-engine.

SPAN: 36 ft. 2 in.

LENGTH: 24 ft.

LOADED WEIGHT: 2,400 lb.

MAX. SPEED: 135 m.p.h.

CEILING: 16,000 ft.

RANGE: 460 miles at 112 m.p.h.

RECOGNITION FEATURES

Distinctive features include fixed, spindly undercarriage, triple fins and aerofoil flaps behind wing trailing edge.

REMARKS

Original design was for a wartime liaison aircraft. Produced for private owners as the Messenger 2A with Cirrus engine; ex-R.A.F. aircraft converted for civil use as Messenger 4A with Gipsy engine. Data above refers to Cirrus-engined version.

MESSENGER

MILES AIRCRAFT LTD.

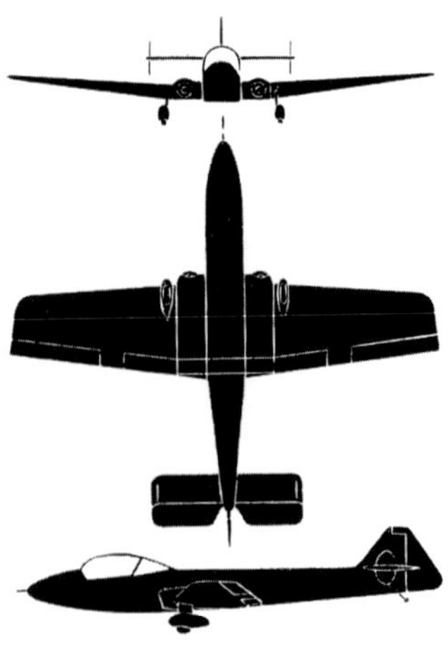

MILES SPARROWJET

F. G. MILES LTD.

TYPE: Racing aircraft.

ACCOMMODATION: 1.

POWERED BY: 2 × 330 lb. thrust Turbomeca Palas turbojets.

SPAN: 28 ft. 8 in. LENGTH: 30 ft. 10 in.

LOADED WEIGHT: 2,400 lb.

MAX. CRUISING SPEED: 220 m.p.h.

RECOGNITION FEATURES

Bears little resemblance to original Sparrowhawk. Slab-sided fuselage, with streamlined nose, blister-type cockpit well forward, triangular fin and rudder. and two small auxiliary fins on plank-like tailplane. Fixed spatted undercarriage. Wings are straight-tapered and broad, with engines mounted in the roots.

REMARKS

First light jet-powered racing aircraft built in the U.K., the Miles M.77 Sparrowjet is a completely rebuilt version of the prototype Sparrowhawk in which F. G. Miles won the first part of the 1935 King's Cup Race.

226

TYPE: Pre-war light aircraft.

ACCOMMODATION: 2.

POWERED BY: 130 h.p. D.H. Gipsy Major 1 piston-engine.

SPAN: 35 ft. 8 in.

LENGTH: 25 ft.

LOADED WEIGHT: 2,000 lb.

MAX. SPEED: 145 m.p.h.

TYPICAL RANGE: 570 miles at 130 m.p.h.

REMARKS

Another typical pre-war Miles cabin monoplane, with broad wings; rectangular tailplane; fixed, spatted undercarriage. Compare with Falcon and Hawk Speed Six.

RECOGNITION FEATURES

A successful two-seat cabin monoplane built in numbers before the War. Several survived war-time service with the R.A.F. as communications aircraft and are still giving good service.

WHITNEY STRAIGHT

MILES AIRCRAFT LTD.

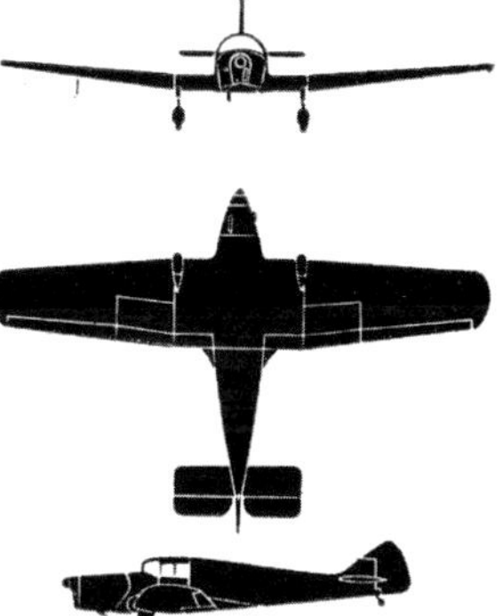

227

CUB J-3

PIPER AIRCRAFT CORP. (U.S.A.)

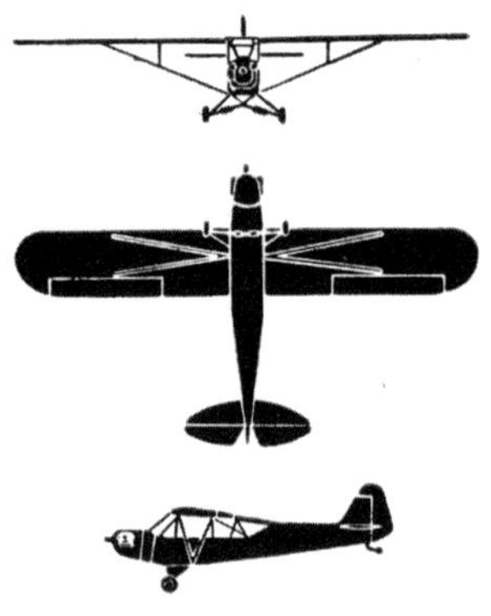

TYPE: Light aircraft.

ACCOMMODATION: 2.

POWERED BY: 65 h.p. Continental A-65 piston-engine.

SPAN: 35 ft. $2\frac{1}{2}$ in.

LENGTH: 22 ft. $4\frac{1}{2}$ in.

LOADED WEIGHT: 1,220 lb.

MAX. SPEED: 87 m.p.h.

CEILING: 11,500 ft.

TYPICAL RANGE: 206 miles at 75 m.p.h.

RECOGNITION FEATURES

Very like Auster series of light 'planes (see Aiglet, page 8), but shorter, snub nose with projecting cylinders, and distinctive rubber shock absorbers between undercarriage wheels.

REMARKS

Standard liaison and observation aircraft with the U.S. Services during World War 2, under the designation L-4 Grasshopper.

228

TYPE: Passenger and freight transport.
ACCOMMODATION: 1 crew + 14-16 passengers.
POWERED BY: 2 × 550 h.p. Alvis Leonides 502/1 piston-engines.
SPAN: 76 ft. 6 in. LENGTH: 45 ft. 3 in.
LOADED WEIGHT: 13,500 lb.
TYPICAL RANGE: 565 miles at 139 m.p.h. at 5,000 ft. with full load.

PRESTWICK TWIN PIONEER

SCOTTISH AVIATION LTD.

RECOGNITION FEATURES

A spotter's gift! Twin-engined high-wing monoplane with three fins and rudders and fixed undercarriage. Bracing struts from undercarriage to wings and engines, with triangular fairings between wheels and fuselage. Unusual wing plan-form caused by tapered centre-section and parallel chord outer panels.

REMARKS

Produced as a result of successful development of the earlier single-engined Pioneer (page 66), the Twin Pioneer has also been designed to operate from very small landing fields. Its wings are fitted with extensive slots, Fowler-type flaps and slotted ailerons. The prototype is due to fly during 1955 and the illustration is, consequently, of a model.

SOLENT

SOLENT 3
(and HYTHE)

SHORT BROS. AND HARLAND LTD.

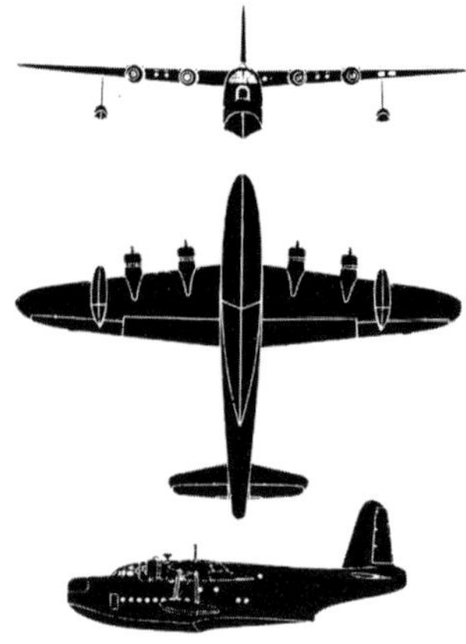

HYTHE

TYPE: Passenger transport flying-boat.

ACCOMMODATION: 7 crew+42 passengers.

POWERED BY: 4×2,000 h.p. Bristol Hercules 637V piston-engines.

SPAN: 112 ft. 9½ in. LENGTH: 88 ft. 7 in.

LOADED WEIGHT: 78,600 lb.

MAX. SPEED: 267 m.p.h.

CEILING: 15,500 ft.

TYPICAL RANGE: 2,200 miles at 190 m.p.h. at 9,250 ft. with 32 passengers and 428 lb. freight.

RECOGNITION FEATURES

Deep, roomy fuselage with two "steps" and upswept tail. Solent has "pointed" nose and tail; Hythe (see silhouette) has blunt, faired-over gun turrets. Tapered, pointed wings with slight dihedral, four mid-set engines and fixed floats. Tall tapered fin and rudder, with dorsal fin on Solent only.

REMARKS

Last big British flying boat to be used commercially. Developed at end of War from Seaford military patrol boat (Sunderland 4). Silhouette shows the Hythe, civil version of the Sunderland 5, with 4 Pratt & Whitney R-1830-90 engines, which is generally similar, but has faired-over gun turrets at nose and tail. Hythe and Solent are used by Aquila Airways. Data applies to Solent.

230

["*Flight*"]

TAYLORCRAFT PLUS D

TAYLORCRAFT AEROPLANES LTD.

TYPE: Pre-war light aircraft.
ACCOMMODATION: 2.
POWERED BY: 90 h.p. Blackburn Cirrus Minor I piston-engine.
SPAN: 36 ft.
LENGTH: 22 ft. 10 in.
LOADED WEIGHT: 1,450 lb.
MAX. SPEED: 120 m.p.h.
RANGE: 250-375 miles at 102 m.p.h.

RECOGNITION FEATURES

Similar to Aiglet Trainer (page 8), but longer-span wings, shorter Perspex cockpit hooding and no exhaust pipe under engine.

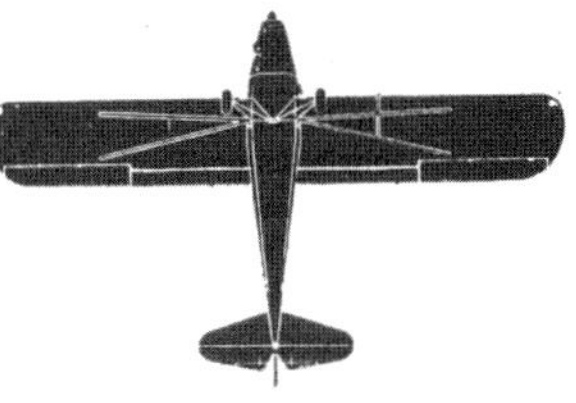

REMARKS

The Plus Model D was the first major production type of the British Taylorcraft company, following the Lycoming-engined Plus C. Upon it was based the war-time Auster 1 Army AOP; most Plus D's used by clubs and private owners today are in fact surplus Austers.

TIPSY TRAINER

TIPSY AIRCRAFT LTD.

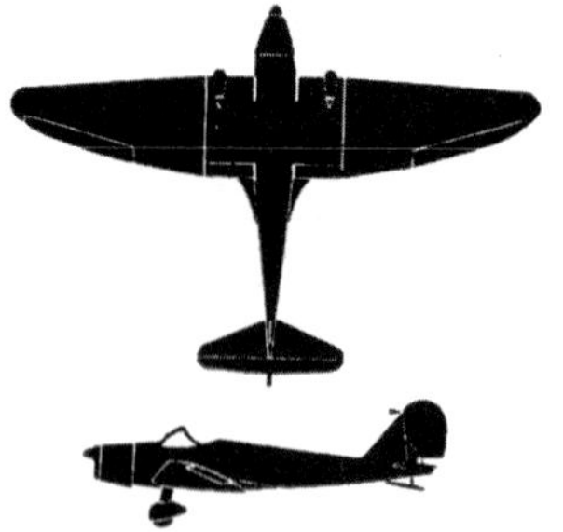

TYPE: Pre-war light aircraft.

ACCOMMODATION: 2.

POWERED BY: 62 h.p. Walter Mikron II piston-engine.

SPAN: 31 ft. 2 in.

LENGTH: 22 ft.

LOADED WEIGHT: 1,074 lb.

MAX. SPEED: 112 m.p.h.

CEILING: 19,000 ft.

TYPICAL RANGE: 400 miles at 100 m.p.h.

RECOGNITION FEATURES

Side-by-side two-seater, with distinctive semi-elliptical wings, big windscreen and unusual "semi-detached" rudder. Fixed, spatted undercarriage.

REMARKS

Of Belgian origin, and also built in small numbers by Tipsy Aircraft Co., Ltd. in this country. Used privately and by Royal Naval Flying Club.

TYPE: Medium-range passenger transport.

ACCOMMODATION: 4 crew + 24-38 passengers.

POWERED BY: 2 × 1,690 h.p. Bristol Hercules 634 piston-engines.

SPAN: 89 ft. 3 in.

LENGTH: 65 ft. 2 in.

LOADED WEIGHT: 34,000 lb.

MAX. SPEED: 304 m.p.h.

CEILING: 23,750 ft.

TYPICAL RANGE: 1,130 miles at 210 m.p.h. at 5,000 ft.

RECOGNITION FEATURES

Short, very fat circular fuselage with pug-nose and sharply-tapering tail. High, typically-Vickers fin and rudder and, again typically-Vickers, tapered wings. Engines set fairly high on wings; tailplane mid-set on fuselage.

REMARKS

First British post-war passenger transport, and mainstay of B.E.A. continental network 1946-1952. The Corporation retired the last of its fleet in 1954, and they are being sold to supplement the Vikings already in service with independent companies and the Queen's Flight.

VIKING 1B

VICKERS-ARMSTRONGS LTD.

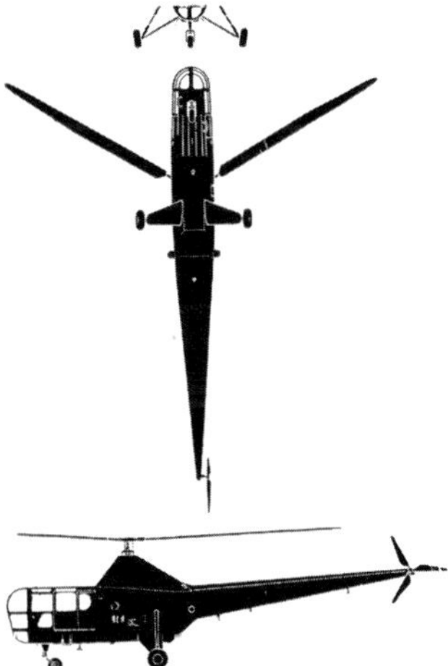

VISCOUNT Series 700

VICKERS-ARMSTRONGS LTD.

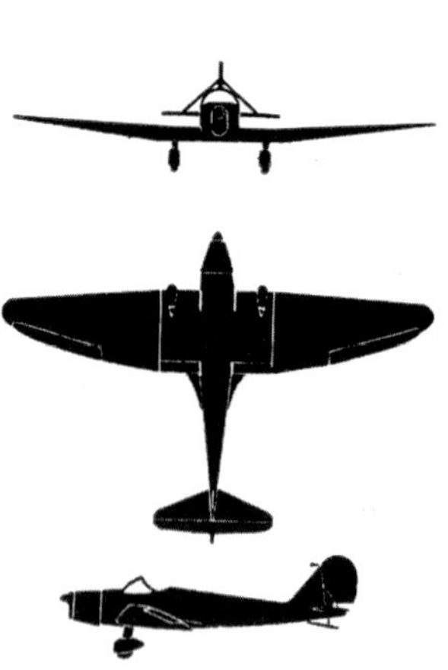

TYPE: Medium-range transport.

ACCOMMODATION: 3-4 crew+40-48 passengers.

POWERED BY: 4×1,530 h.p. Rolls-Royce Dart 505 propeller-turbines.

SPAN: 94 ft.   LENGTH: 81 ft. 2 in.

LOADED WEIGHT: 56,000 lb.

MAX. SPEED: 370 m.p.h.

CEILING: 28,500 ft.

TYPICAL RANGE: 750 miles at 301 m.p.h. at 22,500 ft. with 13,000 lb. payload.

RECOGNITION FEATURES

Big, circular streamlined fuselage with typical Vickers "shark fin" tail and dihedral tailplane. Comparatively small, sharply tapered wings, set well back and carrying four long, pencil thin engine nacelles.

REMARKS

First successful propeller-turbine passenger transport. Original model was Type 630 with shorter fuselage and 89 ft. span—illustrations show production-type Series 700. B.E.A. have in service or on order 26 *Discovery* Class Viscount 701s. Viscounts of Aer Lingus (Type 707) and Air France (708) can also be seen in Britain; and B.E.A. have ordered 12 Series 800 Viscounts with more powerful engines and increased capacity.

5

234

SIKORSKY S-51

WESTLAND AIRCRAFT LTD.

TYPE: Passenger and freight helicopter.
ACCOMMODATION: 4.
POWERED BY: 520 h.p. Alvis Leonides 521/1 or 450 h.p. Pratt & Whitney Wasp Junior R-985-4B piston-engine.
ROTOR DIAMETER: 48 ft.
LENGTH: 45 ft. 0½ in.
LOADED WEIGHT: 5,700 lb.
MAX. SPEED: 103 m.p.h.
CEILING: 14,000 ft.
TYPICAL RANGE: 225 miles at 85 m.p.h. at 5,000 ft.

RECOGNITION FEATURES

" Suitcase"-shaped fuselage, with long straight tapered boom carrying tail rotor. Rotor carried above big pyramid fairing. Compare with Bristol 171 (page 17).

REMARKS

World's first successful commercial helicopter. Original American-built aircraft used on experimental passenger and mail services by B.E.A. Now being produced under licence by Westland with Leonides for British Services as the Dragonfly, and for civil operators.

SIKORSKY S-55
WESTLAND AIRCRAFT LTD.

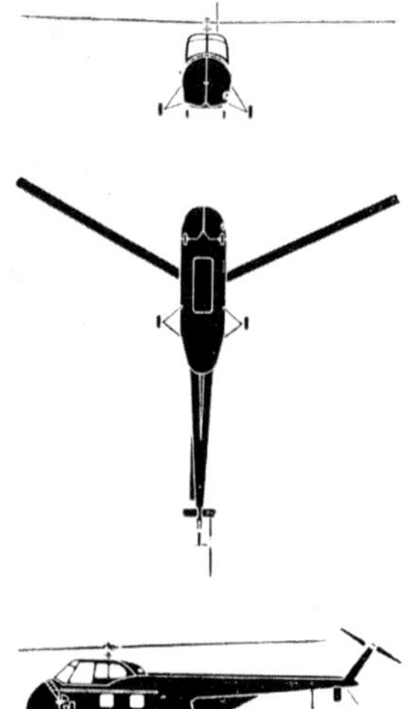

TYPE: General purpose helicopter.
ACCOMMODATION: Up to 12.
POWERED BY: 600 h.p. P. & W. R-1340-40 piston-engine.
ROTOR DIAMETER: 53 ft.
FUSELAGE LENGTH: 41 ft. 8½ in.
LOADED WEIGHT: 7,200 lb.
MAX. SPEED: 112 m.p.h.
CEILING: 12,000 ft.
TYPICAL RANGE: 300 miles at 86 m.p.h

RECOGNITION FEATURES

Massive bull-nosed fuselage, like that of Bristol Freighter, but with tail rotor carried on stalky boom. Flight deck raised above passenger/freight cabin. Rotor mounted close to top of fuselage. Unmistakable!

REMARKS

B.E.A. have bought two Westland-built S-55s, for their regular passenger service between London Airport and the South Bank site near Waterloo Air Station. These aircraft are now fitted with pontoon undercarriage, to permit emergency " landings " on the river, and carry only four passengers.

MINOR TYPES

THE 39 aircraft types described and illustrated on the next 10 pages are of lesser importance than those in the main part of this book, either because they are rarely seen over this country, or because only one or two examples are still flying. But most of them appear from time to time at air displays and races, and keen spotters and collectors would obviously have been disappointed if we had left them out.

AERONCA 100

Type: Pre-war ultra-light monoplane.
Accommodation: 2.
Powered by: 36 h.p. J.A.P. J.99.
Span: 36 ft.
Loaded Weight: 1,020 lb.
Max. speed: 95 m.p.h.
Typical Range: 175 miles at 70 m.p.h.

About four of these diminutive lightplanes still fly. They were built in this country, under American licence.

ARROW J/2

Auster Aircraft Ltd.

Type: Light aircraft.
Accommodation: 2.
Powered by: 75 h.p. Continental C-75.
Span: 36 ft.
Loaded Weight: 1,450 lb.
Max. Speed: 98 m.p.h.
Typical Range: 320 miles at 87 m.p.h.

Close relative of the Autocrat (see page 10) with smaller engine and cabin seating only two.

AUSTER J/4

Auster Aircraft Ltd.

Type: Light aircraft.
Accommodation: 2.
Powered by: 90 h.p. Cirrus Minor I
Span: 36 ft.
Loaded Weight: 1,600 lb.
Max. Speed: 108 m.p.h.
Range: 317 miles at 92 m.p.h.

The J/4 is basically similar to the Arrow but with more powerful engine. It is used largely by flying clubs in the U.K.

CLUB CADET

A. V. Roe and Co. Ltd.

Type Pre-war light aircraft.
Accommodation: 2.
Powered by: 130 h.p. D.H. Gipsy
   Major I or 135 h.p. A.S. Genet
   Major.
Span: 34 ft.
Loaded Weight: 2,000 lb.
Max. Speed: 116 m.p.h.

A popular pre-war club aircraft,
built in several forms. G-ACHP is
sole " in-line " survivor today, and
G-ADIE the only " radial ".

SWALLOW 2

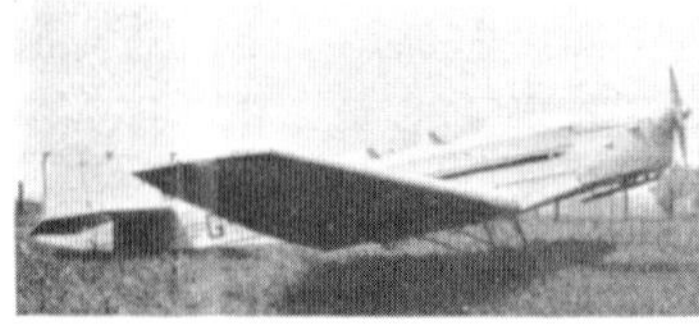

British Aircraft

Type: Pre-war light aircraft.
Accommodation: 2.
Powered by: 92 h.p. Pobjoy Cataract
   III or 90 h.p. Cirrus Minor.
Span: 42 ft. 8 in.
Loaded Weight: 1,500 lb.
Max. Speed: 104 m.p.h.
Typical Range: 355 miles at 92 m.p.h.

Derived from German Klemm
L.25; built in this country. Examples
with both radial and in-line engines
still exist.

DRONE

B.A.C.

Type: Pre-war ultra-light monoplane.
Accommodation: 1.
Powered by: 30 h.p. Carden Ford or
   32 h.p. Bristol Cherub 3.
Span: 39 ft. 8 in.
Loaded Weight: 680 lb.
Max. Speed: 73 m.p.h.
Typical Range: 300 miles at 65 m.p.h.

An interesting venture initiated in
1932 by the late C. H. Lowe-Wylde,
carrying a motor-cycle engine above
the wing of a glider.

BELL 47B-3

Bell Aircraft Corp. (U.S.A.)

Type: Light helicopter.
Accommodation: 3.
Powered by: 178 h.p. Franklin
   6V4-178-B32.
Rotor diameter: 35 ft. 1½ in.
Loaded Weight: 2,200 lb.
Max. Speed: 92 m.p.h.
Range: 215 miles at 80 m.p.h.
Two Bell 47's (*King Arthur* Class)
are used by B.E.A.'s Helicopter
Unit for experimental flying. Another
will be used for aerial photography.

Blackburn Aircraft Ltd.

Type: Pre-war trainer.
Accommodation: 2
Powered by: 130 h.p. D.H Gipsy Major I.
Span: 30 ft 2 in
Loaded Weight: 1,850 lb.
Max. Speed: 112 m.p.h.
Range: 320 miles at 100 m.p.h.

Sole survivor of this once-famous R.A F. side-by-side trainer is G-AEBJ. which is still airworthy.

Boulton Paul Aircraft Ltd.

Type: Advanced Trainer.
Accommodation: 2.
Powered by: 1,280 h.p. Rolls-Royce Merlin 35.
Span: 39 ft. 4 in.
Loaded Weight: 8,410 lb.
Max. Speed: 288 m.p.h.
Range: 650 miles at 222 m.p.h.

Civil-Registered demonstration model of the standard Balliol T.Mk.2 military trainer.

Chrislea Aircraft Co. Ltd.

Type: Light aircraft.
Accommodation: 4.
Powered by: 145 h.p. D.H. Gipsy Major 10.
Span: 36 ft.
Loaded Weight: 2,350 lb.
Max. Speed: 126 m.p.h.
Range: 400 miles at 112 m.p.h.

Super Ace was an interesting project with simplified control system and tricycle undercarriage. The Series 4 Skyjeep has "tail down" undercarriage, more roomy cabin and hinged rear decking to accommodate a stretcher or freight.

Comper Aircraft Co. Ltd.

Type: Pre-war racing monoplane.
Accommodation: 1.
Powered by: 90 h.p. Pobjoy Niagara III or 75 h.p. Pobjoy R.
Span: 24 ft.
Loaded Weight: 985 lb.
Max. Speed: 140 m.p.h.
Range: More than 600 miles.

Famous pre-war racing and sporting monoplane, which has gained new laurels in post-war events. A few survive—one with enclosed cabin and wheel spats.

BLACKBURN B-2

BALLIOL T. Mk. 2

SUPER ACE Series 2 (and SKYJEEP)

["Flight"

COMPER SWIFT

239

KITTEN

[" *The Aeroplane* "

Dart Aircraft

Type: Pre-war ultra-light monoplane.
Accommodation: 1.
Powered by: 36 h.p. J.A.P. J.99.
Span: 31 ft. 9 in.
Loaded Weight: 752 lb.
Max. Speed: 95 m.p.h.
Typical Range: 340 miles at 83 m.p.h.

Designed in 1936 for the amateur flyer. Two built pre-war and one other (Kitten III) completed in 1952.

DRAGON

de Havilland Aircraft Co. Ltd.

Type: Pre-war light transport.
Accommodation: Pilot+6-8 passengers.
Powered by: 2×130 h.p. D.H. Gipsy Major I.
Span: 47 ft.
Loaded Weight: 4,500 lb.
Max. Speed: 134 m.p.h.
Range: 550 miles.

First de Havilland twin-engined light transport, designed as simple, sturdy, economical " twin-engined Moth" for British local airlines. Predecessor of Dragon Rapide.

DRAGONFLY

["*Flight*"

de Havilland Aircraft Co. Ltd.

Type: Pre-war taxi 'plane.
Accommodation: 5.
Powered by: 2×130 h.p. D.H. Gipsy Major ID.
Span: 43 ft.
Loaded Weight: 4,000 lb.
Max. Speed: 147 m.p.h.
Typical Range: 885 miles at 122 m.p.h.

An early attempt to provide a multi-engine, multi-seat private-owner type, but mostly used on charter and feeder-line services.

FOX MOTH

de Havilland Aircraft Co. Ltd.

Type: Pre-war light aircraft and taxi.
Accommodation: 4-5.
Powered by: 130 h.p. D.H. Gipsy Major.
Span: 30 ft. 10 in.
Loaded Weight: 2,100 lb.
Max. Speed: 110 m.p.h.
Typical Range: 450 miles at 96 m.p.h.

Nearly 100 Fox Moths were built before the war; two are still flying in this country.

240

de Havilland Aircraft Co. Ltd.

Type: Pre-war light aircraft.
Accommodation: 2.
Powered by: 65 h.p. Cirrus I.
Span: 29 ft.
Loaded Weight: 1,234 lb.
Max. Speed: 91 m.p.h.
Typical Range: 430 miles.

World's most famous light 'plane, which virtually started the world-wide light aircraft and club movement. A few still exist.

de Havilland Aircraft of Canada Ltd.

Type: Light transport.
Accommodation: 2 crew + 9-13 passengers.
Powered by: 600 h.p. P. & W. R-1340-S3H1-G.
Span: 58 ft. *Loaded Weight:* 7,200 lb.
Max. Speed: 163 m.p.h.
Max. Range: 1,100 miles.
The DHC-3 Otter has been put into production as a result of the success of the smaller DHC-2 Beaver " bush " transport. One is used by the parent company at Hatfield, England.

Fairchild Aircraft

Type: Light aircraft.
Accommodation: 4.
Powered by: 165 h.p. Warner Super Scarab R-500-7.
Span: 36 ft. 4 in.
Loaded Weight: 2,800 lb.
Max. Speed: 110 m.p.h.
Range: 555 miles at 104 m.p.h.
Built during the war as light transport and communications aircraft for U.S. Services and R.A.F. A few ex-R.A.F. machines still flying over U.K. in civil markings; some based in Europe have Ranger in-line engine as shown in photograph.

Avions Fairey S.A. (Belgium)

Type: Ultra-light monoplane.
Accommodation: 1.
Powered by: 62 h.p. Walter Mikron.
Span: 22 ft. 8 in.
Loaded Weight: 770 lb.
Max. Speed: 112 m.p.h.
Typical Range: 340 miles at 100 m.p.h.
Two built in Belgium by Avions Fairey S.A., registered OO TIT and OO-ULA. The latter now on British Register as G-AMVP.

MOTH

OTTER

FAIRCHILD ARGUS

FAIREY JUNIOR

["*The Aeroplane*"

CYGNET

General Aircraft Ltd.

Type: Pre-war light aircraft.
Accommodation: 2.
Powered by: 150 h.p. Cirrus Major II.
Span: 34 ft. 6 in.
Loaded Weight: 2,200 lb.
Max. Speed: 135 m.p.h.
Typical Range: 445 miles at 115 m.p.h.

One of the first British light planes with a tricycle undercarriage.

GLADIATOR

Gloster Aircraft Co. Ltd.

Type· Sporting biplane.
Accommodation: 1.
Powered by: 840 h.p. Bristol Mercury VIIIA.
Span: 32 ft. 3 in.
Loaded Weight: 4,750 lb.
Max. Speed: 250 m.p.h.
Typical Range: 400 miles.

Sole survivor of the famous " last of the biplane fighters ", operated as a sporting type.

METEOR

Gloster Aircraft Co. Ltd.

Type: Advanced trainer.
Accommodation: 2.
Powered by: 2 × 3.500 lb. thrust Rolls-Royce Derwent 8.
Span: 37 ft. 2 in.
Loaded Weight: 14,140 lb.
Max. Speed: 585 m.p.h.
Range: 470 miles without external tanks.

Demonstration model of the Meteor advanced jet trainer. Basically similar to standard T.Mk. 7, but with Mk. 8 type tail unit and tip-tanks.

CYGNET

Hawker Aircraft Ltd.

Type: Pre-war ultra-light biplane.
Accommodation: 1.
Powered by: 32 h.p. Bristol Cherub 3.
Span: 28 ft.
Loaded Weight: 900 lb.
Max. Speed: 75 m.p.h.

Oldest-but-one aircraft in Britain with current Airworthiness Certificate. Winner of the " Daily Mail " Light Aeroplane Competitions in 1926.

Hawker Aircraft Ltd.

Type: Pre-war demonstration bomber.
Accommodation: 2.
Powered by: 670 h.p. Rolls-Royce Kestrel 16 Special.
Span: 37 ft. 3 in.
Loaded Weight: 4,635 lb.
Max. Speed: 184 m.p.h.
Typical Range: 430 miles at 170 m.p.h.

A well-known " special ", used by Hawker's since pre-war days as a mount for photographers, and for demonstration and display.

Hawker Aircraft Ltd.

Type: Sporting monoplane.
Accommodation: 1.
Powered by: 1,280 h.p. Rolls-Royce Merlin 24.
Span: 40 ft.
Loaded Weight: 7,600 lb.
Max. Speed: 334 m.p.h.

" The Last of the Many " (PZ865), the last Hurricane built, preserved by Hawkers as part of their "flying museum ", and frequently raced.

Hawker Aircraft Ltd.

Type: Pre-war trainer and light aircraft.
Accommodation: 2.
Powered by: 150 h.p. A.S. Mongoose IIIC.
Span: 28 ft. 6 in.
Loaded Weight: 2,100 lb.
Max. Speed: 124 m.p.h.
Range: 350 miles.

Designed as an R.A.F. trainer in 1928, and built in numbers for the Service and private-owner. Only one survivor, flown by Neville Duke.

Hiller Helicopters Inc. (U.S.A.)

Type: Light helicopter.
Accommodation: 3.
Powered by: 178 h.p. Franklin 6V4-178-B33.
Rotor diameter: 35 ft.
Loaded Weight: 2,247 lb.
Cruising Speed: 76 m.p.h.

Hiller 360s used by Pest Control Ltd. in this country and overseas are normally fitted with spray-bars and insecticide containers as shown in photograph.

HART

HURRICANE 2C

[Cyril Peckham

TOMTIT

HILLER 360

243

PROVOST

Hunting Percival Aircraft Ltd.
Type: Basic trainer.
Accommodation: 2.
Powered by: 550 h.p. Alvis Leonides 25.
Span: 35 ft. 2 in.
Loaded Weight: 4,400 lb.
Max. Speed: 200 m.p.h.
Range: 700 miles at 177 m.p.h.

Demonstration model of the R.A.F.'s standard basic training aircraft.

Q-6

Percival Aircraft Ltd.
Type: Pre-war light transport.
Accommodation: 7.
Powered by: 2 × 205 h.p. D.H. Gipsy Six II.
Span: 46 ft. 8 in.
Loaded Weight: 5,500 lb.
Max. Speed: 195 m.p.h.
Typical Range: 700 miles at 172 m.p.h.

Pre-war light air liner, available with either fixed or retractable undercarriage.

AEROVAN

Miles Aircraft Ltd.

Type: Light transport.
Accommodation: 2 crew + 9 passengers or 2,240 lb. freight.
Powered by: 2 × 155 h.p. Cirrus Major 3.
Span: 50 ft.
Loaded Weight: 5,800 lb.
Max. Speed: 127 m.p.h.
Typical Range: 800 miles at 112 m.p.h.

Several of these interesting light freighters remain on Register. One example (Mk. 6) has two Lycoming engines.

Miles Aircraft Ltd.
Type: Pre-war light aircraft.
Accommodation: 3.
Powered by: 200 h.p. D.H. Gipsy Six I.
Span: 35 ft.
Loaded Weight: 2,525 lb.
Max. Speed: 180 m.p.h.

A Falcon Six, flown by Tommy Rose, won the 1935 Kings Cup Race at 176 m.p.h. and later set up a new England-Cape Town record. Some served with the wartime R.A.F. on communications duties, and are now back in civil markings together with 4-seat Falcon Majors (130 h.p. Gipsy Major I).

FALCON

244

Miles Aircraft Ltd.

Type: Pre-war Racing monoplane.
Accommodation: 1.
Powered by: 200 h.p. D.H. Gipsy Six H.C.
Span: 33 ft.
Max. Speed: 185 m.p.h.

Special racing version of two-seat Hawk Major. Surviving example has enormous bubble hood.

Miles Aircraft Ltd.

Type: Light aircraft.
Accommodation: 3-4.
Powered by: 155 h.p. Blackburn Cirrus Major III or 145 h.p. D.H. Gipsy Major 2A.
Span: 30 ft. 6 in.
Loaded Weight: 2,500 lb.
Max. Speed: 175 m.p.h.
Typical Range: 700 miles at 169 m.p.h.

Designed for communications and training duties during the war, but not built in quantity.

Société Nationale de Constructions Aéronautiques du Nord (France)

Type: Light touring aircraft.
Accommodation: 4.
Powered by: 135 h.p. Régnier 4LO.
Span: 33 ft. 6 in
Loaded Weight: 2,313 lb.
Max. Speed: 174 m.p.h.
Range: 560 miles at 137 m.p.h.

These popular French lightplanes are regular visitors to the U.K. Their acute wing dihedral is a distinctive recognition feature.

[Barry Jones

Svenska Aeroplan A.B. (Sweden)

Type: Light touring aircraft.
Accommodation: 4.
Powered by: 190 h.p. Lycoming O-435-A.
Span: 34 ft. 9 in.
Loaded Weight: 2,686 lb.
Max. Speed: 168 m.p.h.
Range: 560 miles at 141 m.p.h.

One example of the Swedish Saab-91C Safir came on to the British Civil Register in 1954. It is G-ANOK.

245

PRINCESS

[Barry Jones

Saunders-Roe Ltd.
Type: Long-range passenger-carrying flying boat.
Accommodation: More than 100 passengers.
Powered by: 10 3,200 h.p. Bristol Proteus 600 series propeller-turbines.
Span: 219 ft. 6 in.
Loaded Weight: 320,000 lb.
Cruising Speed: 380 m.p.h.
  Biggest all-metal flying boat ever built. Designed to fly non-stop service Southampton - U.S.A. throughout year. Three built, and now Cocooned, awaiting more powerful engines.

SKEETER 6

Saunders-Roe Ltd.
Type: Training and private-owner helicopter.
Accommodation: 2.
Powered by: 200 h.p. D.H. Gipsy Major 30.
Rotor Diameter: 32 ft.
Loaded Weight: 2,200 lb.
Max. Speed: 115 m.p.h.
Range: 260 miles at 101 m.p.h.
  Smallest post-war British helicopter. Civil Mks. 5 (with Cirrus Bombardier) and 6 are flying. Also under development for military and naval use.

PRESTWICK PIONEER 2

Scottish Aviation Ltd.
Type: Light passenger/freighter.
Accommodation: 4-5.
Powered by: 550 h.p. Alvis Leonides 502/4.
Span: 49 ft. 9 in.
Loaded Weight: 5,400 lb.
Max. Speed: 162 m.p.h.
Range: 400 miles at 120 m.p.h.
  First modern all-Scottish design, the Pioneer has outstanding slow-flying characteristics. One is on the Civil Register. Others are serving with the R.A.F. in Malaya.

SHORT SEALAND

Short Bros. and Harland Ltd.
Type: Light passenger transport amphibian.
Accommodation: 2 crew + 5-8 passengers.
Powered by: 2 345 h.p. D.H. Gipsy Queen 70-3.
Span: 61 ft. 6 in.
Loaded Weight: 9,100 lb.
Max. Speed: 185 m.p.h.
Typical Range: 471 miles at 161 m.p.h. at 8,000 ft. with 5 passengers and baggage.
  Post-war light transport, in service in small numbers throughout the world.

EUROPE'S FINEST AIR FLEET

BEA fly more people about Europe than any other
airline; within Britain, to the Continent, the Mediterranean and
North Africa. Nearly all BEA's international flights
are by Europe's finest pressurized airliners — the turbo-prop
Viscount and spacious Elizabethan.

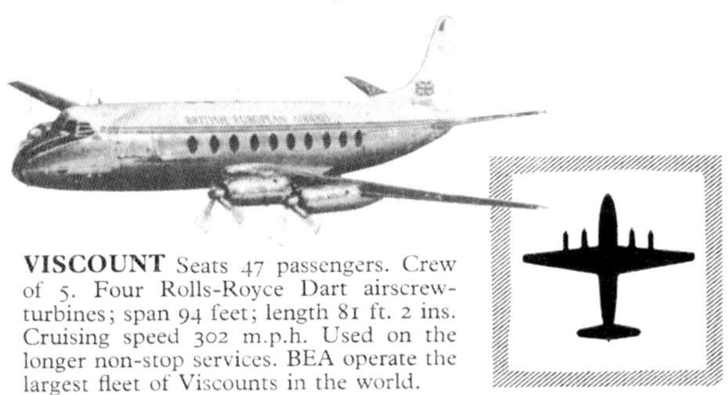

VISCOUNT Seats 47 passengers. Crew
of 5. Four Rolls-Royce Dart airscrew-
turbines; span 94 feet; length 81 ft. 2 ins.
Cruising speed 302 m.p.h. Used on the
longer non-stop services. BEA operate the
largest fleet of Viscounts in the world.

ELIZABETHAN Seats 47 passengers.
Crew of 5. Two Bristol-Centaurus engines;
span 115 ft.; length 81 ft. 3 ins. Cruising
speed 245 m.p.h. 'Landscape' windows set
below the wings give passengers wide
panoramic views.

fly **BEA**

BRITISH   EUROPEAN   AIRWAYS

AIRCRAFT FUELLERS

TYNE Capacity 4,000 Imperial gallons: max. delivery rate per hose, 180 g.p.m. Leyland chassis. Among the largest fuellers in the world; used for servicing trans-Atlantic airliners.

DORSET Capacity 3,000 Imperial gallons: max. delivery rate per hose, 200 g.p.m. Leyland chassis. Originally designed for underwing fuelling of the D.H. Comets with aviation turbine fuel.

STEER Capacity 2,200 Imperial gallons; max. delivery rate per hose, 150 g.p.m.; Leyland chassis. Used at London Airport only for servicing medium-sized aircraft.

LINCOLN Capacity 1,500 Imperial gallons; max. delivery rate per hose 100 g.p.m. Bedford chassis. Designed for over and underwing fuelling of medium sized airliners.

TWEED Capacity 1,200 Imperial gallons; max. delivery rate per hose, 60/70 g.p.m. Ford chassis. Used for servicing aircraft covering moderate distances on European routes.

T. B. MOBILE. Capacity 500 Imperial gallons; max. delivery rate per hose, 30/40 g.p.m. Special 3-wheel chassis. Stationed on the smaller airfields for servicing private and club aircraft.

At all the major airfields in Britain you can see one or more of these different types of fuellers operating Shell and BP Aviation Service. International airlines, charter companies and private owners alike know they can always expect quick, efficient service from the friendly crews of these Service Vehicles.

SHELL AND BP AVIATION SERVICE

Sand Strip—*Seamew* base

Simplicity of design ensures simplicity of maintenance—and economy in initial cost and in use of spares and manpower. Removable panels make components easily accessible.

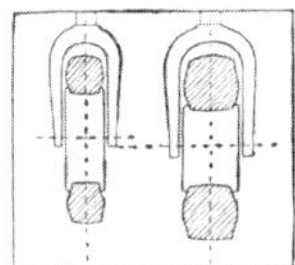

The wheels of the Seamew can be swiftly changed, with differing sizes of tyre to suit the surfaces from which it operates.

Seamew—a tough, economical, all-weather submarine hunter. Airborne in a short distance from any rapidly constructed airstrip—or even a stretch of beach—the Seamew can conduct a maritime search with up-to-date radar equipment and use a variety of weapons to effect a kill. Its high manœuvrability, low stalling speed and fixed shock-absorbing undercarriage enable the Seamew to land back safely after operating in weather conditions impossible for other anti-submarine aircraft.

The *Short* answer is the *Seamew*

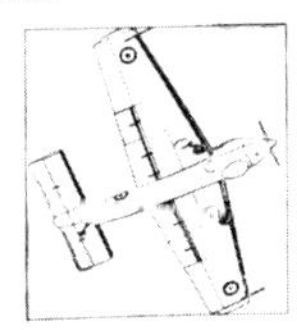

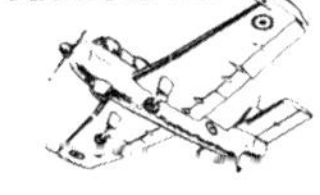

Generous flap surfaces contribute to the very low stalling and landing speeds. The Seamew requires the minimum length of runway on emergency airstrip or escort carrier deck.

NOW IN PRODUCTION FOR R.A.F. COASTAL COMMAND AND THE ROYAL NAVY

Short Brothers, & Harland Limited, Queens Island, Belfast, N. Ireland.   The first manufacturers of aircraft in the world.

See Iceland!

Scheduled air services between Reykjavik and London, Glasgow, Copenhagen, Oslo, Stockholm, Hamburg.

For further information consult our Agents in Great Britain:
BRITISH EUROPEAN AIRWAYS

or

6B PRINCES ARCADE, PICCADILLY, LONDON
MEMBER INTERNATIONAL AIR TRANSPORT ASSOCIATION

The **RIVIERA** *this summer*

AIR FRANCE

of course

The easiest and most comfortable service to the gay places

Four Services daily to Nice, including the Viscount night flight— $2\frac{3}{4}$ hours—(London-Nice £28.0.0. 23-day tourist night return fare).

Thirteen services weekly to Marseilles for Western Riviera (London-Marseilles direct service, £30.12.0. tourist return: or night flight via Paris, £26.0.0. 23-day tourist night return).

Also twenty flights weekly to ITALY, fourteen to SPAIN, two weekly to DINARD and LA BAULE; daily flights to DEAUVILLE and two weekly to BIARRITZ.

Bookings and information through your Travel Agent. Send for European Timetable giving details of all services.

AIR FRANCE

52 HAYMARKET · LONDON · S.W.1

In *1954* the critics said . . . .

" We can most highly recommend it to all who are working in or who are interested in the helicopter field."—
Journal of the Helicopter Association of G.B.

" In short, this is a "must" for all concerned with heli-copters."—*Passenger Transport*

" Mr. Taylor seems to have succeeded once more in cramming a quart of useful pictures and data into a pint-sized book."—*Flight*

In *1955* they will again praise the

ABC of HELICOPTERS

by John W. R. Taylor

2/6

Obtainable from all leading bookstalls and booksellers or from

Ian Allan Ltd

CRAVEN HOUSE   HAMPTON COURT

AIRCRAFT TODAY

by John W. R. Taylor

" For quantity and quality this book is real value. Mr. Taylor is to be congratulated not only on securing contributions from—amongst others—Sir Frederick Handley Page, "Mike" Lithgow, Air Marshal Sir Robert Saundby, and Rear-Admiral H. E. Horan, but in collecting rare photographs of exotic prototypes . . . "—FLIGHT

" . . . A fascinating survey of aviation, with many fine photographs of modern aircraft and their ancestors. John Taylor . . . . has deliberately avoided repetition of facts and figures that can be found elsewhere . . . . well worth 9s. 6d, and its contents are presented in a straightforward way that makes it simple to grasp principles which hitherto have been rather hazy to many."—MODEL AIRCRAFT

9/6

Ian Allan Ltd

CRAVEN HOUSE · HAMPTON COURT

Ian Allan Ltd
COUPON

2

UNITS

Take your cycle to the Continent

BY THE

SILVER CITY
AIR FERRY

You can be on the road in France within thirty minutes of leaving Lydd, Silver City's new airport on the Kentish coast. There are frequent daily services. Travel on the Air Ferry calls for no special preparations and your pedal cycle requires no travel documents of any kind. Get full details from your local Travel Agent, Cyclist's Touring Club, or direct from Silver City Airways.

SILVER CITY AIRWAYS LTD.

One Great Cumberland Place, W.I.   AMB. 1611

'Silver City - the First Name in Foreign Touring'

Published by Ian Allan Ltd., Craven House, Hampton Court, Surrey and
Printed by Crampton & Sons, Ltd., Sawston, Cambridge

Ian Allan
abc
LONDON AIRPORT
BRITISH EUROPEAN AIRWAYS
-CROSS-
SECOND EDITION
with full colour inset
2/6

NEW EDITION

by
John
W.R.
Taylor

abc CIVIL AIRCRAFT MARKINGS

★ Registrations of ALL British civil aircraft
★ Fleet list of all overseas airliners
     serving the United Kingdom
★ More than fifty of the latest photographs
★ 88 pages of information - pocket edition

Available from all bookshops or direct from the publishers

2'6

Ian Allan Ltd HAMPTON COURT, SURREY

AIR
FRANCE
THE
WORLD'S LARGEST
AIRLINE

GET TO KNOW THE NEW R.A.F.
Can you identify this fighter?*

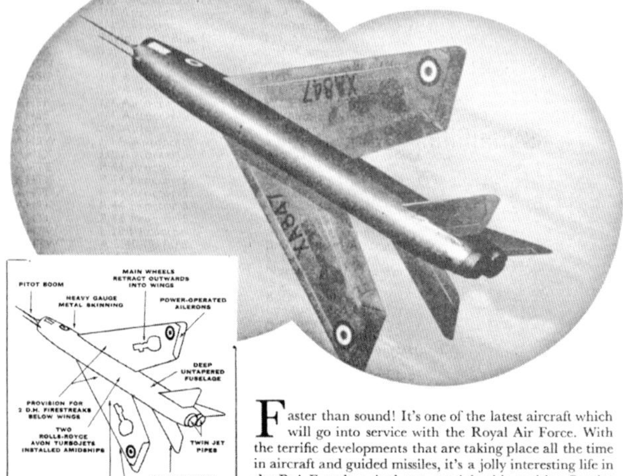

Faster than sound! It's one of the latest aircraft which will go into service with the Royal Air Force. With the terrific developments that are taking place all the time in aircraft and guided missiles, it's a jolly interesting life in the R.A.F. today. And you can join this exciting Service as an Apprentice between 15 and 17. Post the coupon *now* for full details.

There's a career for you in the R.A.F.

To: ROYAL AIR FORCE (F.O.76), Victory House, London, W.C.2.

I am over 14. Please send me details of entry for R.A.F. Aircraft and Administrative Apprentices.

NAME ....

ADDRESS ....

....

....

.... **Date of Birth** ....

(Applicants from British Isles only)

If you're too young for the R.A.F.—join the Air Training Corps!

** This is the English Electric P. 1B, Britain's superb new single-seat fighter which flies far above the speed of sound. Wing span 36 ft. . . . length 52 ft. The P. 1B has provision for Firestreak guided missiles and 30 mm. Aden guns. It is powered by two Rolls-Royce Avon turbojets with reheat.*

2

TCA—One of the World's Great Air Lines

Linking Europe with Canada

and the U.S.A.

TRANS-CANADA AIR LINES

27 PALL MALL, LONDON, S.W.1

also at Glasgow, Manchester, Paris, Düsseldorf, Shannon

3

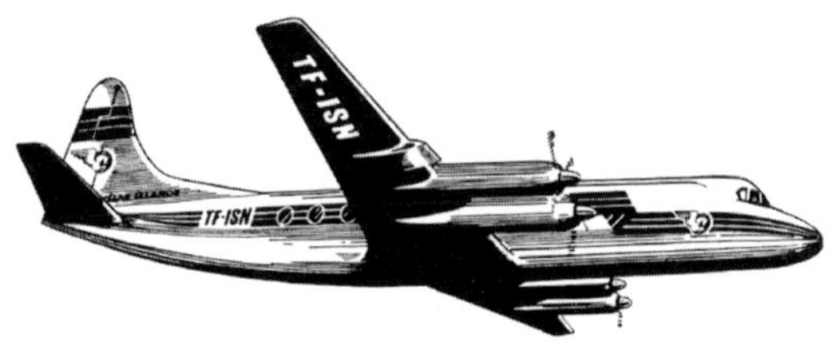

FLY *VISCOUNT*

TO ICELAND

SCHEDULED VISCOUNT SERVICES BETWEEN LONDON, GLASGOW, COPENHAGEN, OSLO, HAMBURG AND REYKJAVIK.

DIRECT VISCOUNT FLIGHTS IN $2\frac{1}{2}$ HOURS BETWEEN GLASGOW AND COPENHAGEN

*For full details and reservations consult
any B.E.A. Office or*

LONDON OFFICE: 161 PICCADILLY, W.1   HYDE PARK 7661-2

4

a b c

LONDON
AIRPORT

BY

Maurice Allward & Roy McLeavy

SECOND EDITION

LONDON

Ian Allan Ltd

The striking memorial to Alcock and Brown. When they made the first non-stop Atlantic crossing on June 14th, 1919, few could have imagined that within a quarter of a century the North Atlantic would be the world's busiest air route. More than 3,000 crossings are made every month.

6

Introduction

AS the mother country of a great family of overseas nations it was, perhaps, to be expected that Britain would be a focal point of air routes. But few foresaw that Britain would become the great international cross-roads of the air she is today.

London Airport is the hub on which the air routes converge ; forty-two airlines from thirty-two countries now operate regular services there. For most of the hundreds of thousands of people arriving in Britain by air, London Airport is the gateway through which they enter and which gives them their all-important first impression of our country. For thousands of other people, the airport is an international gateway to the world at large, providing a last impression for them to take on their journey.

As for the sightseers—ordinary men, women and children—who descend on the airport by coach, car and cycle every fine weekend, few can suppress a thrill as they enter the long tunnel leading to " L.A.P. Central."

The imposing vista of red brick, glass and fluttering flags that greets one when emerging from the tunnel forms the subject of this book. It tells you not only how the airport works, but what you can see while you are there.

Of most interest is, of course, the ceaseless hustle on the concrete aprons in front of the passenger buildings. Twenty-two of the airliners most likely to be seen here are described in detail. To help the enthusiast identify the various aircraft, the international markings of civil aircraft are listed, along with the fleets of some of the airlines using the airport.

We hope the mixture adds to your enjoyment.

M. A.

R. McL.

Thank you . . .

- *to the Press Officers of B.E.A. and B.O.A.C. ;*
- *to the airlines who helped with data and photographs ;*
- *to John W. R. Taylor for his advice and helpful criticism.*

7

The main passenger building in the central terminal area, with its imposing modernistic façade of red brick and glass. Below is the building's Main Concourse, which runs the full length of the first floor. Here are airline booking desks and banks to cope with the currency needs of visitors from all over the world.

Springboard to the shrinking world

IN an age when most sizeable achievements are hailed as the Finest, Biggest or Greatest, London Airport commands as full and imposing a share of superlatives as any. Largest of European airports, it is also the busiest in terms of international airline traffic. Functionally and artistically its buildings are among the finest ; its massive, two-feet thick concrete runways among the longest ; and it claims more " firsts " among its comprehensive array of gadgetry to control air and ground traffic than any other terminal.

" L.A.P.", as it is familiarly known, is Britain's springboard to the air age world—a world which speeding transport planes are shrinking so fast that distances are no longer measured in miles but in minutes. In these sleek silver carriers the glitter of Paris is but 65 minutes away, Rome three hours, Istanbul nine. And in one mighty leap the biggest and fastest of these planes will whisk you across the broad expanse of the North Atlantic to New York between breakfast and tea.

Already the term " intercontinental flight " is being outmoded, for the higher speeds of the advancing jet era bear promise of a world unified on a neighbourly capital-to-capital basis, with even the most distant metropolis less than twenty-four hours away.

Nearly 87 million people of every flag, colour and faith fly on scheduled airline services every year ; more people are nowadays visiting more places, more swiftly than ever before.

The air age has become the greatest sociological mixing force ever known. Reflecting its power is L.A.P.'s huge passenger hall, where the unfamiliar in languages, clothes and customs brings the visitor into fleeting contact with every continent — for every continent is now on London's doorstep.

Paradoxically, L.A.P., though one of the greatest of all civil airports, was born not of peace but war, and owes its origin to the R.A.F.'s need in 1943 for a large transport base near London. It was appreciated that the capital would need a new civil airport when peace returned, and so consideration was given to this by the Air Ministry when they chose the present site at Heathrow. Bounded by the Bath Road to the north and the Staines Road to the south, and only 14 miles west of Charing Cross, the site has proved as ideal as any could be so close to central London.

Copter's-eye view of the central area. In the foreground
is the 127 feet high control tower and behind it the passenger
building. To the left is the Queen's Building.

Construction started in May, 1944, following the classical R.A.F. pattern of three runways arranged in a triangle. But the war ended before its completion, and so it was decided that Heathrow should be handed over to the civil authorities for immediate development as the main London air terminal.

Operations from the new airport began on January 1st, 1946, when a Lancastrian of British South American Airways, now incorporated with B.O.A.C., took-off on a long-distance proving flight to South America. A short while after two American airlines then flying into the wartime trans-Atlantic airfield at Hurn asked to use the new airport because of the difficulties in transporting their passengers from the Bournemouth area to the capital. In July, 1946, B.O.A.C. (until then also at Hurn) followed suit. Newly-revived continental operators began using the terminal and by 1950 it had blossomed into the busiest airport in Europe.

Acute shortage of accommodation in the early days led to immigration, Customs and other departments being housed in caravans and marquees. But behind the scenes all the time an advisory panel was hard at work evolving plans for new permanent buildings, new runways and advanced new facilities. From their recommendations, which were first generally made known in 1947, has sprung the great international terminal we know today.

On the R.A.F.'s original triangular layout of three runways a second triangle has been superimposed, forming what is approximately a huge " Star of David " pattern, and providing a pair of long parallel runways in each of three directions. The great advantage of this arrangement is that two airliners can land and take-off into wind simultaneously on separate runways.

But the airport of today is more than just a piece of land decorated with ribbons of concrete. In the interests of both safety and efficiency it supervises all incoming aircraft from 100 or more miles away until they come to a halt by the passenger buildings. For the same reason it guides them from take-off until they make the great air lanes. To avoid the possibility of collision on the runways, taxiways or aprons, the vehicles for servicing and re-fuelling are controlled just as closely. Arriving and departing passengers

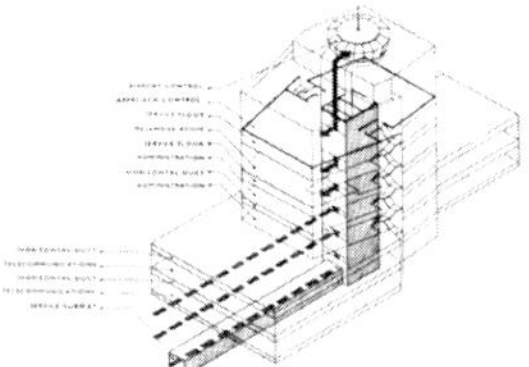

TOWER OF (Air Age) LONDON

Dominating the central area, the control tower is the nerve centre of the whole airport. Its distinctive angular shape minimises the interference which the large flat surfaces of a rectangular building would cause to radio approach and landing aids. The purpose of the tower is to raise the traffic controllers to a height where an unobstructed view may be had of the runways. Controllers in the circular penthouse supervise movement on taxiways and runways. Immediately below is the approach control room which looks after aircraft approaching and leaving the airport and those on the duty runways. The lower floors house the M.T.C.A. headquarters, a medical centre and amenities for all Ministry staff in the central area. A central services core extends to the full height of the structure and contains the lifts, ventilation trunking and cable ducts. *Below:* The penthouse interior.

have to be supervised also, to ensure their smooth and orderly progress through immigration and Customs formalities.

To handle the 129,000 aircraft, $3\frac{1}{2}$ million passengers, and 60,000 tons of freight which pass through London Airport each year is the full-time job of some 25,000 people.

While not all of these are engaged upon the running of the terminal itself, but on associated tasks such as the maintenance of the aircraft, the

figure gives a clear idea of the enormous volume of work that goes on there. The airport is a city within itself, requiring personnel to run its own bus services, hospital, police force, shops, restaurants, post office and fire engines, in addition to those concerned directly with the business of air travel, such as air traffic control, Customs and immigration, baggage and freight, and many other activities.

The permanent buildings are sited in the

central area of the airport, which was deemed the most suitable passenger area since it involved the least taxi-ing. Here too, is the impressive red brick Control Building, the tower of which rises 127 feet high, and is the nerve centre of the whole airport.

Up top, in the compact glass-walled penthouse, is the Ground Controller who supervises the ground movements over the taxiways and runways. The windows of his circular eyrie slope outwards to eliminate reflected light from the sky, and are double glazed, firstly

External and internal balconies around the approach control room permit technicians and officials to visit the room without interfering with work. *Right:* Approach room radar controllers at work.

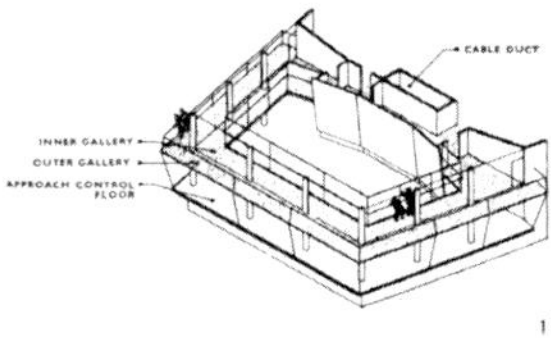

11

Feature of the luxurious passenger lounge overlooking the Main Concourse is the array of "flying saucer" skylights.

to minimise the effect of external noise, and secondly to provide an air space through which de-misting air can be circulated. On a clear day the view embraces West London, Windsor Castle, Harrow and the Surrey hills.

To help him see the position of aircraft and vehicles on every part of the airfield, however bad the visibility, he is aided by special Q-band radar, the revolving "half-cheese" scanner of which is mounted on the penthouse roof. London Airport is the first in the world to be equipped with this system, which scans the surface of the airport with a very narrow beam, and produces a sharply defined picture of all traffic, moving or stationary—and even pedestrians !—on a 12-inch cathode ray tube.

So clear is this picture, that on one occasion when a visitor parked his car in a remote part of the airport then couldn't trace it, the Ground Controller was able to tell him where it was.

The complexity of the airport layout is such that a simple and thoroughly foolproof method had to be found of directing taxi-ing aircraft across the multiplicity of runways between the parking areas and loading aprons. It was decided the most satisfactory method was a block system, similar to that used by many railways. When an airliner has touched down and come to rest, the Controller can see at a glance the quickest route to the unloading apron, and by pressing switches he can turn on a row of green lights down the centre of the taxiway the pilot is to follow. In no case is this green centre-line less than 50 feet away from the edge of the runway or taxiway, and the captain can therefore follow this line with confidence, knowing that as long as his plane's undercarriage straddles the lights he will not leave the hard surface.

Paths in use by another aircraft are closed by a bar of red lights across the threshold. A mimic display in the control room portrays by means of miniature lamps sunk beneath the surface which lights are in use on the airfield itself.

In daylight, route indicator boards are used which are fitted with red traffic lights to isolate sections being used by a taxi-ing aircraft from adjacent tracks.

Aircraft approaching or leaving the airport and those on the duty runway are the responsibility of the Approach Control room situated directly beneath.

Baggage passes up on the conveyor belt to await Customs clearance.

From his vantage point on top of the main restaurant, the apron marshal controls activity on the apron.

V.H.F. radio-telephones are used extensively to control the movement of servicing and refuelling vehicles.

Since it is necessary to start guiding an incoming aircraft when it is still many miles away, and since the importance of this room reaches its greatest when visibility is least, direct vision plays little part in these operations. Aircraft approaching by one of the recognised airways are under the direction of the Southern Air Traffic Control Centre, which controls all air traffic over the South of England. From the airway the airliner is directed, if necessary, to one of the two stacking points at Epsom and Watford where aircraft await their turn to land. At these points the captains orbit about the radio " holding " beacons until called in by one of the Airport's Approach Control officers.

Successive aircraft in the stack adopt an altitude of 1,000 feet higher than the one ahead.

The lower aircraft in the stack is the next to land, and when he leaves all the others move down one place.

From the radio beacon the aircraft is guided to a point in line with the runway, about 6 or 7 miles away, still out of sight, but constantly checked for position by intersecting radio fixes or radar, and then handed over to the talk-down controller.

In poor visibility the final landing approach is made under the G.C.A. system, in which the controller, checking the height and position of the aircraft by radar, gives the pilot direct instructions by radio. Once on the final approach path the pilot can be guided to a point about 400 yards from his touchdown position. Each G.C.A. approach takes about three minutes ; but under normal conditions at peak periods a landing can be made every one and a half minutes.

Another of the magnificent buildings in the central area is the passenger terminal on the southern face, with its imposing, modernistic façade of red brick and glass. Perhaps the most remarkable feature of this building is the system of departure " channels," through which the passenger is speedily transferred from the airline bus to his aircraft. Passengers are decanted from their bus in front of one of ten numbered bays or entrances, each of which is pre - allocated to a particular aircraft flight

The cross-bars of the Calvert lighting system provide the pilot with an artificial horizon, assisting him to keep his aircraft level as he approaches the runway at night.

number. Those passing through Channel 4, say, will enter the lower hall and ascend by the Channel 4 escalator to the vast concourse gallery that runs the whole length of the building at first-floor level. Meanwhile their luggage will have been unloaded and transported by moving belt up to the Channel 4 Customs bay on the floor above. After examination it continues on the belt to the apron loading bays.

After passing through Customs and Immigration, the passengers arrive at the south-east face itself, with its remarkable Airside Gallery, comprising a series of luxurious waiting-rooms—each allocated to a particular passenger channel—behind a massive glassed-in corridor overlooking the apron. As the departure time approaches receptionists escort the passengers out along the Gallery and down the flying bridges to the apron gates, from which they go straight to their aircraft.

All the channels are quickly reversible for incoming services, and the whole unique system has proved remarkably trouble-free.

On the roof of this building are the attractive gardens and terraces of the public enclosure, with shelters, lawns, and cafes giving the impression of a seaside promenade. From here visitors have a panoramic view of the aprons and the airport as a whole. A fine restaurant overlooks the marshalling apron and friends can greet arrivals from an appropriately named "waving base" on the roof of the passenger building. Cantilevered out from the restaurant roof is a glazed box from which the marshalling supervisor controls the movement of aircraft on the apron below.

On the London side of the south-east face block is the Queen's Building or Eastern Apex, which provides accommodation for airline operation staffs and aircrews as well as further amenities for the general public. These include a news cinema, with a seating capacity for 160, an exhibition hall, a post office, a buffet and a grill room.

The grill room occupies the southern half of the sweeping bow front on the airside elevation of the building. A novel feature is the arrange-ment of the tables into four tiers to give all diners a clear view of the apron below.

The roof of the Queen's Building has been designed as a further series of spectacular gardens which are planted with attractive flowers, some of them blooming even in winter conditions, shrubs and ornamental trees. There is even a circular pool in the centre of the southern garden with a fountain playing. On the airside there are terraces on five separate levels so that the maximum number of visitors may enjoy the view.

Naturally, care has been taken to keep the operational side of activities in the building quite separate from the public, and the airline staff have different entrances. On the ground floor are flight planning and briefing rooms, airline operations offices, meteorological personnel, and the crew Customs hall.

Roof of the Queen's Building has a series of spectacular roof gardens.

The famous Alcock and Brown memorial, now remote from the central area on the north side marshalling apron, is eventually to face the public entrance to this building.

Undoubtedly we shall soon see the foundations of yet another building in the central terminal area — the northern face passenger building—from which will eventually operate all the long-distance international services, including those of B.O.A.C., who are still at London Airport North. A section of this building will also handle some of the short-haul services overflowing from the south-east passenger building.

14

270

Entrance to the half-mile tunnel, showing the two 20 feet wide carriageways flanked by footpaths and cycle tracks.

The rapid growth of air travel has startled even the sturdiest of optimists, and the need for the remaining accommodation planned for the central area is borne out by the incredible rise in passenger traffic. The number of passengers handled has shot up from 523,000 in 1950 to 3,520,000 in 1957. By 1960 this figure is expected to approach 5,000,000.

Because the central area is surrounded by runways and taxiways, access is by means of a half-mile-long tunnel, which itself ranks as one of the terminal's main engineering feats. Since the nature of the gravel subsoil precluded a conventional boring operation, it was built by the " cut and cover ' method. A huge trench was dug and into this was built a massive, reinforced concrete shell, more than 2,000 feet long, 86 feet wide and 23 feet high. High enough, in fact, to permit London Transport to run a regular double-deck bus service to the passenger buildings. Subdivisions in the tunnel provide paths for inbound and outbound pedestrians, tracks for cyclists and flanking dual carriageways for motor

B.O.A.C.'s headquarters building covers an area of 8½ acres. It includes four hangars, each with an unobstructed entrance of 300 feet. Four stories of office accommodation flank the walls.

Above: One of B.O.A.C.'s lastest 90-passenger turboprop Britannia airliners. Lined up in front are the Britannia's aircrew and M.T.C.A. and B.O.A.C. staff who handle the arrival and departure of the big aircraft.

Left: To speed the servicing of Viscounts B.E.A. uses a unique system of permanent maintenance docks giving easy access to all parts requiring attention.

16

Right: Every fifth traveller at London Airport has either feathers, fur or four legs. Here a Silky Hew monkey receives treatment at the specially equipped R.S.P.C.A. Animal Hostel.

Passengers' meals are prepared in superbly equipped kitchens below the passenger building, one of which is seen above. In the air these are served by capable stewardesses of many nationalities, including P.I.A.'s Miss Azra Khan, *below*.

vehicles. The tunnel is air-conditioned and fluorescent lighting is provided.

East of the central area, across the mass of runways, are the giant engineering bases of the two British Air Corporations. Each of these massive structures covers $8\frac{1}{2}$ acres and provides hangarage, workshops and stores. In addition to this B.O.A.C.'s building accommodates the complete headquarters staff of the Corporation, so that, to all intents and purposes, it houses the greater part of B.O.A.C. in England.

The building cost about £3 million, and three Britannias can be accommodated with ease in any one of the four massive hangars it provides. One of the many interesting structural features of this building is the use of two tremendously long cantilevers to give wide, uninterrupted door openings of 300 feet. Supporting the cantilevers are two concrete pylons, each carrying a load of more than 4,000 tons and mounted on massive concrete foundations measuring 72 feet by 36 feet.

B.E.A.'s building is primarily an engineering base, and basically comprises two long hangars arranged back-to-back, along the rear of which are the workshops and stores. Each of these hangars is equipped with an overhead crane for the speedy movement of wings, engines and other heavyweight components from one part of the hangar to the other.

One of the most striking sights in the hangars are B.E.A.'s unique permanent maintenance docks. Each comprises a series of platforms and decks which

17

Above: The Central Terminal Area of London Airport, showing the passenger-handling buildings and roof gardens, and the fine 127-feet high control tower in the background.

Left: Loading a dinghy into a K.L.M. DC-4 with the aid of a fork-lift. More than 60,000 tons of freight and mail pass through London Airport each year.

completely embrace an aircraft requiring overhaul after it has been towed in tail first. Easy access is provided by the decks to all parts requiring attention : engines, ailerons, flaps, tail surfaces and fuselage skin joints. Each dock is a complete workshop in itself, with all the necessary electrical supplies, compressed air and lubrication points installed at the appropriate positions.

The crews flying into London Airport express great enthusiasm for its advanced landing aids. One of these is the Calvert line-and-bar approach lighting sited close to the ends of the main east-west runways, to help pilots to land in poor visibility and at night. The system consists of a straight line of lights 3,000 feet long leading directly to the end of the runway. Every 500 feet there are cross-bars of light at right angles to the central line. The cross-bars become smaller as they approach the runway, so the pattern as seen from the air resembles a funnel with the wide neck reaching towards the approaching aircraft and leading to the beginning of the runway. The cross-bars provide an artificial horizon, assisting the pilot to keep his aircraft level as he comes in to land.

So successful has it proved that I.A.T.A. have recommended its use at all international airports.

The air age has come of age and air transport is now one of the world's major industries. It is also one of the busiest, and at London Airport the activity goes on 24 hours a day, 7 days a week, as the big silver planes land and leave with their precious cargoes of passengers and freight in continuous procession. Year by year an increasing amount of freight is carried, and in 1957 60,000 tons of freight and mail passed through London Airport alone. The air has opened fresh markets and brought trade expansion throughout the world. Cargoes carried into and out of London have ranged from cameras to computers and from flowers to furniture. The carriage of urgent cargoes is a speciality. It cost a lot of money to fly a six-ton propeller shaft to a ship broken down in a Pakistan port not long ago. But the vessel, which was costing the owner more than £1,000 per day while idle, was quickly repaired at a big saving.

Air transport is also attractive to people who ship animals and want them delivered with a minimum of discomfort, and the airlines have made animal care a major study. They carefully look after their feeding and domestic habits, water them regularly and sometimes even provide them with special attendants. For dogs some airlines provide sumptuous portable kennels, complete with deodorisers.

To look after creatures in transit the R.S.P.C.A. have built a special Animal Hostel at London Airport north. In one hectic month this unique animal hostel was used by 47,000 creatures, from panthers and penguins to pumas and pythons.

As business booms in all directions, the winged argosies of the air age world are fast developing the terminal at Heathrow into a new Port of London.

Flying with both feet on the ground . . . .

This incredible electronic simulator enables B.O.A.C. to train aircrew in all aspects of flying the Britannia—but on the ground. Pilots hear the noise of the engines, wind and touch-down tyre squeal. They feel the controls respond to airspeed, altitude of the aircraft and the position of the wheels and flaps. If they don't manœuvre correctly the trainer will " crash." Crews can be instructed at all times regardless of weather and the cost is only one-tenth of that of training in the air. Pictured here are the nose of the " grounded " Britannia and the flight compartment.

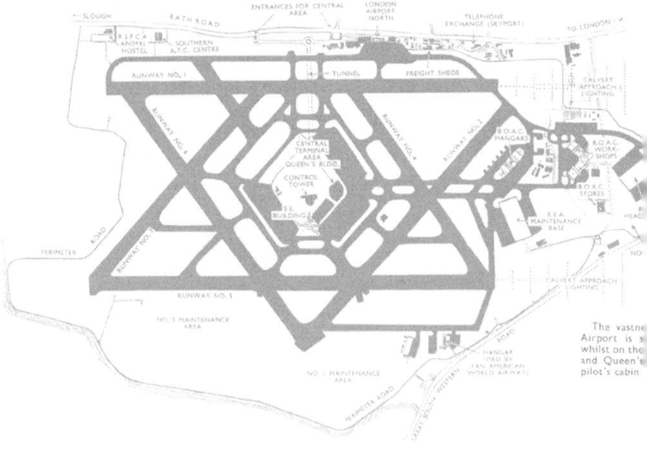

The vastne[ss of London] Airport is s[hown] whilst on the[...] and Queen's [...] pilot's cabin

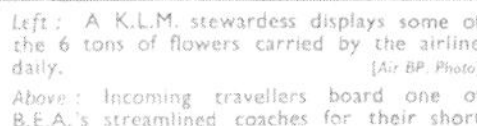

Left : A K.L.M. stewardess displays some of the 6 tons of flowers carried by the airline daily.
[*Air BP. Photo*]

Above : Incoming travellers board one of B.E.A.'s streamlined coaches for their short journey from the airport to the centre of London. [*B.E.A. Photo*]

Right : Passengers disembarking from a K.L.M. Super Constellation.
[*Air BP. Photo*]

e area covered by London the plan on the left impressive control tower are pictured from the opter.
[*B.E.A. Photo*]

PISTON. That the modern airliner is complicated is evident from the photograph above of the cockpit of one of B.O.A.C.'s Stratocruisers. Even the roof is used to mount a battery of switches, knobs and levers. One suspects that, if the pilots were not really firm about it, the windows themselves would soon be covered by instruments!

INSIDE THE

COCKPIT

TURBOPROP. In some respects the turboprop airliner is simpler than its predecessors. Below, the First Officer (right) adjusts the Decca Flight Log in the cockpit of a B.E.A. Viscount. This is an ingenious electronic device on which a pen traces the position of the aircraft with remarkable accuracy on a slowly unwinding map. All in all, however, the new generation of turboprop and turbojet airliners will demand more skill than ever before.

INSIDE THE CABIN

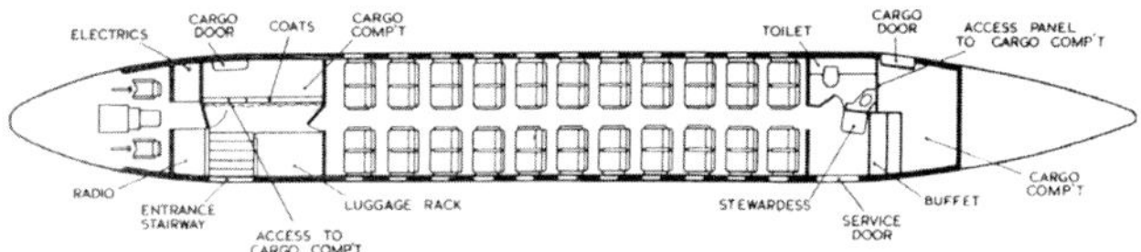

METROPOLITAN. This medium-range airliner seats 44 passengers in one large cabin. Unusual feature is the passenger door forward of the wing, the conventional position is aft. [*Flight drawing*

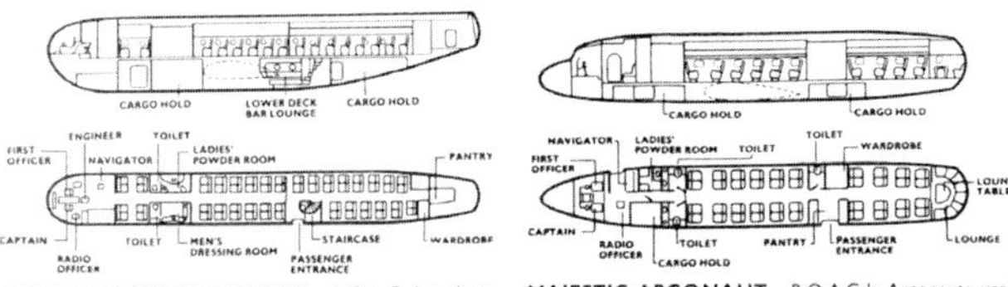

MONARCH STRATOCRUISER. B.O.A.C. has three standard cabin layouts for its fleet of Stratocruisers: 60 seats for the *Monarch* luxury trans-Atlantic service, 81 seats for *Coronet* tourist services, and 68 for the mixed *Majestic Coronet*, luxury tourist services.

MAJESTIC ARGONAUT. B.O.A.C.'s Argonauts used for *Majestic* luxury services are divided into two cabins separated by a broad central aisle, giving a spacious atmosphere not found in many larger aircraft. A comfortable lounge at the back of the rear cabin has seats for six.

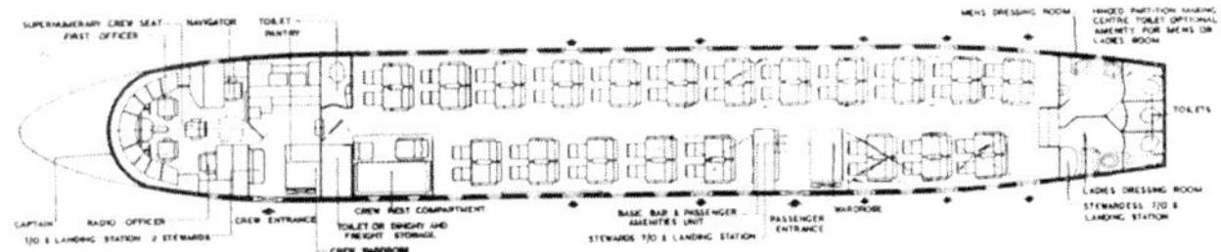

BRITANNIA. One of the many seating arrangements available for the spacious cabin of the Britannia is this luxurious First Class 40 slumberette layout. An alternative layout seating 32 includes a cocktail bar and lounge.

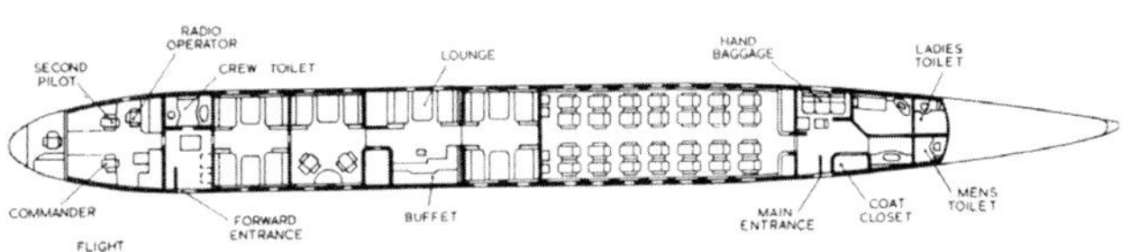

TU 104. Already a " regular " visitor to London Airport, Russia's twin-jet airliner is now being offered for sale in competition with those of the West. The 54-seat luxury cabin (shown above) includes lounges forward fitted with tables and facing double seats. [*Flight drawing*

23

INTERNATIONAL REGISTRATION MARKINGS

AIRCRAFT, like motor cars, have to be registered, and civil machines are allotted a marking consisting of a number of letters. As they travel from country to country it is important that the markings of individual aircraft do not coincide with one another and to avoid this the registrations are allotted on an international basis, certain letters, or groups of letters, being reserved for a particular country. Thus, if the code is known, by looking at the first part of the marking on an aircraft, one can tell its country of origin. The complete marking will tell you the individual airline or company which actually owns the aircraft. The markings of all civil aircraft registered in Britain are given in a companion ABC book entitled *Civil Aircraft Markings*.

Given below are the international prefixes of the most important countries of the world. Those marked * indicate countries whose aircraft may be seen at London Airport.

Prefix	Country	Prefix	Country	Prefix	Country
AN	NICARAGUA	*OD	LEBANON	VQ–B	BARBADOS
*AP	PAKISTAN	*OE	AUSTRIA	VQ–C	CYPRUS
B	FORMOSA	*OH	FINLAND	VQ–F	FIJI ISLANDS
CC	CHILE	*OK	CZECHOSLOVAKIA	VQ–G	GRENADA
*CCCP	SOVIET UNION	*OO	BELGIUM	VQ–H	ST. HELENA
*CF	CANADA	*OY	DENMARK	VQ–L	ST. LUCIA
CN	MOROCCO	*PH	NETHERLANDS	VQ–M	MAURITIUS
CB, CP	BOLIVIA	PI	PHILIPPINE REPUBLIC	VQ–S	SEYCHELLE ISLANDS
CR	PORTUGUESE COLONIES	PJ	NETHERLANDS ANTILLES	VQ–Z	BASUTOLAND, BECHUANA-
*CS	PORTUGAL	PK	UNITED STATES OF		LAND, SWAZILAND
CU	CUBA		INDONESIA	VR–A	ADEN
CX	URUGUAY	*PP,PT	BRAZIL	VR–B	BERMUDA
CZ	MONACO	PZ	SURINAM	VR–G	GIBRALTAR
*D	GERMANY	*SE	SWEDEN	VR–H	HONG KONG
*EC	SPAIN	SN	SUDAN	VR–L	SIERRA LEONE
*EI, EJ	IRELAND	*SP	POLAND	VR–N	NIGERIA, BRITISH CAMER-
EL	LIBERIA	*SU	EGYPT		OONS
EP	IRAN	*SX	GREECE	VR–O	NORTH BORNEO
ET	ETHIOPIA	TC	TURKEY	VR–R	MALAYAN FEDERATION
*F	FRANCE, COLONIES AND	*TF	ICELAND	VR–S	SINGAPORE
	PROTECTORATES	TG	GUATEMALA	VR–T	TANGANYIKA
*G	UNITED KINGDOM	TI	COSTA RICA	VR–U	BRUNEI
HA	HUNGARY	TJ	JORDAN	VR–W	SARAWAK
*HB	SWITZERLAND	*VH	AUSTRALIA	*VT	INDIA
HC	ECUADOR	VP, AA	GHANA	XA, XB, XC	MEXICO
HH	HAITI	VP–B	BAHAMAS	XH	HONDURAS
HI	DOMINICAN REPUBLIC	VP–F	FALKLAND ISLANDS	XT	REPUBLIC OF CHINA
HK	COLOMBIA	VP–G	BRITISH GUIANA	XY, XZ	BURMA
HL	REPUBLIC OF KOREA	VP–H	BRITISH HONDURAS	YA	AFGHANISTAN
HP	PANAMA	VP–J	JAMAICA	YE	YEMEN
HS	THAILAND	VP–K	KENYA	*YI	IRAQ
HZ	SAUDI ARABIA	VP–L	LEEWARD ISLANDS	YJ	NEW HEBRIDES
*I	ITALY	VP–M	MALTA	YK	SYRIA
JA	JAPAN	VP–N	NYASALAND	YR	RUMANIA
JY, TJ	JORDAN	VP–P	ISLANDS OF WESTERN	YS	EL SALVADOR
JZ	NETHERLANDS NEW		PACIFIC HIGH	YU	YUGOSLAVIA
	GUINEA		COMMISSION	YV	VENEZUELA
*LN	NORWAY	VP–R	NORTHERN RHODESIA	ZA	ALBANIA
*LQ	ARGENTINE REPUBLIC	VP–S	SOMALILAND	ZK, ZL, ZM	NEW ZEALAND
LX	LUXEMBOURG	VP–T	TRINIDAD AND TOBAGO	ZP	PARAGUAY
LZ	BULGARIA	VP–U	UGANDA	*ZS, ZT, ZU	UNION OF SOUTH AFRICA
MC	MONTE CARLO	VP–V	ST. VINCENT	3W	VIETNAM
*N	UNITED STATES OF	VP–X	GAMBIA	*4R	CEYLON
	AMERICA	*VP–Y	SOUTHERN RHODESIA	*4X	ISRAEL
OB	PERU	VP–Z	ZANZIBAR	5A	LIBYA

Most countries favour an all-letter registration, usually of five letters, with a hyphen between the first and second, or second and third letters. These markings are usually painted on each aircraft in at least two prominent places. British aircraft usually have the registration marked boldly across the underside of the wing and on either side of the fin, or rear of the fuselage.

American aircraft have the registration in large letters below the port wing, on top of the starboard wing, and on each side of the fin and rudder.

The majority of British aircraft have a registration commencing G-A, followed by three letters. The current series began with G-AAAA and will continue until G-ZZZZ is reached. At the time of going to press, British aircraft are being registered in the G-APAA group.

Argonaut

This fine airliner is the result of co-operation between three countries : Britain, Canada and the United States. A development of the famous Douglas DC (Douglas Commercial) series, it is basically a DC-4 with four Rolls-Royce Merlin in-line engines instead of the usual Twin-Wasp radials, although it incorporates the stronger wing, undercarriage and longer rear fuselage of the DC-6. It remains the only airliner on the North Atlantic route utilising liquid-cooled, in-line piston engines.

Designed to meet the requirements of the Royal Canadian Air Force and Trans-Canada Airlines for a 40-56 seat transport, early versions are in service as North Star transports, those for the R.C.A.F. being un-pressurised. Then came the pressurised Canadair Four with more powerful Rolls-Royce engines which are now in service with T.C.A., as North Star Skyliners, and B.O.A.C., as Argonauts.

The fleet of Argonauts operated by B.O.A.C. carry a crew of 7 and 40 First Class or up to 54 Tourist passengers.

ENGINES: 4 × 1,760 h.p. Rolls-Royce Merlin 724 in-lines.

SPAN: 117 ft. 6 in.

SPEED: Cruising, 265 m.p.h.; maximum: 353 m.p.h.

LENGTH: 93 ft. 8 in.

LOADED WEIGHT: 82,000 lb.

ENGINES: 2 × 1,900 h.p. M82Ts

SPAN: 104 ft.

SPEED: Cruising, 200 m.p.h.

LENGTH: 73 ft. 2 in.

LOADED WEIGHT: 38,000 lb.

Avia 14

This sturdy Dakota-type aircraft is a Czech-built version of the well-known Soviet IL-14. A medium to short-range airliner, the Avia 14 has cabin layouts for 24, 28 and 32 passengers ; in addition there is a luxuriously appointed executive version. A product of the Czech national aircraft industry, the aircraft was produced under the direction of the Ministry of Machinery.

Its two 1,900 h.p. two-row 14-cylinder direct-injection engines give an impressive take-off performance, a service ceiling of 22,000 feet and a range of 1,250 miles. Navigational equipment includes duplicated radio, radio compass, radar altimeter, omni-range equipment, auto-pilot and I.L.S.-type approach aid.

As might be expected the aircraft is fully equipped for cold weather operation, and the makers are offering the aircraft for sale abroad with an extensive selection of spares and servicing tools.

Britannia

Fine proportions and remarkable quietness tend to belittle the size of the Britannia, which is, in fact, one of the biggest and fastest airliners in the world. Recent adverse publicity of teething troubles has also tended to obscure the fact that the Britannia, powered by near-4,000 e.h.p. turbine engines driving propellers and carrying up to 90 passengers at high speeds, is also an exceptionally economical airliner.

Initial aircraft, with a 114 feet fuselage, are known as Series 100s. A " stretched " variant, with the fuselage lengthened by 10 ft. 3 in. and fitted with more powerful engines is known as the Series 300. A long-range version, Series 310, is essentially the same as the 300, except for increased fuel tankage giving a range of nearly 6,000 miles. Picture shows a Series 312.

One of the 18 long-range aircraft on order by B.O.A.C. became the first British passenger-carrying airliner and also the first turbine-powered aircraft ever to go into regular commercial service on the arduous North Atlantic route.

ENGINES: 4 × 4,120 e.h.p. Proteus 755 turboprops (Series 310).

SPEED: Cruising, 391 m.p.h., average.

SPAN: 142 ft. 3 in.

LENGTH: 124 ft. 3 in.

LOADED WEIGHT: 175,000 lb.

Dakota

Originally introduced over *twenty years* ago as the DST—Douglas Sleeper Transport—the Dakota is undoubtedly the best-known airliner ever built. More than 400 were in use by 1940, and nearly 11,000 were built during the war to transport troops and tug gliders. Many more were built under licence in Russia as the LI-2.

Today it is still the workhorse of many airlines and air forces all over the world. One veteran, built in 1937, now rests in an American museum, having covered 8½ million miles during more than 55,000 flying hours—equal to a total stay of 6 years in the air.

B.E.A. uses an improved version known as the Pionair. Weighing 28,000 lb., this has a special door incorporating built-in steps, and can carry 32 passengers, against the normal 21.

Although Dakota replacements appear at the rate of about three a year, there is little doubt that " Daks " will continue to be used for many years to come, particularly in the less developed areas of the world.

ENGINES: 2 × 1,200 h.p. Wright Cyclone, or Pratt and Whitney Twin-Wasp R-1830 radials.

SPEED: Cruising, 165 m.p.h.; maximum, 230 m.p.h.

SPAN: 95 ft.

LENGTH: 64 ft. 5 in.

LOADED WEIGHT: 25,500 lb.

26

DC-4

Under a special war-time agreement America, beyond the range of enemy bombers, provided all the transport aircraft required by the Allies. One of the aircraft developed during this period was the C-54 Skymaster, 1,163 of which had been delivered by the end of 1945. This was a military version of the DC-4, deliveries of which had just commenced when America entered the war.

About 500 of these were " re-converted " into airliners to supplement the 74 built since the war. Second only in fame to its smaller but elder brother the DC-3 (Dakota) it is thus in world wide service with many airlines, including Air France, Iberia, Iceland Airways, K.L.M., Sabena, S.A.S., Seaboard and Western, Swissair, T.A.E., and T.A.P.

With the advent of Tourist Services, many DC-4s have been modified to carry up to 60 passengers compared with the normal 44.

ENGINES: 4 × 1,450 Pratt and Whitney Twin-Wasp R-2000 radials.

SPAN: 117 ft. 6 in.

SPEED: Cruising, 200 m.p.h.; maximum, 280 m.p.h.

LENGTH: 93 ft. 11 in.

LOADED WEIGHT: 73,000 lb.

DC-6

The DC-6 is a " stretched " improvement of the DC-4, the fuselage, lengthened by 12 feet and now pressurised, accommodating up to 92 passengers, and more powerful engines.

The lengthened fuselage is not easily discerned in the air but, fortunately, the makers also introduced square windows (round on the DC-4) so that a DC-6 is readily " spotted ".

Original DC-6s had a length of 100 ft. 7 in., but this was increased by 5 ft. for the DC-6A Liftmaster, an all-freight machine produced in 1949. This could carry up to 15 tons of cargo, or about 12 tons across the Atlantic. In turn, a passenger version was developed from this and designated DC-6B, and about 150 of these have been delivered to 17 different operators. Last of the series is the DC-6C, a convertible passenger-freighter, with a loaded weight of 107,000 lb. and accommodation for 76 passengers. This can be quickly converted from one version to the other and has a movable bulkhead to separate cargo from passengers when both are carried.

ENGINES: 4 × 2,500 h.p. Pratt and Whitney Double Wasp R-2800 CB17 radials.

SPAN: 117 ft. 6 in.

SPEED: Cruising, 310 m.p.h.; maximum, 360 m.p.h.

LENGTH: 105 ft. 7 in.

LOADED WEIGHT: 107,000 lb.

27

DC-7C

Fastest of the world's piston-engined airliners, the DC-7 (Douglas Commercial No. 7) is a larger and more powerful version of the DC-6.

The original DC-7 is flown extensively in the United States where it is shaping anew the country's travel habits by speeding non-stop from coast-to-coast in eight hours. This model was followed by the DC-7B, with increased fuel capacity and improved take-off performance, and more recently by the DC-7C. Popularly known as the Seven Seas, this new plane is designed to fly the North Atlantic non-stop, taking in its stride the bitter 90 m.p.h. headwinds which in winter months have the effect of lengthening the east-west crossing by as much as 1,000 miles. Basically a " stretched " DC-7B, it has more powerful engines, increased span to accommodate new wing-root tanks, a longer fuselage, and enlarged vertical tail surfaces.

ENGINES: 4 × 3,400 h.p. Wright R - 3350 - EA - I Turbo-Compound radials.

SPAN: 127 ft. 6 in.

SPEED: Cruising, 354 m.p.h.; maximum, 410 m.p.h.

LENGTH: 112 ft. 3 in.

LOADED WEIGHT: 143,000 lb.

Elizabethan

Known as the *Elizabethan*-class, Airspeed Ambassadors are in service with B.E.A. on medium-range European routes.

The *Elizabethan* is not only one of the most graceful aircraft flying, but also one of the most popular, the high wing position —unusual feature on a large airliner — being particularly attractive to passengers, affording as it does an excellent unobstructed downward view through every one of its large windows. Also liked is the roomy and comfortable 47-seat cabin. The *Elizabethan*, together with the Convair Metropolitan, probably represents the last word in twin-piston-engined airliner comfort.

Now tried and proved by years of service the *Elizabethans* are B.E.A.'s most economical aircraft on certain routes, but following the company's policy of maintaining its routes with the most modern aircraft, they are soon to be replaced by Viscounts.

The two prototype Ambassadors are being experimentally re-engined with Napier Eland and Rolls-Royce RB109 turboprops.

ENGINES: 2 × 2,625 h.p. Bristol Centaurus 661 radials.

SPAN: 115 ft.

SPEED: Cruising, 270 m.p.h.; maximum, 312 m.p.h.

LENGTH: 82 ft.

LOADED WEIGHT: 55,000 lb.

Hermes 4

Civil counterpart of the well-known Handley Page Hastings—the R.A.F.'s standard long-range transport—the Hermes was Britain's first long-range post-war airliner.

Twenty-five were built for use by B.O.A.C. on Commonwealth routes, but today the majority of these are flown by British independent airlines on general charter services and government air trooping schemes. During 1956 a number of Hermes 4s served with Kuwait Airways and Middle East Airlines. Normal seating is for a crew of 5 and 40 passengers, but alternative arrangements provide for a maximum of 74 passengers.

Characteristics distinguishing the Hermes from the Douglas DC4/6/7 series are its "square" wing centre section, as opposed to the straight-tapered wings of the latter, and the pronounced "sweep back" on the leading edge of its tailplane.

ENGINES: 4 × 2,100 h.p. Bristol Hercules 773 radials.

SPAN: 113 ft.

SPEED: Cruising, 276 m.p.h.; maximum, 355 m.p.h.

LENGTH: 96 ft. 10 in.

LOADED WEIGHT: 86,000 lb.

Heron

A four-engined "big-sister" to the smaller Dove, the 14-17 seat Heron provides four-engined safety in an airliner of a size not normally incorporating such a feature.

Apart from the multiple engines, the Heron is a sturdy and simple machine, admirably suited to both the big city airports and less lavish out-town landing fields between which it normally operates. It is, perhaps, one of the nearest approaches yet to an air-bus, and is used every day by many people who regard it as a swift means of going about their everyday business with little more fuss than is needed on boarding an ordinary wheeled bus.

Originally, the Heron had a fixed undercarriage, but this is made retractable on Series 2 aircraft.

Apart from its eminence as a feeder-liner, the Heron makes an admirable executive or V.I.P. aircraft. Three Herons have been bought for the Queen's Flight. The one occupied by the Queen is fitted with much additional radio, radar and other special safety equipment.

ENGINES: 4 × 250 h.p. Gipsy Queen 30 inlines.

SPAN: 71 ft. 6 in.

SPEED: Cruising, 183 m.p.h.

LENGTH: 48 ft. 6 in.

LOADED WEIGHT: 13,500 lb.

29

285

ENGINES: 2 × 2,500 h.p. Pratt and Whitney Double Wasp R-2800 CB17 radials.
SPAN: 105 ft. 4 in.

SPEED: Cruising, 290 m.p.h.; maximum, 350 m.p.h.
LENGTH: 79 ft. 2 in.
LOADED WEIGHT: 49,100 lb.

Metropolitan

Developed from the Convair 240 and 340 series of airliners which virtually monopolised the best medium air routes of the world since the end of the war until the appearance of Britain's turbopropped Viscount, the Metropolitan is probably the last piston-engined aircraft of its kind.

Carrying up to 44 passengers, over ranges up to 1,000 miles, the Metropolitan incorporates many detail improvements over the earlier 340s affecting general equipment and comfort. Cabin soundproofing has been revised and the distinctive twin-exhaust pipes of earlier Convairliners have been replaced by a new system with a neater rectangular outlet.

About 100 Metropolitans have been sold which, together with about 350 240s and 340s sold to 35 operators, and an equal number of military versions, has raised the production run of the Convair liner family to more than 1,000.

Stratocruiser

A large, luxurious, long-range passenger transport, the Stratocruiser is a development of the war-time Superfortress bomber, and the Stratofreighter cargo transport. It has the same wings, engines, undercarriage and tail as the famous bomber and cabin space was provided by the " simple " expedient of building another, larger, fuselage on top of the original. The rather bluff appearance of the Stratocruiser is the result of this freighter parentage, for which utility, not external beauty, was the governing factor.

In service with three airlines (Pan American Airways, B.O.A.C., and Northwest Airlines) the Stratocruiser is an exceptionally luxurious, quiet and smooth airliner, carrying up to 100 passengers. It has the novel attraction of a " downstairs " lounge and cocktail bar in the centre of the lower fuselage. This enables passengers to take a " walk " and stretch their legs, a facility much appreciated as any regular long distance traveller will readily confirm.

ENGINES: 4 × 3,500 h.p. Pratt and Whitney Wasp Major R-4360 radials.
SPAN: 141 ft. 3 in.

SPEED: Cruising, 315 m.p.h.; maximum, 375 m.p.h.
LENGTH: 110 ft. 4 in.
LOADED WEIGHT: 145,800 lb.

30

286

Super Constellation

Since the first design work started on the Constellation in June, 1939, a Project Engineering Group has been at work continuously adding improvements to the design in the light of operating experience.

To accommodate more passengers and reduce operating costs, the enlarged Lockheed 1049 Super Constellation was produced. This incorporated the biggest single " stretch " yet applied to any aircraft, with just over 18 feet of fuselage being added. The original Constellation lifted 72,000 lb. including its own weight. Pakistan International's Model L1049C shown here lifts 133,000 lb.

The Model L1049C is fitted with the Wright DA1 Turbo-Compound engine, a cross between a piston engine and a propjet. The exhaust gases are used to operate turbines which are geared back into the engine to produce additional power without using more fuel.

ENGINES: 4 × 3,250 h.p. Wright R-3350 DAI. Turbo-compounds

SPAN: 123 ft.

SPEED: Cruising, 330 m.p.h.; maximum, 376 m.p.h.

LENGTH: 113 ft. 7 in.

LOADED WEIGHT : 133,000 lb.

ENGINES: 4 × 3,400 h.p. Wright R-3350 Turbo-compounds.

SPAN : 150 ft.

SPEED: Maximum cruising, 350 m.p.h.

LENGTH: 116 ft. 2 in.

LOADED WEIGHT: 156,000 lb.

Starliner (Super Constellation 1649)

Outstanding feature of this latest — and probably last — development of the Constellation series is the 150 foot span wing. Much energy and ingenuity have been concentrated to produce what is probably the most efficient long-range aerofoil in the world. Designed for ultra-long ranges up to 5,300 miles, this great range is achieved by using almost the whole of the wing, from tip to tip, as an integral fuel tank.

Most Constellation 1649s will probably carry 62 passengers in four-abreast seats of a new design; although up to 93 Tourist seats can be fitted if desired. Model 1649s have been ordered by several airlines using London Airport and there is a good chance of seeing one of these new and remarkable machines. Its wide-span narrow-chord wing will make it easy to spot.

Viking

B.E.A.'s first scheduled flight to Europe — from Northolt to Copenhagen on September 1st, 1946 — was made by a Vickers Viking.

Six months later, B.E.A. possessed a fleet of 29 and by the time they were replaced in October, 1954, these reliable aircraft had flown a total of 65 million miles and carried 2,748,000 passengers.

Many Vikings are still plying their way across the world's skyways in the liveries of Britain's independent airlines and several overseas operators. Vikings and spare parts valued at £2.5 million have been exported to seven different countries.

Two military variants, the Valetta transport and the Varsity crew-trainer, are in service with the R.A.F.

The standard Viking 1B has a crew of 3 and seats 24-38 passengers.

ENGINES: 2 × 1,690 h.p. Bristol Hercules 634.

SPAN: 89 ft. 3 in.

SPEED: Cruising, 263 m.p.h.; maximum, 304 m.p.h.

LENGTH: 65 ft. 2 in.

LOADED WEIGHT: 34,000 lb.

Viscount

No other medium-range airliner yet flying approaches the phenomenal Viscount in either performance or passenger appeal. The world's first propjet-powered civil transport the Viscount entered regular airline service in 1953 when B.E.A. introduced their Discovery Class Viscount 701s.

Popular with passengers for its smooth, vibration-free flights and with airlines for its economy, the Viscount is used or ordered by 40 different operators.

The Viscount 701 normally accommodates a crew of 3-4 and 47 passengers, but up to 59 may be carried on high density air coach services.

Like Topsy, the Viscount has "just growed." The original 32-seat Viscount turned the scales at 40,000 lb. and was only 74 feet long. B.E.A.'s new 70 seat Viscount Major weighs 69,000 lb., is 86 feet long—and even bigger models are on the way.

ENGINES: 4 × 1,400 h.p. Rolls-Royce Dart 505 propjets.

SPAN: 94 ft.

SPEED: Cruising. 317 m.p.h.; maximum 350 m.p.h.

LENGTH: 81 ft. 2 in.

LOADED WEIGHT: 58,500 lb.

32

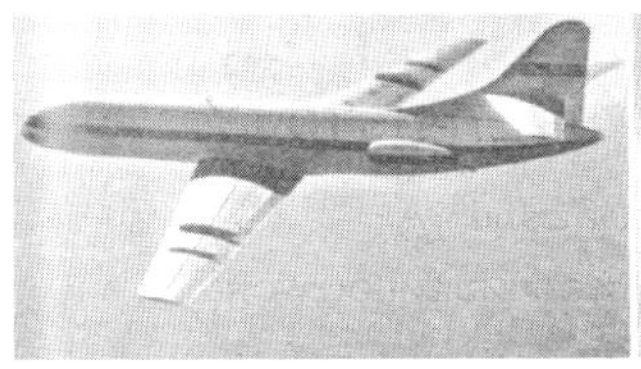

SUD-AVIATION CARAVELLE. Designed for medium ranges, the French Caravelle is a jetliner of which any company will be proud. Seating up to 70 passengers, the Caravelle cruises at 495 m.p.h.

DE HAVILLAND COMET 4. Based on the experience gained on the earlier Comet Is, the Comet 4, almost identical externally to the Comet 3 above, will not only be the most thoroughly tested airliner in the world, but also one of the most economical over all but the very longest routes. It will carry 58–76 passengers, and will have a

FOKKER FRIENDSHIP. Powered by two Rolls-Royce Dart propeller turbines of the type made famous in the Viscount, the Friendship was designed as a replacement for the now ageing Dakota. It may be seen at London Airport.

VICKERS VANGUARD. A large turboprop airliner carrying up to 115 passengers, this is designed to supersede the Viscount in the early 1960s. Unusual feature is the exceptionally big under-cabin cargo hold giving the " double-bubble " shape to the fuselage.

TU 104. This impressive 70-seat Russian turbojet airliner is thought to be one of the aircraft Aeroflot will operate on its proposed Moscow–London service. Maximum cruising speed is around 550 m.p.h.

BOEING STRATOLINER. Fifteen of these big, 100-ton 100-passenger, 600 m.p.h. airliners have been ordered by B.O.A.C. for use over the North Atlantic, as Britain has not yet produced a jet aircraft for this difficult route. First model will enter service with P.A.A. in 1959.

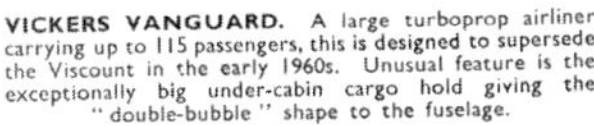

Airline Fleet List

Listed below are over 280 aircraft registered with the six British home-based airline companies using London Airport. For the enthusiast a space is provided for the date to be marked alongside those aircraft seen.

Shortage of space has prevented the listing of all the aircraft of the remaining 36 companies using the airport, but the markings of all civil aircraft seen regularly in Britain are given in a companion ABC book entitled Civil Aircraft Markings.

Registration	Name	When seen	Registration	Name	When seen
AIRWORK LIMITED			**Dakota Fleet—Pionair Class**		
Hermes Fleet			G–AGHJ	Albert Ball	
			G–AGHL	Lanoe Hawker	
G–ALDA			G–AGHM	Edward Maitland	
G–ALDC			G–AGHP	Bert Hinkler	
G–ALDG			G–AGHS	Horace Short	
G–ALDO			G–AGIP	Horatio Phillips	
			G–AGIU	Edward Busk	
Viking Fleet			G–AGJV	John Porte	
			G–AGJW	Wilfred Parke	
G–AHOP			G–AGJZ	John Stringfellow	
G–AIXR			G–AGNK	Edward Mannock	
G–AJFR			G–AGYX	George Holt Thomas	
G–AJFS			G–AGZB	Robert Smith-Barry	
G–AJFT			G–AGZC	Samuel Cody	
G–AKTU			G–AGZD	Percy Pilcher	
G–AKTV			G–AHCU	Charles Ulm	
			G–AHCV	Sir George Cayley	
Viscount Fleet			G–AHCX	Spenser Grey	
			G–AHCZ	Charles Samson	
G–AODG			G–AIWD	John Dunne	
G–AODH			G–AJDE	Sir David Henderson	
			G–AJHY	William Henson	
BRITISH EUROPEAN AIRWAYS			G–AJHZ	Bentfield Hucks	
Ambassador Fleet—Elizabethan Class			G–AJIA	Sir John Alcock	
			G–AJIB	Griffith Brewer	
G–ALZN	Elizabethan (Flagship)		G–AJIC	Roy Chadwick	
G–ALZO	Christopher Marlowe		G–AKJH	Edward Hillman	
G–ALZP	Sir Richard Grenville		G–AKNB	Sir Sefton Brancker	
G–ALZS	William Shakespeare		G–ALCC	Harry Hawker	
G–ALZT	Sir John Hawkins		G–ALLI	Sir Samuel Instone	
G–ALZV	Earl of Leicester		G–ALPN	Sir Godfrey Paine	
G–ALZW	Sir Francis Walsingham		G–ALTT	Charles Grey	
G–ALZY	Sir Philip Sydney		G–ALXK	Rex Pierson	
G–ALZZ	Edmund Spenser		G–ALXL	Charles Rolls	
G–AMAA	Sir Francis Knollys		G–ALXM	William Rhodes-Moorhouse	
G–AMAC	Sir Robert Cecil		G–ALXN	Sir Henry Royce	
G–AMAF	Lord Howard of Effingham				
G–AMAG	Sir Thomas Gresham				

Registration	Name	When seen	Registration	Name	When seen
G–ALYF	Pionair (Flagship)		G–AOHT	Ralph Fitch	
G–AMDB	Claude Johnson		G–AOHU	Sir George Strong Nares	
G–AMDZ	Frank Barnwell		G–AOHV	Sir John Barrow	
G–AMFV	Richard Howard-Flanders		G–AOHW	Sir Francis Younghusband	
G–AMGD	George Brackley		G–AOJA	Sir Samuel White Baker	
G–AMJX	Reginald Mitchell		G–AOJB	Stephen Borough	
G–AMJY	James McCudden		G–AOJC	Robert O'Hara Burke	
G–AMKE	Frederick Lanchester		G–AOJD	Sebastian Cabot	
G–AMNV	Sir Eric Geddes		G–AOJE	Sir Alexander Mackenzie	
G–AMNW	Frank Searle		G–AOJF	Sir George Somers	
			G–AORC	Richard Lander	
			G–AORD	Arthur Phillip	

Viscount Fleet—Discovery Class
Viscount 701

Registration	Name	When seen
G–ALWF	Sir John Franklin	
G–AMNY	Sir Ernest Shackleton	
G–AMNZ	James Cook	
G–AMOA	George Vancouver	
G–AMOB	William Baffin	
G–AMOC	Richard Chancellor	
G–AMOD	John Davis	
G–AMOE	Sir Edward Parry	
G–AMOF	Sir Martin Frobisher	
G–AMOG	Robert Falcon Scott	
G–AMOH	Henry Hudson	
G–AMOI	Sir Hugh Willoughby	
G–AMOJ	Sir James Ross	
G–AMOK	Sir Humphrey Gilbert	
G–AMOL	David Livingstone	
G–AMON	Thomas Cavendish	
G–AMOO	John Oxenham	
G–AMOP	Mungo Park	
G–ANHA	Anthony Jenkinson	
G–ANHB	Sir Henry Stanley	
G–ANHC	Sir Leopold McClintock	
G–ANHD	William Dampier	
G–ANHE	Gino Watkins	
G–ANHF	Matthew Flinders	
G–AOFX	Sir Joseph Banks	

Viscount 802

Registration	Name	When seen
G–AOHG	Richard Hakluyt	
G–AOHH	Sir Robert McClure	
G–AOHI	Charles Montagu Doughty	
G–AOHJ	Sir John Mandeville	
G–AOHK	John Hanning Speke	
G–AOHL	Charles Sturt	
G–AOHM	Robert Machin	
G–AOHN	Alexander Gordon Laing	
G–AOHO	Samuel Wallis	
G–AOHP	James Weddell	
G–AOHR	Sir Richard Burton	
G–AOHS	Robert Thorne	

Viscount 806

Registration	Name	When seen
G–AOYF	Michael Faraday	
G–AOYG	Charles Darwin	
G–AOYH	William Harvey	
G–AOYI	Sir Humphrey Davy	
G–AOYJ	Edward Jenner	
G–AOYK	Edmund Cartwright	
G–AOYL	Lord Joseph Lister	
G–AOYM	John Loudon McAdam	
G–AOYN	Sir Isaac Newton	
G–AOYO	Adam Smith	
G–AOYP	John Napier	
G–AOYR	Sir Richard Arkwright	
G–AOYS	George Stephenson	
G–AOYT	James Watt	
G–APEX	John Harrison	
G–APEY	William Murdock	

BRITISH OVERSEAS AIRWAYS
Argonaut Fleet (Canadair DC–4M)

Registration	Name	When seen
G–ALHC	Ariadne	
G–ALHD	Ajax	
G–ALHG	Aurora	
G–ALHH	Attica	
G–ALHI	Antares	
G–ALHJ	Arcturas	
G–ALHK	Atalanta	
G–ALHN	Argosy	
G–ALHP	Aethra	
G–ALHR	Antiope	
G–ALHS	Astra	
G–ALHT	Athena	
G–ALHU	Artemis	
G–ALHV	Adonis	
G–ALHW	Aeolus	
G–ALHX	Astraea	
G–ALHY	Arion	

Registration	Name	When seen	Registration	Name	When seen
Britannia Fleet—Series 102			G–APDF		
			G–APDG		
G–ANBA			G–APDH		
G–ANBB			G–APDI		
G–ANBC			G–APDJ		
G–ANBD			G–APDK		
G–ANBE			G–APDL		
G–ANBF			G–APDM		
G–ANBG			G–APDN		
G–ANBH			G–APDO		
G–ANBI					
G–ANBJ			**Douglas DC–7C Fleet**		
G–ANBK					
G–ANBL			G–AOIA		
G–ANBM			G–AOIB		
G–ANBN			G–AOIC		
G–ANBO			G–AOID		
			G–AOIE		
Britannia Fleet—Series 312			G–AOIF		
			G–AOIG		
G–AOVA			G–AOIH		
G–AOVB			G–AOII		
G–AOVC			G–AOIJ		
G–AOVD					
G–AOVE			**Stratocruiser Fleet**		
G–AOVF					
G–AOVG			G–AKGH	Caledonia	
G–AOVH			G–AKGI	Caribou	
G–AOVI			G–AKGJ	Cambria	
G–AOVJ			G–AKGK	Canopus	
G–AOVK			G–AKGL	Cabot	
G–AOVL			G–AKGM	Castor	
G–AOVM			G–ALSB	Champion	
G–AOVN			G–ALSC	Centaurus	
G–AOVO			G–ALSD	Cassiopeia	
G–AOVP			G–ANTX	Cleopatra	
G–AOVR			G–ANTY	Coriolanus	
G–AOVS			G–ANTZ	Cordelia	
G–AOVT			G–ANUA	Cameronian	
G–AOVU			G–ANUB	Calypso	
G–AOVV			G–ANUC	Clio	
G–AOVW			G–ANUM	Clyde	
G–AOVX					
			Dove Fleet		
Comet 2E Fleet					
			G–AKCF	(Training)	
G–AMXD			G–AMZY	(Training)	
G–AMXK			G–AODN	(Training)	
			G–AOFI	(Training)	
Comet 4 Fleet					
			EAGLE AVIATION		
G–APDA			**Viking Fleet**		
G–APDB					
G–APDC			G–AGRS	Sir Charles Beresford	
G–APDD					
G–APDE					

Registration	Name	When seen	Registration	Name	When seen
G–AGRT	Lord Collingwood		G–AGRW		
G–AHPM	Lord Rodney		G–AHOY		
G–AIHA	Sir Richard Kempenfelt		G–AHPB		
G–AIVH	Lord Howe		G–AHPC		
G–AIVL	Lord Hawke		G–AHPJ		
G–AIVO	Edward Vernon		G–AKBG		
G–AJBN	Lord Nelson		G–AMNK		
G–AJBP	Sir Edward Hughes				
G–AJBW	Sir William Cornwallis		**Vickers Viscount Fleet**		
G–AJCD	Lord Barham		G–ANRR		
G–AJPH	Lord Dundonald		G–ANRT		
G–AKBH	Sir Henry Morgan				
G–AMGG	Sir Robert Calder		**Avro York Fleet**		
G–AMGI	Sir Henry Harwood		G–AMUS		
G–AMNX	Sir Philip Broke		G–AMUU		
G–APAT	Lord Hood		G–AMXM		
			G–ANGF		
Viscount 805 Fleet			**STARWAYS**		
G–APDW			G–AMJU	Dakota C–47	
G–APDX			G–AMPO	Dakota C–47	
			G–AMPY	Dakota C–47	
HUNTING-CLAN			G–AMSN	Dakota C–47	
Vickers Viking Fleet			G–APEZ	Skymaster DC–4	
G–AGRP			G–APIN	Skymaster DC–4	
G–AGRV					

FOREIGN AIRLINES

Given below are the names of airlines, the aircraft of which may be seen at London Airport. Under each is listed the types and numbers of aircraft operated:—

AER LINGUS (Ireland)
Dakota (13); Viscount 700 (4); Viscount 800 (3); Friendship (7)—Delivery of these aircraft commences in August, 1958.

AEROFLOT (U.S.S.R.)
AN-10; TU-104.

AEROLINEAS ARGENTINAS (Argentine)
Douglas DC-6 (6).

AIR CEYLON (Ceylon)
Constellation (1)—PH–LDP Mahadevi, operated on behalf of Air Ceylon by K.L.M.

AIR FRANCE
Breguet 763 Deux Ports (12); Constellation L–749 (16); Douglas DC–3 (8); Super Constellation L–1049G (14); Starliner L–1649 (10); Viscount 708 (11).

AIR INDIA INTERNATIONAL
Constellation L–749A (3); Super Constellation L–1049 (8).

ALITALIA (Italy)
Convairliner; Douglas DC–3; Douglas DC–6B; Viscount; Starliner 1649.

AUSTRIA
Viscount.

CENTRAL AFRICAN AIRWAYS
Viscount 748 (5).

CZECHOSLOVAKIAN AIRLINES
Avia 14; IL–12; TU–104A.

EAST AFRICAN AIRWAYS
Argonaut

EL AL (Israel)
Constellation L–049 (3); Constellation L–149 (1); Britannia 313 (4).

FINNAIR (Finland)
Convairliner 440 Metropolitan (6).
IBERIA (Spain)
Convairliner 440 Metropolitan (5); Super Constellation L–1049 (5).

ICELANDAIR
Viscount 700.

ICELANDIC AIRLINES
Douglas DC–4 (6).

IRAQI AIRLINE
Viscount.
K.L.M. (Royal Dutch Airlines)
Constellation L–749 (10); Convairliner 240 (2); Convairliner 340 (10); DC–4 (5); DC–6 (6); DC–6A (1); DC–6B (7); DC–7C (15); Super Constellation L–1049 (20); Viscount (9).
LOT (Poland)
Convairliner 240; IL–12; IL–14.
LUFTHANSA (Germany)
Convairliner 340 (4); Convairliner 440 (2); Super Constellation L–1049G (8); Starliner 1649A (4); Viscount.

MIDDLE EAST AIRLINES (Lebanon)
Viscount (7); York Freighter (3).

MISRAIR (Egypt)
Viscount.

OLYMPIC AIRWAYS
Douglas DC–6B.
PAKISTAN INTERNATIONAL AIRWAYS
Super Constellation.
PAN AMERICAN AIRWAYS
Douglas DC–4 (8); Douglas DC–6A (1); Douglas DC–6B (19); Douglas DC–7C (17); Stratocruiser (8).
PANAIR DO BRASIL
Constellation (11); Douglas DC–7C (4).
QANTAS EMPIRE AIRWAYS (Australia)
Super Constellation L–1049 (16).
SABENA BELGIAN AIRLINES
Douglas C–47 (10); Douglas DC–3 (16); Douglas DC–4 (9); Douglas DC–6 (3); Douglas DC–6B (8); Douglas DC–6C (2); Douglas DC–7C (10).
SCANDINAVIAN AIRLINES SYSTEM
Denmark: Convairliner 440 Metropolitan (5); Douglas DC–3 (3); Douglas DC–6 (3); Douglas DC–6B (4); Douglas DC–7C (4).
Norway: Convairliner 440 Metropolitan (4); Douglas DC–3 (1); Douglas DC–6 (3); Douglas DC–6B (5); Douglas DC–7C (4).
Sweden: Convairliner 440 Metropolitan (7); Douglas DC–3 (2); Douglas DC–6 (6); Douglas DC–7C (6).
SEABOARD AND WESTERN (U.S.A.)
Super Constellation L–1049 (10); Douglas DC–4 (3).
SOUTH AFRICAN AIRWAYS
Constellation L–749A (4); Douglas DC–7B (4).
SWISSAIR
Convairliner 440 Metropolitan (11); Douglas DC–3 (8); Douglas DC–4 (3); Douglas DC–6B (6); Douglas DC–7C (4).
TRANSPORTES AEROS PORTUGESES
Douglas DC–4 (3); Super Constellation L–1049G (3).
TRANS CANADA AIRLINES
Super Constellation L–1049 (9).
TRANS WORLD AIRLINES
Constellation L–749A (26); Douglas DC–4 (1); Starliner L–1649A (25); Super Constellation L–1049G (28).
WEST AFRICAN AIRWAYS
Argonaut Stratocruiser. (Operated by B.O.A.C.).

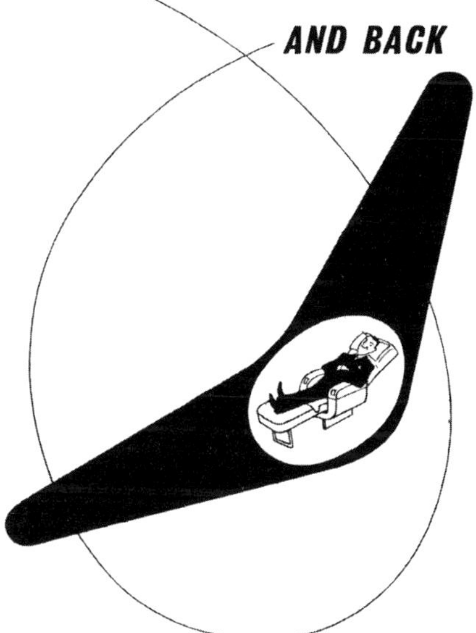

Daily flights via European capitals
and the Middle East to Bombay;
onward flights to the Far East and Australia
Super-G Constellations with
luxurious slumberettes and sleepers

AIR-INDIA
International

66 Haymarket London SW1 TRAfalgar 4541: and in Manchester, Birmingham, Glasgow

39

AIRCRAFT FUELLERS

TYNE Capacity 4,000 Imperial gallons; max. delivery rate per hose, 180 g.p.m. Leyland chassis. Among the largest fuellers in the world; used for servicing trans-Atlantic airliners.

CORNWALL Capacity 3,200 Imperial gallons; max. delivery rate per hose 250 g.p.m. Foden or Leyland chassis. Designed for over and underwing fuelling of large airliners.

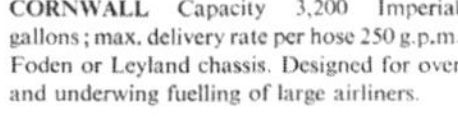

DORSET Capacity 3,000 Imperial gallons; max. delivery rate per hose, 200 g.p.m. Leyland chassis. Designed for over and underwing fuelling of large airliners.

STEER Capacity 2,200 Imperial gallons; max. delivery rate per hose, 150 g.p.m.; Leyland chassis. Used at London Airport only for servicing medium-sized aircraft.

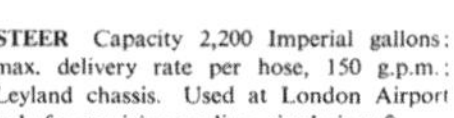

LINCOLN Capacity 1,500 Imperial gallons; max. delivery rate per hose, 100 g.p.m. Bedford chassis. Designed for over and underwing fuelling of medium sized airliners

CLYDE Capacity 1,500 Imperial gallons; max. delivery rate per hose, 200 g.p.m.; Albion chassis. Designed for over and underwing fuelling of short-haul aircraft.

TWEED Capacity 1,200 Imperial gallons; max. delivery rate per hose, 60/70 g.p.m. Ford chassis. Used for servicing aircraft covering moderate distances on European routes.

At all the major airfields in Britain you can see one or more of these different types of fuellers operating Shell and BP Aviation Services. International airlines, charter companies and private owners alike know they can always expect quick, efficient service from the friendly crews of these Service Vehicles

SHELL AND BP AVIATION SERVICES

the world's largest airliner . . . . .

THE TUPOLEV TU.114 — one of more than 100 illustrations in

abc RUSSIAN AIRCRAFT

The only book available today in which are described, with the aid of many hitherto unpublished photographs and specially drawn silhouettes, all known Russian civil and military aircraft

ther aircraft books . . .

abc ROYAL AIR FORCE
abc FLEET AIR ARM
abc CIVIL AIRCRAFT RECOGNITION

SIMILAR IN DESIGN TO abc LONDON AIRPORT, AND CONTAINING LATEST INFORMATION, PICTURES AND SILHOUETTES

abc CIVIL AIRCRAFT MARKINGS

1958 EDITION — GIVING DETAILS OF ALL BRITISH CIVIL AIRCRAFT

to be published during 1958 . . .

abc ROCKETS AND MISSILES

A NEW ASSESSMENT OF WORLD MISSILE POWER

FROM ALL BOOKSELLERS **2/6** OR THE PUBLISHERS

Ian Allan Ltd
CRAVEN HOUSE
HAMPTON COURT
SURREY

COUPON

I UNIT

Ian Allan Ltd

Save these coupons. Vouchers for new books will be sent against the following quantities:—
25—2/6; 50—5/-; 100—11/-

736/476/175/358 Published by Ian Allan Ltd., Hampton Court, Surrey, and printed by McCorquodale, London, S.E.

WHY? Because they've learned that only B.O.A.C. can offer them *everything* that's required for the perfect journey. They know they'll travel in the world's finest, fastest airliners, relax in wonderful comfort, enjoy magnificent food. And they know they'll receive friendly, personal attention, making them feel at home though thousands of miles away. Fly B.O.A.C. yourself — to any one of 51 countries — and see how B.O.A.C. takes good care of *you*.

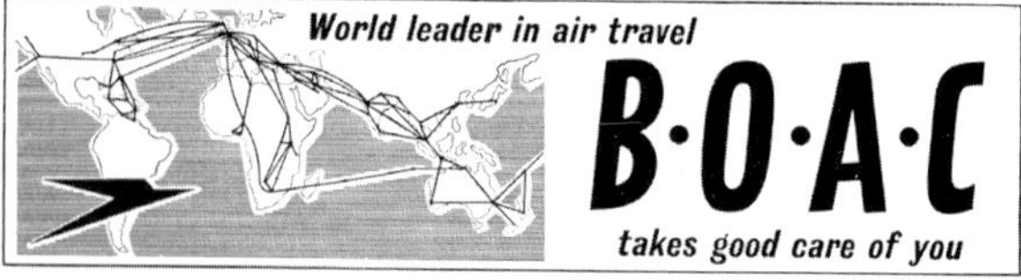

BRITISH OVERSEAS AIRWAYS CORPORATION WITH S.A.A., C.A.A., QANTAS AND TEAL

Military Aircraft of the 1950s

COMBINED VOLUME

For many people, the 1950s was the golden era of military aircraft development, and a time when the world's air forces boasted probably the most varied and eclectic fleet of aircraft ever seen in peacetime. Aircraft in active military service ranged from a few left over World War Two designs, through first generation jets and 1940's re purposed aircraft, to new machines at the cutting edge of aerospace technology, some of which would continue in service for decades to come.

For many, this book will be pure nostalgia for a lost era of classic military aviation; but it is also an important historical record of its time, highlighting the contrast between the break neck pace of military aircraft development for the front line, alongside the classic wartime aircraft still to be found operating in many parts of the world.

ISBN: 9781800353428 **£13.50**

Available at **crecy.co.uk**

ABC
CIVIL
AIRCRAFT MARKINGS
An Ian Allan Publication
2'6

Careers for Boys

ROLLS-ROYCE OFFERS ENGINEERING
APPRENTICESHIP TRAINING IN THE
MANUFACTURE OF AERO-ENGINES.

The Engineering Apprenticeship Scheme is designed to train technicians, mainly as engineers but also as physicists and metallurgists. Applications should be made at the beginning of the final school term for entry in September. Acceptance is provisional on the results of the General Schools Certificate examination. The general academic qualifications required are as follows.

FOR BOYS WHOSE AGE ON SEPTEMBER 1st IS:

(a) *Between 16 and 17 years*

General Certificate, with passes at ordinary level in at least five subjects, including Maths., Physics, and/or Chemistry.

(b) *Between 17 and 18 years*

General Certificate with passes in five subjects of which at least one of the following must be at advanced level : Maths., Physics, Chemistry.

(c) *Between 18 and 19 years*

General Certificate giving University preliminary exemption. The advanced level subjects should be Maths., Physics and Chemistry.

Every opportunity and encouragement (including day release, with pay) is given to Apprentices to continue their education and obtain technical qualifications.

The Welfare Society caters for every type of outdoor and indoor sport and activity.

Details from and applications to:

**THE   TRAINING   MANAGER,   ROLLS-ROYCE   LIMITED
NIGHTINGALE   ROAD,   DERBY.**

DETAILED DATA

on every aspect of the world's aircraft

FLIGHT's many sources of information at home and abroad enable it to provide the most reliable, up-to-the-minute data on all types of the world's aircraft — including Russian. Its illustrated descriptions of new features and items of equipment, together with fully illustrated annual reviews of the various classes — civil, military, research, etc. —make FLIGHT a particularly valuable source of information, especially for those interested in recognition. Order a regular copy TODAY!

AIRCRAFT FUELLERS

TYNE Capacity 4,000 Imperial gallons; max. delivery rate per hose, 180 g.p.m. Leyland chassis. Among the largest fuellers in the world; used for servicing trans-Atlantic airliners.

DORSET Capacity 3,000 Imperial gallons; max. delivery rate per hose, 200 g.p.m. Leyland chassis. Designed for underwing fuelling of the new D.H. Comets with aviation turbine fuel.

STEER Capacity 2,200 Imperial gallons; max. delivery rate per hose, 150 g.p.m. Leyland chassis. Used at London Airport only for servicing medium-sized air craft.

TWEED Capacity 1,200 Imperial gallons; max. delivery rate per hose, 60/70 g.p.m. Ford chassis. Used for servicing aircraft covering moderate distances on European routes.

T. B. MOBILE Capacity 500 Imperial gallons; max. delivery rate per hose, 30/40 g.p.m. Special 3-wheel chassis. Stationed on the smaller aerodromes for servicing private and club aircraft.

There are twenty-five aerodromes in Britain where you can see one or more of these different types of fuellers operating Shell and BP Aviation Service. International airlines, charter companies and private owners alike know they can always expect quick, efficient service from the friendly crews of these Service Vehicles.

SHELL AND BP AVIATION SERVICE

FLY WITH US
TO SUNNY SPAIN

IBERIA . SPANISH AIRLINES
4 CONDUIT STREET · LONDON W.I
Tel. GROSvenor 6131

Regular Services to

MADRID · BARCELONA · PALMA MAJORCA

Hawker P.1067

"...the finest

fighter aircraft

in the world."

HAWKER AIRCRAFT LTD., KINGSTON-ON-THAMES, SURREY

Member of the Hawker Siddeley Group / Pioneer...and World Leader in Aviation

The ABC of
CIVIL AIRCRAFT MARKINGS

by

JOHN W. R. TAYLOR

author of "Wings for Tomorrow", "Spitfire",
"Ian Allan Aircraft Annual", etc.

LONDON

Ian Allan Ltd

Iceland Airways' DC–4 *Gullfaxi* over the Westman Islands, off the Icelandic coast.

2

INTRODUCTION

Many kind reviews of the first *ABC of Civil Aircraft Markings*, published in 1950, have encouraged us to follow the same general layout in this completely new, bigger and, we hope, better edition.

Larger page size has enabled us to do justice to the illustrations this time, and to avoid the previous necessity of abbreviating some company names in the list of aircraft owners. We have not adopted the suggestion that these owners' names should be omitted as, although privately-owned aeroplanes change hands frequently, the same is by no means true of larger aircraft. We feel that most of our readers will prefer to have as much information as possible, which they can supplement and correct from time to time by their own observations.

We should like to acknowledge the help of John Stroud, who has again checked patiently the overseas airline fleet tables; Barry Jones, who designed the cover; and all the airline and aircraft manufacturing companies who have kindly supplied data and photographs for this new edition.

J. W. R. T.

LIST OF ABBREVIATIONS

AIRCRAFT TYPE DESIGNATIONS
(e.g. A.S.65 = Airspeed type 65)

A.S.	Airspeed
B.A.	British Aircraft
C.	Cierva
C.H.	Chrislea
C.L.A.	Comper
D.H.	de Havilland
F.	Fairchild
G.	Gloster
G.A.L.	General Aircraft
G.C.	Globe
H.P.	Handley Page
L	Lockheed
M	Miles
P	Percival
S	Short
S.R.	Stinson

STANDARD ABBREVIATIONS

B.E.A.	British European Airways
B.O.A.C.	British Overseas Airways Corporation
C.I.	Channel Islands
Corpn.	Corporation
Dist.	District
I.O.M.	Isle of Man
K.L.M.	Royal Dutch Airlines
M.C.A.	Ministry of Civil Aviation
M.o.S.	Ministry of Supply
P. & W.	Pratt and Whitney
Ptnr.	Partner

British Civil
Aircraft Registrations

(Correct to February 15th, 1952)

in alphabetical order

Registration	Type	Owner or Operator	Where and when seen
G–EBLV	D.H.60 Moth	de Havilland Aircraft Co.	
G–EBMB	Hawker Cygnet 1	Hawker Aircraft	
G–EBRN	Widgeon 3	N. C. Anderson	
G–EBWD	D.H.60X Moth	Mrs. D. C. Shuttleworth	
G–AACN	H.P.39 Gugnunc	Science Museum	
G–AAHW	Klemm L–25–1A	G. R. Lush	
G–AAIN	Parnall Elf	Shuttleworth Trust	
G–AAPZ	Desoutter 1 (mod.)	Shuttleworth Trust	
G–AAWO	D.H.60G Moth	T. H. Marshall & ptnr.	
G–AAYX	Miles Martlet	U.L.A.A.	
G–AAZP	D.H.80A Puss Moth	Mrs. E. M. Bianchi	
G–ABAG	D.H.60G Moth	P. M. A. Hull	
G–ABDF	D.H.80A Puss Moth	J. M. Banks & ptnr.	
G–ABEE	Avro 594 Avian 4M	R. P. Green & ptnrs.	
G–ABJJ	D.H.60G Moth	W. R. Suffern	
G–ABLM	Cierva C.24	Science Museum	
G–ABMR	Hart 2	Hawker Aircraft	
G–ABNX	Redwing 2	College of Aeronautical & Automobile Engineering	
G–ABTC	CLA.7 Swift	J. A. Kent & ptners.	
G–ABUS	CLA.7 Swift	A. L. Cole	
G–ABUU	CLA.7 Swift	D. Heaton	
G–ABWP	Spartan Arrow	Shuttleworth Trust	
G–ABYA	D.H.60G Moth	M. C. Harley	
G–ACCB	D.H.83 Fox Moth	Giro Aviation	
G–ACDI	D.H.82A Tiger Moth	Air Service Training	
G–ACEJ	D.H.83 Fox Moth	Giro Aviation	
G–ACIT	D.H.84 Dragon	Air Navigation & Trading Co.	
G–ACLL	D.H.85 Leopard Moth	C. P. L. Godsal	
G–ACMA	D.H.85 Leopard Moth	de Havilland Aircraft Co.	
G–ACMN	D.H.85 Leopard Moth	de Havilland Aircraft Co.	
G–ACPP	D.H.89A Dragon Rapide	Air Couriers (Properties)	
G–ACRW	D.H.85 Leopard Moth	F. T. Bingham	
G–ACTF	CLA.7 Swift	R. E. Clear	
G–ACUU	C.30A Autogiro	G. S. Baker	
G–ACVA	Kay Gyroplane	Kay Gyroplanes	
G–ACYO	M.2F Hawk Major	H. C. Blumenthal	
G–ACYR	D.H.89A Dragon Rapide	Reid & Sigrist	
G–ACZP	D.H.86	Lancashire Aircraft Corpn.	
G–ADAH	D.H.89A Dragon Rapide	E. L. Gandar Dower	
G–ADBE	Pitcairn PA–19		
G–ADDI	D.H.84 Dragon	Air Navigation & Trading Co.	
G–ADFH	M.3A Falcon	R. A. Drean	
G–ADGP	M.2L Hawk Six	R. R. Paine	
G–ADGX	D.H.82A Tiger Moth	Wiltshire School of Flying	
G–ADHE	D.H.60G3 Moth Major	N. D. Norman	
G–ADIA	D.H.82A Tiger Moth	Brooklands Aviation	
G–ADIE	Avro 643 Cadet	M. Marron	
G–ADIH	D.H.82A Tiger Moth	P. N. D. Skingley	
G–ADIJ	D.H.82A Tiger Moth	Brooklands Aviation	
G–ADKC	D.H.87B Hornet Moth	P. Q. Reiss	

4

Registration	Type	Owner or Operator	Where and when seen
G-ADKK	D.H.87B Hornet Moth	C. B. Mills	
G-ADKM	D.H.87B Hornet Moth	Mrs. M. K. Wilberforce & ptnr.	
G-ADLI	M.3A Falcon	J. W. Haggas & ptnr.	
G-ADLY	D.H.87B Hornet Moth	Viscountess Mairi Bury	
G-ADMT	D.H.87B Hornet Moth	London Aero Club	
G-ADMW	M.2H Hawk Major	A. E. H. Coltman	
G-ADNB	D.H.87B Hornet Moth	West London Aero Services	
G-ADND	D.H.87B Hornet Moth	W. D. Macpherson	
G-ADNE	D.H.87B Hornet Moth	West London Aero Services	
G-ADNL	M.5 Sparrowhawk	Oldham Tyre Cord Co.	
G-ADOT	D.H.87B Hornet Moth	Herts. & Essex Aero Club	
G-ADPJ	B.A.C. Drone	A. C. Waterhouse	
G-ADPR	P.3 Gull	Percival Aircraft	
G-ADPS	B.A. Swallow 2	Walker & Thompson	
G-ADTD	M.3B Falcon	Wiltshire School of Flying	
G-ADUF	D.H.86B	Gulf Aviation Co.	
G-ADUR	D H.87B Hornet Moth	London Aero Club	
G-ADVJ	D.H.86B	Gulf Aviation Co.	
G-ADWL	D.H.82A Tiger Moth	R. H. Braime & ptnr.	
G-ADWO	D.H.82A Tiger Moth	T. H. Marshall	
G-ADWT	M.2W Hawk Major	T. Shipside Ltd.	
G-AEAL	D.H.89 Dragon Rapide	Hunting Aerosurveys	
G-AEBJ	Blackburn B-2	Blackburn & General Aircraft	
G-AECC	M.3B Falcon Six	James Rush & Co. (Northern)	
G-AEGI	Hendy Heck 2C	—	
G-AEHM	Pou-du-Ciel	Science Museum	
G-AEKV	Kronfeld Drone	—	
G-AEKY	D.H.87B Hornet Moth	West London Aero Services	
G-AELG	B.A. Swallow 2	Swansea Flying School	
G-AELO	D.H.87B Hornet Moth	Airborne Taxi Services	
G-AEMH	D.H.89 Dragon Rapide	G. Clifton	
G-AEML	D.H.89A Dragon Rapide	Sir W. G. Armstrong Whitworth Aircraft	
G-AEMW	B.A. Swallow 2	L.F.P. Walters	
G-AENU	Wicko I	Air Navigation & Trading Co.	
G-AEOA	D.H.80A Puss Moth	Airways Aero Associations	
G-AERN	D.H.89A Dragon Rapide	Gibraltar Airways	
G-AERP	Dart Kitten	W. S. Ogilvie	
G-AERV	M.11A Whitney Straight	H. W. H. Moore	
G-AESE	D.H.87B Hornet Moth	Wilfred T. Scutt (Sales) Ltd.	
G-AESP	Aeronca 100	Airways Aero Associations	
G-AESR	D.H.89A Dragon Rapide	Airwork Ltd.	
G-AESV	Phoenix	A. R. Pilgrim	
G-AESZ	Chilton D.W.I	W. L. James	
G-AEUJ	M.11A Whitney Straight	Hawker Aircraft	
G-AEUT	Hillson Praga	Lt. Cmdr. G. A. J. Goodhart	
G-AEUZ	M.11A Whitney Straight	H. S. Brown	
G-AEVA	M.11A Whitney Straight	J. C. Rice	
G-AEVG	M.11A Whitney Straight	Air Service Training	
G-AEVL	M.11A Whitney Straight	R. K. Dundas Ltd.	
G-AEVS	Aeronca 100	B. J. Snook	
G-AEWA	M.11A Whitney Straight	S. J. Burt	
G-AEWI	B.A. Swallow 2	Central Aeronautical Bureau	
G-AEWL	D.H.89A Dragon Rapide	H. C. Kennard	
G-AEWU	Aeronca 100	P. J. Colbourne	
G-AEWV	Aeronca 100	F. Gill	

Registration	Type	Owner or Operator	Where and when seen
G-AEWY	D.H.87B Hornet Moth	G. & A. Morgan Trust	
G-AEWZ	D.H.90A Dragonfly	Silver City Airways	
G-AEXD	Aeronca 100	Airways Aero Associations	
G-AEXF	P.6 Mew Gull	H. E. Scrope & ptnr.	
G-AEXT	Dart Kitten	W. G. A. Harrison	
G-AEXY	Taylor Cub J-2	F. H. Bird	
G-AEYC	P.10 Vega Gull	Lambskin Exports	
G-AEYE	P.16 Q-Six	W. J. Twitchell	
G-AEZF	S.16 Scion	F. J. Parsons	
G-AEZG	D.H.87B Hornet Moth	D. A. Graham	
G-AEZM	B.A. Swallow 2	D. Kirk	
G-AFBC	P.10 Vega Gull	Lady Sherborne	
G-AFBF	M.3B Falcon	British Aviation Insurance Co.	
G-AFBS	M.14A Hawk Trainer	Airways Aero Associations	
G-AFCL	B.A. Swallow 2	C. D. Street & ptnrs.	
G-AFCR	M.17 Monarch	Air Schools Ltd.	
G-AFEA	P.10 Vega Gull	D. F. Little	
G-AFEH	P.10 Vega Gull	Lancashire Aircraft Corpn.	
G-AFEZ	D.H.89A Rapide (Islander)	B.E.A. *Lord Shaftesbury*	
G-AFFB	D.H.89A Dragon Rapide	Lambert's Trust	
G-AFFD	P.16A Q-Six	R. H. Braime & ptnr.	
G-AFFH	Piper Cub J-2	A. R. Frogley	
G-AFFJ	Piper Cub J-3	E. V. Pyle & ptnr.	
G-AFFN	Tipsy S-2	G. A. Chamberlain	
G-AFGC	B. A. Swallow 2	H. Plain	
G-AFGE	B.A. Swallow 2	G. C. Taylor	
G-AFGI	Chilton D.W.1	H. McC. Kendall	
G-AFGK	M.11A Whitney Straight	F. H. Wilson	
G-AFHC	B.A. Swallow 2	B. Arden	
G-AFHH	B.A. Swallow 2	F. L. Haigh	
G-AFHS	B.A. Swallow 2	J. Heath	
G-AFIH	B.A. Swallow 2	Doncaster Ultra Light Aircraft Group	
G-AFJA	Watkinson Ding Bat	J. A. Allan & ptnr.	
G-AFJB	Wicko G.M.1	Mrs. P. M. Booth & ptnr.	
G-AFJO	Taylorcraft A	Rotol Flying Club	
G-AFJP	Taylorcraft A	E. F. Norris	
G-AFJR	Tipsy Trainer 1	Tattersall's Garages Ltd.	
G-AFJS	Tipsy Trainer 1	Cardiff Ultra Light Aeroplane Club	
G-AFJU	M.17 Monarch	Furzehill Laboratories	
G-AFKP	Tipsy Trainer 1	W. C. Jelliss	
G-AFLT	M.65 Gemini 1A	Iliffe & Sons, Ltd.	
G-AFLU	Ely 700	Airways Aero Associations	
G-AFLW	M.17 Monarch	Rolls-Royce Ltd.	
G-AFMF	D.H.89A Dragon Rapide	J. W. Adamson	
G-AFMJ	D.H.89A Dragon Rapide	Air Enterprises *The Shanklin Flyer*	
G-AFMS	Mosscraft M.A.2	Moss Bros. Aircraft	
G-AFNG	D.H.94 Moth Minor	S. J. Burt	
G-AFNI	D.H.94 Moth Minor	R. S. Spackman	
G-AFNJ	D.H.94 Moth Minor	J. Cooper	
G-AFOB	D.H.94 Moth Minor	J. R. McConnell	
G-AFOI	D.H.89A Dragon Rapide	Airmotive (Liverpool) Ltd.	
G-AFOJ	D.H.94 Moth Minor	London Aero Club	
G-AFOZ	D.H.94 Moth Minor	J. A. Allan	
G-AFPD	D.H.94 Moth Minor	Airways Aero Associations	
G-AFPN	D.H.94 Moth Minor	R. Hutchings	
G-AFPP	Piper Cub Coupe J-4	W. Smyth	
G-AFPR	D.H.94 Moth Minor	Miss J. L. Bird	
G-AFRE	D.H.87B Hornet Moth	H. V. A. Franklin	

6

Registration	Type	Owner or Operator	Where and when seen
G-AFRK	D.H.89A Rapide (Islander)	B.E.A. *Rudyard Kipling*	
G-AFRR	D.H.94 Moth Minor	F. C. Lewis	
G-AFRU	Tipsy Trainer 1	L. D. Birkett	
G-AFRV	Tipsy Trainer 1	J. H. Reed	
G-AFRY	D.H.94 Moth Minor	G. S. Meek	
G-AFSC	Tipsy Trainer 1	Cardiff Ultra Light Aeroplane Club	
G-AFSH	D.H.82A Tiger Moth	W. A. Rollason Ltd.	
G-AFSJ	D.H.82A Tiger Moth	Light Planes (Lancashire)	
G-AFSV	Chilton D.W.1A	A. R. Ward	
G-AFSZ	Piper Cub J–4A	J. S. Sproule	
G-AFTA	Hawker 41H Tom Tit	Hawker Aircraft	
G-AFTN	Taylorcraft Plus C–2	H. Plain	
G-AFVN	Tipsy Trainer 1	E. G. S. Tomley & ptnrs.	
G-AFVR	G.A.L.42 Cygnet 2	T. F. W. Gunton	
G-AFVT	S.R.10C Reliant	The Fairey Aviation Co.	
G-AFWM	Taylorcraft Plus C–2	The Earl of Cardigan	
G-AFWN	J/1 Autocrat	S. K. Davies *Pembroke*	
G-AFWO	Taylorcraft Plus D	G. E. S. Seymour	
G-AFWT	Tipsy Trainer 1	West London Aero Services	
G-AFXA	M.14A Hawk Trainer	R. A. Short & ptnr.	
G-AFXS	Piper Cub Coupe J–4A	J. Dilks	
G-AFYH	D.H.95 Flamingo	British Air Transport	
G-AFZE	Heath Parasol	F. G. Lowe	
G-AFZI	Taylorcraft Plus D	Miss S. M. Cox	
G-AFZP	Fokker F.22	Scottish Aviation	
G-AGAK	Hirtenberg H.S.9A	D. D. Budworth	
G-AGAX	G.A.L.42 Cygnet	L. V. D. Scorah	
G-AGBA	G.A.L.42 Cygnet	R. L. Whyham	
G-AGBD	Dakota 2	B.O.A.C.	
G-AGBN	G.A.L.42 Cygnet	A. Costella	
G-AGDM	D.H.89A Dragon Rapide	Airviews	
G-AGDP	D.H.89A Dragon Rapide	Modern Transport (Wolverhampton) Ltd.	
G-AGEE	D.H.89A Dragon Rapide	Gibraltar Airways	
G-AGER	S.25 Sunderland 3	Aquila Airways *Hadfield*	
G-AGEU	S.25 Sunderland 3	Aquila Airways *Hampshire*	
G-AGHJ	Dakota 3 (Pionair)	B.E.A. *Albert Ball*	
G-AGHL	Dakota 3 (Pionair)	B.E.A. *Lanoe Hawker*	
G-AGHM	Dakota 3 (Pionair)	B.E.A. *Edward Maitland*	
G-AGHP	Dakota 3 Freighter	B.E.A. *Bert Hinkler*	
G-AGHS	Dakota 3 (Pionair)	B.E.A. *Horace Short*	
G-AGIP	Dakota 3 (Pionair)	B.E.A. *Horatio Phillips*	
G-AGIS	Dakota 3 Freighter	B.E.A. *Sir Ross Smith*	
G-AGIU	Dakota 3 (Pionair)	B.E.A. *Edward Busk*	
G-AGIZ	Dakota 3 Freighter	B.E.A. *Sir Oliver Swann*	
G-AGJB	Type 685 York 1	B.O.A.C. *Marathon*	
G-AGJC	Type 685 York 1	B.O.A.C. *Malmesbury*	
G-AJGE	Type 685 York 1	Lancashire Aircraft Corpn.	
G-AGJG	D.H.89A Dragon Rapide	Adie Aviation	
G-AGJN	S.25 Sunderland 3	Aquila Airways *Hudson*	
G-AGJV	Dakota 3 (Pionair)	B.E.A. *John Porte*	
G-AGJW	Dakota 3 (Pionair)	B.E.A. *Wilfred Parke*	
G-AGJZ	Dakota 3 (Pionair)	B.E.A. *John Stringfellow*	
G-AGKX	S.25 Sandringham 1	Aquila Airways *Himalaya*	
G-AGKY	S.25 Sunderland 3	Aquila Airways *Hungerford*	
G-AGLK	Auster 5	M.C.A.	
G-AGLP	D.H.89A Dragon Rapide	C. L. Burton	
G-AGLR	D.H.89A Dragon Rapide	Don Everall (Aviation)	
G-AGND	Dakota 3	Cyprus Airways	

Registration	Type	Owner or Operator	Where and when seen
G-AGNH	D.H.89A Dragon Rapide	M.C.A.	
G-AGNK	Dakota 3 (Pionair)	B.E.A. *Edward Mannock*	
G-AGNL	Type 685 York I	B.O.A.C.	
G-AGNM	Type 685 York I	Eagle Aviation	
G-AGNN	Type 685 York I	B.O.A.C. *Atlantic Trader*	
G-AGNP	Type 685 York I	B.O.A.C. *Manchester*	
G-AGNS	Type 685 York I	B.O.A.C. *Pacific Trader*	
G-AGNT	Type 685 York I	B.O.A.C. *Mandalay*	
G-AGNU	Type 685 York I	B.O.A.C. *Montgomery*	
G-AGNV	Type 685 York I	B.O.A.C. *Moville*	
G-AGNW	Type 685 York I	Lancashire Aircraft Corpn.	
G-AGNY	Type 685 York I	Eagle Aviation	
G-AGNZ	Type 685 York I	Eagle Aviation	
G-AGOB	Type 685 York I	Lancashire Aircraft Corpn.	
G-AGOD	Type 685 York I	Lancashire Aircraft Corpn.	
G-AGOE	Type 685 York I	B.O.A.C.	
G-AGOH	J/1 Autocrat	W. S. Shackleton. Ltd.	
G-AGOJ	D.H.89A Dragon Rapide	Lancashire Aircraft Corpn.	
G-AGOR	D.H.89A Dragon Rapide	Iraq Petroleum Transport Co.	
G-AGOY	M.48 Messenger 3	C. Alexander	
G-AGPG	Avro 19 Srs.1	A. V. Roe & Co.	
G-AGPJ	D.H.104 Dove I	M.o.S.	
G-AGPW	Type 167 Brabazon I	M.o.S.	
G-AGPX	M.38 Messenger 3	D. M. B. Carnegie	
G-AGRA	D.H.82A Tiger Moth	M.C.A.	
G-AGRB	D.H.82A Tiger Moth	M.C.A.	
G-AGRF	Type 688 Tudor 4B	M.C.A.	
G-AGRG	Type 688 Tudor Freighter I	M.C.A.	
G-AGRH	Type 688 Tudor Freighter I	M.C.A.	
G-AGRI	Type 688 Tudor Freighter I	M.C.A.	
G-AGRJ	Type 688 Tudor Freighter I	M.C.A.	
G-AGRP	Type 498 Viking I	Hunting Air Transport	
G-AGRR	Type 498 Viking 1A	Britavia	
G-AGRV	Type 498 Viking 1A	Hunting Air Transport	
G-AGRW	Type 498 Viking 1A	Hunting Air Transport	
G-AGRY	Type 689 Tudor 2	Fairflight	
G-AGSH	D.H.89A Rapide (Islander)	B.E.A. *James Keir Hardie*	
G-AGSI	D.H.89A Dragon Rapide	Olley Air Service	
G-AGSK	D.H.89A Rapide (Islander)	B.E.A. *Lord Kitchener*	
G-AGSL	Type 685 York I	Lancashire Aircraft Corpn.	
G-AGSO	Type 685 York I	B.O.A.C. *Marston*	
G-AGSP	Type 685 York I	B.O.A.C. *Marlborough*	
G-AGSX	P.31C Proctor 4	Hunting Air Transport	
G-AGTC	P.44 Proctor 5	Percival Aircraft	
G-AGTE	P.44 Proctor 5	B. R. W. Betts	
G-AGTF	P.44 Proctor 5	Cambridge University Gliding Club	
G-AGTL	Lockheed 12A	F. S. Cotton	
G-AGTM	D.H.89A Dragon Rapide	Iraq Petroleum Transport Co.	
G-AGTN	D.H.89A Dragon Rapide	Iraq Petroleum Transport Co.	
G-AGTO	J/1 Autocrat	M. Walker	
G-AGTP	J/1 Autocrat	T. Carlyle	
G-AGTR	J/1 Autocrat	R. H. Braime & ptnr.	
G-AGTT	J/1 Autocrat	A. G. Statham	
G-AGTV	J/1 Autocrat	G. S. Pine	

8

Registration	Type	Owner or Operator	Where and when seen
G–AGTX	J/I Autocrat	W. Nadin	
G–AGTY	J/I Autocrat	H. Tempest (Cardiff)	
G–AGUB	H.P.74 Hermes 2	M.o.S.	
G–AGUD	Avro 19 Srs. I	M.C.A.	
G–AGUF	D.H.89A Dragon Rapide	J. A. R. Helps & ptnrs.	
G–AGUG	D.H.89A Dragon Rapide	Lancashire Aircraft Corpn.	
G–AGUH	Avro 19 Srs. I	Armstrong Siddeley Motors	
G–AGUP	D.H. 89A Rapide (Islander)	B.E.A. *Sir Robert Peel*	
G–AGUR	D.H.89A Rapide (Islander)	B.E.A. *Lord Roberts*	
G–AGUS	M.65 Gemini 2	Walter Instruments	
G–AGUU	D.H.89A Rapide (Islander)	B.E.A. *Sir Colin Campbell*	
G–AGUV	D.H.89A Rapide (Islander)	B.E.A. *General Gordon*	
G–AGVA	Avro 19 Srs. I	M.C.A.	
G–AGVB	Type 170 Wayfarer 21	Bowmaker Ltd.	
G–AGVC	Type 170 Freighter 21	Silver City Airways	
G–AGVF	J/I Autocrat	Loxham's Flying Services	
G–AGVG	J/I Autocrat	W. Westoby	
G–AGVI	J/I Autocrat	Merton Motors	
G–AGVJ	J/I Autocrat	British Air Transport	
G–AGVL	J/I Autocrat	Bembridge & Sandown Aero Club	
G–AGVM	J/I Autocrat	Bristol & Wessex Aeroplane Club	
G–AGVN	J/I Autocrat	Len Hayward (Wolverhampton) & Co.	
G–AGVO	J/I Autocrat	W. S. Shackleton Ltd.	
G–AGVP	J/I Autocrat	Wiltshire School of Flying	
G–AGVU	J/I Autocrat	Air Couriers	
G–AGVX	M.28 Mercury 4	Ind Coope & Allsopp	
G–AGWA	Avro 19 Srs. I	M.C.A.	
G–AGWC	D.H.89A Dragon Rapide	Lambert's Trust	
G–AGWE	Avro 19 Srs. I	M.C.A.	
G–AGWF	Avro 19 Srs. I	Sperry Gyroscope Co.	
G–AGWN	Lockheed 12A	Zinc Corporation Ltd.	
G–AGWP	D.H.89A Dragon Rapide	Morton Air Services	
G–AGWR	D.H.89A Dragon Rapide	Morton Air Services	
G–AGWS	Dakota 3	Scottish Aviation	
G–AGWT	M.7A Nighthawk	R. Crewdson	
G–AGWV	P.28B Proctor I	Prince Alexander	
G–AGWY	J/I Autocrat	T. Carlyle	
G–AGXB	J/I Autocrat	J. J. Dykes	
G–AGXC	J/I Autocrat	D. H. Eastwood	
G–AGXD	J/I Autocrat	Lancashire Aircraft Corpn.	
G–AGXF	J/I Autocrat	Southern Flying Schools	
G–AGXG	J/I Autocrat	A. J. Linnell	
G–AGXH	J/I Autocrat	Eagle Aviation	
G–AGXJ	J/I Autocrat	R. W. Powe	
G–AGXK	J/I Autocrat	Midland Aero Club	
G–AGXM	J/I Autocrat	R. G. Parker	
G–AGXN	J/I Autocrat	G. Brady & Co.]	
G–AGXO	J/IA Autocrat	G. W. Asher	
G–AGXP	J/I Autocrat	Private Flying (Ipswich) Ltd.	
G–AGXS	J/I Autocrat	M. A. Crouch	
G–AGXT	J/I Autocrat	Elstree Flying Club	
G–AGXU	J/I Autocrat	Fairey Aviation Co.	
G–AGXV	J/I Autocrat	R. C. Presland	
G–AGXY	J/I Autocrat	Gulf Aviation Co.	
G–AGYB	P.28B Proctor I	J. Drennan	

9

Registration	Type	Owner or Operator	Where and when seen
G-AGYC	P.28B Proctor I	W. A. Rollason Ltd.	
G-AGYD	J/I Autocrat	Herts. & Essex Aero Club	
G-AGYF	J/I Autocrat	W. E. Wigg & Sons	
G-AGYH	J/I Autocrat	Coventry (Civil) Aviation	
G-AGYI	J/I Autocrat	Royal Artillery Aero Club	
G-AGYK	J/I Autocrat	R. J. Bowers	
G-AGYL	J/I Autocrat	W. A. Munro	
G-AGYM	J/I Autocrat	M. W. B. May	
G-AGYN	J/I Autocrat	London Aero Club	
G-AGYP	J/I Autocrat	J. L. Shaw	
G-AGYT	J/I Autocrat	J. H. Watts (Cambrian Air Services) Cardigan	
G-AGYU	D.H.82A Tiger Moth	Marshall's Flying School	
G-AGYX	Dakota 3 (Pionair)	B.E.A. George Holt Thomas	
G-AGYZ	Dakota 3 Freighter	B.E.A. Sir Charles Kingsford Smith	
G-AGZB	Dakota 3 (Pionair)	B.E.A. Robert Smith-Barry	
G-AGZC	Dakota 3 (Pionair)	B.E.A. Samuel Cody	
G-AGZD	Dakota 3 (Pionair)	B.E.A. Percy Pilcher	
G-AGZF	Dakota 3	Scottish Aviation	
G-AGZG	Dakota 3	Scottish Aviation	
G-AGZJ	D.H.89A Dragon Rapide	J. H. Watts & ptnrs.	
G-AGZK	D.H.89A Dragon Rapide	Iraq Petroleum Transport Co.	
G-AGZM	P.28B Proctor I	Herts. & Essex Aero Club	
G-AGZO	D.H.89A Dragon Rapide	Marshall's Flying School	
G-AGZP	H.P.70 Halton I	Lancashire Aircraft Corpn.	
G-AGZT	Avro 19 Srs. I	M.C.A.	
G-AGZU	D.H.89A Dragon Rapide	Herts. & Essex Aero Club	
G-AGZV	Stinson SR.10C Reliant	Southern Aircraft (Gatwick)	
G-AGZW	Stinson 10 Voyager	R. R. Harrington	
G-AHAA	M.28 Mercury 6	Adie Aviation	
G-AHAB	P.28B Proctor I	C. E. Berens	
G-AHAD	Taylorcraft Plus D	A. Reeves	
G-AHAE	Taylorcraft Plus D	Newcastle Aero Club	
G-AHAG	D.H.89A Dragon Rapide	North Sea Air Transport	
G-AHAI	Taylorcraft Plus D	Denham Flying Club	
G-AHAL	J/I Autocrat	G. Neal & ptnrs.	
G-AHAM	J/I Autocrat	H. N. Gregg	
G-AHAO	J/I Autocrat	Air Schools	
G-AHAP	J/I Autocrat	Air Schools	
G-AHAT	J/I Autocrat	F. J. R. Elliott	
G-AHAU	J/I Autocrat	C. W. D. Rowe	
G-AHAV	J/I Autocrat	J. S. Bancroft	
G-AHAY	J/I Autocrat	Fairey Aviation Co.	
G-AHBA	P.44 Proctor 5	Dunlop Rubber Co.	
G-AHBC	P.44 Proctor 5	Donaldson Bros. (Alloa 1937) Ltd.	
G-AHBD	P.44 Proctor 5	Sir W. G. Armstrong Whitworth Aircraft	
G-AHBH	P.44 Proctor 5	Western Airways	
G-AHBI	P.44 Proctor 5	R. B. Pursey	
G-AHBJ	P.44 Proctor 5	Yellow Air Taxis	
G-AHBL	D.H.87B Hornet Moth	L. Grecel	
G-AHBO	Taylorcraft Plus D	Wycombe Flying Club	
G-AHBS	P.28B Proctor I	L. H. B. Roper	
G-AHCG	Taylorcraft Plus D	Boston Air Transport	
G-AHCK	J/I Autocrat	British Air Transport	
G-AHCL	J/I Autocrat	E. Brett	
G-AHCM	J/I Autocrat	R. Ward	
G-AHCN	J/I Autocrat	Bristol & Wessex Aeroplane Club	

Above: Caledonia, one of the ten Stratocruisers used on B.O.A.C's North Atlantic service.

Right: Britain's biggest land-plane, the eight-engined Brabazon I.

Below: Constellations of nine companies can be seen regularly at British airports. This one belongs to South African Airways.

317

Above: S.A.S. aircraft, like this DC–6, carry the dragon emblem of the Viking longboats through 20th century skies.

Left : Britain's lead in jet development is symbolised by these Comets, the world's first jet air liners.

Below : *Hampshire*, one of Aquila's superb flying boats, in Funchal Harbour, Madeira.

Registration	Type	Owner or Operator	Where and when seen
G–AHCO	J/1 Autocrat	T. G. Stephenson	
G–AHCR	Taylorcraft Plus D	L. A. Strange	
G–AHCT	Dakota 3 Freighter	B.E.A. *Sir Hiram Maxim*	
G–AHCU	Dakota 3 Freighter	B.E.A. *Charles Ulm*	
G–AHCV	Dakota 3 (Pionair)	B.E.A. *Sir George Cayley*	
G–AHCX	Dakota 3 Freighter	B.E.A. *Spenser Grey*	
G–AHCZ	Dakota 3 (Pionair)	B.E.A. *Charles Samson*	
G–AHDD	D.H.82A Tiger Moth	J. Chipperfield	
G–AHDJ	P.28B Proctor 1	—	
G–AHDV	H.P.70 Halton 1	Lancashire Aircraft Corpn.	
G–AHDZ	A.S.40 Oxford 2	Scottish Aviation	
G–AHEA	D.H.89A Dragon Rapide	Lancashire Aircraft Corpn.	
G–AHED	D.H.89A Dragon Rapide	Marshall's Flying School	
G–AHEF	A.S.65 Consul	de Havilland Aircraft Co.	
G–AHEG	A.S.65 Consul	A. G. de Q. Colley	
G–AHEI	Taylorcraft Plus D	D. H. Tapp	
G–AHEJ	L.49-46 Constellation	B.O.A.C. *Bristol*	
G–AHEK	L.49-46 Constellation	B.O.A.C. *Berwick*	
G–AHEL	L.49-46 Constellation	B.O.A.C. *Bangor*	
G–AHEM	L.49-46 Constellation	B.O.A.C. *Balmoral*	
G–AHES	P.28B Proctor 1	Mrs. V. O. Hosie	
G–AHET	P.10C Vega Gull	Essex Aero Ltd.	
G–AHEU	P.28B Proctor 1	J. H. Watts (Cambrian Air Enterprises) *Montgomery*	
G–AHEV	P.28B Proctor 1	J. H. Watts (Cambrian Air Enterprises) *Denbigh*	
G–AHEY	Type 685 York 1	B.O.A.C.	
G–AHFA	Type 685 York 1	Lancashire Aircraft Corpn.	
G–AHFB	Type 685 York 1	Lancashire Aircraft Corpn.	
G–AHFC	Type 685 York 1	Lancashire Aircraft Corpn.	
G–AHFD	Type 685 York 1	Lancashire Aircraft Corpn.	
G–AHFE	Type 685 York 1	Lancashire Aircraft Corpn.	
G–AHFF	Type 685 York 1	Lancashire Aircraft Corpn.	
G–AHFG	Type 685 York 1	Lancashire Aircraft Corpn.	
G–AHFH	Type 685 York 1	Lancashire Aircraft Corpn.	
G–AHFK	P.34A Proctor 3	Kelvin & Hughes Ltd.	
G–AHFN	Walrus 1	Charles Mauritzen Ltd.	
G–AHFP	M.38 Messenger 4	B. R. Turner	
G–AHFR	P.31C Proctor 4	Rolls-Royce Ltd.	
G–AHFT	A.S.65 Consul	Morton Air Services	
G–AHFY	P.28B Proctor 1	L. G. S. Payne	
G–AHGA	P.28B Proctor 1	Stewart Smith & Co. Ltd.	
G–AHGC	D.H.89A Dragon Rapide	Hawker Aircraft	
G–AHGD	D.H.89A Dragon Rapide	L. H. Riddell	
G–AHGF	D.H.89A Dragon Rapide	F. A. Hill	
G–AHGG	D.H.89A Dragon Rapide	Olley Air Service	
G–AHGH	D.H. 89A Dragon Rapide	Patrick Motors Ltd.	
G–AHGI	D.H. 89A Dragon Rapide	Patrick Motors Ltd.	
G–AHGJ	P.44 Proctor 5	B. N. White-Spunner Ltd.	
G–AHGL	P.44 Proctor 5	E. S. Davis	
G–AHGM	P.44 Proctor 5	Hunting Air Transport	
G–AHGR	P.44 Proctor 5	D. J. Bennett	
G–AHGS	P.44 Proctor 5	V. H. Bellamy	
G–AHGU	A.S.40 Oxford 2	Bristol Aeroplane Co.	
G–AHGW	Taylorcraft Plus D	Short Bros. & Harland	
G–AHGX	Taylorcraft Plus D	Wiltshire School of Flying	
G–AHGZ	Taylorcraft Plus D	Carlight Trailers Ltd.	
G–AHHB	Taylorcraft Plus D	Light Planes (Lancashire)	
G–AHHK	J/1 Autocrat	Chipperfield's Circus & Zoo	

13

Registration	Type	Owner or Operator	Where and when seen
G-AHHL	J/I Autocrat	Yellow Air Taxis	
G-AHHM	J/I Autocrat	Westland Aircraft	
G-AHHN	J/I Autocrat	F. B. Austin	
G-AHHO	J/I Autocrat	G. S. Pine	
G-AHHP	J/I Autocrat	E. E. Kimbell	
G-AHHR	J/I Autocrat	Misses I. L. & Q. A. Perren	
G-AHHS	J/I Autocrat	D. H. Clarke	
G-AHHT	J/I Autocrat	C. Cruickshank	
G-AHHU	J/I Autocrat	Colt Ventilation Ltd.	
G-AHHW	J/I Autocrat	J. C. Hoyland	
G-AHHX	Taylorcraft Plus D	Light Planes (Lancashire)	
G-AHHY	Taylorcraft Plus D	S. Gillaspry	
G-AHHZ	Taylorcraft Plus D	G. C. Mawer	
G-AHIB	Avro 19 Srs. I	Thorne Aviation (R. L. Whyham)	
G-AHIC	Avro 19 Srs. I	College of Aeronautics	
G-AHIE	Avro 19 Srs. I	Thorne Aviation (R. L. Whyham)	
G-AHIG	Avro 19 Srs. I	R. L. Whyham	
G-AHIH	Avro 19 Srs. I	M.C.A.	
G-AHIJ	Avro 19 Srs. I	Sperry Gyroscope Co.	
G-AHIL	S.45 Solent 2	M.C.A.	
G-AHIM	S.45 Solent 2	M.C.A.	
G-AHIN	S.45 Solent 2	M.C.A.	
G-AHIO	S.45 Solent 2	Trans-Oceanic Airways Pty.	
G-AHIR	S.45 Solent 2	M.C.A.	
G-AHIS	S.45 Solent 2	M.C.A.	
G-AHIT	S.45 Solent 2	M.C.A.	
G-AHIU	S.45 Solent 2	M.C.A.	
G-AHIW	S.45 Solent 2	M.C.A.	
G-AHIY	S.45 Solent 2	M.C.A.	
G-AHIZ	D.H.82A Tiger Moth	London Aero Club	
G-AHJA	D.H.89A Dragon Rapide	Vickers-Armstrongs (Supermarine)	
G-AHJD	Type 170 Freighter 21	—	
G-AHJP	Type 170 Freighter 21	Silver City Airways	
G-AHJS	D.H.89A Dragon Rapide	Fairey Aviation Co.	
G-AHJZ	A.S.65 Consul	de Havilland Aircraft Co.	
G-AHKA	D.H.89A Dragon Rapide	de Havilland Aircraft Co.	
G-AHKB	D.H.89A Dragon Rapide	Vickers-Armstrongs (Supermarine	
G-AHKH	Type 652A Anson I	British Air Transport	
G-AHKL	M.65 Gemini IA	Smithfield Refrigerator Co.	
G-AHKO	Taylorcraft Plus D	Mrs. Y. M. Grace	
G-AHKP	M.14A Hawk Trainer 3	D. M. Spencer-Smith	
G-AHKS	D.H.89A Rapide (Islander)	B.E.A. *Robert Louis Stevenson*	
G-AHKT	D.H.89A Rapide (Islander)	B.E.A. *Lord Tennyson*	
G-AHKU	D.H.89A Rapide (Islander)	B.E.A.	
G-AHKV	D.H.89A Rapide (Islander)	B.E.A. *Sir James Outram*	
G-AHKX	Avro 19 Srs. 2	Smith's Aircraft Instruments	
G-AHKY	Miles M.18/2	H. B. Iles	
G-AHLA	D.H.82A Tiger Moth	Aerocontacts Ltd.	
G-AHLB	D.H.82A Tiger Moth	Air Service Training	
G-AHLF	D.H.89A Dragon Rapide	Westland Aircraft	
G-AHLH	Lockheed 12A	Earl of Granard	
G-AHLI	Auster 3	Vickers-Armstrongs (Supermarine)	
G-AHLJ	Taylorcraft Plus D	Vickers-Armstrongs (Weybridge)	
G-AHLK	Auster 3	Vickers-Armstrongs (Supermarine)	

14

Registration	Type	Owner or Operator	Where and when seen
G-AHLL	D.H.89A Rapide (Islander)	B.E.A. *Sir Henry Lawrence*	
G-AHLM	D.H.89A Dragon Rapide	Marshall's Flying School	
G-AHLN	D.H.89A Dragon Rapide	North-West Airlines (I.O.M.)	
G-AHLO	D.H.80A Puss Moth	R. P. Potgeiter	
G-AHLT	D.H.82A Tiger Moth	Walker & Thompson	
G-AHLV	Type 685 York I	Skyways *Sky Courier*	
G-AHMD	A.S.65 Consul	Lancashire Aircraft Corpn.	
G-AHME	D.H.82A Tiger Moth	J. W. Tomkins & ptnr.	
G-AHMM	D.H.82A Tiger Moth	Brooklands Aviation	
G-AHMN	D.H.82A Tiger Moth	Brooklands Aviation	
G-AHMO	Luton Minor	R. S. Finch	
G-AHMP	P.28B Proctor I	de Havilland Engine Co.	
G-AHMT	P.28B Proctor I	Scottish Aviation	
G-AHMV	P.28B Proctor I	Airwork Ltd.	
G-AHNA	P.28B Proctor I	A. S. K. Paine	
G-AHNB	P.30B Proctor 2	Cinque Ports Flying Club	
G-AHNC	D.H.82A Tiger Moth	Light Planes (Lancashire)	
G-AHND	D.H.82A Tiger Moth	R. Allerton-Austin	
G-AHNE	M.14A Hawk Trainer 3	Air Navigation & Trading Co.	
G-AHNG	Taylorcraft Plus D	T. J. S. Kidner	
G-AHNI	Type 688 Tudor Freighter 4B	M.C.A.	
G-AHNJ	Type 688 Tudor 4	M.C.A.	
G-AHNK	Type 688 Tudor 4	M.C.A.	
G-AHNL	Type 688 Tudor Freighter 4B	M.C.A.	
G-AHNM	Type 688 Tudor Freighter 4B	M.C.A.	
G-AHNN	Type 688 Tudor 4	M.C.A.	
G-AHNO	Type 688 Tudor Freighter 4B	M.C.A.	
G-AHNS	Type 652A Anson I	Air Service Training	
G-AHNT	Type 652A Anson I	Air Service Training	
G-AHNV	M.14A Hawk Trainer 3	Wolverhampton Aviation	
G-AHNW	M.14A Hawk Trainer 3	H. T. Ryan	
G-AHOM	P.16A Q-Six	Ductile Steels Ltd.	
G-AHON	Type 498 Viking IA	A. J. Gaul	
G-AHOP	Type 498 Viking IA	L. E. P. Airservices	
G-AHOR	Type 498 Viking IA	Trans World Charter	
G-AHOT	Type 498 Viking IA	A. J. Gaul	
G-AHOW	Type 498 Viking IA	Trans World Charter	
G-AHOY	Type 499 Viking I	Hunting Air Transport	
G-AHPB	Type 499 Viking I	Hunting Air Transport	
G-AHPC	Type 499 Viking I	Hunting Air Transport	
G-AHPJ	Type 499 Viking I	Hunting Air Transport	
G-AHPL	Type 610 Viking IB	B.E.A. *Lord Anson*	
G-AHPM	Type 610 Viking IB	B.E.A. *Lord Rodney*	
G-AHPO	Type 610 Viking IB	B.E.A. *Sir Edward Howard*	
G-AHPP	Type 610 Viking IB	B.E.A. *Sir Peter Parker*	
G-AHPR	Type 610 Viking IB	B.E.A. *Prince Rupert*	
G-AHPS	Type 610 Viking IB	B.E.A. *Sir Doveton Sturdee*	
G-AHPT	D.H.89A Dragon Rapide	Aerocontacts	
G-AHPU	D.H.89A Dragon Rapide	J. E. Steel	
G-AHRC	D.H.82A Tiger Moth	J. C. Rice	
G-AHRF	Type 630 Viscount	M.o.S.	
G-AHRH	D.H.89A Dragon Rapide	Gloster Aircraft Co.	
G-AHRI	D.11.101 Dove I	Iraq Petroleum Transport Co.	
G-AHRK	A.S.65 Consul	Silver City Airways	
G-AHRM	D.H.82A Tiger Moth	Universal Flying Services	
G-AHRN	D.H.82A Tiger Moth	Universal Flying Services	
G-AHRR	D.H.82A Tiger Moth	Wolverhampton Aviation	
G-AHRV	D.H.82A Tiger Moth	Fairey Aviation Co.	

15

Registration	Type	Owner or Operator	Where and when seen
G-AHRX	D.H.82A Tiger Moth	Goodhew Aviation Co.	
G-AHRY	P.34A Proctor 3	Herts. & Essex Aero Club	
G-AHSA	Avro 621 Tutor	G. S. K. Haywood	
G-AHSB	Taylorcraft Plus D	D. G. S. Cotter	
G-AHSD	Taylorcraft Plus D	Herts. & Essex Aero Club	
G-AHSG	Taylorcraft Plus D	J. Allen	
G-AHSH	J/I Autocrat	R. A. Young	
G-AHSI	J/I Autocrat	Hampshire School of Flying	
G-AHSJ	Taylorcraft Plus D	J. S. Swanson	
G-AHSK	Taylorcraft Plus D	I. H. Cameron	
G-AHSN	J/I Autocrat	Royal Navy Flying Club	
G-AHSO	J/I Autocrat	Universal Flying Services	
G-AHSP	J/I Autocrat	J. D. Robertson & Co.	
G-AHSR	J/I Autocrat	W. S. Shackleton Ltd.	
G-AHSS	J/I Autocrat	Loxham's Flying Services	
G-AHST	J/I Autocrat	D. Everall	
G-AHSW	J/IA Autocrat	York Flying Club	
G-AHSX	J/I Autocrat	Air Navigation & Trading Co.	
G-AHTE	P.44 Proctor 5	C. G. Wheatley	
G-AHTF	P.44 Proctor 5	B. W. J. Pring	
G-AHTI	P.44 Proctor 5	S. Ball	
G-AHTK	P.44 Proctor 5	Willis Hole Aviation	
G-AHTL	P.44 Proctor 5	Dennis Aviation	
G-AHTV	P.28B Proctor I	Air Service Training	
G-AHTW	A.S.40 Oxford	Boulton Paul Aircraft	
G-AHTX	M.57 Aerovan 3	S. G. Newport	
G-AHTY	D.H.89A Dragon Rapide	North Sea Air Transport	
G-AHTZ	Cierva C.30A	Rota Towels	
G-AHUB	D.H.82A Tiger Moth	London Aero Club	
G-AHUE	D.H.82A Tiger Moth	Airwork	
G-AHUG	Taylorcraft Plus D	G. F. K. Donaldson	
G-AHUI	M.38 Messenger 2A	Derek Crouch (Contractors)	
G-AHUJ	M.14A Hawk Trainer 3	S. D. Henderson	
G-AHUM	Taylorcraft Plus D	Christchurch Aero Club	
G-AHUO	D.H.82A Tiger Moth	Hampshire School of Flying	
G-AHUT	D.H.82A Tiger Moth	Universal Flying Services	
G-AHUU	GC-IB Swift	Helliwells Ltd.	
G-AHUV	D.H.82A Tiger Moth	Airwork	
G-AHUX	P.28B Proctor I	D. J. Jemmett	
G-AHVA	P.28B Proctor I	D. W. Brown & ptnr.	
G-AHVC	P.28B Proctor I	A. T. Leaning	
G-AHVG	P.28B Proctor I	H. Wood	
G-AHVK	P.28B Proctor I	J. A. L. Archer	
G-AHVR	Taylorcraft Plus D	Midland Aero Club	
G-AHVS	Taylorcraft Plus D	Midland Aero Club	
G-AHVU	D.H.82A Tiger Moth	Cardiff Aeroplane Club	
G-AHVV	D.H.82A Tiger Moth	Plymouth & District Aero Club	
G-AHVX	D.H.82A Tiger Moth	Air Service Training	
G-AHVY	D.H.82A Tiger Moth	Air Service Training	
G-AHWA	D.H.82A Tiger Moth	Air Service Training	
G-AHWB	D.H.82A Tiger Moth	Air Service Training	
G-AHWC	D.H.82A Tiger Moth	Air Service Training	
G-AHWD	Taylorcraft Plus D	D. G. S. Cotter	
G-AHWE	D.H.82A Tiger Moth	Weston Aero Club	
G-AHWH	GC-IB Swift	C. G. Wheatley	
G-AHWJ	Taylorcraft Plus D	Bristol & Wessex Aeroplane Club	
G-AHWK	Taylorcraft Plus D	Bristol & Wessex Aeroplane Club	
G-AHWO	P.44 Proctor 5	Gerald C. Judd Ltd.	
G-AHWR	P.44 Proctor 5	North Sea Air Transport	
G-AHWS	P.44 Proctor 5	R. H. Braime & ptnr.	
G-AHWU	P.44 Proctor 5	R.N. Flying Club	
G-AHWV	P.44 Proctor 5	D. Napier & Son	
G-AHWZ	P.44 Proctor 5	Colnbrook Trading Co.	
G-AHXB	D.H.82A Tiger Moth	London Aero Club	

Registration	Type	Owner or Operator	Where and when seen
G–AHXC	D.H.82A Tiger Moth	London Aero Club	
G–AHXE	Taylorcraft Plus D	R. A. McMurtrie	
G–AHXF	Taylorcraft Plus D	J. V. Rushton	
G–AHXG	Taylorcraft Plus D	W. S. Shackleton Ltd.	
G–AHXH	M.57 Aerovan 4	S. G. Newport	
G–AHXK	Avro 19 Srs. I	Sivewright Airways	
G–AHXM	Avro 19 Srs. I	Sperry Gyroscope Co.	
G–AHXN	D.H.82A Tiger Moth	Marshall's Flying School	
G–AHXR	M.38 Messenger 2A	Hon. J. B. Fermor-Hesketh	
G–AHXS	Type 652A Anson I	Fairey Aviation Co.	
G–AHXW	D.H.89A Rapide (Islander)	B.E.A. *John Nicholson*	
G–AHXX	D.H.89A Rapide (Islander)	B.E.A. *Islander*	
G–AHYL	M.14A Hawk Trainer 3	Fairey Aviation Co.	
G–AHYN	Avro 19 Srs. I	Sir W. G. Armstrong Whitworth Aircraft	
G–AHYY	S.25 Sandringham 5	B.O.A.C. *Portsmouth*	
G–AHZA	S.25 Sandringham 5	B.O.A.C. *Penzance*	
G–AHZC	S.25 Sandringham 5	B.O.A.C. *Pembroke*	
G–AHZE	S.25 Sandringham 5	B.O.A.C. *Portsea*	
G–AHZF	S.25 Sandringham 5	Qantas Empire Airways	
G–AHZG	S.25 Sandringham 5	Qantas Empire Airways	
G–AHZH	D.H.82A Tiger Moth	Hampshire School of Flying	
G–AHZS	M.38 Messenger 2A	H. C. Kennard	
G–AHZT	M.38 Messenger 2A	H. Deterding	
G–AHZU	M.38 Messenger 2A	Tractor Spares Ltd.	
G–AHZV	A.S.65 Consul	Lancashire Aircraft Corpn.	
G–AHZW	A.S.65 Consul	Lancashire Aircraft Corpn.	
G–AHZY	P.44 Proctor 5	Esso Petroleum Co.	
G–AIAA	P.44 Proctor 5	T. Wayman-Hales	
G–AIAE	P.44 Proctor 5	A. G. de Q. Colley	
G–AIAF	P.44 Proctor 5	T. W. Dupree	
G–AIAG	P.44 Proctor 5	Air Freight	
G–AIAH	A.S.65 Consul	Morton Air Services	
G–AIAI	M.14A Hawk Trainer 3	Airways Aero Associations	
G–AIAJ	M.38 Messenger 2A	H. Blount	
G–AIAT	A.S.40 Oxford I	Air Service Training	
G–AIAU	A.S.40 Oxford I	B.O.A.C.	
G–AIAW	A.S.40 Oxford I	Short Bros. & Harland	
G–AIAX	A.S.40 Oxford I	Air Service Training	
G–AIBB	D.H.89A Dragon Rapide	F. H. Wilson	
G–AIBC	A.S.65 Consul	R. A. Short	
G–AIBD	M.38 Messenger 2A	T. Carlyle	
G–AIBE	Fulmar 2	Fairey Aviation Co.	
G–AIBF	A.S.65 Consul	Silver City Airways	
G–AIBH	J/I Autocrat	N. S. Grainger	
G–AIBL	J/I Autocrat	Machine Traders Ltd.	
G–AIBM	J/I Autocrat	R. E. O. & Mrs. Velten	
G–AIBN	D.H.82A Tiger Moth	Marshall's Flying School	
G–AIBP	J/I Autocrat	W. S. Shackleton, Ltd.	
G–AIBR	J/I Autocrat	Brooklands Aviation	
G–AIBW	J/I Autocrat	Air Schools	
G–AIBX	J/I Autocrat	R. J. White	
G–AIBY	J/I Autocrat	J. D. H. Radford	
G–AIBZ	J/I Autocrat	Wright Aviation	
G–AICD	M.14A Hawk Trainer 3	Bournemouth Flying Club	
G–AICE	M.14A Hawk Trainer 3	Bournemouth Flying Club	
G–AICM	Type 170 Freighter 21	M.C.A.	
G–AICS	Type 170 Freighter 21	B.E.A. *Yeoman*	
G–AICT	Type 170 Freighter 21	Bristol Aeroplane Co.	
G–AICY	D.H.104 Dove I	Iraq Petroleum Transport Co.	
G–AIDB	D.H.82A Tiger Moth	Lancashire Aircraft Corpn.	
G–AIDD	D.H.82A Tiger Moth	Brooklands Aviation	
G–AIDE	M.17 Monarch	B. G. Heron	

Registration	Type	Owner or Operator	Where and when seen
G-AIDF	M.14A Hawk Trainer 3	A. E. T. Allen	
G-AIDK	M.38 Messenger 2A	Wallis & Linnell Ltd.	
G-AIDL	D.H.89A Dragon Rapide	Fox's Glacier Mints	
G-AIDN	Type 502 Spitfire Tr. 8	Vickers-Armstrongs (Super-marine)	
G-AIDR	D.H.82A Tiger Moth	Herts. & Essex Aero Club	
G-AIDS	D.H.82A Tiger Moth	Herts. & Essex Aero Club	
G-AIDT	D.H.82A Tiger Moth	Herts. & Essex Aero Club	
G-AIDV	D.H.82A Tiger Moth	Herts. & Essex Aero Club	
G-AIDW	A.S.65 Consul	Dexford Motors	
G-AIDX	A.S.65 Consul	Esso Petroleum Co.	
G-AIEB	P.28B Proctor 1	W. S. Shackleton Ltd.	
G-AIED	P.28B Proctor 1	Shell-Mex & B.P.	
G-AIEH	P.30B Proctor 2	R. F. Martin	
G-AIEK	M.38 Messenger 2A	A. J. Linnell	
G-AIEP	P.44 Proctor 5	I. M. Erskine	
G-AIER	P.44 Proctor 5	D. I. Allen	
G-AIES	P.44 Proctor 5	G. W. Roberts	
G-AIET	P.44 Proctor 5	V. Van Damm	
G-AIEV	P.44 Proctor 5	J. H. H. Luxton	
G-AIEX	P.28B Proctor 1	R. H. Braime & ptnr.	
G-AIEY	P.28B Proctor 1	Vosper Ltd.	
G-AIFD	Type 652A Anson 1	Gulf Aviation Co.	
G-AIFE	P.34A Proctor 3	E. G. Davis	
G-AIFM	Type 170 Freighter 21	Silver City Airways	
G-AIFV	Type 170 Wayfarer 21	Bristol Aeroplane Co.	
G-AIFZ	J/1 Autocrat	Midland Aero Club	
G-AIGC	J/1 Autocrat	Wiltshire School of Flying	
G-AIGD	J/1 Autocrat	Loxham's Flying Services	
G-AIGE	J/1 Autocrat	Borough of Southend-on-Sea	
G-AIGF	J/1 Autocrat	F. J. R. Elliott	
G-AIGG	J/1 Autocrat	H. Whitaker	
G-AIGH	J/1 Autocrat	W. H. Binns	
G-AIGI	J/1 Autocrat	Hunting Aerosurveys	
G-AIGK	J/1A Autocrat	D. E. Harrington	
G-AIGL	J/1 Autocrat	East Anglian Flying Services	
G-AIGM	J/1 Autocrat	Eagle Aviation	
G-AIGP	J/1 Autocrat	Wright Aviation	
G-AIGR	J/1 Autocrat	Wolverhampton Aviation	
G-AIGT	J/1 Autocrat	Mrs. B. Weininger	
G-AIGU	J/1 Autocrat	C. R. Manasseh	
G-AIGV	J/1 Autocrat	E. C. Francis	
G-AIHD	P.28B Proctor 1	Lancashire Aircraft Corpn.	
G-AIHF	P.28B Proctor 1	Lancashire Aircraft Corpn.	
G-AIHG	P.28B Proctor 1	Air Enterprises	
G-AIHH	P.28B Proctor 1	Lancashire Aircraft Corpn.	
G-AIHM	M.65 Gemini 1A	R. A. Young	
G-AIHN	D.H.89A Dragon Rapide	Gibraltar Airways	
G-AIHO	D.H.82A Tiger Moth	Coventry (Civil) Aviation Judy	
G-AIHV	H.P.70 Halifax 8	Lancashire Aircraft Corpn.	
G-AIIF	M.65 Gemini 1A	Cambridge University Gliding Club	
G-AIIG	M.57 Aerovan 3	Lancashire Aircraft Corpn.	
G-AIIH	Piper J-3C-65 Cub	W. T. Knapton	
G-AIII	P.28B Proctor 1	Darlington & District Aero Club	
G-AIIL	P.34A Proctor 3	M. L. Cherry	
G-AIIP	P.30B Proctor 2	A. T. Leaning	
G-AIIR	P.28B Proctor 1	Southend-on-Sea Flying Services	
G-AIIU	Taylorcraft Plus D	Airways Aero Associations	
G-AIIW	P.28B Proctor 1	Reid & Sigrist Ltd.	
G-AIIZ	D.H.82A Tiger Moth	L.T. (Central Buses) Sports Association Flying Club	
G-AIJA	D.H.82A Tiger Moth	L.T. (Central Buses) Sports Association Flying Club	

Registration	Type	Owner or Operator	Where and when seen
G-AIJE	Type 624 Viking 1	M.o.S.	
G-AIJI	J/1 Autocrat	Eagle Aviation	
G-AIJK	Auster J/4	F. L. Clark	
G-AIJM	Auster J/4	N. D. Roughsedge	
G-AIJS	Auster J/4	Dr. Louise Hyder	
G-AIJT	Auster J/4	—	
G-AIJZ	J/1 Autocrat	W. H. Watkins	
G-AIKC	Auster 5	J. H. Reyner	
G-AIKE	Auster 5	J. Moore	
G-AIKG	P.28B Proctor 1	Mrs. Y. M. Grace	
G-AIKI	P.28B Proctor 1	R. H. Crofts	
G-AIKJ	P.34A Proctor 3	H. J. G. Turner	
G-AIKK	P.28B Proctor 1	Reid & Sigrist Ltd.	
G-AIKR	A.S.65 Consul	Airwork	
G-AIKS	A.S.65 Consul	Lancashire Aircraft Corpn.	
G-AIKT	A.S.65 Consul	Air Enterprises	
G-AIKX	A.S.65 Consul	Samuel Hodge & Sons	
G-AIKZ	A.S.65 Consul	Lancashire Aircraft Corpn.	
G-AILG	M.65 Gemini 1A	Neptune Continental Merchants	
G-AILH	M.60 Marathon 1	M.o.S.	
G-AILI	M.38 Messenger 2A	W. G. Breen-Turner	
G-AILL	M.38 Messenger 2A	Air Schools	
G-AILM	M.57 Aerovan 4	—	
G-AILO	H.P.70 Halifax 8	Lancashire Aircraft Corpn.	
G-AILP	P.28B Proctor 1	P. Filmer-Sankey	
G-AIME	Type 170 Freighter 21	Silver City Airways	
G-AIML	Type 167 Brabazon 2	M.o.S.	
G-AINL	Type 170 Mk.31	Bristol Aeroplane Co.	
G-AINP	Type 170 Mk.31	Bristol Aeroplane Co.	
G-AINR	Type 170	Bristol Aeroplane Co.	
G-AINS	Type 170	Bristol Aeroplane Co.	
G-AINT	Type 170	Bristol Aeroplane Co.	
G-AINY	D.H.82A Tiger Moth	Hants. & Sussex Aviation	
G-AINZ	Type 652A Anson 1	Southern Aviation Training & Western Airways	
G-AIOA	Type 652A Anson 1	Southern Aviation Training & Western Airways	
G-AIOC	Cierva C.30A	Cierva Autogiro Co.	
G-AIOS	A.S.65 Consul	Morton Air Serivces	
G-AIOT	A.S.65 Consul	Air Enterprises	
G-AIOV	A.S.65 Consul	Air Enterprises	
G-AIOW	A.S.65 Consul	Morton Air Services	
G-AIPA	Type 652A Anson 1	College of Aeronautics	
G-AIPC	Type 652A Anson 1	College of Aeronautics	
G-AIPD	Type 652A Anson 1	College of Aeronautics	
G-AIPE	Auster 5	C. L. Bendall	
G-AIPF	Auster 5	H. H. Mould	
G-AIPG	Auster J/4	B. F. Francis	
G-AIPH	Auster J/4	Wright Aviation	
G-AIPN	Auster 5	P. Parry	
G-AIPR	Auster J/4	H. C. N. Goodhart	
G-AIPV	J/1 Autocrat	J. C. Wilson	
G-AIPW	J/1 Autocrat	Mrs. R. H. Reeves	
G-AIPZ	J/1 Autocrat	C. V. Young	
G-AIRA	J/1 Autocrat	W. S. Shackleton. Ltd.	
G-AIRB	J/1 Autocrat	H. Knight	
G-AIRC	J/1 Autocrat	H. C. Kennard	
G-AIRD	Auster J/4	Boston Air Transport	
G-AIRE	Taylorcraft Plus D	J. T. Hayes	
G-AIRI	D.H.82A Tiger Moth	West London Aero Services	
G-AIRJ	D.H.82A Tiger Moth	West London Aero Services	
G-AIRK	D.H.82A Tiger Moth	West London Aero Services	
G-AIRM	Type 652A Anson 1	Aero & Engineering (Merseyside)	
G-AIRN	Type 652A Anson 1	J. A. Wilson	
G-AIRR	D.H.82A Tiger Moth	Short Bros. & Harland	

Registration	Type	Owner or Operator	Where and when seen
G-AIRS	M.65 Gemini 1A	M.C.A.	
G-AIRX	Type 652A Anson 1	—	
G-AIRZ	A.S.40 Oxford 1	Hunting Aerosurveys	
G-AISA	Tipsy B Srs. 1	Royal Naval Flying Club	
G-AISB	Tipsy B Srs. 1	Royal Naval Flying Club	
G-AISC	Tipsy B Srs. 1	Fairey Aviation Co.	
G-AISF	M.57 Aerovan 4	A. J. Challis	
G-AISL	M.38 Messenger 2A	L. F. P. Walters & ptnr	
G-AISM	M.65 Gemini 1A	A. W. Sawyer	
G-AISN	M.65 Gemini 1A	J. Brockhouse & Co.	
G-AISP	Piper J–3C–65 Cub	G. Reid-Walker	
G-AISR	D.H.82A Tiger Moth	Hampshire School of Flying	
G-AISU	Type 349 Spitfire 5B	A. H. Wheeler	
G-AITB	A.S.40 Oxford 1	Air Service Training	
G-AITD	D.H.82A Tiger Moth	East Riding Flying Club (Speeton)	
G-AITE	D.H.82A Tiger Moth	D. Heaton	
G-AITF	A.S.40 Oxford 1	Air Service Training	
G-AITN	M.14A Hawk Trainer 3	H. F. Buckmaster	
G-AITS	M.14A Hawk Trainer 3	F. G. Miles Ltd.	
G-AIUA	M.14A Hawk Trainer 3	Air Schools	
G-AIUE	M.14A Hawk Trainer 3	H. T. Armstrong	
G-AIUH	A.S.40 Oxford 1	Reid & Sigrist Ltd	
G-AIUK	D.H.89A Dragon Rapide	Air Schools	
G-AIUL	D.H.89A Dragon Rapide	Air Transport (Charter) (C.I.)	
G-AIUS	A.S.65 Consul	Stewart Smith & Co.	
G-AIUX	A.S.65 Consul	B.O.A.C.	
G-AIUY	A.S.65 Consul	Olley Air Service	
G-AIVA	A.S.65 Consul	S. J. Cooke	
G-AIVB	Type 610 Viking 1B	B.E.A. *Robert Blake*	
G-AIVC	Type 610 Viking 1B	B.E.A. *Lord Collingwood*	
G-AIVD	Type 610 Viking 1B	B.E.A. *Lord Duncan*	
G-AIVF	Type 610 Viking 1B	B.E.A. *Sir James Somerville*	
G-AIVG	Type 610 Viking 1B	B.E.A. *Sir George Rooke*	
G-AIVH	Type 610 Viking 1B	B.E.A. *Lord Howe*	
G-AIVI	Type 610 Viking 1B	B.E.A. *Viking*	
G-AIVJ	Type 610 Viking 1B	B.E.A. *Lord Jellicoe*	
G-AIVK	Type 610 Viking 1B	B.E.A. *Lord Keyes*	
G-AIVL	Type 610 Viking 1B	B.E.A. *Lord Hawke*	
G-AIVM	Type 610 Viking 1B	B.E.A. *George Monck*	
G-AIVN	Type 610 Viking 1B	B.E.A. *Sir William Penn*	
G-AIVO	Type 610 Viking 1B	B.E.A. *Edward Vernon*	
G-AIVW	D.H.82A Tiger Moth	Newcastle Aero Club	
G-AIVX	S.A.6 Sealand	Short Bros. & Harland	
G-AIVY	A.S.40 Oxford 1	B.O.A.C.	
G-AIVZ	D.H.82A Tiger Moth	—	
G-AIWA	P.28B Proctor 1	D.C. Dickinson & ptnr.	
G-AIWC	Dakota 3	B.O.A.C.	
G-AIWD	Dakota 3 (Pionair)	B.E.A. *John Dunne*	
G-AIWE	Dakota 3	L.E.P. Airservices	
G-AIWH	Type 652A Anson 1	Gulf Aviation Co.	
G-AIWV	Type 652A Anson 1	British Air Transport	
G-AIXA	Taylorcraft Plus D	Cotswold Aero Club	
G-AIXB	Taylorcraft Plus D	D. G. S. Cotter	
G-AIXD	D.H.82A Tiger Moth	D. L. Lloyd	
G-AIXL	D.H.82A Tiger Moth	Southern Flying Schools	
G-AIXM	F.24W–41a Argus 2	J. J. Mackersy	
G-AIXN	Sokol M.1c	G. Shaw	
G-AIXO	Type 652A Anson 1	Mrs. E. M. A. Black	
G-AIXR	Type 627 Viking 1B	Airwork	
G-AIXS	Type 627 Viking 1B	Airwork	
G-AIXV	Type 652A Anson 1	Transair	
G-AIYA	Type 688 Tudor Freighter 3	M.C.A.	
G-AIYB	M.14A Hawk Trainer 3	Redhill Flying Club	

20

Colourful weekly viistors to London are the DC–4s of Iberia.   [*J.W.R.T.*

A Canadair Four, in service with T.C.A. as the *North Star* and with B.O.A.C. as the *Argonaut*.

One of B.O.A.C.'s Hermes 4s, civil counterparts of the Hastings military transport.

Left: Four engines to Paris. An Air France Languedoc. (*J.W.R.T.*)

Centre: G–AMAV, prototype of B.E.A.'s fine fleet of Viscount propeller - turbine air liners.

Bottom: Cars boarding a Freighter of Silver City's unique cross-Channel air ferry service.

Registration	Type	Owner or Operator	Where and when seen
G-AIYD	M.14A Hawk Trainer 3	Redhill Flying Club	
G-AIYE	D.H.89A Dragon Rapide	Olley Air Service	
G-AIYH	P.28B Proctor 1	Hunting Flying Clubs	
G-AIYK	Avro 19 Srs. 2	Hunting Air Transport	
G-AIYL	M.14A Hawk Trainer 3	J. Neasham	
G-AIYN	A.W.55 Apollo	M.o.S.	
G-AIYO	F.24W-41a Argus 2	Nat. Assoc. of Training Corps for Girls	
G-AIYP	D.H.89A Dragon Rapide	V. H. Bellamy (Flightways)	
G-AIYR	D.H.89A Dragon Rapide	Reid & Sigrist Ltd.	
G-AIYS	D.H.85 Leopard Moth	Autowork (Winchester)	
G-AIYU	Piper J-3C-65 Cub	A. C. Stone & ptnr.	
G-AIYV	Piper J-3C-65 Cub	A. J. Walter	
G-AIYX	Piper J-3C-65 Cub	Crewsair Flying Group	
G-AIYY	D.H.89A Dragon Rapide	Reid & Sigrist Ltd.	
G-AIZA	P.44 Proctor 5	D. Stansfield	
G-AIZB	P.44 Proctor 5	East Hull Press	
G-AIZF	D.H.82A Tiger Moth	H. M. Woodhams	
G-AIZI	D.H.89A Dragon Rapide	Reid & Sigrist Ltd.	
G-AIZK	M.14A Hawk Trainer 3	F. G. Miles Ltd.	
G-AIZL	M.14A Hawk Trainer 3	Wright Aviation	
G-AIZT	Auster J/4	Auster Aircraft	
G-AIZU	J/1 Autocrat	R. A. Davies (Birmingham) Ltd.	
G-AIZV	J/1 Autocrat	Herts. & Essex Aero Club	
G-AIZW	J/1 Autocrat	Wiltshire School of Flying	
G-AIZY	J/1 Autocrat	J. L. Thorne	
G-AIZZ	J/1 Autocrat	H. C. Kennard	
G-AJAB	J/1 Autocrat	H. R. Edenborough	
G-AJAC	J/1 Autocrat	R. L. Hutchins	
G-AJAE	J/1 Autocrat	Royal Artillery Aero Club	
G-AJAH	J/1 Autocrat	G. Hadman	
G-AJAI	J/1 Autocrat	Fen Drains & Excavations	
G-AJAJ	J/1 Autocrat	Isle of Wight Flying Club	
G-AJAK	Auster 5	S. Pearce-Smith	
G-AJAM	J/2 Arrow	A. C. T. Carey	
G-AJAR	J/1 Autocrat	F. M. Dewing	
G-AJAS	J/1 Autocrat	J. L. R. James	
G-AJAT	F.24W-41a Argus	J. J. Hofer	
G-AJBH	Dakota 3	Lambert's Trust	
G-AJBJ	D.H.89A Dragon Rapide	Birkett Air Service	
G-AJBM	Type 610 Viking 1B	B.E.A. *Sir Charles Knowles*	
G-AJBN	Type 610 Viking 1B	B.E.A. *Lord Nelson*	
G-AJBO	Type 610 Viking 1B	B.E.A. *John Benbow*	
G-AJBP	Type 610 Viking 1B	B.E.A. *Sir Hyde Parker*	
G-AJBR	Type 610 Viking 1B	B.E.A. *Sir Bertram Ramsay*	
G-AJBS	Type 610 Viking 1B	B.E.A. *Sir Cloudesley Shovell*	
G-AJBT	Type 610 Viking 1B	B.E.A. *Sir Thomas Troubridge*	
G-AJBU	Type 610 Viking 1B	B.E.A. *Lord Bridport*	
G-AJBV	Type 610 Viking 1B	B.E.A. *Sir Henry Morgan*	
G-AJBW	Type 610 Viking 1B	B.E.A. *Sir William Cornwallis*	
G-AJBX	Type 610 Viking 1B	B.E.A. *Sir Edward Hughes*	
G-AJBY	Type 610 Viking 1B	B.E.A. *Sir Richard Strachan*	
G-AJCA	Type 610 Viking 1B	B.E.A. *Sir Thomas Allin*	
G-AJCD	Type 610 Viking 1D	B.E.A. *Sir Charles Douglas*	
G-AJCE	Type 610 Viking 1B	B.E.A. *Lord Exmouth*	
G-AJCK	Heath Parasol	R. A. Mann	
G-AJCL	D.H.89A Dragon Rapide	Allgood Manufacturing Co.	
G-AJCM	M.14A Hawk Trainer 3	Wolverhampton Aviation	
G-AJCW	P.34A Proctor 3	Herts. & Essex Aero Club	

23

Registration	Type	Owner or Operator	Where and when seen
G–AJCX	P.34A Proctor 3	L. C. Hazard	
G–AJCY	P.34A Proctor 3	R. R. Jeffery	
G–AJCZ	P.34A Proctor 3	R. K. Dundas Ltd.	
G–AJDC	Douglas D.C.3	F. H. Wilson	
G–AJDE	Dakota 3 (Pionair)	B.E.A. *Sir David Henderson*	
G–AJDF	M.38 Messenger 4A	N. B. Williams	
G–AJDG	Douglas D.C.3–G.102A	F. H. Wilson	
G–AJDH	Avro 19 Srs. 2	Secretary of State for Air	
G–AJDI	Type 610 Viking IB	B.E.A. *Sir Christopher Cradock*	
G–AJDJ	Type 610 Viking IB	B.E.A. *Lord Beatty*	
G–AJDK	Type 610 Viking IB	B.E.A. *Richard Kempenfelt*	
G–AJDL	Type 610 Viking IB	B.E.A. *Lord St. Vincent*	
G–AJDM	M.38 Messenger 2A	Boston Air Transport	
G–AJDN	D.H.89A Dragon Rapide	Birkett Air Service	
G–AJDP	D.H.104 Dove I	Morton Air Services	
G–AJDR	M.14A Hawk Trainer 3	C. J. de Vere	
G–AJDS	Piper J.3C–65 Cub	A. J. Walter	
G–AJDT	F.24W–41a Argus	J. M. Hollander	
G–AJDV	J/I Autocrat	Universal Flying Services	
G–AJDW	J/I Autocrat	Brooklands Aviation	
G–AJDY	J/I Autocrat	A. Morralee	
G–AJDZ	J/I Autocrat	A. F. Johnson	
G–AJEA	J/I Autocrat	J. E. L. Drabble	
G–AJEB	J/I Autocrat	Hunting Aerosurveys	
G–AJEC	J/I Autocrat	Fen Drains & Excavations	
G–AJEE	J/I Autocrat	H. F. Buckmaster	
G–AJEH	J/I Autocrat	Redhill Flying Club	
G–AJEI	J/I Autocrat	Herts. & Essex Aero Club	
G–AJEK	J/I Autocrat	R. J. Crosfield	
G–AJEN	J/I Autocrat	Loxham's Flying Services	
G–AJEO	J/I Autocrat	Southend-on-Sea Borough Council	
G–AJEP	J/I Autocrat	Airwork	
G–AJEU	J/I Autocrat	Connaught Motors (Sales)	
G–AJEW	J/I Autocrat	A. W. Bingham	
G–AJEX	M.65 Gemini IA	R. Frogley	
G–AJFC	M.38 Messenger 2A	T. Shipside Ltd.	
G–AJFD	M.65 Gemini IA	F. Briggs	
G–AJFF	M.38 Messenger 2A	G. Clifton	
G–AJFH	M.38 Messenger 2A	I. H. Cameron	
G–AJFK	D.H.89A Dragon Rapide	Aerocontacts	
G–AJFR	Type 627 Viking IB	Airwork	
G–AJFS	Type 627 Viking IB	Airwork	
G–AJFT	Type 627 Viking IB	Airwork	
G–AJFX	Type 652A Anson I	C. R. Toye (Trans Arabia Air Services)	
G–AJGA	A.S.65 Consul	Lancashire Aircraft Corpn.	
G–AJGJ	Auster 5	Walker & Thompson	
G–AJGM	M.14A Hawk Trainer 3	Airways Aero Associations	
G–AJGR	A.S.40 Oxford I	Hunting Aerosurveys	
G–AJGS	D.H.89A Dragon Rapide	Miss C. Brunning	
G–AJGT	D.H.104 Dove 5X	de Havilland Engine Co.	
G–AJGV	D.H.89A Dragon Rapide	Manx Air Charters	
G–AJGW	F.24W–41a Argus	R. A. Short	
G–AJGY	Piper P.A.12 Super Cruiser	C. G. Reid-Walker	
G–AJHA	M.14A Hawk Trainer 3	D. Donaldson-Stiff	
G–AJHB	M.14A Hawk Trainer 3	Darlington & Dist. Aero Club	
G–AJHC	M.14A Hawk Trainer 3	J. Neasham	
G–AJHD	M.14A Hawk Trainer 3	J. Neasham	
G–AJHG	M.14A Hawk Trainer 3	D. C. Black	
G–AJHJ	Auster 5	B. Arden	

Registration	Type	Owner or Operator	Where and when seen
G–AJHO	D.H.89A Dragon Rapide	Brooklands Aviation	
G–AJHP	D.H.89A Dragon Rapide	G. Q. Parachute Co.	
G–AJHS	D.H.82A Tiger Moth	Reid & Sigrist	
G–AJHT	D.H.82A Tiger Moth	Reid & Sigrist	
G–AJHU	D.H.82 A Tiger Moth	Reid & Sigrist	
G–AJHV	Auster 4	L. R. Snook	
G–AJHW	Sikorsky S.51	B.E.A. *Sir Baudwin*	
G–AJHX	D.H.104 Dove 1	Iraq Petroleum Transport Co.	
G–AJHY	Dakota 3 (Pionair)	B.E.A. *William Henson*	
G–AJHZ	Dakota 3 (Pionair)	B.E.A. *Bentfield Hucks*	
G–AJIA	Dakota 3 (Pionair)	B.E.A. *Sir John Alcock*	
G–AJIB	Dakota 3 (Pionair)	B.E.A. *Griffith Brewer*	
G–AJIC	Dakota 3 (Pionair)	B.E.A. *Roy Chadwick*	
G–AJID	J/1 Autocrat	A. C. Kingham	
G–AJIE	J/1 Autocrat	A. L. Willings	
G–AJIG	J/1 Autocrat	East Riding Flying Club (Speeton)	
G–AJIH	J/1 Autocrat	Lightplanes (Lancashire)	
G–AJIK	Auster 5	S. G. Newport	
G–AJIN	J/1 Autocrat	East Riding Flying Club (Speeton)	
G–AJIO	J/1 Autocrat	Newcastle Aero Club	
G–AJIP	J/1 Autocrat	Edinburgh Flying Club	
G–AJIS	J/1 Autocrat	R. A. Gunton	
G–AJIT	J/1 Autocrat	Swansea & Dist. Flying School & Club	
G–AJIU	J/1 Autocrat	W. C. Baker	
G–AJIW	J/1 Autocrat	N. A. Rogers	
G–AJIY	J/1 Autocrat	J. R. Ratcliffe	
G–AJIZ	J/1 Autocrat	Auster Aircraft	
G–AJJB	Auster 5	Bristol & Wessex Aeroplane Club	
G–AJJF	D.H.104 Dove 1	Iraq Petroleum Transport Co.	
G–AJJH	Auster 5A	F. M. J. H. de Malet-Rocquefort	
G–AJJI	M.14A Hawk Trainer 3	Wolverhampton Aviation	
G–AJJJ	Beech D–17S Traveller	D. E. Fox	
G–AJJN	Type 636 Viking 1B	B.E.A. *Sir Charles Napier*	
G–AJKC	Type 688 Tudor Freighter 3	M.C.A.	
G–AJKE	D.H.89A Dragon Rapide	W. A. Rollason Ltd.	
G–AJKG	M.38 Messenger 2A	W. F. I. Stephenson	
G–AJKK	M.38 Messenger 2A	H. Tempest	
G–AJKL	M.38 Messenger 2A	P. Sturgeon	
G–AJKP	M.57 Aerovan 4	Alexander Stair Clips Ltd.	
G–AJKR	M.65 Gemini 1A	J. D. Habin	
G–AJKS	M.65 Gemini 1A	E. Day	
G–AJKT	M.38 Messenger 2A	R. W. Kenny	
G–AJKU	M.57 Aerovan 4	North-West Airlines (I.o.M.)	
G–AJKV	M.65 Gemini 1A	V. A. Ercolani	
G–AJKW	D.H.89A Dragon Rapide	Lancashire Aircraft Corpn.	
G–AJKX	D.H.89A Dragon Rapide	Lancashire Aircraft Corpn.	
G–AJKY	D.H.89A Dragon Rapide	Lancashire Aircraft Corpn.	
G–AJLE	Auster 5	Lancashire Aircraft Corpn.	
G–AJLG	Auster 5	Lancashire Aircraft Corpn.	
G–AJLI	A.S.65 Consul	S. J. Cooke	
G–AJLM	A.S.65 Consul	West Indies Trading Co.	
G–AJLN	A.S.65 Consul	English Electric Co.	
G–AJLR	A.S.65 Consul	Olley Air Service	
G–AJLS	P.28B Proctor 1	D. C. T. Bennett	
G–AJLV	D.H.104 Dove 1	M.C.A.	

Registration	Type	Owner or Operator	Where and when seen
G-AJLW	D.H.104 Dove 2	de Havilland Acft. Co.	
G-AJMH	P.31C Proctor 4	E. Williams	
G-AJMI	P.31C Proctor 4	Whitehouse Industries	
G-AJMP	P.31C Proctor 4	G. C. S. Whyham	
G-AJMW	P.31C Proctor 4	Short Bros. & Harland	
G-AJMX	P.31C Proctor 4	Short Bros. & Harland	
G-AJMY	D.H.89A Dragon Rapide	Melba Airways	
G-AJMZ	S.25 Sandringham 5	B.O.A.C. *Perth*	
G-AJNE	A.S.65 Consul	Air Enterprises	
G-AJNG	A.S.65 Consul	M. J. Conry	
G-AJNN	F.24W–41a Argus 2	F. A. Laker	
G-AJNO	Walrus I	Scottish Aviation	
G-AJOA	D.H.82A Tiger Moth	Short Bros. & Harland	
G-AJOC	M.38 Messenger 2A	C. E. Hickman	
G-AJOD	M.38 Messenger 2A	L. H. Wood & ptnr.	
G-AJOE	M.38 Messenger 2A	Reproducers & Amplifiers	
G-AJOF	M.57 Aerovan 4	E. C. Cathels	
G-AJOH	M.65 Gemini IA	J. R. A. Stroyan	
G-AJOJ	M.65 Gemini IA	Loxham's Flying Services	
G-AJOR	Sikorsky S.51	B.E.A. *Sir Owen*	
G-AJOT	D.H.104 Dove I	Olley Air Services	
G-AJOV	Sikorsky S.51	B.E.A. *Sir Lamorak*	
G-AJOW	F.24W–41a Argus	R. MacKisray	
G-AJOZ	F.24W–41a Argus	I.D.A. Wickins & ptnr.	
G-AJPE	F.24W–41a Argus	Bond Air Services	
G-AJPI	F.24W–41a Argus	West London Aero Services	
G-AJPR	D.H.104 Dove I	B.O.A.C.	
G-AJPU	J/2 Arrow	J. M. Rollo	
G-AJPW	J/I Autocrat	Miss H. Courtney-Lewis	
G-AJRB	J/I Autocrat	Brooklands Aviation	
G-AJRC	J/I Autocrat	Lancashire Aircraft Corpn.	
G-AJRE	J/I Autocrat	Hampshire School of Flying	
G-AJRF	J/I Autocrat	Aero Industries	
G-AJRH	J/I Autocrat	Newcastle Aero Club	
G-AJRK	J/I Autocrat	H. E. Smead	
G-AJRN	J/I Autocrat	Darlington & Dist. Aero Club	
G-AJRP	J/I Autocrat	P. Brown	
G-AJRS	M.14A Hawk Trainer 3	British Air Transport	
G-AJRT	M.14A Hawk Trainer 3	British Air Transport	
G-AJRU	M.14A Hawk Trainer 3	British Air Transport	
G-AJRV	M.14A Hawk Trainer 3	Darlington & Dist. Aero Club	
G-AJRZ	F.24W–41a Argus	—	
G-AJSF	M.14A Hawk Trainer 3	W. Holderness	
G-AJSG	F.24W–41a Argus	L. D. Hawthorn	
G-AJSH	F.24W–41a Argus	L. D. Hawthorn	
G-AJSK	D.H.89A Rapide (Islander)	B.E.A. *Lord Lister*	
G-AJSL	D.H.89A Dragon Rapide	Air Charter	
G-AJSN	F.24W–41a Argus	Hon. B. L. Bathurst	
G-AJSP	F.24W–41a Argus	J. J. Hofer	
G-AJSS	F.24W–41a Argus	W. H. Leadbetter	
G-AJSX	F.24W–41a Argus	Industrial & Motor Concessions	
G-AJTC	M.57 Aerovan 4	Western Manufacturing Estate	
G-AJTG	M.65 Gemini 3B	Eddystone Fishing Co.	
G-AJTL	M.65 Gemini IA	L. M. Cooper	
G-AJTM	Auster 5	Wiltshire School of Flying	
G-AJTP	P.31C Proctor 4	A. D. Adnams	
G-AJTV	Auster 5	G. Bickley	
G-AJTW	D.H.82A Tiger Moth	Short Bros. & Harland	
G-AJUD	J/I Autocrat	R. H. Braime & ptnr.	
G-AJUE	J/I Autocrat	Darlington & Dist. Aero Club	
G-AJUF	J/I Autocrat	Miles Car Hire	
G-AJUJ	J/I Autocrat	Weston Aero Club	
G-AJUK	J/I Autocrat	Southend-on-Sea Borough Council	

332

Registration	Type	Owner or Operator	Where and when seen
G-AJUL	J/I Autocrat	Loxham's Flying Services	
G-AJUM	J/I Autocrat	Weston Aero Club	
G-AJUO	J/I Autocrat	Weston Aero Club	
G-AJUP	J/I Autocrat	Southend-on-Sea Borough Council	
G-AJUR	J/I Autocrat	D. K. Gray & ptnrs.	
G-AJUW	J/IB Aiglet	Aerial Spraying Contractors	
G-AJVA	D.H.89A Dragon Rapide	Iraq Petroleum Transport Co.	
G-AJVB	D.H.89A Dragon Rapide	Iraq Petroleum Transport Co.	
G-AJVC	M.38 Messenger 2A	Longford Engineering Co.	
G-AJVD	D.H.C.Ia–I Chipmunk	London Aero Club	
G-AJVE	D.H.82A Tiger Moth	Edinburgh Flying Club	
G-AJVI	F.24W–41a Argus	S. K. Davies	
G-AJVT	Auster 5	Anglo-Continental Air Service	
G-AJVV	Auster 5	Denham Flying Club	
G-AJWA	M.65 Gemini IA	J. J. Hofer	
G-AJWB	M.38 Messenger 2A	Wiltshire School of Flying	
G-AJWC	M.65 Gemini IA	Derek Crouch (Contractors)	
G-AJWD	M.57 Aerovan 4	Western Manufacturing Estate	
G-AJWE	M.65 Gemini IA	T. R. McGeorge	
G-AJWF	M.65 Gemini IA	E. J. Farrow	
G-AJWG	M.65 Gemini IA	R. P. Adler	
G-AJWH	M.65 Gemini IA	H. C. Kennard	
G-AJXA	F.24W–41a Argus	D. B. Monro	
G-AJXB	D.H.89A Rapide (Islander)	B.E.A. *William Gilbert Grace*	
G-AJXC	Auster 5A	A. H. Warminger	
G-AJXE	A.S.65 Consul	M.C.A.	
G-AJXF	A.S.65 Consul	M.C.A.	
G-AJXG	A.S.65 Consul	M.C.A.	
G-AJXH	A.S.65 Consul	M.C.A.	
G-AJXI	A.S.65 Consul	M.C.A.	
G-AJXX	Auster 4	Darlington & Dist. Aero Club.	
G-AJXY	Auster 5	S. Bichan	
G-AJYB	Auster 5	J. G. Crampton	
G-AJYN	J/5B Autocar	J. V. Heriz-Smith	
G-AJYO	J/5B Autocar	T. F. Ringer	
G-AJYP	Auster 4	R. Pointer	
G-AJYR	J/IB Aiglet	Aerial Spraying Contractors	
G-AJYS	Auster J/5E	Auster Aircraft	
G-AJYT	J/IB Aiglet	Aerial Spraying Contractors	
G-AJYV	J/5B Autocar	A. S. Mackenzie-Low	
G-AJYY	J/5B Autocar	Longford Engineering Co.	
G-AJYZ	M.38 Messenger 2A	W. P. Bowles	
G-AJZG	M.57 Aerovan 4	M. J. Conry	
G-AJZH	M.14A Hawk Trainer 3	F. W. Seymour & ptnrs.	
G-AJZJ	M.65 Gemini IA	Air Schools	
G-AJZO	M.65 Gemini IA	Whitbread & Co.	
G-AJZS	M.65 Gemini IA	J. J. Hofer	
G-AKAA	Piper J–3C–65 Cub	R. W. Bates	
G-AKAI	M.38 Messenger 2A	W. S. Shackleton Ltd.	
G-AKAN	M.38 Messenger 2A	B. H. Gutteridge	
G-AKAO	M.38 Messenger 2A	J. C. Elwes	
G-AKAS	M.14A Hawk Trainer 3	Essex Aero	
G-AKAT	M.14A Hawk Trainer 3	Essex Aero	
G-AKAU	M.14A Hawk Trainer 3	Essex Aero	
G-AKAV	M.38 Messenger 2A	W. H. Byars	
G-AKBF	Prestwick Pioneer 2	Scottish Aviation	
G-AKBG	Type 610 Viking IB	B.E.A. *Sir Richard Bickerton*	
G-AKBH	Type 610 Viking IB	B.E.A. *Lord Hood*	
G-AKBM	M.38 Messenger 2A	Plymouth & Dist. Aero Club	
G-AKBO	M.38 Messenger 2A	R. H. Braime & ptnr.	
G-AKBZ	Type 689 Tudor 5	—	
G-AKCA	Type 689 Tudor 5	Surrey Flying Services	

27

333

Registration	Type	Owner or Operator	Where and when seen
G-AKCB	Type 689 Tudor 5	—	
G-AKCD	Type 689 Tudor 5	William Dempster	
G-AKCE	L.49–46 Constellation	B.O.A.C. *Bedford*	
G-AKCF	D.H.104 Dove 1	B.O.A.C.	
G-AKCH	D.H.82A Tiger Moth	Scottish Flying Club	
G-AKCI	D.H.82A Tiger Moth	Scottish Flying Club	
G-AKCO	S.25 Sandringham 7	B.O.A.C. *St. George*	
G-AKDB	M.65 Gemini 1A	J. M. Banks	
G-AKDC	M.65 Gemini 3	J. N. Somers Ltd.	
G-AKDD	M.65 Gemini 1A	M.C.A.	
G-AKDE	M.65 Gemini 1A	L. H. B. Roper	
G-AKDF	M.38 Messenger 2A	Wolverhampton Aviation	
G-AKDI	M.65 Gemini 1A	Gee, Walker & Slater Ltd.	
G-AKDJ	M.65 Gemini 1A	C. F. L. Hersee	
G-AKDK	M.65 Gemini 1A	Mitchell Engineering Co.	
G-AKDN	D.H.C–1a–1 Chipmunk	London Aero Club	
G-AKDW	D.H.89A Dragon Rapide	Short Bros. & Harland	
G-AKDZ	P.44 Proctor 5	Mrs. F. M. D. Houillon	
G-AKEA	P.44 Proctor 5	W. S. Shackleton Ltd.	
G-AKEB	P.44 Proctor 5	Crow Flight	
G-AKEC	H.P.70 Halifax 3	Lancashire Aircraft Corpn.	
G-AKED	D.H.89A Dragon Rapide	Airlines (Jersey)	
G-AKEF	P.31C Proctor 4	E. R. Pyatt & ptnr.	
G-AKEG	M.65 Gemini 1A	S. G. Newport	
G-AKEI	M.65 Gemini 1A	R. R. Carne	
G-AKEJ	M.65 Gemini 1A	North-West Airlines (I.o.M.)	
G-AKEK	M.65 Gemini 1A	M. H. D. McAlpine	
G-AKEL	M.65 Gemini 1A	D. Macartney-Filgate	
G-AKEM	M.65 Gemini 1A	J. A. Wilson	
G-AKEN	M.65 Gemini 1A	C. R. Mauritzen	
G-AKER	M.65 Gemini 1A	Wallis & Linnell Ltd.	
G-AKES	M.65 Gemini 1A	T. Carlyle	
G-AKET	D.H.104 Dove 1	Mrs. P. Churchill	
G-AKEY	Slingsby T.29A Motor-Tutor	Slingsby Sailplanes	
G-AKEZ	M.38 Messenger 2A	F. H. Bird (Netherthorpe Aero Club)	
G-AKFA	Bell 47–B3	B.E.A. *Sir Balin*	
G-AKFB	Bell 47–B3	B.E.A. *Sir Balan*	
G-AKFE	Avro 19 Srs. 2	Secretary of State for Air	
G-AKFK	Type 652A Anson 1	Olds Discount Co.	
G-AKFM	Type 652A Anson 1	Finglands Airways	
G-AKFN	F.24W–41a Argus	L. D. Hawthorn	
G-AKFP	H.P.81 Hermes 4	B.O.A.C. *Hamilcar*	
G-AKFU	M.65 Gemini 1A	E. A. Moffatt	
G-AKFX	M.65 Gemini 1A	Bees Flight	
G-AKFY	M.65 Gemini 1A	H. V. Kennedy	
G-AKGC	M.65 Gemini 1A	T. Shioside Ltd.	
G-AKGD	M.65 Gemini 1A	Platt Bros. & Co.	
G-AKGE	M.65 Gemini 1A	Goodyear Tyre & Rubber Co.	
G-AKGF	D.H.82A Tiger Moth	L.T.(Central Buses) Sports Association Flying Club	
G-AKGH	Type 377 Stratocruiser	B.O.A.C. *Caledonia*	
G-AKGI	Type 377 Stratocruiser	B.O.A.C. *Caribou*	
G-AKGJ	Type 377 Stratocruiser	B.O.A.C. *Cambria*	
G-AKGK	Type 377 Stratocruiser	B.O.A.C. *Canopus*	
G-AKGL	Type 377 Stratocruiser	B.O.A.C. *Cabot*	
G-AKGM	Type 377 Stratocruiser	B.O.A.C. *Castor*	
G-AKGR	M.14A Hawk Trainer 3	Bournemouth Flying Club	
G-AKGS	M.14A Hawk Trainer 3	Bournemouth Flying Club	
G-AKGX	Dakota 3	Cyprus Airways	
G-AKGY	D.H.89A Dragon Rapide	Manx Air Charters	
G-AKHB	M.65 Gemini 1A	R. E. Bibby	
G-AKHC	M.65 Gemini 1A	Bees Flight	

Registration	Type	Owner or Operator	Where and when seen
G–AKHE	M.65 Gemini 1A	L. R. Snook	
G–AKHF	M.57 Aerovan 6	F. G. Miles Ltd.	
G–AKHG	M.57 Aerovan 4	S. G. Newport	
G–AKHJ	M.65 Gemini 1A	H. R. Coxhead	
G–AKHK	M.65 Gemini 1A	Loxham's Flying Services	
G–AKHP	M.65 Gemini 1A	C. Spencer-Thomas	
G–AKHS	M.65 Gemini 1A	Mrs. A. Leadbeater	
G–AKHV	M.65 Gemini 1A	W. T. Franklin	
G–AKHW	M.65 Gemini 1A	Plymouth Airport Ltd.	
G–AKHX	M.65 Gemini 1A	N. D. Norman & ptnr.	
G–AKHY	M.65 Gemini 1A	Smith's Aircraft Instruments	
G–AKHZ	M.65 Gemini 1A	Pasolds	
G–AKIF	D.H.89A Dragon Rapide	Manx Air Charters	
G–AKIG	D.H.82A Tiger Moth	D. Goldstein (Staravia)	
G–AKIH	P.44 Proctor 5	Hon. E. H. K. Digby	
G–AKII	Dakota 3	Cyprus Airways	
G–AKIJ	Dakota 3	Cyprus Airways	
G–AKIK	Dakota 3	Cyprus Airways	
G–AKIM	M.38 Messenger 2A	Don Everall (Aviation)	
G–AKIN	M.38 Messenger 2A	A. J. Spiller	
G–AKIO	M.38 Messenger 2A	Bidgood & Catton Taxi-Planes	
G–AKIR	M.38 Messenger 2A	J. W. Tomkins & ptnr.	
G–AKIS	M.38 Messenger 2A	Porter Spiers (Leicester)	
G–AKIU	P.44 Proctor 5	Rolls-Royce Ltd.	
G–AKIX	P.44 Proctor 5	Shell Co. of Egypt (London)	
G–AKJA	F.24W–41a Argus	—	
G–AKJD	Slingsby T.29B Motor-Tutor	Slingsby Sailplanes	
G–AKJG	D.H.104 Dove 2	Helliwells	
G–AKJH	Dakota 3 (Pionair)	B.E.A. *Edward Hillman*	
G–AKJP	D.H.104 Dove 2	Iraq Petroleum Transport Co.	
G–AKJR	D.H.104 Dove 2	Olley Air Service	
G–AKJS	D.H.89A Dragon Rapide	Fairey Aviation Co.	
G–AKJT	Auster 5	E. W. Kenny	
G–AKJV	M.14A Hawk Trainer 3	Short Bros. & Harland	
G–AKJX	M.14A Hawk Trainer 3	H. C. Kennard	
G–AKJY	D.H.89A Dragon Rapide	Brooklands Aviation	
G–AKJZ	D.H.89A Dragon Rapide	East Anglian Flying Services	
G–AKKB	M.65 Gemini 1A	F. Dunkerley	
G–AKKC	M.38 Messenger 2A	C. A. Mackaness	
G–AKKG	M.38 Messenger 4	Shell-Mex & B.P.	
G–AKKH	M.65 Gemini 1A	S. Bourne & Co.	
G–AKKI	M.38 Messenger 2A	J. Patston	
G–AKKJ	M.57 Aerovan 4	Western Manufacturing Estate	
G–AKKK	M.38 Messenger 2A	Boston Air Transport	
G–AKKM	M.38 Messenger 2A	Newcastle Breweries	
G–AKKN	M.38 Messenger 2A	P. S. Murphy	
G–AKKO	M.38 Messenger 2A	D. Godfrey	
G–AKKR	M.14A Hawk Trainer 3	Airways Aero Associations	
G–AKKS	M.14A Hawk Trainer 3	Airways Aero Associations	
G–AKKV	M.14A Hawk Trainer 3	Airways Aero Associations	
G–AKKW	M.14A Hawk Trainer 3	Airways Aero Associations	
G–AKKY	M.14A Hawk Trainer 3	Airways Aero Associations	
G–AKKZ	M.14A Hawk Trainer 3	Airways Aero Associations	
G–AKLA	D.H.89A Dragon Rapide	Lancashire Aircraft Corpn.	
G–AKLB	P.31C Proctor 4	Lancashire Aircraft Corpn.	
G–AKLD	P.31C Proctor 4	Lancashire Aircraft Corpn.	
G–AKLN	S.A.6 Sealand	Short Bros. & Harland	
G–AKLO	S.A.6 Sealand 1D	Short Bros. & Harland	
G–AKLP	S.A.6 Sealand 1A	Short Bros. & Harland	
G–AKLV	S.A.6 Sealand	Short Bros. & Harland	
G–AKLX	S.A.6 Sealand	Short Bros. & Harland	

Registration	Type	Owner or Operator	Where and when seen
G–AKLY	S.A.6 Sealand	Short Bros. & Harland	
G–AKLZ	S.A.6 Sealand	Short Bros. & Harland	
G–AKMA	S.A.6 Sealand	Short Bros. & Harland	
G–AKMB	Auster 5	M. J. Conry	
G–AKMG	D.H.89A Dragon Rapide	Sivewright Airways	
G–AKMH	D.H.89A Dragon Rapide	Isle of Wight Flying Club	
G–AKMI	Auster 5	Willis Hole Aviation	
G–AKMN	M.14A Hawk Trainer 3	Wolverhampton Aviation	
G–AKMU	M.14A Hawk Trainer 3	C. J. de Vere	
G–AKNB	Dakota 3 (Pionair)	B.E.A. *Sir Sefton Brancker*	
G–AKNE	D.H.89A Dragon Rapide	M. L. Thomas	
G–AKNF	D.H.89A Dragon Rapide	Airlines (Jersey)	
G–AKNM	Dakota 4	Fairey Aviation Co.	
G–AKNN	D.H.89A Dragon Rapide	Air Couriers (Properties)	
G–AKNT	S.45 Solent 3	M.C.A.	
G–AKNU	S.45 Solent 3	Aquila Airways *Sydney*	
G–AKNV	D.H.89A Dragon Rapide	Lancashire Aircraft Corpn.	
G–AKNX	D.H.89A Dragon Rapide	Patrick Motors	
G–AKNY	D.H.89A Dragon Rapide	Patrick Motors	
G–AKOA	D.H.89A Dragon Rapide	M. L. Thomas	
G–AKOB	D.H.89A Dragon Rapide	Air Enterprises *The Sandown Flyer*	
G–AKOD	D.H.89A Dragon Rapide	Lancashire Aircraft Corpn.	
G–AKOE	D.H.89A Dragon Rapide	Lancashire Aircraft Corpn.	
G–AKOH	D.H.89A Dragon Rapide	North-West Airlines (I.o.M.)	
G–AKOK	D.H.89A Dragon Rapide	Mannin Airways	
G–AKOO	D.H.89A Dragon Rapide	Southern Aircraft (Gatwick)	
G–AKOR	D.H.89A Dragon Rapide	Skyways	
G–AKOT	Auster 5	A. D. Daly	
G–AKOV	D.H.89A Dragon Rapide	Wolverhampton Aviation	
G–AKOX	Auster 5	N. C. Anderson	
G–AKOY	D.H.89A Dragon Rapide	Lancashire Aircraft Corpn.	
G–AKOZ	Dakota 4	Air Transport (Charter) (C.I.)	
G–AKPA	D.H.89A Dragon Rapide	Midland Metal Spinning Co.	
G–AKPE	M.14A Hawk Trainer 3	D. C. Jemmett	
G–AKPF	M.14A Hawk Trainer 3	Wards Motolympia	
G–AKPH	Auster 5	N. B. Ewing	
G–AKPI	Auster 5	J. E. Onions	
G–AKPL	M.14A Hawk Trainer 3	Eagle Aviation	
G–AKRC	Auster 4	R. J. Jones	
G–AKRD	A.S.57 Ambassador 1	M.o.S. *Golden Lion*	
G–AKRH	M.14A Hawk Trainer 3	Loxham's Flying Services	
G–AKRM	M.14A Hawk Trainer 3	S. B. Reece	
G–AKRN	D.H.89A Dragon Rapide	East Anglian Flying Services	
G–AKRO	D.H.89A Dragon Rapide	Lancashire Aircraft Corpn.	
G–AKRP	D.H.89A Dragon Rapide	Short Bros. & Harland	

Right: Typical of the rare birds which pass through London Airport was this Convair-liner of Ethiopian Air Lines.

Centre: Well-named—G–ALZN, flagship of B.E.A.'s graceful fleet of *Elizabethans.*

Bottom: Sir Henry Royce, first of B.E.A.'s two Dart-engined Dakota freighters.

Sturdy and reliable, Vikings have been B.E.A.'s mainstay since September 1946.

Above: One of the greatest air liners ever flown: a Dakota of Aer Lingus at Dublin Airport.
Below: Four engines, three fins, 22 seats—a Marathon in the colours of West African Airways.   [*The Aeroplane.*

32

Registration	Type	Owner or Operator	Where and when seen
G-AKRR	D.H.89A Dragon Rapide	Short Bros. & Harland	
G-AKRS	D.H.89A Dragon Rapide	Air Enterprises	
G-AKRT	M.14A Hawk Trainer 3	Swansea & Dist. Flying School	
G-AKRU	M.14A Hawk Trainer 3	Short Bros. & Harland	
G-AKRV	M.14A Hawk Trainer 3	E. Day	
G-AKRW	M.14A Hawk Trainer 3	Short Bros. & Harland	
G-AKSC	D.H.89A Dragon Rapide	Demolition & Construction Co.	
G-AKSD	D.H.89A Dragon Rapide	Windmill Theatre Transport Co.	
G-AKSE	D.H.89A Dragon Rapide	Manx Air Charters	
G-AKSG	D.H.89A Dragon Rapide	R. L. Whyham	
G-AKSK	D.H.104 Dove 1	Olley Air Service	
G-AKSL	D.H.89A Dragon Rapide	Goodhew Aviation Co.	
G-AKSV	D.H.104 Dove 1	Vickers-Armstrongs	
G-AKSW	D.H.104 Dove 2	Enfield Rolling Mills	
G-AKSY	Auster 5	H. Wigley	
G-AKSZ	Auster 5	A. Robinson	
G-AKTF	Auster 5	Lancashire Aircraft Corpn.	
G-AKTU	Type 634 Viking 1B	Airwork	
G-AKTV	Type 634 Viking 1B	Airwork	
G-AKTW	Westland Sikorsky S.51A	Westland Aircraft	
G-AKTZ	D.H.89A Dragon Rapide	Birkett Air Service	
G-AKUA	M.14A Hawk Trainer 3	Fairey Aviation Co.	
G-AKUB	D.H.89A Dragon Rapide	J. H. Watts (Cambrian Air Enterprises) *Glamorgan*	
G-AKUC	D.H.89A Dragon Rapide	J. H. Watts (Cambrian Air Enterprises) *Monmouth*	
G-AKUV	C.H.3 Srs. 2 Super Ace	J. Chapman (Jnr.)	
G-AKUW	C.H.3 Srs. 2 Super Ace	F. G. Fox	
G-AKUX	C.H.3 Srs. 2 Super Ace	Enterprise Aviation Services (London)	
G-AKVA	C.H.3 Srs. 2 Super Ace	W. A. Eley	
G-AKVB	C.H.3 Srs. 2 Super Ace	C. E. Harper Aircraft Co.	
G-AKVD	C.H.3 Srs. 2 Super Ace	Autocars (Worcester)	
G-AKVH	Chrislea C.H.3	C. E. Harper Aircraft Co.	
G-AKVI	Chrislea C.H.3	C. E. Harper Aircraft Co.	
G-AKVJ	Chrislea C.H.3	C. E. Harper Aircraft Co.	
G-AKVK	Chrislea C.H.3	C. E. Harper Aircraft Co.	
G-AKVL	Chrislea C.H.3	C. E. Harper Aircraft Co.	
G-AKVM	Chrislea C.H.3	C. E. Harper Aircraft Co.	
G-AKVN	Chrislea C.H.3	C. E. Harper Aircraft Co.	
G-AKVO	C.H.3 Srs. 4 Skyjeep	C. E. Harper Aircraft Co.	
G-AKVP	C.H.3 Srs. 4 Skyjeep	C. E. Harper Aircraft Co.	
G-AKVS	C.H.3 Srs. 4 Skyjeep	C. E. Harper Aircraft Co.	
G-AKVU	D.H.89A Dragon Rapide	Goodhew Aviation	
G-AKVV	P.28B Proctor 1	D. Goldstein (Staravia)	
G-AKVW	Type 652A Anson 1	Gulf Aviation Co.	
G-AKVZ	M.38 Messenger 4A	Thomas Ratcliffe & Co.	
G-AKWB	P.34A Proctor 3	W. A. Rollason. Ltd.	
G-AKWD	P.28B Proctor 1	A. M. Lowe	
G-AKWE	P.34A Proctor 3	C. M. Chown	
G-AKWF	P.34A Proctor 3	R. K. Dundas Ltd.	
G-AKWJ	P.34A Proctor 3	A. L. McLeod	
G-AKWK	Auster 5	Furzehill Laboratories	
G-AKWL	P.31C Proctor 4	Southend-on-Sea Borough Council	
G-AKWM	P.34A Proctor 3	J. B. Treacy	
G-AKWN	P.34A Proctor 3I	D. Goldstein (Staravia)	

Registration	Type	Owner or Operator	Where and when seen
G-AKWO	P.34A Proctor 3	Lord Malcolm A. Douglas-Hamilton	
G-AKWP	P.34A Proctor 3	Aikman Airways	
G-AKWR	P.34A Proctor 3	Aikman Airways	
G-AKWS	Auster 5	C. J. Greenough	
G-AKWV	P.34A Proctor 3	J. P. Crowther	
G-AKWY	D.H.82A Tiger Moth	Isle of Wight Flying Club	
G-AKXC	D.H.82A Tiger Moth	B. J. Doyle	
G-AKXD	D.H.82A Tiger Moth	R. H. Braime (Yorkshire Aeroplane Club)	
G-AKXG	D.H.82A Tiger Moth	Spray-and-Win	
G-AKXJ	P.34A Proctor 3	H. C. Kennard	
G-AKXK	P.34A Proctor 3	Autocars (Worcester)	
G-AKXO	D.H.82A Tiger Moth	Midland Aero Club	
G-AKXP	Auster 5	Air Service Training	
G-AKXR	Auster 5	Air Service Training	
G-AKXS	D.H.82A Tiger Moth	Air Service Training	
G-AKXZ	P.34A Proctor 3	P. W. Bayliss	
G-AKYA	P.44 Proctor 5	T. Clay	
G-AKYC	P.44 Proctor 5	Wing Cmdr. W. M. Bisdee	
G-AKYD	P.44 Proctor 5	Gloster Aircraft Co.	
G-AKYG	P.28B Proctor I	R. L. Whyham	
G-AKYJ	P.31C Proctor 4	Lancashire Aircraft Corpn.	
G-AKYK	P.31C Proctor 4	Lancashire Aircraft Corpn.	
G-AKYR	D.H.82A Tiger Moth	Cardiff Aeroplane Club	
G-AKYS	D.H.104 Dove 2	David Brown & Sons (Huddersfield)	
G-AKYU	Auster 5	Southern Flying Schools	
G-AKZB	D.H.89A Rapide (Islander)	B.E.A. *Lord Baden-Powell*	
G-AKZC	M.38 Messenger 4A	C. F. Westley	
G-AKZE	P.34A Proctor 3	R. L. Whyham	
G-AKZG	P.34A Proctor 3	P. R. Jefferies	
G-AKZH	D.H89A Dragon Rapide	Kenning Aviation	
G-AKZK	D.H.82A Tiger Moth	Air Service Training	
G-AKZL	D.H.82A Tiger Moth	Air Service Training	
G-AKZM	D.H.82A Tiger Moth	Air Service Training	
G-AKZN	P.34A Proctor 3	Air Service Training	
G-AKZO	D.H.89A Dragon Rapide	J. Nesbit-Evans & Co.	
G-AKZP	D.H.89A Dragon Rapide	E. Holden	
G-AKZR	P.34A Proctor 3	Hyland Ltd.	
G-AKZS	P.34A Proctor 3	Hyland Ltd.	
G-AKZT	D.H.89A Dragon Rapide	R. L. Whyham	
G-AKZU	M.38 Messenger 4A	R. H. Crofts	
G-AKZW	D.H.89A Dragon Rapide	Morton Air Services	
G-AKZX	M.38 Messenger 4A	N. M. Browning	
G-AKZZ	D.H.82A Tiger Moth	T. H. Marshall	
G-ALAB	J/IB Aiglet	Aerial Spraying Contractors	
G-ALAD	D.H.82A Tiger Moth	Wiltshire School of Flying	
G-ALAE	M.38 Messenger 4A	A. R. Adair	
G-ALAF	M.38 Messenger 4A	R. P. Sayer	
G-ALAG	M.38 Messenger 4A	J. C. Rice	
G-ALAH	M.38 Messenger 4A	E. P. Jenks Ltd.	
G-ALAI	M.38 Messenger 4A	L. W. Hamp & ptnrs.	
G-ALAJ	M.38 Messenger 4A	L. W. Farrer	
G-ALAK	L.749–79 Constellation	B.O.A.C. *Brentford*	
G-ALAL	L.749–79 Constellation	B.O.A.C. *Banbury*	
G-ALAM	L.749–79 Constellation	B.O.A.C. *Belfast*	
G-ALAN	L.749–79 Constellation	B.O.A.C. *Beaufort*	
G-ALAO	L.749–79 Constellation	B.O.A.C. *Braemar*	
G-ALAP	M.38 Messenger 4A	Porter Spiers (Leicester)	

Registration	Type	Owner or Operator	Where and when seen
G-ALAR	M.38 Messenger 4A	H. P. Jennings	
G-ALAT	D.H.89A Dragon Rapide	J. H. Watts (Cambrian Air Enterprises) *Anglesey*	
G-ALAV	M.38 Messenger 4A	M. B. Neaum	
G-ALAW	M.38 Messenger 4A	Skegness Steam Laundry Co.	
G-ALAX	D.H.89A Dragon Rapide	Saunders-Roe	
G-ALBA	D.H.89A Dragon Rapide	Skegness Airport	
G-ALBB	D.H.89A Dragon Rapide	E. A. Taylor	
G-ALBC	D.H.89A Dragon Rapide	M. H. D. McAlpine	
G-ALBD	D.H.82A Tiger Moth	College of Aeronautics	
G-ALBE	M.38 Messenger 4A	E. W. Westbrook	
G-ALBF	D.H.104 Dove 1	Iraq Petroleum Transport Co.	
G-ALBH	D.H.89A Dragon Rapide	Scottish Aviation	
G-ALBI	D.H.89A Dragon Rapide	Scottish Aviation	
G-ALBJ	Auster 5	R. H. Elkington	
G-ALBK	Auster 5	V. G. Manton	
G-ALBM	D.H.104 Dove 5B	de Havilland Aircraft Co.	
G-ALBN	Bristol Type 173	M.o.S.	
G-ALBO	Type 175 Britannia	M.o.S.	
G-ALBP	M.38 Messenger 4A	J. P. Gunner	
G-ALBS	H.P.70 Halifax 8	Lancashire Aircraft Corpn.	
G-ALBT	H.P.70 Halifax 8	Lancashire Aircraft Corpn.	
G-ALBW	Auster 5	Photoflight	
G-ALCC	Dakota 3 (Pionair)	B.E.A. *Harry Hawker*	
G-ALCK	P.34A Proctor 3	Lancashire Aircraft Corpn.	
G-ALCL	P.34A Proctor 3	W. Jamison	
G-ALCM	P.50 Prince 1	Percival Aircraft	
G-ALCN	P.34A Proctor 3	R. Watson	
G-ALCS	M.65 Gemini 3A	J. M. Houlder	
G-ALCT	Auster 5	Lancashire Aircraft Corpn.	
G-ALCU	D.H.104 Dove 2	E. P. Jenks Ltd.	
G-ALDA	H.P.81 Hermes 4	B.O.A.C. *Hecuba*	
G-ALDB	H.P.81 Hermes 4	B.O.A.C. *Hebe*	
G-ALDC	H.P.81 Hermes 4	B.O.A.C. *Hermione*	
G-ALDD	H.P.81 Hermes 4	B.O.A.C. *Horatius*	
G-ALDE	H.P.81 Hermes 4	B.O.A.C. *Hanno*	
G-ALDF	H.P.81 Hermes 4	B.O.A.C. *Hadrian*	
G-ALDG	H.P.81 Hermes 4	B.O.A.C. *Horsa*	
G-ALDH	H.P.81 Hermes 4	B.O.A.C. *Heracles*	
G-ALDI	H.P.81 Hermes 4	B.O.A.C. *Hannibal*	
G-ALDJ	H.P.81 Hermes 4	B.O.A.C. *Hengist*	
G-ALDK	H.P.81 Hermes 4	B.O.A.C. *Helena*	
G-ALDL	H.P.81 Hermes 4	B.O.A.C. *Hector*	
G-ALDM	H.P.81 Hermes 4	B.O.A.C. *Hero*	
G-ALDN	H.P.81 Hermes 4	B.O.A.C. *Horus*	
G-ALDO	H.P.81 Hermes 4	B.O.A.C. *Heron*	
G-ALDP	H.P.81 Hermes 4	B.O.A.C. *Homer*	
G-ALDR	H.P.81 Hermes 4	B.O.A.C. *Herodotus*	
G-ALDS	H.P.81 Hermes 4	B.O.A.C. *Hesperides*	
G-ALDT	H.P.81 Hermes 4	B.O.A.C. *Hestia*	
G-ALDU	H.P.81 Hermes 4	B.O.A.C. *Halcyone*	
G-ALDV	H.P.81 Hermes 4	B.O.A.C. *Hera*	
G-ALDW	H.P.81 Hermes 4	B.O.A.C. *Helios*	
G-ALDX	H.P.81 Hermes 4	B.O.A.C. *Hyperion*	
G-ALDY	H.P.81 Hermes 4	B.O.A.C. *Honor*	
G-ALEJ	D.H.89A Dragon Rapide	Lancashire Aircraft Corpn.	
G-ALEO	P.31C Proctor 4	Birkett Air Service	
G-ALER	P.34A Proctor 3	R. C. Preston	
G-ALES	P.34A Proctor 3	A. Bilbe-Robinson	
G-ALEU	H.P.82 Hermes 5	M.o.S.	

Registration	Type	Owner or Operator	Where and when seen
G—ALEV	H.P.82 Hermes 5	M.o.S.	
G—ALFA	Auster 5	A. Harrison	
G—ALFD	Type 652A Anson I	Transair	
G—ALFE	M.14A Hawk Trainer 3	Redhill Flying Club	
G—ALFF	P.34A Proctor 3	G. Cribb	
G—ALFG	D.H.82A Tiger Moth	I. H. L. Grant & ptnr. (R.E. Flying Club)	
G—ALFP	Type 652A Anson I	Finglands Airways	
G—ALFR	A.S.57 Ambassador Srs. 2	M.o.S. *Golden Hind*	
G—ALFT	D.H.104 Dove 2	M.C.A.	
G—ALFU	D.H.104 Dove 2	M.C.A.	
G—ALFX	P.34A Proctor 3	Autocars (Worcester)	
G—ALFY	P.34A Proctor 3	Murray Chown Aviation	
G—ALGA	Kirby Kitten	Airways Aero Associations	
G—ALGB	D.H.89A Dragon Rapide	R. H. Braime (Yorkshire Aeroplane Club)	
G—ALGC	D.H.89A Dragon Rapide	Melba Airways	
G—ALGE	D.H.89A Dragon Rapide	Melba Airways	
G—ALGH	Piper J–3C–65 Cub	H. Tinsley	
G—ALGI	D.H.89A Dragon Rapide	W. Westoby	
G—ALGJ	M.14A Hawk Trainer 3	W. L. Foster	
G—ALGM	D.H.89A Dragon Rapide	K. J. Nalson	
G—ALGN	D.H.89A Dragon Rapide	Aerocontacts	
G—ALGP	P.34A Proctor 3	K. J. Nalson	
G—ALGS	P.34A Proctor 3	G. P. Reece	
G—ALGT	Type 379 Spitfire 14	Rolls-Royce	
G—ALGU	D.H.98 Mosquito 19	Flight Refuelling	
G—ALGW	Auster 6	K. J. Nalson	
G—ALGX	D.H.82A Tiger Moth	H. B. Showell	
G—ALGY	P.34A Proctor 3	J. W. E. Newby	
G—ALHC	Canadair C–4 (Argonaut)	B.O.A.C. *Ariadne*	
G—ALHD	Canadair C–4 (Argonaut)	B.O.A.C. *Ajax*	
G—ALHE	Canadair C–4 (Argonaut)	B.O.A.C. *Argo*	
G—ALHF	Canadair C–4 (Argonaut)	B.O.A.C. *Atlas*	
G—ALHG	Canadair C–4 (Argonaut)	B.O.A.C. *Aurora*	
G—ALHH	Canadair C–4 (Argonaut)	B.O.A.C. *Attica*	
G—ALHI	Canadair C–4 (Argonaut)	B.O.A.C. *Antares*	
G—ALHJ	Canadair C–4 (Argonaut)	B.O.A.C. *Arcturus*	
G—ALHK	Canadair C–4 (Argonaut)	B.O.A.C. *Atalanta*	
G—ALHL	Canadair C–4 (Argonaut)	B.O.A.C. *Altair*	
G—ALHM	Canadair C–4 (Argonaut)	B.O.A.C. *Antaeus*	
G—ALHN	Canadair C–4 (Argonaut)	B.O.A.C. *Argosy*	
G—ALHO	Canadair C–4 (Argonaut)	B.O.A.C. *Amazon*	
G—ALHP	Canadair C–4 (Argonaut)	B.O.A.C. *Aethra*	
G—ALHR	Canadair C–4 (Argonaut)	B.O.A.C. *Antiope*	

Registration	Type	Owner or Operator	Where and when seen
G-ALHS	Canadair C-4 (Argonaut)	B.O.A.C. *Astra*	
G-ALHT	Canadair C-4 (Argonaut)	B.O.A.C. *Athena*	
G-ALHU	Canadair C-4 (Argonaut	B.O.A.C. *Artemis*	
G-ALHV	Canadair C-4 (Argonaut)	B.O.A.C. *Adonis*	
G-ALHW	Canadair C-4 (Argonaut)	B.O.A.C. *Aeolus*	
G-ALHX	Canadair C-4 (Argonaut)	B.O.A.C. *Astraea*	
G-ALHY	Canadair C-4 (Argonaut)	B.O.A.C. *Arion*	
G-ALIF	Type 652A Anson 11	R. L. Whyham	
G-ALIH	Type 652A Anson 11	J. A. Wilson	
G-ALIK	Westland Sikorsky S.51 Srs. 1A	Westland Aircraft	
G-ALIM	M.14A Hawk Trainer 3	Short Bros. & Harland	
G-ALIO	M.14A Hawk Trainer 3	L. G. S. Thomas & ptnr. (R.E. Flying Club)	
G-ALIS	P.34A Proctor 3	Mrs. D. E. Bartlam	
G-ALIT	P.34A Proctor 3	B. C. Barton & Son Ltd.	
G-ALIV	D.H.82A Tiger Moth	Wolverhampton Aviation	
G-ALIX	D.H.82A Tiger Moth	London Aero Club	
G-ALJB	Auster 5	A. E. Morris	
G-ALJF	P.34A Proctor 3	Darlington & Dist. Aero Club	
G-ALJH	P.34A Proctor 3	J. A. Longmoor (Vendair)	
G-ALJJ	Beechcraft C-18S	Stewart Smith & Co.	
G-ALLI	Dakota 3 (Pionair)	B.E.A. *Sir Samuel Instone*	
G-ALMA	Piper J-3C-65 Cub	E. N. Haywood	
G-ALMR	D.H.104 Dove 1B	English Electric Co.	
G-ALMS	P.34A Proctor 3	K. C. Millican	
G-ALMU	M.65 Gemini 3A	Fairway Engineering Co., Ltd.	
G-ALMV	—	—	
G-ALNA	D.H.82A Tiger Moth	Bembridge and Sandown Aero Club	
G-ALND	D.H.82A Tiger Moth	Air Service Training	
G-ALNS	D.H.89A Dragon Rapide	S. G. Newport	
G-ALNT	D.H.89A Dragon Rapide	Hampshire School of Flying	
G-ALNV	Auster 5	Tattersalls Garages	
G-ALNW	Auster 5	R. A. Short & ptnr.	
G-ALNX	M.14A Hawk Trainer 3	R. A. Short & ptnr.	
G-ALNY	M.14A Hawk Trainer 3	R. A. Short & ptnr.	
G-ALNZ	M.14A Hawk Trainer 3	R. A. Short & ptnr.	
G-ALOA	M.14A Hawk Trainer 3	R. A. Short & ptnr.	
G-ALOB	M.14A Hawk Trainer 3	R. A. Short & ptnr.	
G-ALOE	M.14A Hawk Trainer 3	R. A. Short & ptnr.	
G-ALOF	M.14A Hawk Trainer 3	R. A. Short & ptnr.	
G-ALOG	M.14A Hawk Trainer 3	Wright Aviation	
G-ALOK	P.34A Proctor 3	Miss B. John	
G-ALOL	P.34A Proctor 3	Thomas Sol Ltd.	
G-ALOV	D.H.89A Dragon Rapide	Short Bros. & Harland	
G-ALOW	D.H. C.2 Beaver	de Havilland Aircraft Co.	
G-ALOX	D.H.82A Tiger Moth	Airways Aero Associations	
G-ALPF	Type 694 Lincoln 2	Fairflight	
G-ALPK	D.H.89A Dragon Rapide	Lancashire Aircraft Corpn.	
G-ALPN	Dakota 3 (Pionair)	B.E.A. *Sir Godfrey Paine*	
G-ALRW	D.H.89A Dragon Rapide	J. H. Watts (Cambrian Air Enterprises) *Merionydd*	
G-ALRX	Type 175 Britannia	Bristol Aeroplane Co.	
G-ALRY	P.54 Prince 1	Hunting Aerosurveys	
G-ALSA	Type 377 Stratocruiser	B.O.A.C. *Cathay*	

Registration	Type	Owner or Operator	Where and when seen
G-ALSB	Type 377 Stratocruiser	B.O.A.C. *Champion*	
G-ALSC	Type 377 Stratocruiser	B.O.A.C. *Centaurus*	
G-ALSD	Type 377 Stratocruiser	B.O.A.C. *Cassiopeia*	
G-ALSH	D.H.82A Tiger Moth	Wiltshire School of Flying	
G-ALSJ	Type 170 Freighter 31	Bristol Aeroplane Co.	
G-ALSM	P.34A Proctor 3	L. W. Watkins & ptnr.	
G-ALSP	Bristol 171 Mk.3	Bristol Aeroplane Co.	
G-ALSR	Bristol 171 Mk.3	Bristol Aeroplane Co. (B.E.A.)	
G-ALSS	—	—	
G-ALST	—	—	
G-ALSU	—	—	
G-ALSV	Bristol 171 Mk. 3	Bristol Aeroplane Co.	
G-ALSW	Bristol 171 Mk. 3	Bristol Aeroplane Co.	
G-ALSX	Bristol 171 Mk. 3	Bristol Aeroplane Co.	
G-ALSY	Bristol 171 Mk. 3	Bristol Aeroplane Co.	
G-ALSZ	Bristol 171 Mk. 3	Bristol Aeroplane Co.	
G-ALTA	Bristol 171 Mk. 3	Bristol Aeroplane Co.	
G-ALTB	Bristol 171 Mk. 3	Bristol Aeroplane Co.	
G-ALTC	Bristol 171 Mk. 3	Bristol Aeroplane Co.	
G-ALTD	Bristol 171 Mk. 3	Bristol Aeroplane Co.	
G-ALTE	Bristol 171 Mk. 3	Bristol Aeroplane Co.	
G-ALTM	D.H.104 Dove 2	B.O.A.C.	
G-ALTP	A.S.40 Oxford 1	Air Service Training	
G-ALTR	A.S.40 Oxford 1	Air Service Training	
G-ALTT	Dakota 3 Freighter	B.E.A. *Harold Burchall*	
G-ALTW	D.H.82A Tiger Moth	Marshall's Flying School	
G-ALTZ	A.S.65 Consul	B.O.A.C.	
G-ALUA	Zaunkoenig	Ulair	
G-ALUB	M.60 Marathon 1	M.o.S. *Rob Roy*	
G-ALUC	D.H.82A Tiger Moth	Coventry (Civil) Aviation	
G-ALUE	J/1 Autocrat	G. Morgan-Harris	
G-ALUG	M.65 Gemini 1A	J. P. G. Daly	
G-ALUI	P.34A Proctor 3	Darlington & Dist. Aero Club	
G-ALUJ	P.34A Proctor 3	Darlington & Dist. Aero Club	
G-ALUK	P.34A Proctor 3	Darlington & Dist. Aero Club	
G-ALUM	Type 652A Anson 1	Transair	
G-ALUR	Type 652A Anson 1	Crewsair	
G-ALUX	M.14A Hawk Trainer	Universal Flying Services	
G-ALUY	P.34A Proctor 3	D. Goldstein (Staravia)	
G-ALUZ	—		
G-ALVD	D.H.104 Dove 2	Dunlop Rubber Co.	
G-ALVE	P.34A Proctor 3	D. Goldstein (Staravia)	
G-ALVF	D.H.104 Dove 1	College of Aeronautics	
G-ALVG	D.H.106 Comet Srs. 1	M.o.S.	
G-ALVP	D.H.82A Tiger Moth	Midland Aero Club	
G-ALVR	Piper J–3C–65 Cub	G. Whyte	
G-ALVS	D.H.104 Dove 2	M.C.A.	
G-ALVU	D.H.89A Dragon Rapide	G. C. S. Whyham	
G-ALVV	Auster 4	G. C. S. Whyham	
G-ALVW	M.60 Marathon 1	M.o.S.	
G-ALVX	M.60 Marathon 1	M.o.S.	
G-ALVY	M.60 Marathon 1	M.o.S.	
G-ALWB	D.H. C.1. Chipmunk 10	de Havilland Aircraft Co.	
G-ALWC	Dakota 4	Fairey Aviation Co.	
G-ALWE	Type 701 Viscount	B.E.A. *Discovery*	
G-ALWF	Type 701 Viscount	B.E.A. *Sir John Franklin*	
G-ALWI	D.H.89A Dragon Rapide	Short Bros. & Harland	
G-ALWJ	D.H.89A Dragon Rapide	Short Bros. & Harland	
G-ALWK	D.H.89A Dragon Rapide	H. C. Kennard	
G-ALWL	D.H.89A Dragon Rapide	Southern Aerowork	
G-ALWN	D.H.89A Dragon Rapide	Southern Aerowork	

Registration	Type	Owner or Operator	Where and when seen
G-ALWT	D.H.82A Tiger Moth	Air Service Training	
G-ALWU	D.H.82A Tiger Moth	Air Service Training	
G-ALWW	D.H.82A Tiger Moth	Air Service Training	
G-ALWX	Type 652A Anson 1	Transair	
G-ALWY	D.H.89A Dragon Rapide	Air Enterprises *The Ventnor Flyer*	
G-ALXA	D.H.89A Dragon Rapide	W. S. Shackleton Ltd.	
G-ALXB	Type 652A Anson 1	Transair	
G-ALXC	Type 652A Anson 1	Transair	
G-ALXF	Type 652A Anson 1	Mrs. D. Whyham	
G-ALXG	Type 652A Anson 1	Mrs. D. Whyham	
G-ALXH	Type 652A Anson 1	Mrs. D. Whyham	
G-ALXI	D.H.89A Dragon Rapide	W. Stevens	
G-ALXK	Dakota 3 (Pionair)	B.E.A. *Rex Pierson*	
G-ALXL	Dakota 3 (Pionair)	B.E.A. *Charles Rolls*	
G-ALXM	Dakota 3 (Pionair)	B.E.A. *William Rhodes-Moorhouse*	
G-ALXN	Dart-Dakota	B.E.A. *Sir Henry Royce*	
G-ALXP	Firth Helicopter	Firth Helicopters	
G-ALXR	M.60 Marathon 1	M.o.S.	
G-ALXZ	Auster 5	S. J. Cooper	
G-ALYA	H.S.1 Herald	Hants. & Sussex Aviation	
G-ALYB	Auster 5	L. R. Vandome	
G-ALYD	Auster 4	D. G. S. Cotter	
G-ALYF	Dakota 3 (Pionair)	B.E.A. *Pionair*	
G-ALYG	Auster 5	W. Sturrock	
G-ALYH	Auster 5	I. Kendall	
G-ALYO	D.H.104 Dove 4	Secretary of State for Air	
G-ALYP	D.H.106 Comet Srs. 1	B.O.A.C.	
G-ALYR	D.H.106 Comet Srs. 1	B.O.A.C.	
G-ALYS	D.H.106 Comet Srs. 1	B.O.A.C.	
G-ALYT	D.H.106 Comet Srs. 2	M.o.S.	
G-ALYU	D.H.106 Comet Srs. 1	B.O.A.C.	
G-ALYV	D.H.106 Comet Srs. 1	B.O.A.C.	
G-ALYW	D.H.106 Comet Srs. 1	B.O.A.C.	
G-ALYX	D.H.106 Comet Srs. 1	B.O.A.C.	
G-ALYY	D.H.106 Comet Srs. 1	B.O.A.C.	
G-ALYZ	D.H.106 Comet Srs. 1	B.O.A.C.	
G-ALZA	—	—	
G-ALZB	—	—	
G-ALZC	—	—	
G-ALZD	—	—	
G-ALZE	Britten Norman BN-1F	F. R. J. Britten & ptnr.	
G-ALZF	D.H.89A Dragon Rapide	—	
G-ALZG	M.65 Gemini 1A	P. Blamire	
G-ALZH	D.H 89A Dragon Rapide	Aerocontacts	
G-ALZJ	D.H.89A Dragon Rapide	J. H. Watts (Cambrian Air Enterprises) *Caernarvon*	
G-ALZK	D.H.106 Comet Srs. 1	M.o.S.	
G-ALZL	D.H.114 Heron Srs. 1	de Havilland Aircraft Co.	
G-ALZM	Auster 5	T. H. Marshall	
G-ALZN	A.S.57 Ambassador Srs. 2 (Elizabethan)	B.E.A. *Elizabethan*	
G-ALZO	A.S.57 Ambassador (Elizabethan)	B.E.A. *Christopher Marlowe*	
G-ALZP	A.S.57 Ambassador Srs. 2 (Elizabethan)	B.E.A. *Sir Richard Grenville*	
G-ALZR	A.S.57 Ambassador Srs. 2 (Elizabethan)	B.E.A. *Sir Walter Raleigh*	
G-ALZS	A.S.57 Ambassador Srs. 2 (Elizabethan)	B.E.A. *William Shakespeare*	

345

Registration	Type	Owner or Operator	Where and when seen
G-ALZT	A.S.57 Ambassador Srs. 2. (Elizabethan	B.E.A. *Sir John Hawkins*	
G-ALZU	A.S.57 Ambassador (Elizabethan)	B.E.A. *Lord Burghley*	
G-ALZV	A.S.57 Ambassador (Elizabethan)	B.E.A. *Earl of Leicester*	
G-ALZW	A.S.57 Ambassador (Elizabethan)	B.E.A. *Sir Francis Walsingham*	
G-ALZX	A.S.57 Ambassador (Elizabethan)	B.E.A. *Sir John Norris*	
G-ALZY	A.S.57 Ambassador (Elizabethan)	B.E.A. *Sir Philip Sidney*	
G-ALZZ	A.S.57 Ambassador (Elizabethan)	B.E.A. *Edmund Spenser*	
G-AMAA	A.S.57 Ambassador (Elizabethan)	B.E.A. *Sir Francis Knollys*	
G-AMAB	A.S.57 Ambassador (Elizabethan)	B.E.A. *Sir Francis Bacon*	
G-AMAC	A.S.57 Ambassador (Elizabethan)	B.E.A. *Sir Robert Cecil*	
G-AMAD	A.S.57 Ambassador (Elizabethan)	B.E.A. *Sir Francis Drake*	
G-AMAE	A.S.57 Ambassador (Elizabethan)	B.E.A. *Earl of Essex*	
G-AMAF	A.S.57 Ambassador (Elizabethan)	B.E.A. *Lord Howard of Effingham*	
G-AMAG	A.S.57 Ambassador (Elizabethan)	B.E.A. *Sir Thomas Gresham*	
G-AMAH	A.S.57 Ambassador (Elizabethan)	B.E.A. *Sir Christopher Hatton*	
G-AMAI	D.H.89A Dragon Rapide	A. G. Sheppard	
G-AMAJ	D.H.82A Tiger Moth	M. J. Spence	
G-AMAM	D.H.89A Dragon Rapide	Martin Baker Aircraft	
G-AMAN	P.28B Proctor I	Hants. & Sussex Aviation	
G-AMAO	Auster 5	R. A. Short	
G-AMAP	Auster 5	J. Green	
G-AMAR	D.H.82A Tiger Moth	Central Aeronautical Bureau	
G-AMAU	Hurricane 2C	Hawker Aircraft	
G-AMAV	Type 700 Viscount	M.o.S.	
G-AMAW	Luton Minor	J. R. Coates	
G-AMAX	M.60 Marathon I	M.o.S.	
G-AMAY	M.60 Marathon I	M.o.S.	
G-AMAZ	F.24W–41a Argus	Gulf Aviation Co.	
G-AMBA	F.24W–41a Argus	Gulf Aviation Co.	
G-AMBB	D.H.82A Tiger Moth	Central Aeronautical Bureau	
G-AMBC	Type 652A Anson I	R. L. Whyham (Thorne Aviation)	
G-AMBD	D.H.82A Tiger Moth	Defford Aero Club (Worcestershire)	
G-AMBE	Type 652A Anson I	Transair	
G-AMBH	M.65 Gemini IA	E. G. Hayes	
G-AMBI	D.H.82A Tiger Moth	Wiltshire School of Flying	
G-AMBK	D.H.82A Tiger Moth	Bristol & Wessex Aeroplane Club	
G-AMBL	Youngman-Baynes H.L.	R. T. Youngman	
G-AMBM	M.14A Hawk Trainer 3	All-Power Transformers	
G-AMBN	M.14A Hawk Trainer 3	Universal Flying Services	
G-AMBS	P.34A Proctor 3	F. J. R. Elliott	
G-AMBW	Dakota 4	Airwork	
G-AMCA	Dakota 4	Fairey Aviation Co.	
G-AMCH	A.W.55 Apollo	M.o.S.	
G-AMCM	D.H.82A Tiger Moth	R.A.E. Aero Club	
G-AMCN	D.H.82A Tiger Moth	R. Ward	
G-AMCO	P.34A Proctor 3	R. K. Dundas Ltd.	
G-AMCP	P.44 Proctor 5	Mrs. V. L. Dhome	

40

Top: Big brother to the Dove, the Heron combines simplicity and reliability with good performance.

Centre: This Dove is used by staff of the British Embassy, Washington.

Right: Fast, comfortable and safe even on one engine — the Short Sealand amphibian.

Left: An Oxford trainer of Air Service Training. Basically similar to the Consul transport.

Centre : Popular Prince : ordered by airlines, the Royal Navy and Royal Air Force for worldwide service.

[*The Aeroplane.*

Bottom: The Rapide, still unsurpassed for cheap, safe local services.

42

Registration	Type	Owner or Operator	Where and when seen
G–AMCR	Type 170 Freighter 31	Bristol Aeroplane Co.	
G–AMCT	D.H.89A Dragon Rapide	Short Bros. & Harland	
G–AMCU	A.S.40 Oxford	de Havilland Aircraft Co.	
G–AMCV	A.S.40 Oxford	de Havilland Aircraft Co.	
G–AMCW	A.S.40 Oxford	de Havilland Aircraft Co.	
G–AMCY	A.S.40 Oxford	de Havilland Aircraft Co.	
G–AMCZ	A.S.40 Oxford	de Havilland Aircraft Co.	
G–AMDA	Type 652A Anson 1	Air Navigation & Trading Co.	
G–AMDB	Dart-Dakota	B.E.A. *Claude Johnson*	
G–AMDC	W. 14 Skeeter 5	Cierva Autogiro Co.	
G–AMDD	D.H.104 Dove 2	Shell Refining & Marketing Co.	
G–AMDE	M.65 Gemini 3A	L. S. Dawson	
G–AMDH	M.60 Marathon 1	M.o.S.	
G–AMDJ	M.75 Aries	F. G. Miles Ltd.	
G–AMDN	Hiller 360	Pest Control	
G–AMDO	Hiller 360	Pest Control	
G–AMDZ	Dakota 3 (Pionair)	B.E.A. *Frank Barnwell*	
G–AMED	P.44 Proctor 5	Field Aircraft Services	
G–AMEJ	M.65 Gemini 1A	Balfour (Marine) Engineering Co.	
G–AMEK	M.60 Marathon 1	M.o.S.	
G–AMEL	M.60 Marathon 1	M.o.S.	
G–AMEM	M.60 Marathon 1	M.o.S.	
G–AMEO	M.60 Marathon 1	M.o.S.	
G–AMEP	M.60 Marathon 1	M.o.S.	
G–AMER	M.60 Marathon 1	M.o.S.	
G–AMES	—	—	
G–AMET	M.60 Marathon 1	M.o.S.	
G–AMEU	M.60 Marathon 1	M.o.S.	
G–AMEV	M.60 Marathon 1	M.o.S.	
G–AMEW	M.60 Marathon 1	M.o.S.	
G–AMEY	D.H.82A Tiger Moth	C. G. Wheatley (York Flying Club)	
G–AMEZ	D.H.82A Tiger Moth	C. G. Wheatley (York Flying Club)	
G–AMFL	A.S.40 Oxford	Aerocontacts	
G–AMFN	D.H.82A Tiger Moth	Defford Aero Club (Worcestershire)	
G–AMFO	J/5B Autocar	Sissleys Cycles (Essex)	
G–AMFP	J/5B Autocar	Aviation Traders	
G–AMFR	Auster 5	Warden Aviation Co.	
G–AMFS	Auster 5	Warden Aviation Co.	
G–AMFU	D.H.104 Dove 1	W. F. Martin	
G–AMFV	Dakota 3 (Pionair)	B.E.A. *Richard Howard-Flanders*	
G–AMGC	D.H.82A Tiger Moth	Air Navigation & Trading Co.	
G–AMGD	Dakota 3 (Pionair)	B.E.A. *George Brackley*	
G–AMGE	P.34A Proctor 3	A. J. Whittemore & Co	
G–AMGF	M.65 Gemini 3A	Shell Refining and Marketing Co.	
G–AMGG	Type 635 Viking 1B	B.E.A. *Sir Robert Calder*	
G–AMGH	Type 635 Viking 1B	B.E.A. *Sir John Duckworth*	
G–AMGI	Type 635 Viking 1B	B.E.A. *Sir Henry Harwood*	
G–AMGJ	Type 635 Viking 1B	B.E.A. *Sir John Warren*	
G–AMGK	Type 685 York 1	Eagle Aviation	
G–AMGL	Type 685 York 1	Surrey Flying Services	
G–AMGM	Type 685 York 1	Surrey Flying Services	
G–AMGN	M.60 Marathon 1	M.o.S.	
G–AMGO	M.60 Marathon 1	M.o.S.	
G–AMGP	M.60 Marathon 1	M.o.S.	
G–AMGR	M.60 Marathon 1	M.o.S.	
G–AMGS	M.60 Marathon 1	M.o.S.	
G–AMGT	M.60 Marathon 1	M.o.S.	
G–AMGU	M.60 Marathon 1	M.o.S.	
G–AMGV	M.60 Marathon 1	M.o.S.	

Registration	Type	Owner or Operator	Where and when seen
G-AMGW	M.60 Marathon 1A (Clansman)	M.o.S. *Clansman*	
G-AMGX	M.60 Marathon 1A (Clansman)	M.o.S. *Macleod*	
G-AMGY	Hiller 360	Pest Control	
G-AMHC	Westland-Sikorsky S.51 Srs. 1B	Westland Aircraft	
G-AMHD	Westland-Sikorsky S.51 Srs. 1B	Westland Aircraft	
G-AMHE	A.S.40 Oxford	Aerocontacts	
G-AMHF	D.H.82A Tiger Moth	Southern Flying Schools	
G-AMHG	D.H.82A Tiger Moth	Southern Flying Schools	
G-AMHI	D.H.82A Tiger Moth	H. A. McCarthy	
G-AMHJ	Dakota 3	Cyprus Airways	
G-AMHK	Sikorsky S.55	Westland Aircraft	
G-AMHM	D.H.104 Dove 2	Trader Navigation Co.	
G-AMHP	D.H.82A Tiger Moth	Wiltshire School of Flying	
G-AMHR	M.60 Marathon 1A (Clansman)	M.o.S. *MacDonald*	
G-AMHS	M.60 Marathon 1A (Clansman)	M.o.S. *MacNeil*	
G-AMHT	M.60 Marathon 1	M.o.S.	
G-AMHU	M.60 Marathon 1	M.o.S.	
G-AMHV	M.60 Marathon 1A (Clansman)	M.o.S. *MacGregor*	
G-AMHW	M.60 Marathon 1A (Clansman)	M.o.S. *MacKenzie*	
G-AMHX	M.60 Marathon 1A (Clansman)	M.o.S. *MacDuff*	
G-AMHY	M.60 Marathon 1A	M.o.S.	
G-AMHZ	M.60 Mraathon 1A	M.o.S.	
G-AMIA	M.60 Marathon 1A	M.o.S.	
G-AMIB	M.60 Marathon 1	M.o.S.	
G-AMIC	M.60 Marathon 1	M.o.S.	
G-AMID	A.S.65 Consul	de Havilland Aircraft Co.	
G-AMIH	J/1B Aiglet	T. W. Hayhow	
G-AMIJ	D.H.82A Tiger Moth	Short Bros. & Harland	
G-AMIK	D.H.82A Tiger Moth	Short Bros. & Harland	
G-AMIL	D.H.82A Tiger Moth	Short Bros. & Harland	
G-AMIM	D.H.82A Tiger Moth	Short Bros. & Harland	
G-AMIN	D.H.82A Tiger Moth	Short Bros. & Harland	
G-AMIO	D.H.82A Tiger Moth	Short Bros. & Harland	
G-AMIP	D.H.82A Tiger Moth	Short Bros. & Harland	
G-AMIR	D.H.82A Tiger Moth	Short Bros. & Harland	
G-AMIS	D.H.82A Tiger Moth	Short Bros. & Harland	
G-AMIT	D.H.82A Tiger Moth	Short Bros. & Harland	
G-AMIU	D.H.82A Tiger Moth	Short Bros. & Harland	
G-AMIV	D.H.82A Tiger Moth	Short Bros. & Harland	
G-AMIW	D.H.82A Tiger Moth	Short Bros. & Harland	
G-AMIX	D.H.82A Tiger Moth	Short Bros. & Harland	
G-AMIY	D.H.82A Tiger Moth	Short Bros. & Harland	
G-AMIZ	D.H.82A Tiger Moth	Short Bros. & Harland	
G-AMJA	D.H.82A Tiger Moth	Short Bros. & Harland	
G-AMJB	D.H.82A Tiger Moth	Short Bros. & Harland	
G-AMJC	D.H.82A Tiger Moth	Short Bros. & Harland	
G-AMJD	D.H.82A Tiger Moth	Short Bros. & Harland	
G-AMJE	J/1B Aiglet	Aerial Spraying Contractors	
G-AMJF	D.H.82A Tiger Moth	A. R. H. Van Baerle	
G-AMJG	D.H.82A Tiger Moth	W. S. Shackleton Ltd.	
G-AMJH	Non-rigid Airship	T.A.C. (Bournemouth)	
G-AMJI	Bristol 173	M.o.S.	
G-AMJJ	D.H.104 Dove 4	Secretary of State for Air	
G-AMJK	D.H.89A Dragon Rapide	Fairey Aviation Co.	
G-AMJL	D.H.82A Tiger Moth	Newcastle-upon-Tyne Aero Club	
G-AMJN	D.H.82A Tiger Moth	Aerocontacts	

44

Registration	Type	Owner or Operator	Where and when seen
G–AMJO	D.H.82A Tiger Moth	Aerocontacts	
G–AMJP	Kitten 3	Dart Aircraft	
G–AMJT	Westland Sikorsky S.55	Westland Aircraft	
G–AMJU	Dakota 3	Scottish Aviation	
G–AMJV	Auster 4	Darlington & Dist. Aero Club	
G–AMJW	Westland-Sikorsky S.51	Westland Aircraft	
G–AMJX	Dakota 3 (Pionair)	B.E.A. *Reginald Mitchell*	
G–AMJY	Dakota 3 (Pionair)	B.E.A. *James McCudden*	
G–AMJZ	D.H.104 Dove 1	Gulf Aviation Co.	
G–AMKE	Dakota 3 (Pionair)	B.E.A. *Frederick Lanchester*	
G–AMKF	J/5F Aiglet Trainer	Auster Aircraft	
G–AMKG	J/5G Autocar	Auster Aircraft	
G–AMKH	D.H.82A Tiger Moth	Wiltshire School of Flying	
G–AMKI	D.H.82A Tiger Moth	W. S. Shackleton Ltd.	
G–AMKJ	D.H.82A Tiger Moth	J. A. Longmoor (Vendair)	
G–AMKK	P.50 Prince 3	Shell Refining & Marketing Co.	
G–AMKL	Auster B.4	Auster Aircraft	
G–AMKT	D.H.104 Dove 1B	B.O.A.C.	
G–AMKU	J/1B Aiglet	Pest Control	
G–AMKV	D.H.82A Tiger Moth	R. H. Haygarth (The Northolt Group)	
G–AMKW	P.54 Prince 3B	M.C.A.	
G–AMKX	P.54 Prince 3B	M.C.A.	
G–AMKY	P.54 Prince 3B	M.C.A.	
G–AMKZ	M.65 Gemini 3A	Wolverhampton Aviation	
G–AMLA	D.H.82A Tiger Moth	W. A. Rollason Ltd.	
G–AMLB	D.H.82A Tiger Moth	Wolverhampton Aviation	
G–AMLC	D.H. C.1 Chipmunk 21	College of Aeronautics	
G–AMLE	D.H.82A Tiger Moth	Hants. & Sussex Aviation	
G–AMLF	D.H.82A Tiger Moth	Wiltshire School of Flying	
G–AMLH	D.H.82A Tiger Moth	Newcastle-upon-Tyne Aero Club	
G–AMLI	J/5B Autocar	W. S. Shackleton, Ltd.	
G–AMLJ	Bristol 170 Mk. 31	Bristol Aeroplane Co.	
G–AMLK	Bristol 170 Mk. 31	Bristol Aeroplane Co.	
G–AMLL	Bristol 170 Mk. 31	Bristol Aeroplane Co.	
G–AMLM	Bristol 170 Mk. 31	Bristol Aeroplane Co.	
G–AMLN	Bristol 170 Mk. 31	Bristol Aeroplane Co.	
G–AMLO	Bristol 170 Mk. 31	Bristol Aeroplane Co.	
G–AMLP	Bristol 170 Mk. 31	Bristol Aeroplane Co.	
G–AMLR	Bristol 170 Mk. 31	Bristol Aeroplane Co.	
G–AMLS	Bristol 170 Mk. 31	Bristol Aeroplane Co.	
G–AMLT	Bristol 170 Mk. 31	Bristol Aeroplane Co.	
G–AMLU	Auster 4	Boardsides Aircraft Servicing	
G–AMLV	D.H.82A Tiger Moth	Halton Aero Club	
G–AMLW	P.50 Prince 3	Shell Refining & Marketing Co.	
G–AMLX	P.50 Prince 3	Shell Refining & Marketing Co.	
G–AMLY	P.50 Prince 3	Shell Refining & Marketing Co.	
G–AMLZ	P.50 Prince 3	Shell Refining & Marketing Co.	
G–AMMA	D.H. C.1 Chipmunk 21	M.C.A.	
G–AMMB	P.50 Prince 2 (Mod.)	Percival Aircraft	
G–AMMC	M.14A Hawk Trainer 3	W. A. Rollason Ltd.	
G–AMME	M.65 Gemini 3A	Ind, Coope and Allsopp	
G–AMMF	D.H.82A Tiger Moth	M. J. Spence	
G–AMMG	D.H.82A Tiger Moth	M. J. Spence	
G–AMMH	D.H.82A Tiger Moth	M. J. Spence	
G–AMMJ	Dakota 4	B.O.A.C.	
G–AMMN	D.H.82A Tiger Moth	Wiltshire School of Flying	
G–AMMO	D.H.82A Tiger Moth	Wiltshire School of Flying	
G–AMMP	D.H.82A Tiger Moth	Wiltshire School of Flying	
G–AMMR	J/1B Aiglet	W. S. Shackleton Ltd.	
G–AMMS	J/5F Aiglet Trainer	Auster Aircraft	
G–AMMU	Auster J/5	R. K. Dundas Ltd.	
G–AMMV	D.H.82A Tiger Moth	M. J. Spence	
G–AMMW	D.H.82A Tiger Moth	M. J. Spence	
G–AMMX	D.H.82A Tiger Moth	M. J. Spence	

Registration	Type	Owner or Operator	Where and when seen
G-AMMY	Hiller 360	Pest Control	
G-AMMZ	J/5B Autocar	Hunting Aerosurveys	
G-AMNA	Avro 19 Srs. 1	Secretary of State for Air	
G-AMNB	J/5B Autocar	Royal Artillery Aero Club	
G-AMNC	J/5B Autocar	Bristol Aeroplane Co.	
G-AMNE	—	—	
G-AMNF	D.H.82A Tiger Moth	Hants. & Sussex Aviation	
G-AMNG	D.H.82A Tiger Moth	Hants. & Sussex Aviation	
G-AMNI	Auster 5	Willis Hole Aviation	
G-AMNJ	Type 635 Viking 1B	B.E.A. *Lord Fisher*	
G-AMNK	Viking 1B	Field Aircraft Services	
G-AMNL	Dakota 4	Hunting Air Transport	
G-AMNM	J/5F Aiglet Trainer	R. K. Dundas	
G-AMNN	D.H.82A Tiger Moth	Aeronautical Educational Trust	
G-AMNO	D.H.82A Tiger Moth	Airtrade	
G-AMNP	D.H.82A Tiger Moth	Hants. & Sussex Aviation	
G-AMNR	Type 635 Viking 1B	B.E.A. *Lord Charles Beresford*	
G-AMNS	Type 635 Viking 1B	B.E.A. *Sir Dudley Pound*	
G-AMNT	—		
G-AMNU	Auster 5	Air Service Training	
G-AMNV	Dakota	B.E.A.	
G-AMNW	Dakota	B.E.A.	
G-AMNX	Type 635 Viking 1B	B.E.A. *Sir George Callaghan*	
G-AMOR	Auster 5	Hants. & Sussex Aviation	
G-AMOS	J.5F Aiglet Tr.	T. W. Hayhow	
G-AMOT	P.50 Prince 3	Hunting Aerosurveys	
G-AMOU	D.H.82A Tiger Moth	Hants. & Sussex Aviation	
G-AMOV	J.5F Aiglet Tr.	D. Martyn	
G-AMOW	W.S.51	Westland Aircraft	
G-AMOX	W.S.51	Westland Aircraft	
G-AMOY	J.5G Autocar	Pest Control	
G-AMOZ	J.5G Autocar	Pest Control	
G-AMPA	J.5G Autocar	Pest Control	
G-AMPB	J.5G Autocar	Pest Control	
G-AMPC	J.5G Autocar	Pest Control	

Foreign Airline Fleet List

(Air liners serving U.K. only)

SHOWING INSIGNIA OF THE AIRLINES CONCERNED

CANADA (CF)

Registration	Type	Operator	Where and when seen
CF–TFA	North Star	Trans-Canada Air Lines	
CF–TFB	North Star	Trans-Canada Air Lines	
CF–TFC	North Star	Trans-Canada Air Lines	
CF–TFD	North Star	Trans-Canada Air Lines	
CF–TFE	North Star	Trans-Canada Air Lines	
CF–TFF	North Star	Trans-Canada Air Lines	
CF–TFG	North Star	Trans-Canada Air Lines	
CF–TFH	North Star	Trans-Canada Air Lines	
CF–TFI	North Star	Trans-Canada Air Lines	
CF–TFJ	North Star	Trans-Canada Air Lines	
CF–TFK	North Star	Trans-Canada Air Lines	
CF–TFL	North Star	Trans-Canada Air Lines	
CF–TFM	North Star	Trans-Canada Air Lines	
CF–TFN	North Star	Trans-Canada Air Lines	
CF–TFO	North Star	Trans-Canada Air Lines	
CF–TFP	North Star	Trans-Canada Air Lines	
CF–TFQ	North Star	Trans-Canada Air Lines	
CF–TFR	North Star	Trans-Canada Air Lines	
CF–TFS	North Star	Trans-Canada Air Lines	
CF–TFT	North Star	Trans-Canada Air Lines	

PORTUGAL (CS)

Registration	Type	Operator	Where and when seen
CS–TSA	Douglas DC–4	Transportes Aereos Portugueses	
CS–TSB	Douglas DC–4	Transportes Aereos Portugueses	
CS–TSD	Douglas DC–4	Transportes Aereos Portugueses	

47

SPAIN (EC)

Registration	Type	Operator	Where and when seen
EC–ACD	Douglas DC–4	Iberia	
EC–ACE	Douglas DC–4	Iberia	
EC–ACF	Douglas DC–4	Iberia	
EC–AEK	Douglas DC–4	Iberia	
EC–AEO	Douglas DC–4	Iberia	
EC–AEP	Douglas DC–4	Iberia	

EIRE (EI)

Registration	Type	Operator	Where and when seen
EI–ACD	Douglas C–47	Aer Lingus St. Patrick	
EI–ACE	Douglas D6–3D	Aer Lingus St. Colmcille	
EI–ACF	Douglas C–47	Aer Lingus St. Kieran	
EI–ACG	Douglas C–47	Aer Lingus St. Malachy	
EI–ACH	Douglas C–47A	Aer Lingus St. Brigid	
EI–ACI	Douglas C–47	Aer Lingus St. Aidan	
EI–ACK	Douglas C–47A	Aer Lingus St. Albert	
EI–ACL	Douglas C–47	Aer Lingus St. Declan	
EI–ACM	Douglas C–47	Aer Lingus St. Fintan	
EI–ACT	Douglas C–47A	Aer Lingus St. Colman	
EI–AFA	Douglas C–47A	Aer Lingus St. Laurence O'Toole	
EI–AFB	Douglas C–47A	Aer Lingus St. Brendan	
EI–AFC	Douglas DC–3F	Aer Lingus St. Enda	

FRANCE (F)

Registration	Type	Operator	Where and when seen
F–BAIF	Douglas DC–3	Air France	
F–BAIH	Douglas DC–3	Air France	
F–BAII	Douglas DC–3	Air France	
F–BATB	Languedoc	Air France	
F–BATE	Languedoc	Air France	
F–BATJ	Languedoc	Air France	
F–BATN	Languedoc	Air France	
F–BATP	Languedoc	Air France	
F–BATQ	Languedoc	Air France	
F–BATR	Languedoc	Air France	
F–BATS	Languedoc	Air France	
F–BATV	Languedoc	Air France	
F–BATX	Languedoc	Air France	
F–BATZ	Languedoc	Air France	
F–BAXH	Douglas DC–3	Air France	

Registration	Type	Operator	Where and when seen
F–BAXI	Douglas DC–3	Air France	
F–BAXL	Douglas DC–3	Air France	
F–BAXP	Douglas DC–3	Air France	
F–BAXR	Douglas DC–3	Air France	
F–BAXS	Douglas DC–3	Air France	
F–BBBA	Douglas DC–3	Air France	
F–BBDA	Douglas DC–4	Air France *Ciel de Bretagne*	
F–BBDD	Douglas DC–4	Air France *Ciel de Bourgogne*	
F–BBDF	Douglas DC–4	Air France *Ciel d'Artois*	
F–BBDG	Douglas DC–4	Air France *Ciel de Champagne*	
F–BBDH	Douglas DC–4	Air France *Ciel de Bearn*	
F–BBDI	Douglas DC–4	Air France *Ciel de Provence*	
F–BBDJ	Douglas DC–4	Air France *Ciel Ille de France*	
F–BBDK	Douglas DC–4	Air France *Ciel de Normandie*	
F–BBDN	Douglas DC–4	Air France *Ciel de Lorraine*	
F–BBDP	Douglas DC–4	Air France	
F–BBDQ	Douglas DC–4	Air France	
F–BBDR	Douglas DC–4	Air France	
F–BCUA	Languedoc	Air France	
F–BCUB	Languedoc	Air France	
F–BCUF	Languedoc	Air France	
F–BCUG	Languedoc	Air France	
F–BCUH	Languedoc	Air France	
F–BCUJ	Languedoc	Air France	
F–BCUK	Languedoc	Air France	
F–BCUL	Languedoc	Air France	
F–BCUN	Languedoc	Air France	
F–BCUO	Languedoc	Air France	
F–BCUQ	Languedoc	Air France	
F–BCUR	Languedoc	Air France	
F–BCUS	Languedoc	Air France	
F–BCYD	Douglas DC–3	Air France	
F–BCYT	Douglas DC–3	Air France	
F–BCYU	Douglas DC–3	Air France	
F–BCYV	Douglas DC–3	Air France	
F–BCYX	Douglas DC–3	Air France	
F–BEFM	Douglas DC–3	Air France	
F–BEFN	Douglas DC–3	Air France	
F–BEIK	Douglas DC–3	Air France	
F–BELC	Douglas DC–4	Air France	
F–BELD	Douglas DC–4	Air France	
F–BELE	Douglas DC–4	Air France	
F–BELF	Douglas DC–4	Air France	
F–BELH	Douglas DC–4	Air France	
F–BELI	Douglas DC–4	Air France	
F–BELJ	Douglas DC–4	Air France	
F–BELK	Douglas DC–4	Air France	
F–BELL	Douglas DC–4	Air France	
F–BELM	Douglas DC–4	Air France	
F–BELN	Douglas DC–4	Air France	
F–BELP	Douglas DC–4	Air France	
F–BELQ	Douglas DC–4	Air France	
F–BELR	Douglas DC–4	Air France	
F–BELS	Douglas DC–4	Air France	
F–BFGM	Douglas DC–3	Air France	

49

SWITZERLAND (HB)

Registration	Type	Operator	Where and when seen
HB–IBA	Douglas DC–6B	Swissair *Zurich*	
HB–IBE	Douglas DC–6B	Swissair *Geneve*	
HB–ILA	Douglas DC–4	Swissair	
HB–ILI	Douglas DC–4	Swissair *Basel*	
HB–IRA	Douglas DC–3	Swissair	
HB–IRB	Douglas DC–3	Swissair	
HB–IRC	Douglas DC–3	Swissair	
HB–IRD	Douglas DC–3	Swissair	
HB–IRE	Douglas DC–3	Swissair	
HB–IRF	Douglas DC–3	Swissair	
HB–IRG	Douglas DC–3	Swissair	
HB–IRH	Douglas DC–3	Swissair	
HB–IRI	Douglas DC–3	Swissair	
HB–IRK	Douglas DC–3	Swissair	
HB–IRL	Douglas DC–3	Swissair	
HB–IRM	Douglas DC–3	Swissair	
HB–IRN	Douglas DC–3	Swissair	
HB–IRO	Douglas DC–3	Swissair	
HB–IRP	Convair-Liner	Swissair	
HB–IRS	Convair-Liner	Swissair	
HB–IRT	Convair-Liner	Swissair	
HB–IRV	Convair-Liner	Swissair	
HB–IRX	Douglas DC–3	Swissair	

ITALY (I)

I–DALT	Douglas DC–4	Alitalia *Citta di Milano*	
I–DALU	Douglas DC–4	Alitalia *Citta di Palermo*	
I–DALV	Douglas DC–4	Alitalia *Citta di Napoli*	
I–DALZ	Douglas DC–4	Alitalia *Citta di Roma*	

NORWAY (LN)

LN–IAD	Douglas DC–4	Scandinavian Airlines System *Hakon*	
LN–IAE	Douglas DC–4	Scandinavian Airlines System *Olav*	

356

Right: The rugged seven-seat Beaver, designed for Canadian "bush flying."

Centre: Made in Scotland. The remarkable Prestwick Pioneer has slow - flying performance to rival the helicopter.

Bottom: The versatile Auster Ambulance / Freighter, smallest of Britain's flying boxcars.

One of the popular Miles family of sporting aircraft, the twin-engined Gemini

Above: Proctor 3, wearing its British air racing colours.   [*The Aeroplane.*
Below: One of the few pre-war Monarchs still in service.   [*Flight.*

Registration	Type	Operator	Where and when seen
LN–IAF	Douglas DC–3	Scandinavian Airlines System *Fridtjof*	
LN–IAK	Douglas DC–3	Scandinavian Airlines System *Knut*	
LN–IAL	Douglas DC–3	Scandinavian Airlines System *Erling*	
LN–IAP	Douglas DC–3	Scandinavian Airlines System *Halvdan*	
LN–IAR	Douglas DC–3	Scandinavian Airlines System *Roald*	
LN–IAS	Douglas DC–3	Scandinavian Airlines System *Steinar*	
LN–IAT	Douglas DC–3	Scandinavian Airlines System *Terje*	
LN–IKG	Douglas DC–3	Scandinavian Airlines System *Guttorm*	
LN–IKH	Douglas DC–3	Scandinavian Airlines System *Hallvard*	
LN–IKI	Douglas DC–3	Scandinavian Airlines System *Einar*	
LN–KLK	Scandia	Scandinavian Airlines System *Nial*	
LN–KLL	Scandia	Scandinavian Airlines System *Sigurd*	
LN–LAG	Douglas DC–6	Scandinavian Airlines System *Sverre*	
LN–LAH	Douglas DC–6	Scandinavian Airlines System *Harald*	

N.B. Scandinavian Airlines System aircraft names are suffixed *Viking* (e.g. LN–LAH is *Harald Viking*).

ARGENTINA (LV)

LV–ADR	Douglas DC–6	Aerolineas Argentinas	
LV–ADS	Douglas DC–6	Aerolineas Argentinas	
LV–ADT	Douglas DC–6	Aerolineas Argentinas	
LV–ADU	Douglas DC–6	Aerolineas Argentinas	
LV–ADV	Douglas DC–6	Aerolineas Argentinas	
LV–ADW	Douglas DC–6	Aerolineas Argentinas	

Now you should get a copy of:

A.B.C. of MILITARY AIRCRAFT

by JOHN W. R. TAYLOR

THE FIRST OF ITS KIND YET PUBLISHED

Illustrated throughout with half-tones and silhouettes **2/6**

53

U.S A. (N)

Registration	Type	Operator	Where and when seen
N1023V	Stratocruiser	Pan American World Airways *Golden Gate*	
N1027V	Stratocruiser	Pan American World Airways *Friendship*	
N1028V	Stratocruiser	Pan American World Airways *Flying Cloud*	
N1029V	Stratocruiser	Pan American World Airways *Golden Eagle*	
N1030V	Stratocruiser	Pan American World Airways *Southern Cross*	
N1031V	Stratocruiser	Pan American World Airways *Mayflower*	
N1032V	Stratocruiser	Pan American World Airways *United States*	
N1033V	Stratocruiser	Pan American World Airways *Seven Seas*	
N1034V	Stratocruiser	Pan American World Airways *Westward Ho*	
N1035V	Stratocruiser	Pan American World Airways *Flying Eagle*	
N1036V	Stratocruiser	Pan American World Airways *Washington*	
N1037V	Stratocruiser	Pan American World Airways *Fleetwing*	
N1038V	Stratocruiser	Pan American World Airways *Constitution*	
N1039V	Stratocruiser	Pan American World Airways *Good Hope*	
N1040V	Stratocruiser	Pan American World Airways *Invincible*	
N1041V	Stratocruiser	Pan American World Airways *Yankee*	
N1042V	Stratocruiser	Pan American World Airways *Morning Star*	
N54705	Douglas DC–3	Pan American World Airways	
N6001C	Constellation 749A	Trans World Airlines *New Jersey*	
N6002C	Constellation 749A	Trans World Airlines *Kansas*	
N6003C	Constellation 749A	Trans World Airlines *Texas*	
N6005C	Constellation 749A	Trans World Airlines *New York*	
N6006C	Constellation 749A	Trans World Airlines *Pennsylvania*	

54

Registration	Type	Operator	Where and when seen
N6007C	Constellation 749A	Trans World Airlines *Ohio*	
N6008C	Constellation 749A	Trans World Airlines *Indiana*	
N6009C	Constellation 749A	Trans World Airlines *Michigan*	
N6010C	Constellation 749A	Trans World Airlines *Illinois*	
N6011C	Constellation 749A	Trans World Airlines *Missouri*	
N6012C	Constellation 749A	Trans World Airlines *Massachusetts*	
N6013C	Constellation 749A	Trans World Airlines *New Mexico*	
N6014C	Constellation 749A	Trans World Airlines *Delaware*	
N6015C	Constellation 749A	Trans World Airlines *Arizona*	
N6016C	Constellation 749A	Trans World Airlines *California*	
N6017C	Constellation 749A	Trans World Airlines *the District of Columbia*	
N6018C	Constellation 749A	Trans World Airlines *Nevada*	
N6019C	Constellation 749A	Trans World Airlines *Minnesota*	
N6020C	Constellation 749A	Trans World Airlines *Kentucky*	
N6021C	Constellation 749A	Trans World Airlines *West Virginia*	
N6022C	Constellation 749A	Trans World Airlines *Virginia*	
N6023C	Constellation 749A	Trans World Airlines *Iowa*	
N6024C	Constellation 749A	Trans World Airlines *Nebraska*	
N6025C	Constellation 749A	Trans World Airlines *Colorado*	
N6026C	Constellation 749A	Trans World Airlines *Connecticut*	
N6518C	Douglas DC–6B	Pan American World Airways *Liberty Bell*	
N88832	Constellation	Pan American World Airways *Flora Temple*	
N88836	Constellation	Pan American World Airways *Yankee Ranger*	
N88837	Constellation	Pan American World Airways *Challenge*	
N88838	Constellation	Pan American World Airways *Donald McKay*	
N88846	Constellation	Pan American World Airways *Great Republic*	
N88847	Constellation	Pan American World Airways *Hotspur*	
N88850	Constellation	Pan American World Airways *Intrepid*	
N88855	Constellation	Pan American World Airways *Undaunted*	
N88857	Constellation	Pan American World Airways *Unity*	
N88859	Constellation	Pan American World Airways *Talisman*	
N88861	Constellation	Pan American World Airways *Winged Arrow*	
N88868	Constellation	Pan American World Airways *Golden Fleece*	
N88944	Douglas DC–4	Pan American World Airways	
N88945	Douglas DC–4	Pan American World Airways	
N88947	Douglas DC–4	Pan American World Airways	
N88948	Douglas DC–4	Pan American World Airways	
N88954	Douglas DC–4	Pan American World Airways *Pacific Trader*	
N88955	Douglas DC–4	Pan American World Airways	
N90806	Douglas DC–6A	Slick Airways	
N90807	Douglas DC–6A	Slick Airways *Miss Judy*	
N90808	Douglas DC–6A	Slick Airways	

361

Registration	Type	Operator	Where and when seen
N90902	Douglas DC–4	Pan American World Airways	
N90905	Douglas DC–4	Pan American World Airways *Berlin*	
N90908	Douglas DC–3	Pan American World Airways	
N90921	Constellation	Pan American World Airways *Jupiter Rex*	
N90922	Constellation	Pan American World Airways *Mount Vernon*	
N90923	Constellation	Pan American World Airways *Golden Rule*	
N90924	Constellation	Pan American World Airways *Lafayette*	
N90925	Constellation	Pan American World Airways *Courier*	
N90926	Constellation	Pan American World Airways *Ocean Herald*	
N90927	Constellation	Pan American World Airways *Wings of the Morning*	

N.B. Pan American aircraft names are prefixed *Clipper* (e.g. N90927 is *Clipper Wings of the Morning*).

Trans World aircraft names are prefixed *Star of* (e.g. N6026C is *Star of Connecticut*).

Slick Airways DC-GA's operate into London under charter to Pan American World Airways

BELGIUM (OO)

Registration	Type	Operator	Where and when seen
OO–AUL	Douglas DC–3	Sabena	
OO–AUM	Douglas DC–3	Sabena	
OO–AUN	Douglas DC–3	Sabena	
OO–AUO	Douglas DC–3	Sabena	
OO–AUP	Douglas DC–3	Sabena	
OO–AUV	Douglas DC–3	Sabena	
OO–AUW	Douglas C–47B	Sabena	
OO–AUX	Douglas DC–3	Sabena	
OO–AUY	Douglas DC–3	Sabena	
OO–AUZ	Douglas DC–3	Sabena	
OO–AWF	Douglas C–47A	Sabena	
OO–AWG	Douglas DC–3	Sabena	
OO–AWJ	Douglas C–47A	Sabena	
OO–AWK	Douglas C–47A	Sabena	
OO–AWL	Douglas DC–3	Sabena	
OO–AWM	Douglas C–47	Sabena	
OO–AWN	Douglas DC–3	Sabena	
OO–AWO	Convair-Liner	Sabena	
OO–AWP	Convair-Liner	Sabena	
OO–AWQ	Convair-Liner	Sabena	
OO–AWR	Convair-Liner	Sabena	
OO–AWS	Convair-Liner	Sabena	

362

Registration	Type	Operator	Where and when seen
OO–AWT	Convair-Liner	Sabena	
OO–CBB	Douglas DC–3	Sabena	
OO–CBC	Douglas DC–3	Sabena	
OO–CBD	Douglas DC–4	Sabena	
OO–CBF	Douglas DC–4	Sabena	
OO–CBH	Douglas DC–4	Sabena	
OO–CBI	Douglas DC–4	Sabena	
OO–CBP	Douglas DC–4	Sabena	
OO–CBQ	Douglas DC–4	Sabena	
OO–CBR	Douglas DC–4	Sabena	
OO–SBC	Douglas DC–3	Sabena	
OO–SBD	Douglas DC–3	Sabena	
OO–UBJ	Douglas DC–3	Sabena	
OO–UBT	Douglas C–47	Sabena	

DENMARK (OY)

Registration	Type	Operator	
OY–DCE	Douglas DC–3	Scandinavian Airlines System	Gorm
OY–DCO	Douglas DC–3	Scandinavian Airlines System	Orm
OY–DCU	Douglas DC–3	Scandinavian Airlines System	Ulf
OY–DCY	Douglas DC–3	Scandinavian Airlines System	Sten
OY–DDY	Douglas DC–3	Scandinavian Airlines System	Trym
OY–DFI	Douglas DC–4	Scandinavian Airlines System	Dan
OY–DFO	Douglas DC–4	Scandinavian Airlines System	Rolf
OY–DFY	Douglas DC–4	Scandinavian Airlines System	Sigvard
OY–KLE	Douglas DC–3	Scandinavian Airlines System	Arv
OY–KLO	Douglas DC–6	Scandimavian Airlines System	Skjold
OY–KLU	Douglas DC–6	Scandinavian Airlines System	Skjalm
OY–KLY	Douglas DC–6	Scandinavian Airlines System	Alf

N.B. Scandinavian Airlines System aircraft names are all suffixed *Viking* (e.g. OY–KLU is *Skjalm Viking*).

Ian Allan **TRAINS DIARY 1953**

Place an order for one of our famous diaries now by sending a postal order for 3/3 to cover cost and postage.   It's a money value buy.

NETHERLANDS (PH)

Registration	Type	Operator	Where and when seen
PH–TAY	Douglas DC–3	K.L.M.	
PH–TBI	Douglas DC–3	K.L.M.	
PH–TBM	Douglas DC–3	K.L.M.	
PH–TBP	Douglas DC–3	K.L.M.	
PH–TBZ	Douglas DC–3	K.L.M.	
PH–TCB	Douglas DC–3	K.L.M.	
PH–TCE	Douglas DC–4	K.L.M. Edam	
PH–TCI	Douglas DC–3	K.L.M.	
PH–TCL	Douglas DC–3	K.L.M.	
PH–TCT	Douglas DC–3	K.L.M.	
PH–TCY	Douglas DC–3	K.L.M.	
PH–TDB	Constellation L749	K.L.M. Walcheren	
PH–TDC	Constellation L749	K.L.M. Curacao	
PH–TDD	Constellation L749	K.L.M. Delft	
PH–TDE	Constellation L749	K.L.M. Eindhoven	
PH–TDG	Constellation L749	K.L.M. Gouda	
PH–TDH	Constellation L749	K.L.M. Holland	
PH–TDI	Constellation L749	K.L.M. Enschede	
PH–TDK	Constellation L749	K.L.M. Amsterdam	
PH–TDL	Douglas DC–4	K.L.M. Groningen	
PH–TDM	Douglas DC–4	K.L.M. Aalsmeer	
PH–TDN	Constellation L–749A	K.L.M. Vlaardingen	
PH–TDO	Constellation L–749A	K.L.M. Maastricht	
PH–TDP	Constellation L–749A	K.L.M. Rotterdam	
PH–TDU	Douglas DC–3	K.L.M.	
PH–TDZ	Douglas DC–3	K.L.M.	
PH–TEA	Convair-Liner	K.L.M. Adriaen van Ostade	
PH–TEB	Convair-Liner	K.L.M. Rembrandt	
PH–TEC	Convair-Liner	K.L.M. Albert Cuyp	
PH–TED	Convair-Liner	K.L.M. Gerard Terborch	
PH–TEE	Convair-Liner	K.L.M. Jan Steen	
PH–TEF	Convair-Liner	K.L.M. Frans Hals	
PH–TEG	Convair-Liner	K.L.M. Jan van Goyen	
PH–TEH	Convair-Liner	K.L.M. Pieter de Hoogh	
PH–TEI	Convair-Liner	K.L.M. Paulus Potter	
PH–TEK	Convair-Liner	K.L.M. Johannes Vermeer	
PH–TEL	Convair-Liner	K.L.M. Jacob van Ruisdaal	
PH–TEM	Convair-Liner	K.L.M. Meindert Hobbema	
PH–TEP	Constellation L–749	K.L.M. Pontianak	
PH–TES	Constellation L–749	K.L.M. Soerabaja	
PH–TET	Constellation L–749	K.L.M. Tilburg	
PH–TEY	Douglas DC–4	K.L.M. Limburg	
PH–TEZ	Douglas DC–4	K.L.M. Zeeland	
PH–TFD	Constellation L–749A	K.L.M. Arnhem	
PH–TFE	Constellation L–749A	K.L.M. Utrecht	
PH–TFF	Constellation L–749A	K.L.M. Venlo	
PH–TFG	Constellation L–749A	K.L.M. Friesland	
PH–TLW	Douglas DC–4	K.L.M. Overloon	

364

PHILIPPINES (PI)

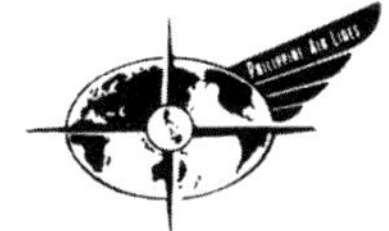

Registration	Type	Operator	Where and when seen
PI–C290	Douglas DC–6	Philippine Air Lines *Bataan*	
PI–C292	Douglas DC–6	Philippine Air Lines *Lingayen*	
PI–C293	Douglas DC–6	Philippine Air Lines *Manila*	
PI–C294	Douglas DC–6	Philippine Air Lines *Mindoro*	

BRAZIL (PP)

PP–PCB	Constellation	Panair do Brasil	
PP–PCF	Constellation	Panair do Brasil	
PP–PCR	Constellation	Panair do Brasil	
PP–PDA	Constellation	Panair do Brasil	
PP–PDC	Constellation	Panair do Brasil	

SWEDEN (SE)

SE–BAA	Douglas DC–3	Scandinavian Airlines System *Arne*	
SE–BAB	Douglas DC–3	Scandinavian Airlines System *Bele*	
SE–BAC	Douglas DC–3	Scandinavian Airlines System *Folke*	
SE–BBA	Douglas DC–4	Scandinavian Airlines System *Sigtrygg*	
SE–BBD	Douglas DC–4	Scandinavian Airlines System *Sigmund*	
SE–BBE	Douglas DC–4	Scandinavian Airlines System *Svavar*	
SE–BBF	Douglas DC–4	Scandinavian Airlines System *Sverker*	
SE–BBO	Douglas DC–3	Scandinavian Airlines System *Orvar*	
SE–BDB	Douglas DC–6	Scandinavian Airlines System *Agne*	
SE–BDD	Douglas DC–6	Scandinavian Airlines System *Algaut*	
SE–BDE	Douglas DC–6	Scandinavian Airlines System *Alrik*	
SE–BDF	Douglas DC–6	Scandinavian Airlines System *Alvar*	
SE–BDL	Douglas DC–6	Scandinavian Airlines System *Asmund*	
SE–BDM	Douglas DC–6	Scandinavian Airlines System *Amund*	

Registration	Type	Operator	Where and when seen
SE–BDO	Douglas DC–6	Scandinavian Airlines System *Arngrim*	
SE–BSB	Scandia	Scandinavian Airlines System *Gardar*	
SE–BSD	Scandia	Scandinavian Airlines System *Grim*	
SE–BSE	Scandia	Scandinavian Airlines System *Jarl*	
SE–BSH	Scandia	Scandinavian Airlines System *Torulf*	
SE–BSI	Douglas DC–3	Scandinavian Airlines System *Ravn*	

N.B. Scandinavian Airlines System aircraft names are all suffixed *Viking* (e.g. SE–BDO is *Arngrim Viking*).

GREECE (SX)

SX–DAC	Douglas DC–4	National Greek Airlines TAE	

ICELAND (TF)

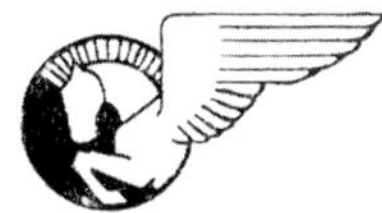

TF–ISE	Douglas DC–4	Flugfelag Islands H.F. *Gullfaxi*	

AUSTRALIA (VH)

VH–EAA	Constellation	Qantas Empire Airways *Ross Smith*	
VH–EAB	Constellation	Qantas Empire Airways *Lawrence Hargrave*	
VH–EAC	Constellation	Qantas Empire Airways *Harry Hawker*	
VH–EAD	Constellation	Qantas Empire Airways *Charles Kingsford Smith*	
VH–EAE	Constellation	Qantas Empire Airways *Bert Hinkler*	
VH–EAF	Constellation	Qantas Empire Airways *Horace Brinsmead*	
VH–INY VH–INZ	See under Ceylon, **page 63**		

Right: Family four-seater—the reasonably-priced Auster Autocar.

Centre: Trim successor to the well-loved Tiger Moth —de Havilland's fully-aerobatic Chipmunk trainer.

Bottom: The Aiglet, in the form shown here, has proved highly successful for crop-spraying work.   [*Shell*.

61

367

Left: A comfortable, sporty two - seater — the veteran Hornet Moth biplane [*Flight.*

Centre: Junior Spitfire—a 32 h.p. Chilton of the type which won the 1951 *Daily Express* race.
[*F. G. Swanborough.*

Bottom : Home-made. A Heath Parasol "ultra-light," designed for sale in kit form for building at home.
[*J.W.R.T.*

62

CEYLON

Registration	Type	Operator	Where and when seen
VH–INY	Douglas DC–4	Air Ceylon *Ratmalana*	
VH–INZ	Douglas DC–4	Air Ceylon *Laxapana*	

These are Australian National Airways aircraft, operated by A.N.A. on behalf of Air Ceylon.

INDIA (VT)

VT–DAR	Constellation L749A	Air India International *Maratha*
VT–DAS	Constellation L749A	Air India International *Himalayan*
VT–DEO	Constellation L749A	Air India International *Bengal*
VT–DEP	Constellation L749A	Air India International *Kashmir*

N.B. All Air India International aircraft names are suffixed *Princess* (e.g. VT–DEP is *Kashmir Princess*).

SOUTH AFRICA (ZS)

ZS–DBR	Constellation L749A	South African Airways *Capetown*
ZS–DBS	Constellation L749A	South African Airways *Johannesburg*
ZS–DBT	Constellation L749A	South African Airways *Pretoria*
ZS–DBU	Constellation L749A	South African Airways *Durban*

ISRAEL (4X)

Registration	Type	Operator	Where and when seen
4X–ACC	Douglas DC–4	El Al	
4X–AKA	Constellation L–249	El Al	
4X–AKB	Constellation L–249	El Al	
4X–AKC	Constellation L–249	El Al	
4X–AQD	Curtiss C–46	El Al	
4X–AQE	Curtiss C–46	El Al	

BRITAIN

Below are the badges of British Overseas Airways Corporation and British European Airways, whose aircraft are, of course, listed in the civil register on pages 4–46.

64

370

MILITARY REGISTRATIONS

Military aircraft, like their civil counterparts, all carry some kind of identification markings, and these "serial numbers" as they are called, form the basis of a fascinating but complicated study. Although they are really outside the scope of this book, the following notes will help readers to understand how military serial numbers are allocated and how they can be distinguished from civil registrations.

Serial numbers for aircraft operated by the Royal Air Force and Royal Navy are allocated by the Ministry of Supply in a co-ordinated system. Each serial consists of a five-symbol group, made up of either one letter followed by four digits or, more recently, two letters followed by three digits. They have run progressively through the years, starting with the prefix A, then B, C, etc., through to Z, which was followed by the prefix AA, then AB, etc., up to WZ, which is in use as this book goes to press.

The serial number on R.A.F. and R.N. aircraft is displayed on each side of the rear fuselage and beneath each wing, in addition to the national red, white and blue roundels. Such a serial number is, therefore, readily distinguishable and can be ignored by those using this book as a means of identifying civil aircraft types.

The Ministry of Supply, in its capacity of foster-mother to many of the civil prototypes developed in this country since the war, has allocated military-type serials to most of these prototypes for the period of their testing by its pilots. But these aircraft also receive normal civil registrations, and these are included in the appropriate section of this book.

Military aircraft of other countries also can be seen flying over the United Kingdom. The identification systems of these countries are too diverse to be dealt with here, but, as a rule, military aircraft can be identified quickly by national insignia on their wings and fuselage. Furthermore, an identification marking which does not fit into the scheme of national civil markings as laid down in this book can be assumed to be a military serial.

Finally, *a word of warning.* Collections of military serial numbers could be of immense value to enemies of this country, as they give a clue to the number of aircraft of each type that we have in service, where they are based, and so on. For that reason, we ask our readers to be careful. Collections of civil markings can hurt nobody: military markings might. So remember that the safety of our country is more important than merely satisfying your collector's urge!

Civil Aircraft Specifications

AIRCRAFT	MANUFACTURER	ENGINES	SEATS	SPAN	Loaded Wt.: (lb.)	Cruising Speed M.P.H.
Aeronca 100	Aeronca (G.B.)	1 × 36 J.A.P.	2	36'	1,005	70
Aerovan	Miles (G.B.)	2 × 155 Cirrus Major	9/Freight	50'	5,800	110
Aiglet	Auster (G.B.)	1 × 130 Gipsy Major	3	36'	2,000	105
Ambassador	Airspeed (G.B.)	2 × 2,600 Centaurus	52	115'	52,000	245
Ambulance/Freighter	Auster (G.B.)	1 × 180 Cirrus Bombardier	2 + 550lb.	37'	2,600	100+
Anson 1	A. V. Roe (G.B.)	2 × 320 Cheetah	9	56' 6"	7,663	158
Apollo	Armstrong Whitworth (G.B.)	4 × 1,270 + 350 lb. Mamba	24-41	92'	45,000	276
Argus	Fairchild (U.S.A.)	1 × 165 Super Scarab	4	36' 4"	2,801	104
Auster 5	Auster (G.B.)	1 × 130 Lycoming	2-3	36'	1,920	112
Auster J/4	Auster (G.B.)	1 × 90 Cirrus	2	36'	1,600	92
Autocar	Auster (G.B.)	1 × 130 Gipsy Major	4	36'	2,400	100
Autocrat	Auster (G.B.)	1 × 100 Cirrus Minor	3	36'	1,850	100
Avro XIX	A. V. Roe (G.B.)	2 × 420 Cheetah	6-9	56' 6"	10,400	155
Beaver	De Havilland (Canada)	1 × 450 Wasp Junior	4-7	48'	4,820	153
Brabazon 1	Bristol (G.B.)	8 × 2,650 Centaurus	101	230'	290,000	250
Bristol Type 170	Bristol (G.B.)	2 × 2,000 Hercules	36/Freight	108'	42,000	166
Bristol Type 171 Helicopter	Bristol (G.B.)	1 × 550 Leonides	4	48' 7" Dia.	5,200	84
Bristol Type 173 Helicopter	Bristol (G.B.)	2 × 550 Leonides	15	48' 7" Dia.	10,600	105
Bristol Type 175	Bristol (G.B.)	4 × 3,200 + 800 lb. Proteus	up to 95	140'	130,000	343
C.30 A Autogiro	Cierva (G.B.)	1 × 140 Genet Major	2	37'	1,900	85
Canadair Four	Canadair (Canada)	4 × 1,760 Merlin	40	117' 6"	82,300	302
Chilton	Chilton (G.B.)	1 × 32 Carden	1	24'	640	103
Chipmunk	De Havilland (G.B.)	1 × 145 Gipsy Major	2	34' 4"	2,000	119
Comet	De Havilland (G.B.)	4 × 5,000 lb. Ghost	36-48	115'	105,000	490
Constellation 749A	Lockheed (U.S.A.)	4 × 2,500 Cyclone	44-64	123'	107,000	309
Consul	Airspeed (G.B.)	2 × 395 Cheetah	5-6	53' 4"	8,250	156
Convair-Liner	Consolidated (U.S.A.)	2 × 2,400 P & W R-2800	40	91' 9"	41,790	270
Cub	Piper (U.S.A.)	1 × 65 Continental	2	35' 2"	1,220	75
Cygnet	Hawker (G.B.)	1 × 30 Cherub	1-2	28'	900	65
DC–3 Dakota	Douglas (U.S.A.)	2 × 1,200 P & W R-1830	21-32	95'	25,200	207
DC–4 Skymaster	Douglas (U.S.A.)	4 × 1,350 P & W R-2000	36-47	117' 6"	73,000	231
DC–6	Douglas (U.S.A.)	4 × 2,150 P & W R-2800	52-68	117' 6"	97,200	313
Dove	De Havilland (G.B.)	2 × 345 Gipsy Queen	8-11	57'	8,500	179
Gemini	Miles (G.B.)	2 × 100 Cirrus Minor	4	36' 2"	3,000	135
Halifax	Handley Page (G.B.)	4 × 1,650 Hercules	11/Freight	104'	65,000	270
Hart	Hawker (G.B.)	1 × 690 Kestrel	2	37' 4½"	4,635	170
Hawk Major	Miles (G.B.)	1 × 130 Gipsy Major	2	33'	1,800	135
Hawk Trainer 3	Miles (G.B.)	1 × 130 Gipsy Major	2	33' 10"	1,900	120
Hermes 4	Handley Page (G.B.)	4 × 2,100 Hercules	40-74	113'	86,000	242
Hermes 5	Handley Page (G.B.)	4 × 2,430 Theseus	40-74	113'	86,000	343

Civil Aircraft Specifications

AIRCRAFT	MANUFACTURER	ENGINES	SEATS	SPAN	Loaded Wt.: (lb.)	Cruising Speed M.P.H.
Heron	De Havilland (G.B.)	4 × 250 Gipsy Queen	14-17	71' 6"	12,500	160
Hornet Moth	De Havilland (G.B.)	1 × 130 Gipsy Major	2	31' 11"	2,000	105
Hythe	Short (G.B.)	4 × 1,010 Pegasus	27	112' 10"	50,000	117
Languedoc	S.N.C.A.S.E. (France)	4 × 1,220 Gnome-Rhone	12-33	96' 5"	45,364	233
M-18	Miles (G.B.)	1 × 150 Gipsy Major	2	31'	1,918	120
Marathon 1	Handley Page (G.B.)	4 × 345 Gipsy Queen	18-22	65'	18,000	209
Messenger	Miles (G.B.)	1 × 155 Cirrus Major	3-4	36' 2"	2,400	112
Monarch	Miles (G.B.)	1 × 130 Gipsy Major	2	35' 8"	2,000	130
Moth Minor	De Havilland (G.B.)	1 × 90 Gipsy Minor	2	36' 7"	1,550	100
Pioneer	Scottish Aviation (G.B.)	1 × 540 Leonides	5	52' 6"	5,400	120
Prince	Percival (G.B.)	2 × 550 Leonides	8-10	56'	11,000	179
Proctor 5	Percival (G.B.)	1 × 208 Gipsy Queen	4	39' 6"	3,500	140
Q-6	Percival (G.B.)	2 × 205 Gipsy Six	6	46' 8"	5,550	181
Rapide	De Havilland (G.B.)	2 × 200 Gipsy Six	5-8	48'	5,550	132
Sealand	Short (G.B.)	2 × 340 Gipsy Queen	5-8	61' 6"	9,100	176
Sea Otter	Vickers (G.B.)	1 × 805 Mercury	5	46'	10,000	100
Sikorsky S-51 Helicopter	Westland (G.B.)	1 × 505 Leonides	4	48' Dia.	5,700	85
Sikorsky S-55 Helicopter	Westland (G.B.)	1 × 600 Wasp	12	53' Dia.	7,300	86
Solent	Short (G.B.)	4 × 2,040 Hercules	24-80	112' 9"	80,000	236
Spitfire Trainer	Vickers (G.B.)	1 × 1,325 Merlin	2	36' 10"	7,400	232
Stratocruiser	Boeing (U.S.A.)	4 × 3,500 P & W R-4360	55-100	141' 3"	145,800	340
Sunderland 3	Short (G.B.)	4 × 1,065 Pegasus	22	112' 9"	55,000	115
Super Ace 2	Chrislea (G.B.)	1 × 145 Gipsy Major	4	36'	2,350	112
Swallow	British Aircraft (G.B.)	1 × 20 Cataract	2	42" 8'	1,500	92
Swift	Comper (G.B.)	1 × 80 Pobjoy 8	1	24'	985	110
Taylorcraft D	Taylorcraft (G.B.)	1 × 90 Cirrus Minor	2	36'	1,400	107
Tiger Moth	De Havilland (G.B.)	1 × 130 Gipsy Major	2	29' 4"	1,825	94
Tipsy Trainer	Tipsy (G.B.)	1 × 52 Mikron	2	31' 2"	1,200	100
Tudor 5	A. V. Roe (G.B.)	4 × 1,740 Merlin	44	120'	80,000	285
Vega Gull	Percival (G.B.)	1 × 200 Gipsy Six	4	39' 6"	3,250	170
Viking	Vickers (G.B.)	2 × 1,690 Hercules	27-38	89' 3"	34,000	210
Viscount 700	Vickers (G.B.)	4 × 1,420 + 325 lb. Dart	40-53	94'	52,500	317
Whitney Straight	Miles (G.B.)	1 × 130 Gipsy Major	2	35' 8"	1,896	130
York	A. V. Roe (G.B.)	4 × 1,280 Merlin	12-56	102'	68,597	255

International Civil Aircraft Markings

Mark	Country	Mark	Country
AN–	Nicaragua	OY–	Denmark
AP–	Pakistan	PH–	Netherlands
B–	China. People's Republic	PI–	Philippine Republic
CB–	Bolivia	PJ–	Netherlands W. Indies
CC–	Chile	PK–	United States of Indonesia
CCCP–	Soviet Union	PP–	Brazil
CF–	Canada	PT–	Brazil
CN–	Morocco	PZ–	Surinam
CP–	Bolivia	RX–	Panama
CR–	Portuguese Colonies	SE–	Sweden
CS–	Portugal	SN–	Sudan
CU–	Cuba	SP–	Poland
CX–	Uruguay	SR–	Syria
CY–	Ceylon	SU–	Egypt
CZ–	Monaco	SX–	Greece
D–	Germany	TC–	Turkey
EC–	Spain	TF–	Iceland
EI–, EJ–	Ireland	TG–	Guatemala
EL–	Liberia	TI–	Costa Rica
EP–	Iran	TJ–	Jordan
ET–	Ethiopia	VH–	Australia
F–	France, Colonies and Protectorates	VP–AAA–VP–AZZ	Gold Coast with Ashanti
G–	United Kingdom	VP–BAA–VP–BZZ	Bahamas
HA–	Hungary	VP–FAA–VP–FZZ	Falkland Islands
HB–	Switzerland	VP–GAA–VP–GZZ	British Guiana
HC–	Ecuador	VP–HAA–VP–HZZ	British Honduras
HH–	Haiti	VP–JAA–VP–JZZ	Jamaica
HI–	Dominican Republic	VP–KAA–VP–KZZ	Kenya
HK–	Colombia	VP–LAA–VP–LZZ	Leeward Islands
HS–	Thailand	VP–MAA–VP–MZZ	Malta
HZ–	Saudi Arabia	VP–NAA–VP–NZZ	Nyasaland
I–	Italy	VP–PAA–VP–PZZ	Islands of Western Pacific High Commission
LN–	Norway	VP–RAA–VP–RZZ	Northern Rhodesia
LR–	Lebanon	VP–SAA–VP–SZZ	Somaliland
LV–	Argentine Republic	VP–TAA–VP–TZZ	Trinidad and Tobago
LX–	Luxembourg	VP–UAA–VP–UZZ	Uganda
LZ–	Bulgaria	VP–VAA–VP–VZZ	St. Vincent
MC–	Monte Carlo	VP–XAA–VP–XZZ	Gambia
N–	United States of America	VP–YAA–VP–YZZ	Southern Rhodesia
OB–	Peru	VP–ZAA–VP–ZZZ	Zanzibar
OE–	Austria	VQ–BAA–VQ–BZZ	Barbados
OH–	Finland	VQ–CAA–VQ–CZZ	Cyprus (not used. Present Cyprus Airways aircraft registered G–).
OK–	Czechoslovakia		
OO–	Belgium	VQ–FAA–VQ–FZZ	Fiji Islands

International Civil Aircraft Markings

Marking	Country	Marking	Country
VQ-GAA–VQ-GZZ	Grenada	XH–	Honduras
VQ-HAA–VQ-HZZ	St. Helena	XT–	China, Nationalist
VQ-LAA–VQ-LZZ	St. Lucia	XY–	Burma
VQ-MAA–VQ-MZZ	Mauritius	XZ–	Burma
VQ-SAA–VQ-SZZ	Seychelle Islands	YA–	Afghanistan
VR-BAA–VR-BZZ	Bermuda	YE–	Yemen
VR-GAA–VR-GZZ	Gibraltar (not used. Present Gibraltar Airways aircraft registered G–).	YI–	Iraq
		YK–	Syria
VR-HAA–VR-HZZ	Hong Kong	YJ–	New Hebrides
VR-JAA–VR-JZZ	Johore	YR–	Rumania
VR-LAA–VR-LZZ	Sierra Leone	YS–	El Salvador
VR-NAA–VR-NZZ	Nigeria, British Cameroons	YU–	Yugoslavia
VR-RAA–VR-RZZ	Malaya and Singapore	YV–	Venezuela
VR-TAA–VR-TZZ	Tanganyika	ZA–	Albania
VR-UAA–VR-UZZ	Brunei (British North Borneo)	ZK–, ZL–, ZM–	New Zealand
VT–	India	ZP–	Paraguay
XA–	Mexico	ZS–, ZT–, ZU–	Union of South Africa
XB–	Mexico	4X–	Israel
XC–	Mexico		

You should get a copy of :

WINGS FOR TOMORROW

by John W. R. Taylor and Maurice F. Allward

**112 pages 16 pages of photographs on art paper,
Foreword by Lord Brabazon of Tara.   7/6.**

What the critics say :—

" A work which seems assured of an enduring place in Aeronautical literature ".

Flight

" This book is utterly comprehensive and accurate ".

C. G. Grey, The Aeroplane.

" We recommend " Wings for Tomorrow " to students of aviation history   Convinced flying-boat supporters will revel in it ".

Air Pictorial.

" As long as books like this are published the controversy about flying-boats will never die ".

R.D.C. Aeronautics.

" Never before have I seen gathered together between two covers such a wealth of information about every aspect of marine aviation ".

Coventry Evening Telegraph.

" It is delightfully written and the authors have obviously spent many hours of research in obtaining the detailed information which appears with its 112 pages ".

The Royal Aero Club Gazette.

Obtainable from W. H. Smith & Son, Wymans and leading booksellers everywhere or direct from the publishers

Ian Allan Ltd

282, VAUXHALL BRIDGE ROAD, LONDON S.W.1.

Top: Hart G–ABMR, last survivor of the famous Hawker bomber family and a favourite mount of air photographers for nearly 20 years.

Centre: Still flying—the Hawker Cygnet which won the *Daily Mail* light aeroplane contest in 1926.

Right: A Cierva C30 Autogiro of the type used during World War II for radar calibration.

[*F. G. Swanborough.*

Top: Bristol 171—in service with B.E.A. and, as the Sycamore, with the British Services.

Centre: B.E.A. used their Sikorsky S–51s to operate the world's first helicopter passenger and night mail services.

Left: Big brother of the S–51, the Sikorsky S–55 is also being built in Britain by Westlands. [*Flight*,

378

A million passengers a year

fly BEA

Scheduled Skymaster services to Reykjavik from London, Prestwick, Copenhagen and Oslo.

For further information consult our Agents in Great Britain:
BRITISH EUROPEAN AIRWAYS

or

6B PRINCES ARCADE, PICCADILLY, LONDON
MEMBER INTERNATIONAL AIR TRANSPORT ASSOCIATION

The Swiss are sure . . . accurate, steady people who take things calmly. And it's in their nature to care for machines, to keep them spotlessly clean and running efficiently. Scratch a Swiss, it's said, and you either find a precision engineer or a watchmaker — or a Maître d'hotel of course. Well . . . that makes for a first class airline. You get there — on time — and you are treated like a lord en route.

REGULAR FLIGHTS TO ZURICH, GENEVA AND BASLE, WITH CONNECTIONS TO MOST EUROPEAN CITIES AND THE NEAR EAST. SWISSAIR, 126, REGENT ST., LONDON, W.1. AND MANCHESTER, GLASGOW

CRC 7

This book is

An *Ian Allan* Publication

Published by

Ian Allan Ltd

Specialists in Transport Books

Write for our up-to-date book list.

NEW YORK   CAIRO   KARACHI   ISRAEL

BELGIUM   CZECHOSLOVAKIA   LEBANON   PERSIA   SYRIA

DENMARK   ANTILLES   ARGENTINE   BRAZIL

EIRE   BUENOS AIRES   URUGUAY   AUSTRIA   CHINA

FRANCE   GERMANY   HONG KONG   INDIA

HOLLAND   GREECE   SIAM   PAKISTAN

CALCUTTA   INDO-CHINA

NORWAY   ITALY   SUDAN   SIERRA LEONE

SWITZERLAND   TANGANYIKA

PORTUGAL   TURKEY   TANGIERS   TUNISIA

SCOTLAND   LIBERIA   ALGERIA   NEW CALEDONIA

SWEDEN   SPAIN   S PACIFIC ISLANDS   KENYA   IVORY COAST

FRENCH CONGO   GUINEA   GAMBIA   CAMEROONS

NIGERIA   MAURITIUS   MADAGASCAR   MOROCCO   GOLD COAST

SENEGAL   REUNION

AIR FRANCE

World Services

The first Airline in the World

AIR FRANCE 52 HAYMARKET, LONDON, S.W.1   WHITEHALL 4455

A New *Ian Allan* Publication

London's Underground

By H. F. Howson

On the London Transport system today, there are nearly 250 miles of railway spread over those routes that are seen on the little pocket maps at the Stations, criss-crossing London, threading the suburbs and reaching out into the country. Every year more passengers go to swell the millions already carried by London's "Underground" and all the time these railways maintain their reputation for remarkable efficiency and safety.

In this book the author tells the story of this great undertaking in a language acceptable not only to the enthusiast but also to the interested layman.

Fully bound   **Fully Illustrated**

12/6

FROM YOUR BOOKSTALL OR BOOKSELLER

FLY with your bike

20 mins TO FRANCE

Half hourly service by Bristol Freighters for Cycles, Motor Cycles, Cars and Passengers from Lympne to Le Touquet, Southampton to Cherbourg, Southend to Ostend.

Cycles .... £1 single
Motor Cycles.. £4 single
Cars ....£12 single

★ *Apply NOW for illustrated Brochure F to your local Travel Agent or DIRECT to :*

SILVER CITY AIRWAYS L^{TD}.

**11, GREAT CUMBERLAND PLACE,
LONDON, W.1.**
Phone : PAD 7040

Operated in Association with B.E.A.

214/65/100 Printed in England by the Falstaff Press, 316, Vauxhall Bridge Road, London, S.W.1